Legal Writing and Analysis

EDITORIAL ADVISORS

ASPEN COURSEBOOK SERIES

Legal Writing and Analysis

Sixth Edition

Linda H. Edwards
E. L. Cord Foundation Professor of Law, Emerita
William S. Boyd School of Law University of Nevada, Las Vegas

Samantha A. Moppett
Professor of Legal Writing
Associate Director, Legal Practice Skills
Suffolk University Law School

ASPEN PUBLISHING

To contact Customer Service, e-mail customer.service@aspenpublishing.com, call 1-800-950-5259, or mail correspondence to:

Aspen Publishing
Attn: Order Department
PO Box 990
Frederick, MD 21705

Printed in the United States of America.

1 2 3 4 5 6 7 8 9 0

ISBN 978-1-5438-5851-8

Library of Congress Cataloging-in-Publication Data

Names: Edwards, Linda Holdeman, 1948- author. | Moppett, Samantha A., author.
Title: Legal writing and analysis / Linda H. Edwards, E. L. Cord Foundation Professor of Law, Emerita, William S. Boyd School of Law, University of Nevada, Las Vegas; Samantha A. Moppett, Professor of Legal Writing, Associate Director, Legal Practice Skills, Suffolk University Law School.
Description: Sixth edition. | Frederick : Aspen Publishing, 2023. | Series: Aspen coursebook series | Includes bibliographical references and index.
Identifiers: LCCN 2022048005 | ISBN 9781543858518 (paperback) | ISBN 9781543858525 (ebook)
Subjects: LCSH: Legal composition. | Legal briefs—United States.
Classification: LCC KF250 .E378 2023 | DDC 808.06/634—dc23/eng/20221115
LC record available at https://lccn.loc.gov/2022048005

About Aspen Publishing

Aspen Publishing is a leading provider of educational content and digital learning solutions to law schools in the U.S. and around the world. Aspen provides best-in-class solutions for legal education through authoritative textbooks, written by renowned authors, and breakthrough products such as Connected eBooks, Connected Quizzing, and PracticePerfect.

The Aspen Casebook Series (famously known among law faculty and students as the "red and black" casebooks) encompasses hundreds of highly regarded textbooks in more than eighty disciplines, from large enrollment courses, such as Torts and Contracts to emerging electives such as Sustainability and the Law of Policing. Study aids such as the *Examples & Explanations* and the *Emanuel Law Outlines* series, both highly popular collections, help law students master complex subject matter.

Major products, programs, and initiatives include:

- **Connected eBooks** are enhanced digital textbooks and study aids that come with a suite of online content and learning tools designed to maximize student success. Designed in collaboration with hundreds of faculty and students, the Connected eBook is a significant leap forward in the legal education learning tools available to students.
- **Connected Quizzing** is an easy-to-use formative assessment tool that tests law students' understanding and provides timely feedback to improve learning outcomes. Delivered through CasebookConnect.com, the learning platform already used by students to access their Aspen casebooks, Connected Quizzing is simple to implement and integrates seamlessly with law school course curricula.
- **PracticePerfect** is a visually engaging, interactive study aid to explain commonly encountered legal doctrines through easy-to-understand animated videos, illustrative examples, and numerous practice questions. Developed by a team of experts, PracticePerfect is the ideal study companion for today's law students.
- The **Aspen Learning Library** enables law schools to provide their students with access to the most popular study aids on the market across all of their courses. Available through an annual subscription, the online library consists of study aids in e-book, audio, and video formats with full text search, note-taking, and highlighting capabilities.
- Aspen's **Digital Bookshelf** is an institutional-level online education bookshelf, consolidating everything students and professors need to ensure success. This program ensures that every student has access to affordable course materials from day one.
- **Leading Edge** is a community centered on thinking differently about legal education and putting those thoughts into actionable strategies. At the core of the program is the Leading Edge Conference, an annual gathering of legal education thought leaders looking to pool ideas and identify promising directions of exploration.

To Frances,
for her unfailing suppport,
and to Emilie and Katherine,
for the inspiration of their courage

—LHE

To my husband,
Jon, and daughters,
Jocelyn and Charlotte

—SAM

Summary of Contents

Contents

Preface

This book is a concise text that tracks the traditional legal writing course syllabus. It identifies the five main stages of the writing process: (1) Reading and analyzing the materials; (2) creating an annotated outline; (3) writing a working draft of the analysis; (4) converting that analysis into a document designed for a reader; and (5) editing for style and technical correctness.

The book groups relevant material together instead of scattering it in different stages of the writing process. Numerous examples are included along with frequent short exercises to encourage students to apply new material. It provides students with the necessary structure for organizing a legal discussion. Finally, it includes discrete materials that offer students the opportunity to explore a deeper level of understanding than its small size would imply.

The Book's Organization: Part One explains the legal system and introduces lawyers' roles within that system. Part Two explains how to work with the raw material for analysis. It introduces briefing and synthesizing cases, analogizing and distinguishing case law, and interpreting statutes. Part Three presents the traditional organizational formats for communicating the analysis of a legal question (the basic IRAC or CREAC structures). Parts Four and Five cover the components of office memos, correspondence (including texts and e-mails), trial-level briefs, and appellate briefs. Part Six presents material on citation and style, and Part Seven introduces oral argument.

How This Book Differs: The primary difference between this book and our earlier text, *Legal Writing: Process, Analysis, and Organization*, is the way the material is grouped. This book is not so unrelenting in its process approach, although it still recognizes writing as a process. The first book presents its material in stages defined entirely by a writer's progress toward completing a particular assignment. Although that approach offers real advantages, course time and resources do not always permit its use and *Process, Analysis, and Organization* is less flexible pedagogically. In contrast, this book groups relevant material together in a more efficient manner while still providing guidance about the writing process. That guidance is identified throughout the book by this recurring symbol shown in the margin.

Examples and Exercises: Another characteristic of this book is its frequent use of examples and exercises. For instance, Chapter 1 succinctly describes the writing roles of planning and prevention, prediction, and persuasion, and then describes several hypothetical situations asking students to decide which kind of writing each situation would require. Later in that chapter, after an introduction to plagiarism and the purposes of citation, students see examples of when to cite and then read a short legal discussion and identify the ideas that need citations. This pattern of examples and exercises continues throughout the book.

Organizing a Legal Discussion: The book explains the standard IRAC and CREAC paradigms and explains how to use those paradigms in discussions of multiple issues. The book introduces the structures inherent in rules and shows students how to use those rule structures to identify issues and to organize their written discussions.

Flexible Levels: Each major section presents its material at a basic introductory level so all the core information is concisely grouped. Courses that have time for a more advanced treatment can also cover optional chapters that take students deeper into the material. For instance, the core chapters of Part Two explain synthesizing cases and interpreting statutes. This material is presented at a level appropriate for all students. Then, Part Two concludes with an optional more advanced chapter explaining the major forms of reasoning lawyers use and providing examples and simple exercises for that material.

Similarly, in Part Three, the core chapters explain how to organize and write a legal analysis, including how to analogize and distinguish cases. This material is presented at a level appropriate for all students. Part Three then ends with an optional chapter showing students how to broaden and deepen their analysis in each part of their IRAC or CREAC structure. This chapter can be assigned as required reading, assigned as optional reading, or omitted entirely.

Finally, in Part Five, the core chapters explain how to write a trial-level and appellate brief. These chapters present everything a first-year student needs to know to write her first brief. Then Part Five ends with an optional online chapter explaining how a lawyer can use her awareness of a judge's legal philosophy to target her argument more effectively. Again, this supplemental chapter can be assigned as required reading, assigned as optional reading, or omitted entirely.

The goal of this book is to provide a pedagogically flexible text for basic legal writing, readily adaptable to fit the needs of any traditional legal writing course. It presents the fundamentals in a concise, lucid style for first-year students. It also offers discrete sections of more advanced material that can be included or omitted at the discretion of the professor. The book includes ample examples and exercises, which relieve the professor of the burden of generating such material, but that may nonetheless be supplemented at any point. It is, in short, a basic text, adaptable to a wide variety of legal writing programs.

The Sixth Edition remains streamlined for today's law students. The detailed material on briefing cases has been moved to the book's website. Other additional material has been enhanced or added in the text, including material on all three categories of sovereign entities in the United States that can make and enforce laws (Chapter 2), e-mail memos (Chapter 13), the proper use of texts as a means of correspondence (Chapter 13), electronic filings and certificates of compliance (Chapter 14), and the proper use of "they" as a singular pronoun (Chapter 20). Finally, the citation and quotation material (Chapter 19) has been revised to match the current editions of the *ALWD Guide to Legal Citation* and *The Bluebook*.

Linda H. Edwards
Samantha A. Moppett

November 2022

Acknowledgments

This book has benefited immeasurably from the assistance and support of many people. First and foremost, I am grateful to all of my Mercer colleagues. Their belief in the importance of legal writing has been manifested again and again through the years and has been the foundation on which this project, among many others, is built. Special thanks go to Susan Bay, Ted Blumoff, Jim Hunt, Mark Jones, Hal Lewis, Adam Milani, Jack Sammons, and Michael Smith for reading and commenting on parts of the book. Two Mercer Deans, Larry Dessem and Mike Sabbath, have assisted in innumerable ways. Billie Blaine and Carrie Murray provided careful research assistance, and Sandy Studdard provided ready administrative support. Finally, I am grateful to my students, whose hard work and probing questions have kept me learning.

I am privileged to be part of a remarkable national legal writing community. Space does not permit listing all of the colleagues who have shared generously of their vision, enthusiasm, wisdom, and experience. I hope they each know how thankful I am for their friendship and for their many contributions to our discipline. Two names cannot be omitted, however: Mary Lawrence, who has mentored generations of legal writing colleagues, and Tom Blackwell, whose memory will continue to guide us for years to come.

The chapters of this book dealing with the grounding of analysis and argument in underlying theories of jurisprudence would not have been possible without the friendship, advice, and encouragement of doctrinal law colleagues, especially Scott Brewer, Martha Minow, and Joseph Singer. Errors, of course, are my own. I owe a debt of gratitude to Darby Dickerson for her invaluable assistance with Chapter 20. Thanks are due also to the wonderful people at Aspen Publishers, especially Carol McGeehan, Melody Davies, Richard Mixter, Betsy Kenny, and Peggy Rehberger. I am especially grateful to the anonymous Aspen reviewers whose comments contributed so significantly to the book.

I would also like to thank the following copyright holder for permission to reprint the map of the federal judicial circuits:

2009 Judicial Staff Directory 963 (C.Q. Press 2009). Copyright © 2009 by Congressional Quarterly, Inc. Phone (202) 729–1817.

And finally, my deepest thanks to Dan Edwards. Yet again, words fail.

—Linda H. Edwards

I would first like to thank Linda Edwards for the privilege of assisting with the Sixth Edition of *Legal Writing* and the honor of having my name appear on the cover along with hers. This project has been one of the highlights of my over twenty-year career teaching legal research and writing.

I would be remiss if I were not to also acknowledge the national legal writing community. This truly wonderful group of people has become like a second family to me and has made my career more rewarding than I would have thought possible. While it would be impossible to list everyone that has influenced my career, I am particularly indebted to Terrill Pollman, Judith Stinson, and Kathleen Elliot Vinson.

I would also like to thank Timothy Bolen, Heidi K. Brown, Adam Eckart, Marnie Hodahkwen, and Dyane O'Leary for their expertise and assistance on some updates to this edition. I am also grateful for the support from my fellow Suffolk colleagues, Suffolk University Law School, and my research assistant, Grayson Barlow.

Finally, a special thanks to Sarah Hains at The Froebe Group and Stacie Goosman at Aspen.

—Samantha A. Moppett

Legal Writing and Analysis

PART ONE

Lawyers and the Legal Landscape

CHAPTER 1

Overview of the Lawyer's Role

Most students entering law school would not call themselves writers; nor would they expect that in three years they will be professional writers, earning a significant part of their income by writing for publication. Yet that is precisely what lawyers do. Most lawyers write and publish more pages than do novelists, and with greater consequences hanging in the balance.

This book introduces the critical skill of legal writing. We begin by exploring the kinds of writing lawyers do, a lawyer's ethical duties, and the obligation to provide attribution to the source of the information placed in a document.

I. WRITING AND A LAWYER'S ROLES

Lawyers write many kinds of documents—court papers, letters, e-mails, texts, legal instruments, and internal working documents. As different as these documents are from each other, they all fall into one of three categories defined by the lawyer's primary role when writing them: (1) planning and preventive writing, (2) predictive writing, and (3) persuasive writing. A lawyer's writing differs significantly depending on which role the lawyer is performing. A lawyer's writing also differs depending on the document's audience and purpose.

A LAWYER'S WRITING ROLES

- Planning and Preventive Writing
- Predictive Writing
- Persuasive Writing

Planning and Preventive Writing. Lawyers engage in planning and preventive writing when they draft transactional documents such as wills, trusts, leases, mortgages, partnership agreements, and contracts. Planning documents define the rights of the parties and the limits of their conduct, much as case law and statutes do for society at large. Thus, planning documents create what is, in effect, the "law" of the transaction. To write these documents, a lawyer needs to be able to foresee any possible future legal issues in any given situation and then prevent them by accounting for all possibilities, and resolving those possibilities before they occur, in the transactional document. The audience for preventive writing is often a client, business people, or other lawyers, rather than judges.

In some ways, planning and preventive writing is the most satisfying of the lawyering roles because it requires creativity and because, typically, there are several paths to a satisfactory result. Through planning and preventive writing, the lawyer creates and structures some of the most important transactions and relationships in an individual client's life or in the commercial world. Also, with careful planning, the lawyer can forestall future disputes because preventive writing occurs before a dispute happens. This timing is quite different from that of other types of legal writing that occur after a dispute has arisen. Lawyers who engage in this type of writing enjoy being able to participate in collaborative and proactive lawyering, helping clients document relationships and prevent injury. Most lawyers would rather help clients prevent injury than recover for injury.

Predictive Writing. Predictive writing is part of another satisfying task—client counseling. Clients often seek a lawyer's advice when they must make an important decision. To help the client decide, the lawyer must research the law and predict a legal result.

Lawyers engage in predictive writing in both transactional and litigation settings. In transactional settings, the lawyer predicts legal outcomes in order to analyze and prevent possible problems. In litigation, the client and the lawyer must decide many questions, ranging from relatively routine matters of litigation management (such as which motions to file) to such fundamental matters as whether to settle the case. To resolve any of these questions, the lawyer must predict the legal outcomes of the possible courses of action and must communicate those predictions to the client or to another lawyer working on the case.

In predictive writing, the lawyer must analyze the relevant law *objectively*, as a judge would do. The most common documents for communicating predictive analysis are the *office memo* or *e-memo* (addressed to another lawyer who has requested the analysis) or the *opinion letter* (addressed to the client). The lawyer's goal is to predict the legal result as accurately as possible, objectively weighing the strengths and weaknesses of the possible arguments. The answer might not be the answer the client or the requesting lawyer wants to hear, but it is the answer they need in order to make a good decision.

Persuasive Writing. Legal problems cannot always be prevented, and some of them inevitably result in litigation or a proceeding before some other decision-maker. When that happens, the lawyer becomes an advocate, taking on a persuasive role. No matter what result the lawyer might have *predicted*, the lawyer now must try to persuade the audience, most frequently the judge, to reach the result most favorable to the client. The lawyer will marshal the strongest arguments in her client's favor and refute opposing arguments. The most common persuasive document is the *brief* (also called a *memorandum of law*).

Although the goals of prediction and persuasion differ, on a fundamental level predictive (objective) analysis and persuasive analysis cannot be separated. To predict a result, a writer must understand the arguments each side would present. To persuade, a writer must understand how the argument will strike a neutral reader. Thus, as you improve your predictive analysis, you will be improving your persuasive analysis as well, and vice versa.

This text focuses on teaching predictive and persuasive writing. That said, the skills necessary to write predictively and persuasively are transferable to preventive writing. Before you go on, turn to Appendix A, which contains a sample office memo; Appendix B, which contains a sample e-memo; and Appendices C and D, which contain sample briefs. We will study the parts of each document in more detail later. The goal at this point is simply to understand the function of each kind of document and to see what the end products will look like before beginning the process of creating them.

EXERCISE 1-1
Recognizing a Lawyer's Role

Identify the primary lawyering role called for in each of the following situations:

1. A client (a widower) has been diagnosed with a fatal form of cancer.
   a. The client asks a lawyer to draft a trust to protect his assets for his children.
   b. The client asks whether there is a procedure by which he can designate a foster family to care for his children after his death and whether it would be wise for him to do so.
   c. The client asks the lawyer to file a lawsuit seeking recovery against his employer for exposure to carcinogens in the workplace.

2. A client has located a piece of real property she wishes to buy and lease to a commercial tenant. The title registry lists an easement allowing the owner of the property next door to use the driveway along the back of the property. The client wishes to expand the existing structure on the property and eliminate the driveway.
   a. The client asks the lawyer whether the easement can be challenged legally.
   b. The client asks the lawyer to approach the owner of the property next door and seek the release of the easement.
   c. The client asks the lawyer to draft the release of the easement and also to draft a lease for the new commercial tenant to sign.

II. OVERVIEW OF A CIVIL CASE

Because most of your first-year courses focus on reading appellate opinions, you'll need an overview of how a civil case proceeds through the litigation process. This section summarizes the course of a fairly simple personal injury lawsuit with only one legal claim against only one defendant and raising no ancillary issues. As you read it, notice how many litigation stages require legal research and the writing of a legal document (identified by italics), even in a relatively simple case.

Initial Research. A civil case begins when a client consults a lawyer about a legal problem. Usually the client has been injured and believes that his injury was caused by the wrongful conduct of someone else. The client wants to know whether he has any legal recourse and, if so, whether he should pursue it.

To decide these questions, the lawyer must gather all the relevant facts and research the relevant legal issues. Rarely will the lawyer already know all the law that will be required to answer these initial questions, and the lawyer might not have time to research all of them herself. She might ask an associate to research some of them for her. The requesting lawyer will write *file memos* to the associate, providing the necessary information and setting out exactly what she needs to know. After finishing the requested research, the associate will write an *office memo* or *e-memo* to the requesting lawyer, communicating the results of the research.

The first lawyer will review the research, analyze the client's possible claims, and provide that analysis to the client. The lawyer and client are likely to discuss the analysis face to face, but often the lawyer also writes an *opinion letter* memorializing the research and her advice. Together the client and the lawyer decide whether to proceed with the claim.

Initial Negotiation Process. The next step is writing a *demand letter* to the party whose conduct appears to have caused the injury (the defendant). Typically, the demand letter will explain the legal basis for believing that the defendant's conduct was wrongful; the legal and factual basis for believing that the conduct caused the plaintiff's injury; and the kinds of damages the law permits in such a case. The lawyer for the defendant will write a *response to the demand letter* explaining the legal and factual bases for the defendant's defenses. The negotiation process may continue for some time, with settlement offers and counteroffers communicated by additional *settlement letters* between the lawyers and *client letters* conveying settlement offers.

Filing a Lawsuit and Resolving Initial Defenses. If the case does not settle, the plaintiff's lawyer chooses the appropriate court and files a *complaint,* a document that sets out the facts of the case and the legal basis for the claim. Once the defendant's lawyer receives the complaint, he has only a few weeks to draft and file a response. His research might have shown that the defendant has one or more defenses that can be raised immediately. If so, the lawyer will raise these defenses in documents called *motions,* which state the defense and ask the court for some kind of action, such as dismissal of the case. Each motion will be supported by a *brief* (also called a *memorandum of law*), explaining the legal and factual basis for the defense. The motions may also be accompanied by other supporting documents, such as *affidavits* from witnesses and copies of documents bearing on the defense.

Each time one party files a motion asking the court to take some action, the other party files a *responsive brief,* usually explaining the legal and factual basis for the argument that the court should deny the motion. The responsive brief may be accompanied by other supporting documents such as *affidavits*. The party who filed the motion (the moving party) will file a *reply brief* addressing the arguments raised in the responsive brief, and there might be a hearing on the motion. The court then decides that issue.

If the court declines to dismiss the case, the defendant's lawyer must file an *answer*, a document that admits or denies all the facts alleged in the complaint and may raise additional defenses as well. The defendant's lawyer also may file a *counterclaim*, a document that alleges some wrongful conduct on the part of the plaintiff. The plaintiff will then file an *answer* to the defendant's counterclaim. The answer admits or denies all the facts alleged in the counterclaim and raises possible remaining defenses against the counterclaim.

Factual Discovery. Now the case is ready for the discovery phase. In this phase, the parties gather all the available evidence in an effort to prepare for trial. During discovery, both parties draft and file *interrogatories* (questions directed to each other) and *responses to interrogatories* (answers to the questions). They draft and file *requests for production of documents, requests for admissions*, and *notices of depositions* (occasions for oral questioning of witnesses under oath). Parties can file *requests for entry on land* (to inspect the premises) or *requests for medical examination* (to subject a person to a physical or psychiatric examination). During the discovery phase, disputes might arise over how much or what kind of information can be sought. These disputes can become the subject of *motions to compel* (filed by the party seeking discovery) or *motions for a protective order* (filed by the party seeking to prevent discovery). Like other motions, discovery motions and responses to them are accompanied by supporting *briefs* and *affidavits*.

Motions for Summary Judgment. After the discovery phase, the parties often draft and file *motions for summary judgment*. A party seeking summary judgment is asking the court to rule on some or all of the claims or defenses without the need for a trial. Summary judgment motions are supported by *briefs*, by *statements of uncontested facts*, and by *affidavits*, excerpts from *depositions*, evidentiary documents, and excerpts from written discovery. The opposing party files a *responsive brief, affidavits*, and other supporting documents resisting the motion, to which the moving party files a *reply brief*. Oral argument is often held. The court might resolve the entire case at the summary judgment stage, or it might resolve some of the claims or defenses, thus narrowing the issues remaining for trial.

Trial. If the case is not resolved, the parties and their lawyers prepare for trial. If the case will be tried to a jury, both parties draft and file a set of proposed *jury instructions*. Jury instructions are statements to be read to the jury to help them understand the law governing the case and their role in the process. Each party also drafts and files a *trial brief*, a document that summarizes the evidence expected to be introduced, raises and argues any evidentiary issues the party anticipates, and argues for the adoption of that party's version of the jury instructions.

Trial begins with jury selection (if the case will be tried to a jury) and opening statements by each party's lawyer. Then the parties call their witnesses and offer their evidence. The trial concludes with closing statements from each lawyer, the reading of the jury instructions (if the case is tried to a jury), and a decision by the judge or the jury. Some *post-trial motions* may be decided, and then a final *judgment* will be entered.

Appeal(s). A party who is dissatisfied with the result at trial usually can file a *notice of appeal* to a higher court. This party is called the appellant. The other party (the appellee) may file a *notice of appeal* as well, raising other objections to the trial court result. A series of documents identify the issues to be argued in the appeal and designate the record of the trial court proceedings that will be sent to the appellate court.

After the record has been prepared and filed, the parties each file *briefs, responsive briefs*, and *reply briefs* arguing the issues raised in the appeal. Oral argument is often held, after which the appellate court issues an opinion. In some circumstances, either or both parties may seek to appeal the appellate court's decision to an even higher court. If so, the appellate process is repeated there. When all appeals are completed, the losing party either complies with the judgment (if applicable) or enforcement proceedings begin. After the judgment has been paid, a *satisfaction of judgment* is filed, and the case is closed.

III. ETHICAL DUTIES

The ethical standards your jurisdiction has adopted for lawyers will govern your legal practice, including your legal writing. These ethical rules bind every lawyer, no matter whether that lawyer is in charge of the case or working under the direction of another lawyer.[1] Most jurisdictions have adopted a version of either the American Bar Association's Model Rules of Professional Conduct or the earlier Model Code of Professional Responsibility. Sanctions for violation of these rules range from private censure to disbarment. No matter what your jurisdiction's ethical rules or your lawyering role, your legal writing must meet at least the following professional obligations:

1. *Competency.* A lawyer must provide competent representation, including legal knowledge, skill, thoroughness, and preparation.[2]
2. *Diligence.* A lawyer's representation must be diligent.[3]
3. *Promptness.* A lawyer must do the client's work promptly.[4]
4. *Confidentiality.* Generally, a lawyer must not reveal a client's confidences except with the client's permission.[5]
5. *Loyalty.* A lawyer's advice must be candid and unbiased, not influenced by conflicting loyalties to another client, to a third party, or to the lawyer's own interests.[6]

---

1. Model R. Pro. Conduct r. 5.2 (Am. Bar Ass'n 2013).
2. *Id.* r. 1.1.
3. *Id.* r. 1.3.
4. *Id.*
5. *Id.* r. 1.6.
6. *Id.* r. 1.7 & 2.1.

In addition to these general standards, your **predictive** legal writing must meet at least the following ethical standards dealing with giving advice:

6. *Criminal or fraudulent activity.* A lawyer must not advise or assist a client to commit a crime or a fraud.[7] When the client expects unethical assistance, the lawyer must explain to the client the ethical limitations on the lawyer's conduct.[8]
7. *Moral, economic, and political factors.* While a lawyer's advice must provide an accurate assessment of the law, it may refer also to moral, economic, social, and political factors relevant to the client's situation.[9] However, the lawyer's representation of a client does not constitute a personal endorsement of the client's activities or views.[10]

Finally, your **persuasive** legal writing must meet at least the following ethical standards:

8. *Statements of law.* A brief-writer must not knowingly make a false statement of law.[11]
9. *Disclosing authority.* A brief-writer must not knowingly fail to disclose to the court directly adverse legal authority in the controlling jurisdiction.[12]
10. *Statements of fact.* A brief-writer must not knowingly make a false statement of fact or fail to disclose a material fact when keeping silent would enable the client to commit a crime or a fraud.[13]
11. *Frivolous arguments.* A brief-writer must not assert a legal argument unless there is a non-frivolous basis for doing so.[14]
12. *Communicating with the judge.* A brief-writer must not communicate ex parte[15] with a judge about the merits of a pending case, unless the particular ex parte communication is specifically permitted by law.[16]
13. *Filing requirements.* A brief-writer must not intentionally disregard filing requirements or other obligations imposed by court rules.[17]

These ethical standards will apply to your legal writing after you are a lawyer. They will also apply, directly or indirectly, to the legal writing you do as a law clerk before you are admitted to the bar. They will be among the standards by which your legal writing teacher evaluates your law school writing. Be sure that every document you write meets these standards of professional responsibility.

---

7. *Id.* r. 1.2(d).
8. *Id.* r. 1.4(a)(5).
9. *Id.* r. 2.1.
10. *Id.* r. 1.2(b).
11. *Id.* r. 3.3(a)(1).
12. *Id.* r. 3.3(a)(3).
13. *Id.* r. 3.3(a)(1) & (2).
14. *Id.* r. 3.1.
15. *Ex parte,* in this context, means without notice to other parties in the litigation.
16. Model R. Pro. Conduct r. 3.5(b).
17. *Id.* r. 3.2 & 3.4(c).

IV. LEGAL CITATION

In addition to their ethical duties, lawyers also have the obligation to provide proper attribution to the sources that they are citing to. An understanding of plagiarism and when it is necessary to cite are integral to professional legal writing.

A. Plagiarism

Plagiarism is the act of presenting someone else's words or ideas as your own. Most of us first encountered the concept of plagiarism in an academic environment. There, plagiarism occurs primarily in one or both of these situations: (1) failing to attribute an idea to the source from which it was drawn; or (2) failing to use quotation marks to show that the words themselves, not just the idea, came from another source. In an academic setting, authoring a document constitutes a representation that the author is the source of all ideas and words not otherwise attributed. Thus, in an academic setting, failure to attribute borrowed words or ideas constitutes plagiarism. It is both a lie and a theft.

In law practice, the concept of plagiarism can be confusing. Lawyers and judges often adapt and use, without attribution or quotation marks, language and ideas drawn from other lawyers' work. Firms keep form files and brief banks so documents prepared by one lawyer can be "recycled" by another. Law clerks write opinions to be signed by their judges. Judges incorporate into their opinions sections of briefs filed by the parties' lawyers. Associates write briefs to be signed by partners. Law publishers publish books of pleadings and other forms designed to be used nearly verbatim.

Some wonder whether the concept of plagiarism applies at all in a law practice setting. They argue that writing in law practice does not carry a representation that the author is the source of all unattributed ideas and words, especially not when the document is asserting a legal point. In legal practice, the writer's goal is not to take personal credit for originating everything in the document, but rather to serve the client efficiently and well. The identity of the writer is irrelevant. Proponents of this position argue that service to a client requires presenting the most effective material in the most effective manner for the least cost. Thus, they assert, a lawyer's signature on a document constitutes only the lawyer's representation that the document is not being presented for any improper purpose, including the purpose of causing needless increase in the cost of litigation; that the legal contentions are not frivolous; and that any factual contentions or denials are reasonably supported by the evidence.[18]

18. Fed. R. Civ. P. 11(b).

No matter what standards might apply to *law practice*, however, remember that your law school writing is being done in an academic environment where the writing assignment has pedagogical goals rather than goals of efficiency and economy. The law school project focuses on enabling the writer *to learn* and the teacher *to evaluate* that learning. You must generate ideas and text on your own so you can learn that skill, and your teacher must be able to identify your ideas and text to be able to evaluate them.

Your school's honor code probably prohibits plagiarism, which it may define to include conduct resulting either from an intent to deceive or from "mere" carelessness. Being charged with an honor code violation is serious business for any student, but especially serious for law students. Soon, you will be applying for admission to the bar, and most Bar Character and Fitness Committees ask questions designed to discover whether you have violated your school's honor code. Any honor code charge brings a risk that the proceeding will have to be reported to the Character and Fitness Committee, that you will have to appear personally to explain the charge, and that your bar admission will be delayed or denied as a result.

So carefully follow your teacher's instructions about using material from another source or working with another student. Be precise in your note-taking so you can remember where you found the ideas you will use and so you can distinguish between paraphrases and quotes. *Unless you have explicit instructions to the contrary, do not use the words or ideas of another without proper attribution and, where appropriate, quotation marks.*[19]

B. When to Cite

Citation to authority has twin purposes. First, citations provide your reader with the authority that supports your assertions about the law. Providing your reader with supporting authority is essential. Your citations should prove that the law is what you say it is and that it means what you say it means.

Second, citations attribute the words and ideas of another author to that author. Because a reader will attribute uncited material to you, a citation is your way of disclaiming credit for the words and ideas you did not create. Therefore, you should cite when you quote and when you paraphrase (that is, when you use your own words to express the authority's idea).

19. See Chapter 19 for a discussion of when quotation marks are appropriate.

WHEN TO USE CITATIONS

1. When you assert a legal principle.

Example:

To recover under an implied warranty of habitability, a tenant must show that she gave the landlord notice of the defect and allowed time for its correction. *King v. Moorehead*, 495 S.W.2d 65, 76 (Mo. Ct. App. 1973).

2. When you refer to or describe the content of an authority.

Example:

In a leading case, the leased premises had faulty sewer pipes, defective wiring, and crumbling ceilings. *Hilder v. St. Peter*, 478 A.2d 202, 206 (Vt. 1984).

3. When you quote.

Example:

An earlier court had observed that today's tenants "seek a well known package of goods and services — a package which includes not merely walls and ceilings, but also adequate heat, light and ventilation, serviceable plumbing facilities, secure windows and doors, proper sanitation, and proper maintenance." *Javins v. First Nat'l Realty Corp.*, 428 F.2d 1071, 1074 (D.C. Cir. 1970).

EXERCISE 1-2
Recognizing Ideas That Need Citations

Read the following passage[20] and identify the statements for which a citation is either necessary or desirable. Be prepared to explain your answers.

A lawyer has a fiduciary relationship with his or her client. The fiduciary aspect of the relationship is said to arise after the formation of the attorney-client relationship, and it applies to a fee agreement reached after the attorney-client relationship has been entered.

At least three reasons support the imposition of fiduciary obligations on a lawyer. First, once the relationship is established, the client likely will have begun to depend on the attorney's integrity, fairness, and judgment. Second, the attorney may have acquired information about the client that gives the attorney an unfair advantage in negotiations between them. Finally, the client generally will not be able to change attorneys easily, but rather will be economically or personally dependent on the attorney's continued representation.

Accordingly, an attorney breaches his fiduciary duty when he abuses his client's trust. For example, in *Benson v. State Bar*, the attorney borrowed money from a current client. The attorney "was heavily in debt, and insolvent, at the time he approached [the client] for these loans." In return for the loans, the attorney gave the client unsecured promissory notes. In disbarring

20. Modified from Stephen Gillers, *Regulation of Lawyers: Problems of Law and Ethics* 61–62 (4th ed. 1995).

the lawyer, the court described the client's trust in the lawyer's judgment and wrote:

> The gravamen of the charge is abuse of that trust, and regardless of petitioner's contention that he never specifically recommended the unsecured loans to [the client], it is undisputed that in soliciting them he failed to reveal the extent of his preexisting indebtedness and financial distress.

In addition, in *People v. Smith*, an attorney was under investigation for drug use. The attorney offered to cooperate with Colorado police as an undercover informant. He secretly recorded a telephone conversation with a former client in which he asked the former client to sell him cocaine. He then met with the former client wearing a body microphone. The recorded conversations ultimately were used to convict the former client of three felony charges. The Colorado Supreme Court held that although the attorney

> no longer represented the [former client], the conduct in all probability would not have occurred had [the attorney] not relied upon the trust and confidence placed in him by the [former client] as a result of the recently completed attorney-client relationship between the two. The undisclosed use of a recording device necessarily involves elements of deception and trickery which do not comport with the high standards of candor and fairness to which all attorneys are bound.

For these and other offenses, the attorney was suspended from the practice of law.

CHAPTER 2

Sources of Law, the Common-Law Process, and Weight of Authority

In this chapter, we begin by discussing the courses of law, with a focus on case law, including the structures and functions of courts and the concepts of precedent, stare decisis, and case holdings. Chapter 3 introduces case briefing, the basic analytical tool for reading and understanding cases. Chapter 3 also explores the ways in which individual cases relate to each other. Then, in Chapter 4, we turn our attention specifically to statutes, exploring methods of interpretation and application of these increasingly important sources of law.

I. SOURCES OF LAW

There are three sovereign entities in the United States with the power to make and enforce laws: the federal government, the states, and the Native American tribes (Figure 2-1). Constitutions are the foundation of most legal systems in the United States, dividing lawmaking powers among three branches of government. These branches are the executive branch, the legislative branch, and the judicial branch. The legislative branch enacts laws, the executive branch implements the laws through rules and regulations, and the judicial branch interprets the laws by deciding cases. Accordingly, these

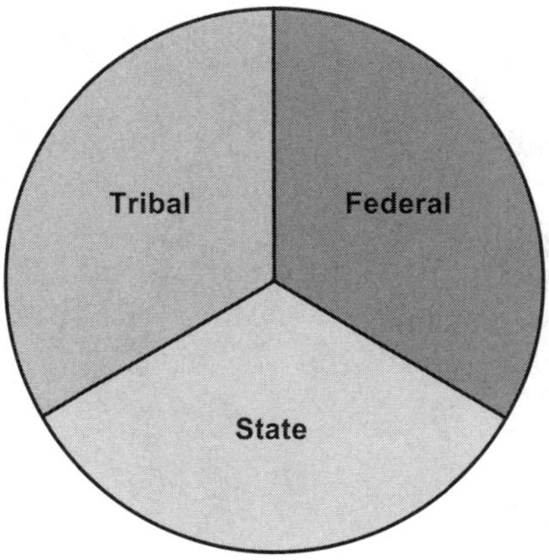

Figure 2-1
Three sovereign entities in the United States

government branches for each of the three sovereign entities create primary sources of law, which include constitutions, statutes, regulations, and cases.

A. The Structure of Court Systems

As mentioned above, there are three sovereign entities within the United States with the power to render legal decisions. Each state has at least two court systems: its own court system and the federal court system. In addition, some states also have tribal court systems (see Figure 2-2). Federal courts have jurisdiction (authority) over cases entrusted to them by the constitution or by federal statutes. For the most part, these are cases raising issues of federal law[1] and cases involving parties from different states when the damages exceed $75,000.[2] State courts also have subject-matter jurisdiction over many of the same cases, so a plaintiff may be able to choose the court system he or she prefers.

The jurisdiction of tribal courts is extremely complicated. Just be aware that before bringing a case that involves a Native American or a tribe, you need to determine whether the tribal court has jurisdiction. Generally, a tribal court's jurisdiction over criminal and civil cases is contingent on whether the parties are Native American and on whether the alleged crime or dispute took place in Native American territory.

We will begin with an overview of the federal court system because it operates in the same way in each state.

1. The Federal Court System

The federal court system has three levels. Litigation usually begins in the United States District Court, which is the trial court of general jurisdiction[3] in

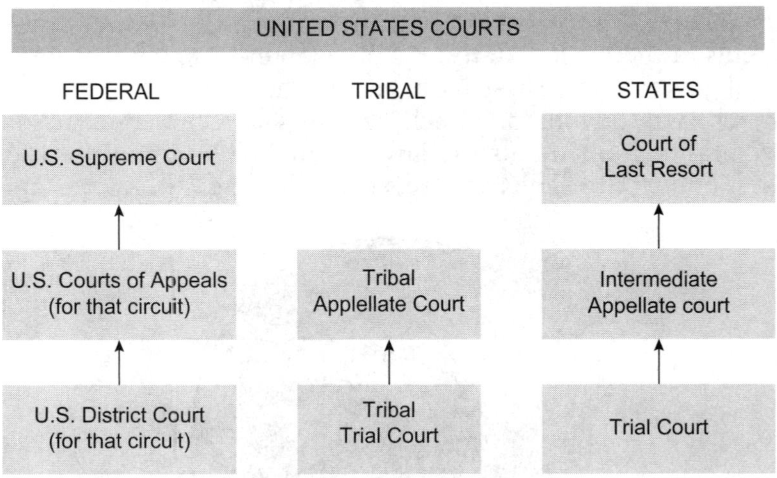

Figure 2-2
United States Courts

1. 28 U.S.C. § 1331.
2. 28 U.S.C. § 1332(a).
3. A court of general jurisdiction is a court whose jurisdiction is not limited to certain kinds of cases. A court whose jurisdiction is limited is called, not surprisingly, a court of limited jurisdiction. An example of a federal court of limited jurisdiction is the United States Tax Court, which may hear only federal tax cases.

the federal system. A federal district court may have a number of judges, but normally a proceeding is heard by only one judge. Other judges of that court are busy in other courtrooms hearing other cases.

Each state has at least one federal district, and many have two or more. For instance, California has four districts: the Southern District, the Northern District, the Eastern District, and the Central District. The full name for the federal trial-level court located in Los Angeles is the United States District Court for the Central District of California. The first four words of that long title identify the court as the trial-level federal court. The remaining words identify the court's particular district.

A district court's decision may be appealed to the intermediate appellate court, the United States Court of Appeals. Normally, an appeal is heard by a panel of three judges, but occasionally a case might be heard by all of the judges of that court. In such a case, we say that the court heard the case *en banc*.

For purposes of this intermediate appellate level, the country is divided into 13 circuits. The First through the Eleventh Circuits cover multistate areas.[4] For instance, decisions appealed from the federal district court in Los Angeles would be heard by the United States Court of Appeals for the Ninth Circuit. Decisions appealed from the federal district court in New York City would be heard by the United States Court of Appeals for the Second Circuit. The first five words of this long title identify the court as the intermediate federal appellate court. The remaining words identify the court's particular circuit.

Figure 2-3 shows the geographic jurisdictions of the federal circuit courts of appeal.

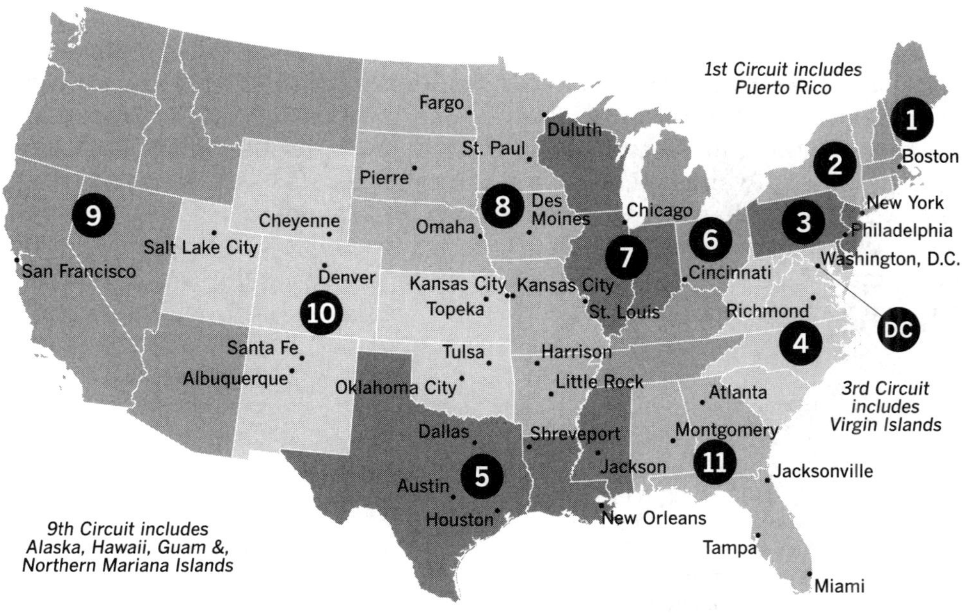

Figure 2-3
The federal judicial circuits as shown in *2009 Judicial Staff Directory* 963 (C.Q. Press 2009)

4. The other two circuits are the United States Court of Appeals for the District of Columbia, which hears appeals from the District of Columbia, and the United States Court of Appeals for the Federal Circuit, which hears appeals from certain specialized federal courts.

Some federal cases ultimately are appealed to the United States Supreme Court, the highest appellate court in the federal system.[5] The United States Supreme Court has the discretion to hear a case and reviews only a fraction of the cases decided by the federal circuit courts each year. At the level of the Supreme Court, some preliminary matters are decided by one justice or a panel of justices, but cases receiving full review are heard by all the justices of the Court.

2. State Court Systems

State court systems resemble the federal court system in many respects. Litigation usually begins in a trial court of general jurisdiction.[6] The names of these trial courts vary from state to state, but common names for them are district courts, circuit courts, courts of common pleas, or superior courts.

Most states have at least one intermediate appellate court. Larger states have several, whose jurisdiction is defined geographically, much as in the federal system. At the intermediate level, most appellate cases are decided by panels of an odd number of judges, often three. Some cases, however, are heard en banc, either initially or after a decision by a panel.

Finally, all states have an appellate court of last resort, the highest appellate court in the state. In most states, this court is called the Supreme Court.[7] Most cases are decided by all justices sitting together. This court decides whether to review a case and is the last and highest forum for deciding matters of state law.

3. Tribal Court Systems

The majority of Native American tribal courts tend to follow the same pattern as the federal and state court systems.[8] Yet, these tribally authorized courts tend to be more informal than state and federal courts and endeavor to integrate traditional values. In addition, the tribal courts focus on a restorative approach rather than the win-lose approach of Anglo-American justice systems. When administering justice, these courts rely on the tribe's constitution, statutes, common law, customs, traditions, and administrative law; and any applicable federal laws.

---

5. The United States Supreme Court can also hear cases from a state's highest appellate court, but only when the state court's ruling was based on federal law.

6. Specialized courts (courts of limited jurisdiction) exist for hearing such matters as juvenile cases, probates of estates, cases alleging small damage amounts, and housing issues.

7. New York is a notable exception. There, the trial court is called the Supreme Court. The intermediate appellate court is called the Supreme Court, Appellate Division. The highest appellate court in New York is called the Court of Appeals.

8. In addition to the tribally authorized courts that are organized similarly to the state and federal court systems, some tribes use traditional courts of justice systems while others use CFR courts. *See* Samantha A. Moppett, *Acknowledging America's First Sovereign: Incorporating Tribal Justice Systems into the Legal Research and Writing Curriculum*, 35 Okla. City U. L. Rev, 267, 295 (2010).

II. THE FUNCTIONS OF TRIAL AND APPELLATE COURTS

The functions of trial courts and appellate courts differ in important ways. Understanding these differences will help you understand the cases you read and the arguments you can make.

A. The Functions of Trial Courts

A trial court has two primary functions: deciding what law applies to the case and deciding who did what to whom. In other words, a trial court decides questions of law and questions of fact.

A court decides *a question of law* when it decides what the law of that jurisdiction says about a legal question. Does the law allow relief for what the defendant is alleged to have done? What kind of evidence does the law permit the court to consider? What kind of relief is the court permitted to grant? These are pure questions of law. They can be answered solely by doing legal research in the law library. To decide them, the court need not decide anything about what actually happened to these parties. The court need only decide what the law will require *if a particular set of facts turns out to be true.*

A court decides *a question of fact* when it decides what actually happened in this case. Did Smith strike Jones? Did Kerry sign the document? Did Newman pull into the right lane? These are pure questions of fact. They cannot be answered by doing research in the law library. To decide them, the court must listen to the testimony, examine the documents and other exhibits, and decide what happened to these parties.

Questions of fact can be decided by a judge or by a jury. If the case is tried to a jury, questions of fact are decided by the jury, not the judge.[9] If the case is a bench trial (that is, a case tried to the judge without a jury), decisions on questions of fact are made by the trial judge. Either way, however, questions of law are decided by the trial judge, not a jury.[10]

B. The Functions of Appellate Courts

A trial court's decision usually can be appealed to a higher court. The party who appeals (the appellant) cannot simply ask the appellate court to decide the entire case again. Appellate courts are error-correcting courts. The

---

9. A trial judge can, however, change a jury's factual findings if no reasonable understanding of the evidence could have resulted in the jury's findings. Thus, the judge acts as a safety net protecting against a jury that has disregarded the evidence.

10. A third category exists: a mixed question of law and fact. We will explore this category in Chapter 17. For our purposes here, it is enough to understand the distinction between pure questions of law and pure questions of fact.

appellant must identify the particular question(s) to be reviewed. Generally, a party seeks appellate review of a question of law or a question of fact.[11]

Because the trial court had the opportunity to observe the witnesses first-hand, the trial court's decision on pure questions of fact will not be disturbed on appeal unless the decision is clearly erroneous. In essence, to reverse a trial court's factual finding, the appellate court must believe that no reasonable interpretation of the evidence would support the trial court's decision. Thus, reversals on pure questions of fact are unusual.

The situation is different for questions of law. On a question of law, the appellate court is free to decide that the trial judge's understanding of the law was wrong. Because it is a higher court, an appellate court's decision on questions of law supersedes the trial judge's opinion. Most reversals involve questions of law.

EXERCISE 2-1
Questions of Law Versus Questions of Fact

Decide whether an appellate court would have to give any deference to the following statements from a trial court's decision.

1. The Defendant cultivated a garden on the property each year between 1994 and 2002.
2. To establish a claim to property by adverse possession, a party must prove that his or her use of the property was open and notorious for the entire statutory period.
3. Abandonment occurs when a person in possession of real property leaves the property with no intention to return.
4. When the Defendant left the property to attend school in another state, her improvements and her household furnishings remained on the property.

III. THE COMMON-LAW PROCESS

The American legal system is a direct descendant of the English legal system that began to develop in 1066, with the Norman invasion of Britain. The most significant characteristic of this Anglo-American legal system is its reliance on the common-law process, that is, the process by which judges "make" law and then adhere to this judge-made law. To understand how the common-law process functions, we must examine four closely related concepts: the doctrine of stare decisis, an opinion's holding, the breadth of a holding, and the distinction between a holding and dicta.

---

11. We will explore this subject in more detail in Chapter 17's discussion of standards of review.

A. Stare Decisis

At the heart of the common-law system is the doctrine of stare decisis. According to this doctrine, when a court has decided a case in a particular way, future similar cases should be decided the same way. Although the doctrine sounds simple and straightforward, in operation it is more complex than it might appear.

First, the doctrine applies only when the pending case is similar enough to the prior case to justify the application. Because all pending cases differ somewhat from prior cases, the question of whether the cases are similar enough will almost always be subject to argument. Second, if there is good reason, a lower court can decline to follow the precedent of a higher court. Conceptually, the justification for such a decision is the belief that the higher court probably would not adhere to the prior decision if the question were now before it. Finally, a court can overrule its own prior decision when the court decides that the law should change. A court might decide that the prior decision was ill-reasoned originally, that its application has produced unanticipated and undesirable results, or that modern conditions now call for a different approach.

A court usually overrules its own decision explicitly, by identifying in its new opinion the case to be overruled and directly stating the intention not to rely on it in the future. A court also can overrule a case implicitly, not mentioning the case at all but applying a different legal standard to the pending case.

B. Holdings

In the common-law process, the part of the precedent case that binds a future court is the holding. A case holding is a statement of the court's decision about the issues actually before it. No doubt you have already heard the term "holding." You might have seen the term defined in materials about how to brief cases, and your professors are probably asking you to state the holdings of the cases you read. A word of clarification is appropriate here.

The term "holding" is used in a number of different ways, varying according to the context, the task at hand, and one's particular legal philosophy. For instance, your professors might want you to state the holding in terms specific to the parties in the case; state the holding as a general principle ready to be applied to future cases; include a rule statement in the holding; or provide a fairly complete statement of the important facts leading to the case's outcome.

Rest assured that each of these professors has a pedagogical purpose in mind, and you should follow each professor's preference in his or her class. The purpose of stating holdings in a law school class is to teach you the basics of case reading, and each professor's approach emphasizes particular parts of that important skill.

In your legal writing class and in law practice, however, you will be identifying holdings for a different purpose—to decide whether and how that precedent case might apply to your client's situation. When you write statements of holdings for a contracts or torts class, you have only the precedent case before you. You rarely have a set of new facts to which the precedent might apply. In your legal writing class and in law practice, you will be reading the case for the purpose of relating it to a particular new set of facts. You will find that when you state holdings for this purpose, you will not need to worry about most of the differences you might have noticed among professors and among books and other materials discussing the term.

For our purposes, you can think of the holding as the court's decision on the particular legal issue plus the important facts—the facts that seemed to make a difference to the result. For instance, consider *Cantwell v. Denton*, a hypothetical case about assumption of the risk in a torts case. In *Cantwell*, faulty wiring in an apartment house caused a fire. A resident of one of the apartments arrived at the scene, observed the fire, entered the building anyway, and sustained injuries in the process. The resident sued the building owner to recover for those injuries, and the defendant raised the defense of assumption of the risk, a doctrine that, in various forms, prevents or limits recovery for damages caused in part by a voluntary assumption of the risk of injury.

Assume that the court in *Cantwell* decided that the doctrine of voluntary assumption of the risk did not apply to this plaintiff because he had entered the building believing his young daughter to be inside. You might state the holding as follows:

> *Holding* Assumption of the risk applies only to voluntary conduct, and a father's choice to enter a burning building is not voluntary if he must choose between entering the building and failing to save his child's life.

No doubt you have already observed great variety in holding statements, even without regard for different preferences among professors. Differences are normal. The next sections explain more about why you should not be surprised to find these differences and how you can use them in representing your clients.

C. The Breadth of Holdings

One of the ways holding statements can differ is in breadth. Consider again our hypothetical torts case, *Cantwell v. Denton*. The holding statement above is stated narrowly. It describes the holding as applying to fathers who are choosing between entering a burning building and failing to save the lives of their children. It does not tell us whether the rule would apply to persons other than fathers, to situations other than burning buildings, or to saving people other than children. It certainly tells us nothing about whether the rule would include saving property rather than lives.

But you might need to argue on behalf of a client in one of those situations. For instance, assume that your firm is representing Mr. and Mrs. Gregory in litigation against Jerico Autoworks, an auto repair business. Jerico advertised oil changes completed in 20 minutes "while you wait." One Saturday, the Gregorys put a turkey in their oven, set the temperature for 325 degrees, and left for town to have Jerico change the oil in their car. Jerico completed the job and turned the car back over to the Gregorys. The Gregorys paid Jerico and began driving the rural road toward their home.

They were only halfway home when they noticed the internal engine heat beginning to climb. They realized that they were running low on oil and surmised, correctly as it turned out, that Jerico had not sufficiently tightened the oil plug. But they also realized that the turkey in their oven was nearly done. They knew that this rural road was traveled so infrequently that the odds were small that they would be able to flag another driver and get home before the burning turkey might cause a fire in their kitchen.

They decided to drive on in the hope that they could get home before their kitchen burned. The Gregorys got close enough to walk the rest of the way and so saved their kitchen, but at the cost of serious engine damage. Your firm has sued Jerico on behalf of the Gregorys, and Jerico has raised the defense of assumption of the risk based on the Gregorys' decision to continue driving.

An attorney in your firm has asked you to write a brief arguing that the decision to continue driving should not be considered an assumption of the risk. Assume that your only authority is *Cantwell v. Denton*. Suppose you stated the holding of *Cantwell* as we did above, that is:

Holding Assumption of the risk applies only to voluntary conduct, and a father's choice to enter a burning building is not voluntary if he must choose between entering the building and failing to save his child.

This holding statement would not tell a court much about whether the Gregorys' decision would constitute assumption of the risk. Can you state the holding more broadly? Whether you will be able to formulate a broader holding statement will depend largely on the court's language in *Cantwell*. Most opinions will contain at least several paragraphs explaining the court's decision, and this language might help you formulate a broader holding. Assume you find these paragraphs in the *Cantwell* opinion:

> A father's choice to enter a burning building is not voluntary where he must choose between entering the building and failing to save his child. The bond between a parent and a child is the strongest human bond. In situations that otherwise would constitute assumption of the risk, the law should not penalize a plaintiff for fulfilling the duties of a parent to a child.
>
> Further, our law places the highest value on human life, and the highest form of courage is to risk one's own life in an attempt to save the life of another. The doctrine of assumption of the risk was not designed to penalize one who demonstrates this kind of courage.
>
> We must remember, after all, that it was the defendant's negligence that placed the plaintiff in the position of having to choose between the threatened harm and an equal or greater harm. A defendant cannot subject the plaintiff to such a Hobson's choice[12] and then defend against his own negligence by pointing to the plaintiff's response.

If the *Cantwell* opinion contains this language, could you formulate a broader holding? What holding might you formulate if you focus primarily on the first paragraph? What if you focus primarily on the second paragraph?

12. Hobson's choice refers to a situation where it appears that there is a choice to be made between two different actions, when in reality there is only one choice to be made.

The third? Which paragraph would allow you to formulate a holding that will accommodate the Gregorys' concern about their kitchen?

The first paragraph grounds the result in the particular obligations of a parent to a child. From that paragraph, you could formulate a holding that applies to parents, not just fathers. You might even be able to formulate a holding that would apply to property damage if protection of the property was a clear parental duty. But the Gregorys' dilemma did not involve parental duty, so the holding you could formulate from the first paragraph would not help the Gregorys very much.

The second paragraph grounds the holding in the special value we place on trying to save human life. From that paragraph you could formulate a holding not limited to a parental obligation, but it still might not cover property damage.

The third paragraph, however, grounds the holding in the observation that the defendant's negligence has caused the necessity to choose between two bad options. That paragraph describes the situations that call for this result as those in which the defendant's negligence has forced the plaintiff to choose between the threatened harm and an equal or greater harm. The third paragraph would allow you to formulate a broader holding like this:

Holding Assumption of the risk requires a voluntary choice. When the defendant's negligence forces the plaintiff to choose between the threatened harm and another equal or greater harm, the plaintiff's choice is not voluntary.

Figure 2-4 demonstrates how this broader holding statement would allow the Gregorys to argue that their decision to continue driving did not constitute assumption of the risk.

We have seen in this section that case analysis is inherently subjective. It is no wonder that holding statements differ so widely from each other. At

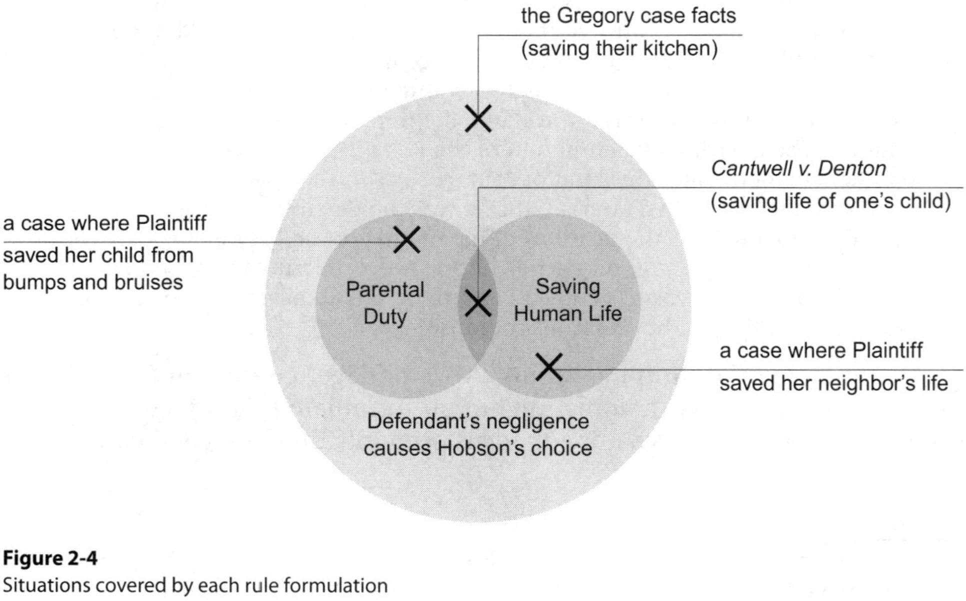

Figure 2-4
Situations covered by each rule formulation

first, you might find this subjectivity unnerving, but it provides lawyers with wonderful opportunities for advocacy on behalf of clients. In the practice of law, you will find that you are grateful for it.

EXERCISE 2-2

Drafting a Holding

Write a statement of the holding for a case your professor has assigned. If your professor has not assigned a case for this exercise, use the well-known contracts case, *Lucy v. Zehmer*, found in Appendix F.

D. Holdings Versus Dicta

We are now ready to explore the last important topic explaining the common-law process—the distinction between *holdings* and *dicta*.[13] This distinction is important because only an opinion's holding is binding on future courts. The doctrine of stare decisis does not apply to dicta. A judge in a future case may *choose* to follow dicta but is not bound to do so.

The holding of an opinion is limited to the court's statements resolving the question(s) *actually at issue in that case*, that is, statements on issues necessary to the result reached. The court might make many other statements about the law, statements other than those necessary to explain the decision. Such statements of law not essential to the outcome of that particular case are *dicta*. They are not part of the holding.

An example may help. Assume that you are reading a contracts opinion dealing with whether a communication without a price would constitute a valid offer. In that opinion, the court might have made some statements about other legal issues. In the course of the opinion, the judge might have stated that a valid contract requires acceptance and consideration. However, the judge did not decide that particular case by considering whether there had been a valid acceptance or sufficient consideration. Those were not the issues the parties raised. Instead, the question before the court and the basis for the result was whether there had been a valid *offer*. Therefore, any statements the judge might have made about *acceptance* or *consideration* would be dicta.

Remember that the primary purpose of distinguishing holding from dicta is to decide whether a future court is *bound* by the language. Although statements of dicta are not binding, a lower court will often give the dicta of a higher court great deference. Many trial and intermediate appellate court judges consider it their role to apply the law as the higher court would, and dicta can be a strong indication of what the higher court would hold. Take care, however, not to mislead the court or another lawyer by presenting dicta as if they were part of the holding. You can convey to the reader that the information that you are relying on is dicta in the text and in a weight of

13. The full term is *obiter dictum*, literally meaning "a remark made in passing." "Dictum" is singular; the plural form is "dicta."

authority parenthetical added to the case citation. Chapter 19 will discuss proper citation form.

Although the distinction between holding and dicta is sometimes clear, as in the contracts example above, it is often debatable. You will not always know for sure whether a certain statement of law was necessary to the court's decision. For instance, consider again the *Cantwell* language in the prior section. If you are trying to persuade the judge that the Gregorys did not assume the risk of injury to their engine, you probably will draw the *holding* from the third paragraph. However, if you represent Jerico, no doubt you will argue that the statements in the third paragraph are *dicta*. You will argue that only the narrower statements in the first and second paragraphs were necessary to decide *Cantwell* and therefore that the broad statements in the third paragraph are "mere dicta."

Once again we see that case analysis is inherently an interpretive project. If you are looking for certainty in the law, you are bound to feel frustrated, for no language can capture completely the whole of human experience. It is this very flexibility of interpretation, however, that provides the opportunity for advocacy.

EXERCISE 2-3
Holding Versus Dicta

Read the following hypothetical opinion. For each statement that follows it, decide whether the statement is part of the holding or dictum. Be prepared to explain your answers.

> This is an action to decide the rightful owner of a painting, which was allegedly given by Harrison Crenshaw to his daughter Alecia Green on her 25th birthday. According to the record below, on the date of Green's birthday, Crenshaw hosted a party for his daughter in his condominium. He told her in the presence of the guests at the party that the painting was hers. Crenshaw said that she could have the painting as soon as he found another to replace it. One month later, before the painting was delivered, Crenshaw died. The trial court held that Crenshaw had made a valid gift to Green. We disagree.
>
> To constitute a valid gift of personal property, the donor must manifest his intention to make the gift and the item must be physically delivered unless physical delivery is not practicable. Physical delivery is not practicable if, for instance, the item is in another city, or locked in a safe deposit box in a bank closed for the weekend, or too heavy to move without arranging moving assistance. This painting, however, was hanging on the wall not ten feet away. It is small and light, and it was hanging freely on a hook. Physical delivery is required when the item can be so easily removed and handed over. Therefore, there was no valid gift of the painting.

1. An item must be physically delivered unless physical delivery would be impracticable.
2. An item locked in a safe deposit box in a bank closed for the weekend need not be physically delivered.
3. A small, light, freely accessible item must be physically delivered to complete a valid gift.
4. To constitute a valid gift of personal property, the donor must manifest his intention to make the gift.

IV. THE WEIGHT OF AUTHORITY

No doubt you already have noticed many different kinds of authorities cited in the cases you are reading and in the note material in your case books. Some of these authorities are actually "law," and some are not. Some of them would bind a particular court, and some would not. Some would trump another authority, and some would not. The principles that govern these questions are critically important for your understanding of law.

A. Primary Authority Versus Secondary Authority

The first important distinction among authorities is the question of which actually constitute "law." Some do, and some are simply commentary on the law or suggestions about what the law ought to be. Authorities that actually constitute law are called "primary authorities." Authorities that merely explain or comment on these primary authorities are called "secondary authorities."

Primary authority is created by an entity that has the legal power to create law. As discussed at the beginning of the chapter, four basic kinds of law exist: (1) constitutions, (2) case law, (3) statutes, and (4) regulations or rulings issued by governmental agencies. Situations to which Michigan law applies will be governed by the Michigan Constitution and by the statutes the Michigan legislature enacts. They will be governed by the case law the Michigan courts create. They will be governed by the administrative law the Michigan state agencies create. They are also governed by applicable federal constitutional provisions and federal case law, statutes, and administrative law. All of these sources are primary authority—the law itself.

Secondary authority is commentary on the law, and it comes in many forms. You might have encountered some secondary sources already, such as treatises or hornbooks on particular subjects, legal encyclopedias, or law review articles. These sources are created by private individuals, organizations, or businesses. They could help you locate primary authority or understand it better once you have found it. For some, respect for the author or for the drafting process might persuade a judge to defer to the source's content, but those private individuals, organizations, or businesses do not have the authority to create law. Thus, a court is not required to follow it.

Relationships Among Primary Authorities. Each jurisdiction has a constitution, a set of statutes, a body of case law, and a body of administrative regulations.[14] The relationships among these primary authorities are, in a sense, hierarchical. Applicable constitutional provisions constrain all other authorities. Thus, a state statute or case opinion found to violate that state's constitution will not be followed. Properly enacted statutes constrain both case law and administrative regulations or rulings. Thus, a judge must follow

14. This might not be the case for the Native American tribes.

a properly enacted statute and may not simply disagree and rule according to her own views. The court does, however, have the authority to interpret the meaning of a constitutional provision or a statute and to decide whether it applies to the situation before the court. The ability to interpret the text and decide whether it applies gives the courts broad powers to define even statutory law. Case law constrains an administrative agency. The agency cannot decline to follow an applicable binding court decision.

EXERCISE 2-4
Comparing Precedential Value

For each question below, which authority carries more precedential value? Assume that the authorities listed in each question address precisely the same issue, that all are in the same jurisdiction, and that each is valid in all respects. Be prepared to explain your answers.

1. A state statute or an opinion of that state's highest court?
2. An agency regulation or a state statute?
3. A state constitutional provision or a state statute?
4. An opinion of the state's highest court or a ruling by a state agency?
5. A state constitutional provision or an opinion of that state's highest court?

B. Mandatory Authority Versus Persuasive Authority

In our discussion of primary authorities, we identified what is actually law, but not all primary authorities will bind every court. To decide which primary authorities will bind a particular court, we must explore another distinction—the distinction between mandatory and persuasive authority. An authority is mandatory in a particular court if it binds that court. An authority is merely persuasive if it does not bind that court. The judge may choose to be persuaded by it, but the judge has a choice.

For instance, an Iowa case would not bind a Nevada trial court on an issue of Nevada law. The Nevada court may find the Iowa opinion persuasive, perhaps because of the strength of its reasoning or because the judge who wrote the opinion is particularly well respected, but the Nevada court would not be *required* to follow it. Thus, in the Nevada trial court, the Iowa opinion would be *persuasive* authority, not mandatory authority.

On the other hand, an applicable opinion of the Nevada Supreme Court would bind the Nevada trial court. The Nevada Supreme Court is the highest appellate court in the state, and the Nevada trial court is bound to follow a Nevada Supreme Court opinion absent some reason to think that the opinion is no longer viable. Thus, the Nevada Supreme Court opinion is *mandatory* authority for the Nevada trial court. Similarly, a Nevada statute would be *mandatory* authority for any Nevada court. Here are the basic principles for identifying mandatory case authority, divided according to whether the issue is a matter of state law or federal law:

On issues of state law, the decisions of a state's highest court are mandatory authority for all other courts of that state as well as for all federal courts applying that state's law. It might surprise you to learn that federal courts can be bound by state courts. However, a state's highest court has the ultimate authority on matters of that state's law. No federal court, not even the United States Supreme Court, can control the state's highest court on matters of that state's law.

Decisions of a state's intermediate appellate courts are binding on trial courts within the geographic boundaries of the intermediate appellate court's jurisdiction. In many states, the decision of an intermediate appellate court also binds any trial court whose own intermediate appellate court has not ruled on the issue. Decisions of federal courts or courts from other states are persuasive but not mandatory on matters of state law.

On issues of federal law, decisions of the United States Supreme Court are binding on all federal and state courts in the country. Decisions of the applicable intermediate federal appellate court are binding on all federal district courts in that circuit. Decisions of other circuits are persuasive only.

Decisions of federal intermediate appellate courts and federal trial courts on issues of federal law are not mandatory authority for state courts. However, as a practical matter, state courts generally give the opinions of those courts significant weight. This is particularly true of state courts within the geographical boundaries of the particular federal court.

EXERCISE 2-5
Gauging the Relative Weights of Authorities

Your firm represents Kay Lang, who sold a piece of commercial property located in Los Angeles to Adam Kornfeld. Kornfeld claims that Lang failed to disclose to him the true condition of the property, and he has filed suit against her for damages in the state trial court. You are researching whether under California law a seller of real property has a duty to disclose to the buyer the condition of the property.

You have found the following authorities: (1) Which are primary authorities? (2) For each authority, describe the precedential value it likely will carry for the dispute between Kornfeld and Lang. Use the following choices: mandatory binding; very persuasive; moderately persuasive; slightly persuasive; no persuasive value.

1. An opinion of the California Supreme Court deciding the duty of a seller to disclose to the buyer the condition of the property.
2. An article in the University of California at Los Angeles (UCLA) Law Review discussing the applicable California rule on the seller's duty to disclose to the buyer the condition of the property.
3. An opinion of the United States Court of Appeals for the Ninth Circuit applying the applicable California rule on the duty of a seller to disclose to a buyer the condition of the property.
4. A California statute on the duty of a seller to disclose to a buyer the condition of the property.
5. An opinion of another California state trial court applying the California rule on the duty of a seller to disclose to a buyer the condition of the property.

6. A section from a California legal encyclopedia explaining the applicable California rule on the duty of a seller to disclose to a buyer the condition of the property.
7. An opinion of the United States Supreme Court applying the California rule on the duty of a seller to disclose to a buyer the condition of the property.

C. Other Characteristics Affecting the Persuasive Value of Cases

The degree of deference a court will give to any particular case will be affected in more subtle ways by additional factors, including the following:

The Relative Level of the Issuing Court. The more prestigious the court, the more persuasive its opinions. For instance, a decision of the United States Supreme Court is powerful persuasive authority, even when it is not mandatory.

The Date of the Opinion. All other things being equal, more recent opinions carry more persuasive value.

The Strength of the Opinion's Reasoning. A well-reasoned opinion is more persuasive than a poorly reasoned one. An opinion that explains the rationale of the decision is more persuasive than one that simply applies existing legal authorities without exploration of the policy rationale.

The Subsequent Treatment of the Opinion by Other Authorities. The more the case has been followed by subsequent cases, the greater its precedential value. The more it has been discussed approvingly in treatises or law review articles, the greater its precedential value.

The Number of Other Jurisdictions That Follow the Same Approach. If a majority of jurisdictions follow this court's approach, the opinion's precedential value is increased. We refer to the approach of the majority of jurisdictions as the "majority rule" and to a minority approach as the "minority rule."

Whether the Court's Statements About the Issue Are Part of the Holding or Dicta. As Section III in this chapter explained, statements that are dicta are not as persuasive as statements that are part of the holding.

How Factually Similar the Opinion Is to the Facts of the Present Situation. The more similar the facts, the surer the judge can be that the authority was meant to apply to situations like the pending case.

The Number of Subscribing Judges. Most federal intermediate-level appellate cases are decided by a panel of the court, often three judges. Far less frequently, a case will be decided by all judges of that court (the court sitting en banc). En banc opinions are binding on future panels of the same court. Other courts generally find them more persuasive than panel decisions.

Unanimous opinions are more persuasive than split decisions. A majority opinion generally is more persuasive than a concurring opinion, which is in turn more persuasive than a dissenting opinion.

Be careful with concurring or dissenting opinions. If the statement of law you are interested in is part of a disagreement between the concurring or dissenting opinion and the majority opinion, the statement in the concurring or dissenting opinion might actually establish that what it says is *not* the law. After all, the opinion is disagreeing with the majority opinion on that point (or agreeing for different reasons), and it is the majority opinion that establishes the law.

En banc opinion	An opinion issued in a case that was heard by all of the judges of the court.
Majority opinion	An opinion subscribed to by a majority of the judges who heard the case.
Concurring opinion	An opinion that agrees with the result reached by the majority opinion but for reasons different from or in addition to those of the majority opinion.
Dissenting opinion	An opinion that disagrees with the result reached by the majority opinion.

Whether the Opinion Is Published. If the opinion does not appear in an official collection of published opinions (an official case reporter), it is not "published." In some jurisdictions, the precedential value of an unpublished opinion is limited or nonexistent. Be sure to check relevant court rules on this point.

The Reputation of the Particular Judge Writing the Case Opinion. Some judges have earned significant respect personally, separate from the position they hold. The opinions of those judges might have added persuasive value.

Trends in the Law. If you can discern a trend among other courts in the nation or in your state, opinions consistent with that trend could have greater precedential value than inconsistent opinions. For instance, if, over the past several years your state's highest court has been extending the liability of manufacturers in various situations, a case opinion consistent with that trend might have more precedential weight than an opinion that questions that trend.

PART TWO

Reading and Analyzing the Law

CHAPTER 3

Reading and Synthesizing Cases

To understand case law, a lawyer must read and interpret the written decisions of judges. The lawyer looks for cues from the language of the opinion, evaluating the meaning and significance of each cue and synthesizing the results. Thus, the lawyer creates an interpretation that synthesizes the facts, the result, and the judge's explanation of that result. One can even say that a lawyer "constructs" the law through this interpretive process. The starting point for learning this interpretive process is the case brief.[1]

I. INTRODUCTION TO READING CASES

During the first few weeks of law school, reading cases might be the most important skill to practice. An early overview of the parts of a case opinion is helpful so you know what information to notice and where to find it. Although judicial opinions don't follow an established formula, most of them roughly follow this format:

- Case name, court, citation, date (at the top of the opinion)
- Facts (what happened to raise the legal issue)
- Procedural history (what happened in prior courts or agencies)
- Legal issue(s) to be decided
- Rule(s) of law (the court's statement of the applicable legal standard)
- Reasoning (the court's reasons for deciding the case as it did)[2]
- Holding (the court's decision on the relevant facts)
- Order (what will happen next; e.g., remanded for trial)

Notice the difference between the governing rule of law, the holding, and the court's reasoning. The *rule* sets out the legal test the court used to decide the

1. The term "brief" is also used to refer to a formal court document a lawyer submits to a judge to advocate for a favorable ruling in a case. A case brief often is called simply a "brief," so some confusion of terminology is possible. Usually, though, the context will clarify the meaning.

2. Chapter 5 identifies the major forms of reasoning.

case (e.g., to revoke a will, a testator must take some action that demonstrates her intent). The *holding* states the court's conclusion about whether the facts of this case meet that legal test (e.g., merely marking a large "X" across only the first page of a five-page will, as the decedent did here, is enough if the other evidence of intent is sufficiently strong). The *reasoning* is the full discussion of why the court decided the legal issue as it did. The court's reasons may include multiple forms of reasoning, including the language of the governing rule of law, comparisons to prior cases, policy rationales, and the court's interpretation of the facts.

II. INTRODUCTION TO CASE BRIEFING

A case brief is a method for reading, analyzing, and making notes about a case. The parts of a case opinion identified above include the key information to include in a case brief. That being said, formats and preferred methods for case briefing vary widely, partly because case briefs are personal study tools. People process information differently, so they develop personalized study methods that best accommodate their own learning styles.

Briefing formats differ also according to the legal task to be performed. When you brief a case for your torts class, your most immediate goal is to be ready to answer classroom questions about the case. Your torts professor might have given you a format to use, or you might be able to devise your own format based on the kinds of questions your professor tends to ask.

When you brief cases for a legal writing assignment, however, your purpose is different in several ways.[3] First, you have a hypothetical client with a set of facts and a specific legal question to answer. Having a discrete task means you can focus your case brief on the aspects of the case most applicable to your client's facts. Second, you will be reading many cases on a particular legal point, not just one or two. Your assignment will require you not only to understand the case you are reading, but also to understand how it relates to a number of other cases on the same point. That means you'll need to notice additional features about the case. Third, you will be writing a document (perhaps an office memo or a memorandum of law) describing the case and referring to its language. Therefore, you will need to be able to find the case again, and you will need to take more careful notes about the parts you anticipate describing in your office memo or memorandum of law. These notes will save you time when you are writing, and they will save you from committing plagiarism.[4]

---

3. Visit the website for this book at www.AspenPublishing.com/Edwards-LWAnalysis6 for a detailed discussion of a suggested format for briefing the cases you read as part of your legal writing assignment. A case and sample case brief are included.

4. See Chapter 1, Section IV.

III. TOOLS FOR FINDING NEW INFORMATION ABOUT THE RULE

When reading and briefing a case for a legal writing assignment, you will also want to look for—in a note on the case brief or elsewhere—new information a case provides you about the rule or its application that you did not know before you read the case. Notice especially anything about this case that could apply in some way to your assignment. Perhaps this opinion modified or expanded the rule. Perhaps the court discussed a part of the rule you have not seen discussed so thoroughly before. Perhaps the court phrased the governing rule in a way particularly helpful to your client's facts. Perhaps the opinion explains the historical developments in this area of the law. You will notice more information in the opinion if you consciously look for new information, and you will be better able to use that information in your assignment if you have made note of it in your case brief. Here are some tools that will help you find new information about a rule:

1. *Notice what the court said about the rule.* In most opinions, the author gives the reader some explanation of the rule before applying it to the facts of that particular case. Here, the author's primary goal is to tell the reader about the rule. Begin with this part of the opinion. The *court's* explicit explanation of the rule gives you the most basic new information from the case.

2. *Notice how the court applied the rule.* After noticing what the court *said* about the rule, look at how the court *applied* the rule to the facts before it. You might expect an opinion to state and explain a rule of law and then to apply that rule of law exactly as the opinion just explained it. Often, that is exactly what happens. But sometimes the court's *application* of the rule differs from the court's explanation of it. One of the best ways to understand the rule is to observe how the court applied it. A court "holds" what it *does*, not what it *says.*

3. *Notice how the court did* not *apply the rule.* After you have observed how the court applied the rule, ask yourself how the court did *not* apply it. A court's unexplained silence rarely can be characterized as a binding rule of law. However, judicial silence can have persuasive value if the most likely reason for the silence is that the ignored topic is not a part of the relevant legal analysis. For instance, in a child custody case, if the facts state that one spouse is Christian and one spouse is Muslim but the opinion does not mention religious differences, you might be able to infer that religious differences will not be relevant to custody decisions.

After all, your goal here is to figure out what rule was governing the judge when deciding the case and how that rule would apply to your client's facts. If you are wondering whether a certain fact true of your client's situation would affect the outcome, ask yourself whether that kind of fact seemed to affect the judge's ruling in the earlier case.

4. *Notice any facts the court emphasized.* When a court sets out the facts or applies the law, it sometimes emphasizes a certain fact. Usually, the opinion will explain why the fact is important, but even without explanation, the opinion's emphasis on the fact implies that the judge found it legally significant.

5. *Find out what leading commentators have said about the case.* Case opinions actually make law, but a wealth of secondary authorities exist. As we saw in Chapter 2, secondary authorities are explanations of the law written by legal commentators. Secondary authorities have persuasive value, depending on factors such as the reputation of the author, the level of detail of the discussion, and the recency of the writing. If you are working with a well-known and influential case, commentators might have discussed it. Finding secondary authority can help you understand the case and its significance for your assignment.

EXERCISE 3-1
Briefing a Case

Prepare a case brief for a case your professor has selected. Bring your brief to class, and be prepared to discuss it. If your professor has not assigned a case, brief *Lucy v. Zehmer*, found in Appendix F.

IV. SYNTHESIZING CASES

Case briefing will help you understand a single case, but a lawyer faced with multiple authorities must do more than analyze each authority separately. Such a discussion would be little more than reading a series of case briefs. Instead, she must explain how the cases fit together to create the law governing her client's issue. She must compare the authorities to find and reconcile any seeming inconsistencies and to combine the content of the authorities so she can present a unified statement of the governing rule of law. Therefore, after you have identified the cases that will be important to your analysis, you must consider how they fit together. This process is called "synthesizing" cases.

A. Using Consistent Cases

Sometimes the cases will use similar language to state the governing rule and will apply that rule consistently. Or perhaps some jurisdictions follow one rule and others follow a different rule. However, the cases within each jurisdiction are consistent with each other. In either of these situations, it will not be difficult to combine the language of the cases into a unified statement of the governing rule with a consistent explanation of how the courts have applied it. Simply identify the points you want to make about the law and its application, and select and discuss the cases that best illustrate each point. Usually those points will include each element or factor[5] and may include

5. See Chapter 7, Section I for a discussion of rule structures.

other observations about how the rule is usually applied. For example, recall our rule on whether a person had effectively revoked her will:

> To revoke a will, a testator must have the intention to revoke and must take some action that demonstrates that intent.

Your written analysis would discuss each element (intention and action) separately. For each element you would identify several cases that best explain that element and discuss them in your description of that element.

Similarly, if jurisdictions are split between two different approaches, your written analysis would discuss each approach separately. For each approach, you would identify several cases that best explain that approach and discuss them in your description of that element. For instance, assume you are writing an office memo on the question of whether parents can recover for the wrongful death of a fetus. You might find that some jurisdictions do not permit recovery at all, whereas others permit recovery if the fetus was medically viable at the time of the injury. You would explain to your reader that jurisdictions disagree and then discuss separately each of the two approaches. For each approach, you would select and discuss the several cases that best illustrate that approach.

B. Reconciling Seemingly Inconsistent Cases

Cases in the same jurisdiction are not always consistent, however. If you find seemingly inconsistent cases in the same jurisdiction, and if these cases are important for your analysis, you must try to reconcile them. Reread carefully all of the language in both opinions, and also look for later cases that might resolve the inconsistency. Even if the later cases do not mention the inconsistency, these later cases will probably articulate and apply a rule. As you study the way these later cases articulate and apply the law, you will probably find clues about how to reconcile the cases.

One possibility is that the later case implicitly overruled the earlier case. As we saw in Chapter 2, a court can overrule an earlier opinion implicitly by ignoring it while reaching an inconsistent result. Another possibility is that the seemingly inconsistent legal rules are meant to apply to different situations. Perhaps one rule is meant to be an exception to the other. In either case, the rule in one of the cases will apply to your client's situation and the other will not. This explanation handily resolves the inconsistency. Analysis that leads to a conclusion that the two opinions apply to different situations is called "distinguishing" cases.

Finally, you might be able to study the language of each opinion and find meanings in the text that will allow you to read the two cases consistently. Identify the seemingly inconsistent aspects of the opinions. Then reread the opinions carefully, exploring whether you can imagine a possible explanation that would reconcile the statements.

Inconsistencies in Rule Statements. Cases can seem inconsistent because they appear to state two different legal rules. For instance, assume that a lawyer is representing Sharon Watson, a sales employee of Carrolton Company, headquartered in Atlanta, Georgia. Watson had sold Carrolton to its present owners. She remained employed by Carrolton and signed a covenant not to compete, an agreement promising not to compete with Carrolton in certain ways for a certain period of time after the termination of her employment. Watson is considering leaving Carrolton to form a new business that would compete with Carrolton. She needs to know whether Carrolton would be able to enforce the covenant against her.

The lawyer researches the issue and finds *Coffee System of Atlanta v. Fox*[6] and *Clein v. Kapiloff*,[7] two Georgia cases dealing with enforcement of covenants not to compete. In *Fox*, the court uses the following language to articulate the rule governing when a covenant is enforceable:

> A covenant not to compete is enforceable if all of the following elements are reasonable: the kind of activity restrained; the geographical area in which it is restrained; and the time period of the restraint.

If *Fox* were the only authority, the lawyer would use this rule to analyze Watson's question. He would analyze the reasonableness of each of the identified characteristics of the Watson covenant. But *Fox* is not the only authority. The lawyer also found *Clein*, and there the court seems to articulate the governing rule differently. In *Clein*, the court stated:

> A covenant not to compete is enforceable if it is reasonable. The test for determining reasonableness is whether the covenant is reasonably necessary to protect the interests of the party who benefits by it; whether it unduly prejudices the interests of the public; and whether it imposes greater restrictions than are necessary.

Fox and *Clein* seem to lay out different rules. There seem to be two different legal standards governing the enforceability of covenants not to compete. Novice legal writers might be tempted to analyze the Watson issue by describing and applying, one at a time, the "rules" set out in *Fox* and in *Clein*. The discussion would first give a sort of "case brief" of *Fox*, describing the facts, the "rule" language that court used, and the result. The discussion would then apply the "rule" from *Fox* to the Watson facts. Then the discussion would do the same thing with *Clein*, setting out the "rule" language from that case and

6. 176 S.E.2d 71 (Ga. 1970).
7. 98 S.E.2d 897 (Ga. 1957).

applying that "rule" to the Watson facts. The organizational structure would look something like this:

Is the Watson covenant not to compete enforceable?

A. The rule in the *Fox* case

The covenant is enforceable if

1. the kind of activity restrained is reasonable;
2. the geographical area of restraint is reasonable; and
3. the duration of the restraint is reasonable.

B. The rule in the *Clein* case

The covenant is enforceable if

1. it is reasonably necessary to protect the employer's interests;
2. it does not unduly prejudice the interests of the public; and
3. it does not impose greater restrictions than are necessary.

This approach is problematic, however. The lawyer needs to know *Georgia's* rule of law on enforcing covenants not to compete. Determining Georgia's rule is the most important analytical task. Organizing by the separate cases here would give the client two possible rules and two possible outcomes. Yet our legal system contemplates that a jurisdiction ordinarily will have only one rule of law on a particular issue so people can know what the law is and how it will apply to their conduct.

The lawyer must try to reconcile these seemingly inconsistent statements in *Fox* and *Clein*. After rereading the cases several times and carefully considering the court's possible meanings, the lawyer might conclude that the language in *Fox* identifies the particular terms that must be reasonable while the language in *Clein* identifies the criteria the court will use to judge whether those terms are reasonable. In other words, each contract term (kind of restraint, area of restraint, and duration of restraint) must meet the three criteria identified in *Clein*. This reconciliation salvages precedential value for each case and combines them into one unified statement of the jurisdiction's legal rule. Here is a rule statement that reconciles *Fox* and *Clein*:

A covenant not to compete is enforceable if the kind of activity restrained, the geographical area of the restraint, and the duration of the restraint are reasonable. Reasonableness is judged according to whether the restraint is necessary to protect the employer's interests, does not unduly prejudice the interests of the public, and does not impose greater restrictions than are necessary.

This reconciled rule statement might produce an analysis organized like this:

Is the Watson covenant not to compete enforceable?

The covenant is enforceable if its terms are reasonable according to the following criteria:

A. Are its terms necessary to protect the employer's interests?
   1. the kind of activity
   2. the geographical area
   3. the duration

B. Do its terms unduly prejudice the interests of the public?
   1. the kind of activity
   2. the geographical area
   3. the duration

C. Do its terms impose greater restrictions than necessary?
   1. the kind of activity
   2. the geographical area
   3. the duration

Inconsistencies in Results. You might find cases that seem to apply the same governing rule to seemingly similar sets of facts but reach puzzlingly different results. To reconcile them, search for factual differences that might explain these results.

Consider this example: To establish adverse possession of land, a claimant must prove several things, one of which is "possession." The kind of possession that will ripen into title is gauged by the kind and degree of the claimant's use of the land. Here are summaries of two hypothetical cases dealing with the issue of whether the kind and degree of use was sufficient. Do they seem inconsistent? If so, can you reconcile them?

> *Allen v. Baxter:* Fifteen years ago, Anne Allen bought Lot A in a suburban neighborhood. Lot B, the vacant and overgrown lot next door, was owned by Jacob Baxter. Allen built a house on Lot A and moved in. In 1981, Allen began gardening on Lot B. During the eight-month growing season, she worked in the garden nearly every day, growing vegetables for herself and her neighbors. During the four remaining months, she seldom went on the lot. The court held that this use did not establish a sufficient degree of "possession" for the purposes of adverse possession.

> *Clay v. Davidson:* Fifteen years ago, Charles Clay bought a lakeside lot in a resort area. The lot already contained a cabin, and Clay built a dock. Every year since then, he has spent about six weekends a year and two weeks during the summer at the cabin. He has now discovered that the legal description of the lot was incorrect in that it actually describes the lot next door. Darlene Davidson is the actual record titleholder of the lot Clay thought to be his. The court held that Clay's facts established a sufficient degree of "possession" for the purposes of adverse possession.

The results in these two cases seem inconsistent. The degree of possession in *Allen* seems much greater than the degree of possession in *Clay*. Allen was physically present on the land for many more days of the year than was

Clay, and Allen did more to the land than did Clay. Yet the court held that Clay possessed the land to a sufficient degree, and Allen did not. Reconciling these cases requires you to search for differences that could explain this seeming inconsistency. Perhaps the court will be satisfied with a lesser degree of possession in the case of vacation property, where an owner would not be expected to be in possession year-round. Perhaps the court counted the continuous presence of Clay's improvements as part of Clay's possession. Or perhaps the court will require a greater degree of possession in the case of a possessor who knows she does not have record title. Any of these explanations could reconcile *Allen* and *Clay*.[8]

EXERCISE 3-2
Synthesizing and Reconciling Rule Statements

Synthesize (and reconcile where necessary) the following four summaries of case opinions setting out the requirements for recovery under the attractive nuisance doctrine. Use the cases to formulate one rule of law. For each part of the rule you formulate, identify the case(s) you would cite for support of that part of the rule. Remember that often you can formulate different rules from the same set of authorities.

Bell v. Grackin (state's highest appellate court, 1959)

Facts. A piece of wire was lying in a neighbor's yard. A child walking by saw the wire and went into the yard to get it. As he was playing with the wire, the child bent it and then let it go. The wire recoiled, hitting the child in the eye. The child sought recovery from the neighbor based on the doctrine of attractive nuisance. The court denied recovery, stating:

> The doctrine underlying the attractive nuisance cases applies only where the instrument or artificial condition is within itself inherently dangerous even while being used properly, such as weapons, explosives, or power tools. It would be extending the doctrine entirely too far to apply it to such commonplace objects as a piece of wire, a pencil, a coat hanger, or a hammer, all objects so commonplace as to be found around any house or yard, but not dangerous in themselves, although they might be attractive to children and capable of inflicting injury if misused.

Andersonville v. Goodden (state's intermediate-level appellate court, 1961)

Facts. A neighbor's pickup truck was parked unattended in the neighbor's yard. A child came into the yard to sell the neighbor candy bars for a school fundraising project. The child saw the truck, climbed on it, fell, and impaled himself on a hook on the end of a chain dangling from the rear of the truck. The child sought recovery from the neighbor based on the doctrine of attractive nuisance. The court denied recovery, stating:

---

8. If you study adverse possession in your property class, you might learn more about how to reconcile these two cases. The purpose of this exercise is simply to give you some practice in *imagining possible reconciliations.*

> The attractive nuisance doctrine was developed for the benefit of children coming upon property even though trespassing. However, the courts of this state have been reluctant to extend the doctrine beyond its restricted application to situations in which the dangerous instrument is found to be one of actual and compelling attraction for children. The courts have not expanded the doctrine to cases where the instrument or artificial condition did not actually draw the children onto the property.

Newcomb v. Roberts (state's highest appellate court, 1982)

Facts. A swimming pool was located in a backyard with no fence, unshielded from view. A child visiting next door and playing hide-and-seek came into the backyard seeking a hiding place. She hid behind a utility shack for a while. Then she began to wonder whether her friends were still looking for her. She decided to go investigate the status of the game. As she was leaving the backyard, walking alongside the pool, she accidentally fell into the pool and suffered serious injury. She brought suit against the property owner under the doctrine of attractive nuisance. The court allowed recovery, stating:

> A landowner is liable for physical harm to trespassing children by an artificial condition if the place where the condition exists is one upon which the possessor knows or has reason to know that children are likely to trespass; if the risk posed by the condition is one that children, because of their youth, will not realize; and if the landowner fails to exercise reasonable care to eliminate the danger or otherwise to protect the children. This landowner should have known that neighborhood children were likely to trespass and that such children would not appreciate the risks posed by a swimming pool. The landowner did not enclose the pool in a fence or take any steps to shield the pool from view. Thus, the landowner is liable for the injuries to the child.

McDaniels v. Lanier (state's highest appellate court, 1987)

Facts. A natural pond lay behind a house located on two acres of property. The pond was visible to passersby, and no fence prevented access. A child saw the pond and decided to swim in the pond. The child suffered abdominal cramps and drowned. The court denied recovery, stating:

> An owner who has reason to know that children are likely to trespass is liable, under the doctrine of attractive nuisance, for injuries sustained by a child if the risk is one that children will not appreciate and if the owner has failed to exercise reasonable care to protect the child [cite to *Newcomb*].
>
> However, here the condition that caused the injury was a naturally occurring condition rather than an artificial condition. While landowners have a duty to protect trespassing children from artificially created conditions on their property, they do not have the duty to protect trespassing children from naturally occurring conditions. Such a duty would often require landowners to take unreasonable or impossible actions such as fencing off huge tracts of land. Thus, the owner is not liable for the injuries to the trespassing child.

EXERCISE 3-3
Reconciling Facts

You are researching an issue dealing with the requirements for making a valid gift. The cases explain that to make a gift, the donor must physically deliver possession of the item to the donee if possible. All of the cases you first find are similar to *Elder v. Fisher* below. Then, you find *Galloway v. Harris*. Does *Galloway* seem inconsistent with *Elder* and the cases like it? If so, how? Can you imagine how you might reconcile *Elder* and *Galloway*?

Elder v. Fisher. Janice Elder had a ruby ring, which she kept in her safe deposit box at a local bank. She wanted to give it to her sister, Darlene, for her birthday. Janice took Darlene to lunch and gave her a birthday card. The card read, "You're the best sister anyone could have. From this moment on, my ruby ring is yours. Meet me at the bank Wednesday at noon, and I'll get it out of the safe deposit box." Janice died on Tuesday, and her executor, Fisher, refused to turn over the ring to Darlene, claiming that no valid gift had been made because the ring was in the same town as the donor and donee but had not been physically handed over. The court held that actual physical delivery was required and that no valid gift had been made.

Galloway v. Harris. Chester Galloway wanted to give his daughter Jane an oil painting that was hanging over his mantel. He gave Jane a birthday party, and in the presence of the guests, he gave Jane a birthday card. Inside the card was a note declaring that the painting was her gift. Chester said that he wanted to keep the painting in place until his house sold and then he would bring it to her. Before Chester's house sold, he died. Jane claimed that the painting was hers, and Chester's executor (Harris) claimed that no valid gift had been made because the painting was in the same room with the donor and donee and had not been physically handed over. The court held that actual physical delivery was not required and that the painting was Jane's.

CHAPTER 4

Interpreting Statutes

While the roots of the American legal system remain in the common law, the 1930s saw the beginning of "an orgy of statute-making."[1] Today, most legal issues are controlled or significantly affected by statutes — written laws passed by a legislative body. Thus, your skills of statutory analysis will be crucial to your success as a lawyer. The skills basic to statutory analysis are (1) reading the statute, (2) identifying the issues, and (3) interpreting the statute's language.

I. READING STATUTES

The starting point for reading a statute is understanding the legislature's relationship to the courts. As we saw in Chapter 2, an applicable statute binds the courts of that jurisdiction, but a court has the authority to interpret the statute's language. Once a court has interpreted the statute, the doctrine of stare decisis applies, and the court's interpretation binds all other courts for whom the opinion is mandatory authority. If the legislature disagrees with the court's interpretation, the legislature is free to amend the statute to clarify its intended meaning. The court is then bound once again, this time by the newly amended statute.

Also, as we saw in Chapter 2, a court has the authority to rule on the constitutionality of the statute. On the question of constitutionality, the court has the last word. The legislature can amend the statute to cure the constitutional infirmity the court identified, but the legislature cannot enact another statute declaring the original statute constitutional. A statute that has been held unconstitutional will not be enforced within the jurisdiction of the court that issued the opinion.

Within the boundaries set by these interlocking roles, courts must read statutory language and tell litigants whether the statute applies to their situation, and if so, what that language means. To advise clients and represent litigants, therefore, lawyers must read statutes precisely, accurately, and

1. Grant Gilmore, *The Ages of American Law* 95 (1977).

sometimes creatively. You can think of the questions critical to this inquiry as similar to the famous five Ws that guide a journalist:[2]

THE FIVE Ws OF READING A STATUTE

Who?	Whose actions are covered?
What?	What kinds of actions are required, prohibited, or permitted?
When?	When was the statute effective?
Where?	Where must the actions have taken place to be covered?
What then?	What consequences follow?

Often, the scope of the material you must read closely is larger than the specific statutory provision you first identify. If you are dealing with an act containing individual separately numbered provisions, you must read carefully at least the following parts of the act:

READ THESE PARTS OF A STATUTE

1. The language of the individual provisions that appear to deal directly with the legal issue;
2. The language of any other individual provisions expressly cross-referenced by the directly applicable provisions;
3. The titles of these individual provisions and of the entire act;
4. Any set of definitions applying to the individual provisions or to the act as a whole;
5. Any statement of purpose and any preamble to the individual provisions or the act as a whole;
6. If length is not prohibitive, read the entire act;
7. If the entire act is too long to read, at least read carefully the titles of all other individual provisions to identify any that might relate to the issue at hand;
8. The dates on which the act as a whole and the individual provisions were enacted and on which they became effective;
9. All of the same information for any amendments to important provisions; and
10. If available, read the same information for any prior versions of important provisions (to understand what changes the legislature intended to make when it enacted the current version).

Read each of these parts of the statute word by word and phrase by phrase, paying attention to every detail. Reading a statute is more like reading an algebraic formula than it is like reading standard prose. Each word and punctuation mark is important. Even the internal tabulation (numbering or lettering) can be significant. Pay particular attention to words that signal structural information.

2. It is said that a journalist asks "five Ws and an H": who, what, when, where, why, and how.

SOME WORDS THAT SIGNAL STRUCTURAL INFORMATION

and	include	unless	other
or	limited to	outweighs	shall
either	except	all	may

Also, notice whether any list set out in the statute is meant to be exclusive. The statute might tell you expressly that the list is not exclusive, using such language as the phrase "and any other factors relevant to the child's best interests." Or the statute might merely imply whether the list is exclusive, for instance, by introducing the list with a word like "including."

EXERCISE 4-1
Reading Statutes

Read this statute, and answer the questions that follow it. If you would need more information to answer the question, identify the information you would need.

> A lawyer's fee shall be reasonable. The factors to be considered in determining the reasonableness of a fee include the following: the time and labor required; the novelty and difficulty of the questions involved; and the skill requisite to perform the legal service properly; the likelihood, if apparent to the client, that the acceptance of the particular employment will preclude other employment by the lawyer; the fee customarily charged in the locality for similar legal services; the amount involved and the results obtained; the time limitations imposed by the client or by the circumstances; the nature and length of the professional relationship with the client; the experience, reputation, and ability of the lawyer or lawyers performing the services; and whether the fee is fixed or contingent.[3]

1. Client *A* asks a lawyer to handle a car accident case. The opposing party is insured by Security Insurance. The lawyer has been hoping to be placed on the list of lawyers approved to represent Security Insurance clients. In setting her fee, can the lawyer consider the fact that acceptance of the client's case might prevent Security Insurance from approving her to represent Security Insurance clients?
2. Client *B* has come to a lawyer to handle a car accident case. In setting her fee, can the lawyer consider the fact that she is certified as a Family Law Mediator?
3. In setting her fee, can the lawyer consider the fact that she is leaving for her vacation at the end of the week and therefore must finish the client's work in only two days?

3. Based on Model R. Pro. Conduct r. 1.5(a) (Am. Bar Ass'n 2013).

II. IDENTIFYING ISSUES

When you brief cases, you should read the whole case through once before you begin to prepare your brief. Similarly, when you are ready to identify statutory issues, read through all the material identified in Section I to establish the context for your analysis and to identify the key provisions of the statute. When you have identified the provisions that will govern your issue, return to those provisions for another and even more careful reading. Read with a pen or pencil in your hand. Read the text of the statute word for word, looking for key terms that tell you what conduct the statute covers.

One way to find the key terms is to focus on the answers to the five Ws set out in Section I. Another way is to ask yourself what someone would have to prove to show that the requirements of the statute were or were not met. Underline each word that tells you something about the answers to those questions. Then circle all the terms that tell you something about the relationships among the key terms (words like "and" or "or"). Consider this example:

The statute:
No cemetery shall be hereafter established within the corporate limits of any city or town; nor shall any cemetery be established within two hundred and fifty yards of any residence without the consent of the owner of the legal and equitable title of such residence.[4]

Key terms:

cemetery	hereafter	established	within	corporate limits
city	town	250 yards	residence	
consent	owner	legal title	equitable title	

Relational terms:

or	nor	and

Notice that each of the key terms raises an issue. Something other than a cemetery would not be covered by this statute, so to know whether this statute would apply to your client's facts, you must find out what the term "cemetery" means in this context. There might be a definition section in this same act, or there might be cases in which prior courts have defined the term.

The same is true with the word "hereafter." The statute does not prohibit all cemeteries; it prohibits only those established "hereafter." After what? The date of the statute's passage? Or the date on which the statute became effective? What are those dates? Another issue to resolve. And what does the term "established" mean? Is a cemetery "established" when construction begins? Ends? When the cemetery first opens for business? Each key term

4. Va. Code, § 56 (Michie 1942), construed in *Temple v. Petersburg*, 29 S.E.2d 357 (Va. 1944).

identified above raises an issue the lawyer must resolve before the lawyer can know whether and how the statute might apply to her client's facts.

Are you surprised to find so many issues raised in one statutory sentence? Statutes are packed tightly with key terms, each of which raises a potential issue. If you were analyzing whether and how this statute applies to your client's facts, you would have at least 12 issues to consider.

One word of caution about identifying key terms: You might be tempted to treat a phrase as a single key term. For example, consider a statute providing that, for a gift to be effective, a donor must transfer possession of the gifted item with "a manifested intent" to part with ownership. You might first think of the words "manifested intent" as a single key term. However, that phrase would require proof of two things, not one: (1) that the donor actually intended to part with ownership and (2) that this intent was sufficiently "manifested" to others. This phrase raises two issues, not one. Your list of key terms should treat these words separately.

One more strategy is helpful for reading statutes and identifying issues: rewriting the statute in your own words. Restating the rule in your own words is an effective tool of analysis, and you often can state the rule more simply and clearly than its original writer did. Do not, however, rephrase the *key terms* of the statute. Those terms will be defined and explained by the authorities; thus, they will have developed their own meaning, and as we saw above, that meaning is the critical question of the analysis.

EXERCISE 4-2
Identifying Issues

The Fair Housing Act, 42 U.S.C. §§ 3601-3619, prohibits housing discrimination. Underline the words or phrases that raise potential legal issues in the following portion of the Act:

> [I]t shall be unlawful . . . to refuse to sell or rent after the making of a bona fide offer, or to refuse to negotiate for the sale or rental of, or otherwise make unavailable or deny, a dwelling to any person because of race, color, religion, sex, familial status, or national origin.

III. INTERPRETING THE STATUTE'S LANGUAGE

Statutes are interpreted by case opinions. If case authority has already told you what the statute means, you can rely on that case law to the extent of its precedential value. But if no binding case law has answered your particular question, you must use other tools of interpretation. The most important of these tools are (1) the text itself, (2) the intent of the legislature, (3) the policies implicated by the possible interpretations, (4) the interpretation of any governmental agencies charged with enforcement of the statute, and (5) the opinions of other courts and of respected commentators.

The Text Itself. The most important inquiry is the "plain meaning" of the text of the statute—what an ordinary or reasonable person would understand the words to mean. When the plain meaning is unambiguous, a court generally will give effect to the plain meaning unless the result would be absurd or at odds with the clearly articulated congressional intent to the contrary. Also look for other parts of the statute or act that might tell you more about the language you are concerned with, such as the section explaining the act's purpose. Many acts contain separate definition sections. Even when your term is not defined, other parts of the statute could give you clues about what the term means.

The Legislature's Intent. If the text of the statute is unclear, many courts will try to decide what the legislature intended. This search for the legislature's intent is problematic at best. The statute was probably enacted by a large group of elected officials who were serving in that office some years ago. The particular language you are concerned with could have been the result of political compromise, and various factions of the legislature might have had vastly different intentions surrounding that language. Quite possibly, your question never occurred to them at all. How can we decide the intent of the legislature as if the legislature were an entity with one mind? Yet, when a statute's language is unclear, a court applying the statute will have to have some basis for a decision. In such a circumstance, the court often will try to discern the legislature's intent.

Many courts are willing to consider the legislative history of the statute as evidence of legislative intent. Legislative history consists primarily of the documents or other records generated by the legislative body during its deliberations about the bill that ultimately became the statute. Legislative history comes in many forms, such as committee reports, speeches, witness testimony, or studies introduced into the record. Your research text will tell you more about legislative history and how to find it.

Policy. Consider the policy concerns implicated by a particular construction of the statute. Some implicated policies probably were part of the legislature's intent, but the legislature might not have foreseen all the policy concerns. If the legislature has not spoken on the issue, a court can consider its own view of which possible interpretation would produce the best result.

Some *kinds* of statutes carry a general policy leaning applicable to all statutes of that particular kind. These policies call for either a strict or a liberal construction of that kind of statute. The most common of these policies are:

- Statutes that change long-standing case law (statutes "in derogation of the common law") should be strictly construed. (A statute is strictly construed when it is read narrowly, so that it changes the legal environment as little as possible.)
- Statutes intended to remedy a problem ("remedial statutes") should be liberally construed to accomplish their remedial purpose. (A statute is liberally construed when it is read broadly to include more kinds of situations than a narrow reading would allow.)
- Statutes making certain conduct a crime ("penal statutes") should be narrowly construed, out of concern for the rights of the accused.

Finally, courts are guided by the general policy that, if possible, the meaning of a statute should be construed in a way that will render the statute constitutional.

Agency Interpretation. When enforcement of a statute is assigned to a particular agency, that agency must decide what the statute means to enforce it. Courts often look to this agency as the entity with the most expertise in the relevant issues and thus defer to the agency's interpretation. Look for agency interpretations in the agency's regulations, in the agency's decisions, and in case law.

Commentators and Other Courts. Finally, courts may recognize persuasive value attaching to the opinions of other courts and of respected commentators. The persuasive value of another court's opinion depends on the factors identified in Chapter 2. The persuasive value of a commentator's opinion depends on the reputation of the commentator and on the commentator's well-reasoned reliance on the other tools of construction.

IV. INTERPRETING STATUTORY LANGUAGE: CANONS OF CONSTRUCTION

To decide how to construe a statute, a court also may consider commonly accepted maxims of interpretation known as "canons of construction." Here are some of the most generally applicable:

- Read the statute as a whole.
- Give effect to rules of grammar and punctuation.
- Construe technical terms technically and ordinary terms in their ordinary sense.
- When the same language is used in various parts of an act, the language is presumed to have the same meaning throughout.
- Where general words (such as "and any other") follow a list, the general words should be construed to refer to things similar to the items in the list. This is the principle of "ejusdem generis," meaning literally "of the same genus."
- Modifying words or phrases refer to the nearest referent.
- Where a statute from state *X* is adopted in state *Y*, the construction given the statute by the courts of state *X* should be followed in state *Y*.
- If the statute does not contain an exception for a particular situation, a court should not create one.
- The court should presume that the legislature did not intend to enact a statute that impairs fundamental societal values.
- Specific description of one or more situations implies the exclusion of other kinds of situations not mentioned.
- Different statutes on the same legal issue (statutes "in pari materia") should be read consistently.
- Sometimes the courts of state *X* will have interpreted a particular word or phrase in a certain way. If, subsequently, the legislature of state *X*

enacts a different statute using that word or phrase, the language in the new statute should be interpreted as having the meaning previously given it by the courts.

- Titles, preambles, and section headings, though not technically part of the statute's text, are persuasive evidence of legislative intent.
- Sometimes courts will have construed the words of a statute in a particular way. Later the legislature may amend the statute in other ways but without changing those words. A court might conclude that the legislature's lack of action to change the judicial construction is evidence of the legislature's approval of that construction.

These maxims are treated as legal principles in and of themselves. Therefore, when you rely on one of them as part of your analysis, cite to a persuasive case opinion that adopts that maxim if you can. Even if you cannot find case authority adopting the maxim, however, a court still will be willing to consider the maxim's logic.

None of these guidelines for interpreting statutes will provide a certain answer. As a matter of fact, when you apply several, they might support contradictory results.[5] However, courts generally will consider these guidelines, so they will help you to predict what a court might decide or to persuade a court to interpret a statute favorably for your client.

5. Karl N. Llewellyn, *Remarks on the Theory of Appellate Decision and Rules or Canons About How Statutes Are to Be Construed*, 5 Green Bag 2d 297, 301 (2002).

CHAPTER 5

Forms of Legal Reasoning

Lawyers and judges use a number of kinds of reasoning to argue and decide cases. They reason by relying on a statement of the law, like a statute or a common-law rule articulated in a case (rule-based reasoning). They reason by comparing the facts of earlier cases to the facts of the present case (analogical reasoning). They reason by pointing to a desirable social or economic result, like promoting economic efficiency (policy-based reasoning). They reason by alluding to norms of conduct and customary expectations common in our society, such as how we expect people to act in certain circumstances (custom-based reasoning). They reason by appealing to a moral principle such as honesty or fairness or a political principle such as equality or democracy (principle-based reasoning). They reason by deciding whether a particular factual conclusion would explain the available evidence (inferential reasoning).

In practice, these forms often overlap, but it is helpful to identify them separately in this chapter so that you can learn to recognize them and to use them in your own analyses. Mastering their use is one of the most important goals of a law school education.

This chapter will also cover one more important way lawyers advocate for a result: narrative. Today, we usually use the term "reasoning" to describe only logical processes like those described above, but an earlier understanding of "reasoning" was much broader. It included processes that transcend logical arguments and may even resemble intuition. For lawyers and judges, the most powerful of these nonlogical processes is narrative. No matter what understanding of the term "reasoning" one prefers, lawyers and judges know that narrative functions just as the logical forms do, to justify and persuade. Therefore, this chapter includes narrative along with the logical forms of reasoning. Together, these forms will provide you with a powerful set of tools for analyzing legal issues and for advocating for a particular legal outcome.

I. RULE-BASED REASONING

Rule-based reasoning is the starting point for legal analysis. It justifies a result by establishing and applying a rule of law directly to the facts of a case. It asserts, "X is the answer because *the rule of law* articulated by the governing authorities mandates it."[1]

RULE-BASED REASONING
Harold Collier should not be bound by the contract he signed because he is a minor, and *A v. B* establishes that minors do not have the capacity to execute binding contracts.

> *Example of Rule-Based Reasoning*
> "[T]he only lawful means to dispossess a tenant who has not abandoned nor voluntarily surrendered . . . is by resort to judicial process. . . . Applying [this principle of law] to the facts of this case, we conclude, as did the trial court, that because Wiley failed to resort to judicial remedies against Berg . . . , his lockout of Berg was wrongful as a matter of law." *Berg v. Wiley*, 264 N.W.2d 145, 151–52 (Minn. 1978).

EXERCISE 5-1
Rule-Based Reasoning

Your client owns rental property. She wants to know whether she can refuse to rent to men. Read the following statute and write one paragraph that uses rule-based reasoning to answer her question.

> It shall be unlawful to refuse to sell or rent after the making of a bona fide offer, or to refuse to negotiate for the sale or rental of, or otherwise make unavailable or deny, a dwelling to any person because of race, color, religion, sex, familial status, or national origin. 42 U.S.C. § 3604(a).

II. ANALOGICAL REASONING: ANALOGIZING AND DISTINGUISHING CASES

Analogical reasoning is another major form of legal reasoning. The most common variety of analogical reasoning justifies a result by making direct factual comparisons between the facts of prior cases and the facts of the client's situation. The comparison can demonstrate factual similarities (leading to a similar result) or factual differences (leading to a different result).[2] A comparison

1. In some discussions of jurisprudence, you may notice scholars distinguishing between "rules" and "standards" or "principles." *See, e.g.*, Ronald M. Dworkin, *The Model of Rules*, 35 U. Chi. L. Rev. 14, 22–29 (1967). We need not be troubled here about that jurisprudential distinction. We will use the term "rule" to refer to all applicable statements of the governing law.

2. Comparisons that show differences are often called "disanalogical" or "counteranalogical" reasoning. For simplicity, however, we use "analogical" reasoning to refer both to pointing out similarities and pointing out differences.

that points out similarities asserts, "X is the answer *because the facts of this case are just like the facts of* A v. B, *and X was the result there.*" Comparing cases to point out similarities is often called "analogizing" cases.

ANALOGICAL REASONING
(Similarities)
Harold Collier should not be bound by the contract he signed because, like the successful defendant in *A v. B,* who was not bound by his contract because he was under the age of eighteen, Harold Collier is only sixteen.

A comparison that points out differences asserts, "Even though X was the answer in *A v. B,* that is not the appropriate answer here *because the facts in this case are different from the facts in A v. B.*" Comparing cases to point out differences is often called "distinguishing" cases.

ANALOGICAL REASONING
(Differences)
Unlike the minor in *C v. D,* who signed a statement asserting that he was 19, Harold Collier never made any statement about his age. Accordingly, the result in *C v. D* does not control Collier's case because he did not intentionally misrepresent his age.

> *Example of Analogical Reasoning*
> "[In *Fahmie,*] property was conveyed to [Fahmie], who had no knowledge of the installation of the culvert [or the violation of state law]. Fahmie made application to the development commission to make additional improvements to the stream and its banks. It was then that the inadequate nine foot culvert was discovered, and the plaintiff was required to replace it.
>
> The case before us raises the same issues as those raised in *Fahmie.* Here, the court found that in 1978 the wetlands area was filled without a permit and in violation of state statute. The alleged violation was unknown to the defendant and was discovered only after the plaintiff attempted to get permission to perform additional improvements to the wetlands area." [The result in the pending case should be the same as the result in *Fahmie.*] *Frimberger v. Anzellotti,* 594 A.2d 1029, 1033 (Conn. 1991) (ellipses omitted).

EXERCISE 5-2
Analogical Reasoning

Your client's mother has just died, and a dispute has arisen over who owns the mother's dining room table and matching chairs. Your client, James, has told you this story: His mother was eighty years old when she died, and her neighbor, Martha, had often taken her to the store or the doctor. Martha has now produced a thank you note from the mother, dated six months before her death, in which the mother wrote, "Dear Martha, I can't thank you enough for all your help through the years. I want you to have my dining room table and chairs. You can come get them anytime you want." You have found a relevant case, *Elder v. Fisher*, which is summarized below. Write a paragraph using analogical reasoning to argue that the attempted gift is not valid. Then switch sides and write a paragraph pointing out differences between *Elder* and Martha's claim, to demonstrate that *Elder* does not mean that Martha should lose.

> *Elder v. Fisher:* Janice Elder had a ruby ring, which she kept in her safe deposit box at a local bank. She wanted to give it to her sister, Darlene, for her birthday. Janice met Darlene and several friends for lunch. In the presence of the friends, Janice said to Darlene, "You're the best sister anyone could have. From this moment on, my ruby ring is yours. Meet me at the bank Wednesday at noon, and I'll get it out of the safe deposit box." Janice died in a car accident on Tuesday, and her executor, Fisher, refused to turn over the ring to Darlene, claiming that no valid gift had been made because the donor had not physically handed over the ring. The court held that actual physical delivery was required where possible and that therefore no valid gift had been made.

III. POLICY-BASED REASONING

Policy-based reasoning justifies a result by analyzing which answer would be the best for society at large. It asserts, "X is the answer *because that answer will encourage desirable results for our society.*"

POLICY-BASED REASONING
Harold Collier should not be bound by the contract he signed because he is only sixteen, and people that young should be protected from the harmful consequences of making important decisions before they are mature enough to consider all the options. Further, contract defaults are likely when minors undertake contractual obligations, and contract defaults dampen economic growth and decrease productivity levels.

> *Example of Policy-Based Reasoning*
> "To approve this lockout [of a defaulting tenant by a landlord] . . . merely because in Berg's absence no actual violence erupted while the locks were being changed, would be to encourage all future tenants, in order to protect their possession, to be vigilant and thereby set the stage for the very kind of public disturbance which it must be our policy to discourage." *Berg v. Wiley*, 264 N.W.2d 145, 150 (Minn. 1978).

EXERCISE 5-3
Policy-Based Reasoning

Your client signed a one-year lease for an apartment, but before he moved in, he lost his job. Without the job, he was unable to afford the rent, so he notified his landlord that he would not be able to take the apartment after all. The landlord has refused to rent the apartment to any other tenant and is holding your client responsible for the entire year's rent. Write a paragraph setting out a policy-based argument in favor of your client. Then switch sides and write a paragraph setting out a policy-based argument in favor of the landlord. For both paragraphs, you can consider both the economic effects and the social effects of a rule that allows landlords to do what this landlord is doing.

IV. PRINCIPLE-BASED REASONING

Principle-based reasoning justifies a result by appealing to a broad principle or character trait valued by our society, such as a principle of morality, justice, fairness, or democracy. It asserts that "X is the answer *because that answer upholds notions of morality, justice, fair-play, equality, democracy, or personal freedom.*"

PRINCIPLE-BASED REASONING
Harold Collier should not be bound by the contract he signed because enforcing contracts like his would encourage sales agents to lie and would reward unfair and dishonest sales practices.

> *Example of Principle-Based Reasoning*
> "[A] succession of trespasses . . . should not . . . be allowed to defeat the record title. . . . [T]he squatter should not be able to profit by his trespass." *Howard v. Kunto*, 477 P.2d 210, 214 (Wash. Ct. App. 1970).

EXERCISE 5-4
Principle-Based Reasoning

Your client bought a house and soon discovered that the roof leaked. The seller had not made any statement to your client about the roof, but your client believes the seller knew about the problem. Up until now, your jurisdiction has not required a seller to tell a buyer about problems like this roof, so long as the seller makes no affirmative statement about the quality of the roof. You want to argue that your jurisdiction should impose a duty on sellers to disclose significant defects of which they are aware. Write a paragraph using principle-based reasoning to argue in favor of this change in the law. You can consider principles like honesty and fairness.

V. CUSTOM-BASED REASONING

Custom-based reasoning justifies a result by reliance on cultural and societal norms of behavior. It asserts, "X is the answer *because that result is consistent with what we expect of people in this society."* Custom-based arguments often are phrased as statements about what is and is not "reasonable." Some legal rules directly incorporate custom-based reasoning as the operative legal standard, such as the negligence standard ("the reasonable person") or the constitutional standard for judging pornography ("falls outside contemporary community standards") or rules that protect people from "undue" influence.

CUSTOM-BASED REASONING
Harold Collier should not be bound by the contract he signed because it is unreasonable to expect a minor to be able to match wits with an experienced and overreaching sales agent. In our society, people do not make contracts with minors; they deal with the minor's parent or guardian.

Example of Custom-Based Reasoning
"[T]here is no . . . reason to deny plaintiff relief for failing to discover a state of affairs which the most prudent purchaser would not be expected to even contemplate." *Stambovsky v. Ackley*, 572 N.Y.S.2d 672, 676 (N.Y. App. Div. 1991).

EXERCISE 5-5
Custom-Based Reasoning

Your client has signed a contract to buy a house. The contract requires the seller to deliver "marketable title," which is a title a reasonable person would accept and pay fair value for. Your client has now discovered that the house extends over the lot line by one foot. The house was built in 1892, and the seller claims that he owns the extra foot under the doctrine of adverse possession. Assume that you have researched the doctrine and the applicable facts, and as far as you can tell, the seller's claim appears true. Can you use custom-based reasoning to argue that, even if the seller's claim appears likely, title partially based on adverse possession instead of actual record title does not satisfy the definition of marketable title?

VI. INFERENTIAL REASONING

Lawyers often use inferential reasoning (abduction) when analyzing a set of facts to decide whether those facts meet the requirements of a rule of law. If a particular factual conclusion would be consistent with the available evidence, that consistency provides some reason to believe that the factual conclusion is true. The possible conclusion would explain the observable facts. For example, assume that a patient had normal blood pressure during all prior phases of treatment and then the doctor changed one of the patient's medications. Immediately after taking the first dose, the patient developed high blood pressure. No other changes in treatment or lifestyle occurred. One could infer from this set of facts that the new medication caused the high blood pressure.

Inferential reasoning is important in analyzing many legal issues. It is especially important when the legal rule calls for a conclusion that cannot be directly observed—questions like causation (as in our prior example), knowledge (whether a person was aware of a certain fact or situation), or motive or intent (whether a person intended to cause a certain result).

INFERENTIAL REASONING
(used to establish whether the sales agent knew or should have known that Collier was a minor)
Collier is a short, smooth-faced boy who looks and acts like the 16-year-old he is. He told the agent about his hopes to be selected next year for the high school cheerleading squad. That hope would make no sense if he were already a senior, the year when most students turn 18. He said that he should probably call his parents to ask their advice. He said that he had never dreamed that he would have a car sooner than any of his friends, a puzzling comment for an 18-year-old to make because many high school students have a car shortly after turning 16. Most telling of all, the sales agent asked to see Collier's driver's license to make a copy of it for the dealership's files. Under these circumstances, the sales agent surely either knew or suspected that Harold Collier was a minor.

Example of Factual Inferences
A will is invalid if it was written when the testator was under the undue influence of someone. In *Estate of Lakatosh*, 656 A.2d 1378, 1379 (Pa. Super. Ct. 1994), the issue was whether Roger exercised undue influence over Rose. The court noted that Roger had met Rose, a woman in her seventies and living alone, and had immediately begun to visit her daily. *Id.* at 1381. Within a couple of months, Roger had suggested to Rose that she give him a power of attorney, which she did. *Id.* at 1381–82. A mere eight months after they met, Rose executed the will at issue in the case. *Id.* at 1382. The will left all but $1,000 of Rose's $268,000 estate to Roger. *Id.* The lawyer who drafted the will was Roger's second cousin, to whom Roger had referred Rose. *Id.*

What inferences can be implied by this description of the *Lakatosh* facts?

EXERCISE 5-6
Inferential Reasoning

Read the facts set out in Exercise 8-2 in Chapter 8. Write a paragraph identifying and explaining all the factual inferences that would support a conclusion that a reasonable person in Virginia's position would have thought that Stewart was making a serious offer. Then write a second paragraph identifying and explaining all the factual inferences that would support a conclusion that a reasonable person in Virginia's position would have thought that Stewart's offer was only in jest.

VII. NARRATIVE

Narrative justifies a result by telling a story whose theme implicitly calls for that result. Narrative uses the components of a story (characterization, context, description, dialogue, theme, and perspective) to appeal to commonly shared notions of justice, mercy, fairness, reasonableness, and empathy. In this sense, narrative is closely related both to principle-based reasoning and to custom-based reasoning, but narrative is far more contextual, placing these other forms of reasoning in a specific situation. Narrative tells the client's story in a way that encodes but does not directly articulate the commonly held principles and values on which these two logical forms rely.

The governing rule might directly adopt a legal standard easily communicated as a narrative theme. For instance, assume that the applicable rule about the enforcement of contracts made by minors allowed enforcement only if the other party to the contract did not use "undue" influence to convince the minor to enter into the contract. Narrative would use storytelling techniques such as description, dialogue, characterization, perspective, and context to establish that the other party's conduct was or was not "undue."

NARRATIVE
(where the use of undue influence is an issue in the governing rule)
Harold Collier should not be bound by the contract he signed because Jenkins, a car dealer for twenty-two years, discouraged Harold from calling his parents to ask advice and told him that another purchaser was looking at the car at that very moment. Jenkins lowered his voice and said, "Tell you what I'll do. I'll knock off $1,000 just for you—just because this is your first car. But you can't tell anyone how low I went. This will have to be our secret."

Even if the applicable rule does not articulate a legal standard based on a narrative theme, narrative can still persuade. A narrative demonstrating the fairness of a particular result can convince a judge to exercise any available discretion in favor of the client, to create an exception to the general rule of law, or to reinterpret or overturn the rule. The law is not insensitive to justice, mercy, fairness, reasonableness, and empathy, even when those commonly shared values are not directly incorporated in the legal rule. As a matter of fact, those notions underlie much of the more abstract rationales in policy-based or principle-based reasoning. Narrative can serve as a powerful partner with policies or principles, providing a real-life example of the policy or principle that justifies the desired result.

For example, recall that the rule prohibiting enforcement of contracts made by minors is supported by the policy rationale that minors should be protected from the harmful consequences of making important decisions before they are mature enough to consider all the options. Narrative reasoning can bolster that policy point:

NARRATIVE
(consequences to minor not part of rule, but part of policy behind rule)
Harold Collier should not be bound by the contract he signed because he is only sixteen; he has never before shopped for a car; he was pressured by a sophisticated sales agent; he did not have the benefit of advice from any advisor; and the car purchase will exhaust the funds he has saved for college.

Each form of reasoning has persuasive power, and each has particular functions in written legal analysis. As we shall see in Part III of this book, the rule establishes the structure of the analysis and organizes the written discussion. Within that structure, a complete analysis includes reasoning based on applicable rules, analogies, policies, principles, norms, factual inferences, and narrative. In addition to its role in the written legal analysis, narrative is paramount in the written fact statement.

Begin to notice the kinds of reasoning you find in the cases you read, the arguments you hear your classmates and your professors make, and your own analysis of hypothetical questions. By next year at this time, your skills in using all of the logical forms of reasoning will have increased dramatically.

EXERCISE 5-7
Forms of Reasoning

Make a photocopy of Section I-A of the sample office memo found in Appendix A. In the margin of the photocopy, identify each form of reasoning you find, and be prepared to explain your labeling.

PART THREE

Writing the Discussion of a Legal Question

CHAPTER 6

The Writing Process and Law-Trained Readers

Now that you understand the legal authorities and the kinds of legal reasoning you will be working with, it is time to turn your attention to the writing process and to the reader for whom you will write.

I. THE WRITING PROCESS

Writing is a process with distinct stages and distinct goals at each stage. Each writing stage serves an important function as you work toward a finished document. This chapter identifies five main stages of a writing task and invites you to use each stage consciously as an opportunity to strengthen your writing.

STAGES OF THE WRITING PROCESS

1. Reading and analyzing the materials.
2. Creating an annotated outline.
3. Writing a working draft of the analysis.
4. Converting that analysis into a document designed for a reader.
5. Editing for style and technical correctness.

This section will describe each stage, and writing process hints will be included at appropriate points throughout the rest of the book. For easy identification, this margin symbol will mark those process hints in future chapters. Two caveats about this description of the writing process are in order, however. First, writing processes are as personal as signatures and fingerprints. The stages presented here represent a common way of approaching a writing task, but your own process will be unique to you. What is important is that you find places in your *own* writing process for the *activities* described here.

Second, the writing process is recursive. While you are working on the tasks of one stage, you often will find yourself returning to the tasks of an earlier stage and anticipating those of a later stage. Writing requires you to circle back again and again as you come to understand more about your legal issue, your client's facts and goals, and the available legal strategies. Your willingness to construct, dismantle, and reconstruct your document will be crucial to achieving a good written product.

Stage 1: Reading and Analyzing the Materials. Start by reading carefully all parts of your assignment, paying particular attention to the assignment's articulation of the issue(s). If you have any trouble understanding the issues, try writing them out in your own words and comparing them to the issue statements in the relevant case law. Clarify any questions with your professor.

Then read all of the relevant legal sources that you locate by conducting legal research. Keep in mind what you learned about weight of authority in Chapter 2. Brief the cases and take notes on the statutes as Chapters 2–5 explained. Use a separate sheet of paper for each source so you can sort them later. Be sure to keep your legal issue in mind, and look particularly for the ways in which each legal source might tell you something about your legal issue. You are looking generally for answers to the following questions:

KEY INFORMATION ABOUT LEGAL AUTHORITIES

1. What is the governing rule?
2. What do its important terms mean?
3. What are some examples of facts that have satisfied the rule's requirements?
4. What are some examples of facts that have *not* satisfied the rule's requirements?
5. What policies or principles does the rule serve?

Make a note about each thought or question that occurs to you, whether or not you think it might be important. There will be time later for sorting and discarding. This is the time for wide, creative perception.

Stage 2: Creating an Annotated Outline. At some point, you must arrive at an outline—the large-scale organization—of your analysis. It is ideal if you can create the outline before you begin to compose a draft, even if later you find you must change it. Start by formulating and outlining the governing rule of law—a statement that explains the test for deciding a legal issue. Then use a version of the rule's outline to create the main categories of your outline. Chapter 7 will explain this process in more detail, but an example here might help. Assume that you have outlined a rule setting out the requirements for revoking a will. The outline of that rule gives you a good starting outline for a written discussion of that issue. Under each element, you would discuss whether your client's facts establish that element.

OUTLINE OF WILL REVOCATION ISSUE
To revoke a will, a testator must
1. have the intention to revoke, and
2. take some action that demonstrates that intent.

Once you have the main categories in place, select one of your authorities and ask yourself what it tells you about the first category (the intention to revoke). Does it help you answer any of the five questions we identified in the box labeled "Key Information About Legal Authorities"? If so, write that information on your case brief or other notes for that authority. *Note the page number on which you find the noted information.* You will have to cite to it when you begin to write, and you will save valuable time if you do not have to look for it again. Then move to the second category (an action demonstrating that intent), and go through the same process. Does this legal authority tell you any of the five kinds of information about the second category? Go through this process with each authority, keeping in mind that some authorities will give you information about more than one category.

After examining each authority, gather all relevant information under the appropriate categories. Use a separate sheet of paper for each category. For each point you have learned, write a complete sentence expressing that information. For instance, under the "intent" category, you might write: "The testator must intend to revoke the will now, not in the future." Under the "action" element, you might write: "The action must not be consistent with any interpretation other than the intent to revoke." These sentences will be the bases for the *thesis sentences* of your paragraphs. And as we shall see in Chapter 20, good thesis sentences are crucial.

Now you are ready for the last step in the outlining stage: selecting the authorities you actually will discuss in your analysis. For each point that you want to make, select the sources that give you the best support or the most important information for that point. Notice that you do not select the *authorities* you will discuss until you have identified the *points* you plan to make. This writing strategy will help you organize according to the relevant substantive points and not simply list and describe cases.

One more point about outlining your analysis: Outlining comes easily for some people; others find it difficult. If you are in the latter group, there is good news and bad news. The bad news is that a tight, linear structure is essential for a good office memo or brief. The good news is that you do not have to create that structure first. Many people find that they must write a very rough draft before they are ready to create an outline. Writing before you outline usually takes longer, but often the resulting outline is more reliable. The key is finding the method that works best for your own writing process.

Stage 3: Writing a Working Draft of the Analysis. After setting forth the large-scale organization of the analysis in an outline, the focus shifts to the small-scale organization, working out your own analysis of the issue. Your primary purpose in writing a working draft is to use the writing process as an analytical tool. Dean and former judge Donald Burnett put it this way:

> Clear expression . . . is not merely a linguistic art. It is the testing ground for ideas. Through the discipline of putting an argument into words, we find out whether the argument is worth making. . . . The secret . . . is to start verbalizing early—while there is still time to learn from the discipline of forming ideas into words. You must begin by identifying your client's goal and the issues to be resolved. Each issue is defined by a cluster of facts and governing legal principle. If you cannot articulate this nexus of law and fact, you do not yet have a grasp of the case.[1]

Your working draft is where you "grasp the case." It guides, deepens, and tests your analysis, and it forms your ideas into the kind of structured, linear reasoning that lawyers must master. Write out your analysis, putting flesh on the outline's bones. Chapters 7–10 will explain how to organize the material. In the working draft stage, focus your attention on the substance and structure of your analysis. Each time you write a statement about what the law is or what an opinion said, note a source and page number. While you are writing your working draft, you need not stop to look up the rules explaining how to cite correctly. The revision stage will give you the chance to correct citation form, spelling, punctuation, and legal usage. In the working draft stage, do the best you can on those matters, but do not let them distract you from your primary task at this stage: creating a solid analysis of your issue.

Try to arrive at the end of Stage 3 with enough time to put down the document for a while. Then return to your draft and revise it, based on what you see when you read with fresh eyes.

Stage 4: Turning the Analysis into a Document Designed for Your Reader. After your analysis is solid, turn your attention toward your reader. The working draft of your analysis will become the Discussion section of your office memo or the Argument section of your brief. In Stage 4 you will check your organization to be sure that it will meet your reader's needs. You will complete the document by writing its statement of facts and its other components.

Stage 5: Editing for Style and Technical Correctness. In this last stage, turn your attention to the fine points of writing. Edit to achieve clarity and correct citation form, punctuation, and grammar. These technical matters are the most easily visible criteria for judging writing. Readers will notice these matters first and draw from them conclusions about the skill and care of the writer. A sloppy document causes a reader to doubt the document's substantive accuracy.

Suggestions for Consciously Using the Writing Process. First, be alert for signs that you need to revisit earlier stages. Although the completed document should take the reader on a linear journey toward the document's conclusion,

1. Donald L. Burnett, Jr., *The Discipline of Clear Expression*, 32 Advocate 8, 8 (June 1989).

you will find that the process of creating the document is far from linear. Rather, the process returns you again and again to earlier stages to reconsider earlier decisions. The willingness to reconsider earlier writing decisions and to revise existing material is one of the hallmarks of a good writer.

Second, experiment with different writing strategies, and observe your own writing process. What works well for you at each stage? Do you work better if you dictate a draft first? Does free-writing help you? How about charts or colored pens? Each writer's creative and analytical processes are unique. Part of your goal in your first few years of legal writing should be to observe as much as you can about your own process so that you can adopt writing strategies that work for you.

Third, be patient. On your first few writing assignments, take the stages in order without trying to combine or compress them. Your goal on these first assignments is to let each stage of the writing process teach you some critical skills. Soon you will have developed those skills well enough to speed up each stage. You will learn to customize each stage to fit your own skill level, the complexity of the assignment, and your own unique creative processes.

Fourth, master the general principles before you decide to try something new. This introductory course on legal writing teaches the basic principles that operate in most situations. First master the basic substantive and organizational principles covered in this course. Soon you will develop the judgment to know when and how you can depart from them.

Finally, start early. Good writing takes time—almost always more time than the writer first expects.

II. LAW-TRAINED READERS

A. Focus on the Reader

The goal of an office memo or a brief is to communicate with a reader. As a matter of fact, you can think of a memo or brief as a conversation with your reader. As in any conversation, the better we know our conversational partners, the more effectively we can communicate. The characteristics of your reader will govern many of the choices you make as a writer.

When you undertake a legal writing task, you might not know your reader well—perhaps not at all. But you can still write with a fairly accurate focus on this unfamiliar reader because law-trained readers share certain characteristics. The general characteristics of law-trained readers in this chapter introduce you to the study of readers, but do not just accept the principles that follow. Notice your own reactions when you read. Try to be a participant-observer of the reading process. Your observations of your own reactions as a reader will be your best writing teacher. Observe, too, the other law-trained readers you know. This way, as the years of your legal practice go by, your writing will become better and better.

B. Attention Levels

Before a speaker can communicate, the audience must be listening. Here is some information about the attention levels of law-trained readers (Figure 6-1):

1. A reader's attention is finite. Even the most diligent reader will eventually run low or run out.
2. On top of a reader's attention being finite, the number of distractions has grown exponentially. While reading, your reader's attention may be drawn away by e-mail alerts, tweets, news notifications, Facebook posts, and Instagram accounts.
3. A reader's investment in the nuances of the topic might not be as great as the writer's. Although the law-trained reader will have a particular need to understand the material, these readers are extraordinarily busy. The judge has many other cases and does not have a personal investment in this one. The senior partner has many other obligations and depends on the memo writer to analyze thoroughly but communicate succinctly.
4. A reader's attention is not evenly distributed. It is greatest in the first several pages, and it decreases rapidly from then on.
5. Readers generally save some attention for the conclusion. They are willing to invest attention there, but only if they can locate the conclusion easily and if the conclusion is clear and compelling enough to warrant the investment.
6. Although readers spend more attention on the document's first few pages and on a compelling conclusion, attention levels revive a bit at internal beginnings and endings, like the start of a new issue or the last few paragraphs of a statement of facts. This revival is more likely if the new issue is marked by a heading or subheading.
7. Stories, especially real-life stories, are engrossing. Many readers pay more attention to facts than to abstract legal concepts. This means, for instance, that attention levels are higher in the middle of an effective Statement of Facts than in the middle of the legal analysis in the Argument or Discussion section. It also means that, even in the middle of a Discussion or Argument section, a reader's attention level will rise a bit when the material begins to apply law to fact.
8. A reader's attention level is lowest about three-fourths of the way through the Discussion section of an office memo or the Argument section of a brief.

These observations about readers underlie an important writing principle: Placement of material is one of the important decisions a writer must make. A good writer places the most important parts of the analysis where the reader can find them quickly and give them first priority for her attention.

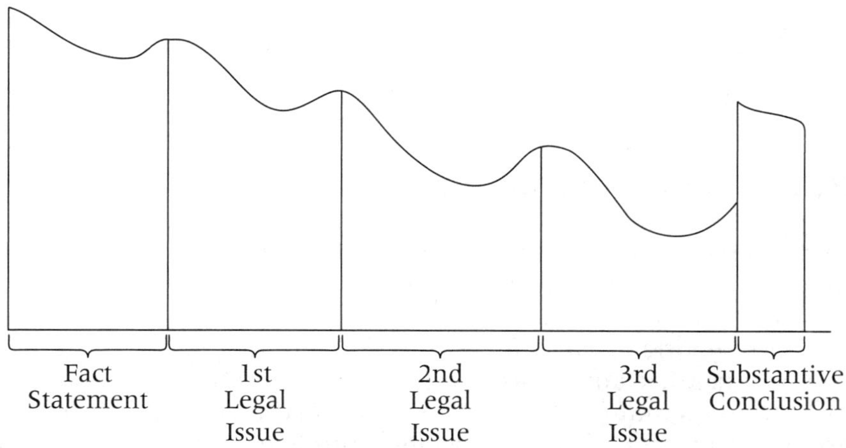

Figure 6.1
Attention levels

C. Road Maps

Most readers want a road map—some sense of where they are and where they are headed. But law-trained readers have an even greater need for an organizational structure. Here's why:

1. A reader's first priority is to understand the law. A law-trained reader's first step in the process of understanding the law is an outline. This process of learning and applying law set out in outline form is how most lawyers and judges studied law. It is basic to the way law-trained readers think. In the first few semesters of law school, this learning style and thinking process probably came more naturally to some than to others, but by the end of law school virtually all lawyers approach legal analysis by some variation of this method. This process is one of the primary components of "thinking like a lawyer."
2. Lawyers and judges do not read the law out of intellectual curiosity but because they have a problem to solve. They are looking to your memo or brief to help them solve it. This means that your discussion of the law must be clearly and closely tied to the facts and issues of the case. Your organizational structure serves as the continuing reminder of how your legal discussion relates to the problem to be solved.
3. A law-trained reader constantly assesses the strength and accuracy of the analysis and the credibility of the writer. The most visible part of the analysis, the part the reader first evaluates, is its organization. Here the law-trained reader expects to find the outline of the law. If a reader doubts the organization of the analysis, the reader wonders whether the content of the analysis is reliable.
4. At some point in their legal education or practice, law-trained readers have studied many of the more common rules of law. Such readers will be used to thinking of those rules in a familiar order or structure. Even if a reader is not already familiar with a particular rule of law, a statute or a leading case might set out the rule in a particular structure. A law-trained reader will be expecting to analyze

the issue in this familiar order or structure. Many law-trained readers are not comfortable with organizational surprises, and an uncomfortable reader is an unreceptive reader.

D. Readers as Commentators

It is easy to assume that writing is a one-way street, with the discourse all flowing in one direction. We tend to think that we, as writers, are the only speakers. We think this because we cannot hear anyone else talking. In reality, the most important party to the conversation, the reader, *is* talking, but we can't hear her. Each of us has a voice in his or her mind—an opinionated, talkative "Commentator." We've already observed this character at work because when a writer mistakenly begins writing to herself, she is writing to her own internal Commentator.

The reader has such a Commentator, too, and that little voice will chatter at every opportunity. The Commentator will be saying things like "No, that's not right, because . . . " or "What in the world do you mean by that?" or "But wait, where is the discussion about . . . ?" Think of yourself as a reader. Haven't you been reading this chapter listening to both the written word and to your own Commentator?[2]

The reader's Commentator will not remain completely silent, and there is nothing the writer can do to change that. The Commentator's participation can even be helpful. Yet each time the Commentator speaks, the reader must listen to two voices at once; the writer must compete with the Commentator for the reader's attention.

The writer, then, has two objectives: (1) The writer wants to keep the reader's Commentator relatively quiet, resolving its concerns at the points where they arise, and (2) when the Commentator does speak, the writer wants it to be saying "OK," "right," or "yes," or perhaps even arriving at the writer's conclusions moments before the writer states them. As a writer, you must anticipate the Commentator's chatter before the conversation occurs and try to preempt that chatter. Your goal is to craft your side of the conversation to keep the Commentator as quiet and agreeable as possible.

E. Judges as Readers

Judges share the characteristics of other law-trained readers. Their attention is finite. They are busy and may become impatient with delay in getting to the bottom line. They generally focus more attention on the beginning and end of a document or a section than on the middle. They find facts engrossing. They want a road map. They value clear organization that sets out the rule of law. But judges tend to have some additional characteristics as well. Here are some other observations about how judges read.

---

2. If so, be grateful to your Commentator. The sort of critical reading the Commentator inspires is essential to legal analysis. When you are studying the law and writing about it, your own Commentator is your best friend.

1. Although any law-trained reader tests the analysis at each step, a judge is particularly apt to do so. This skeptical testing is the heart of a judge's job. Girvan Peck explained it by describing judges as "professional buyers of ideas."[3] However, even a skeptical judge will be less skeptical of the analysis of a lawyer known for careful and honest work than of the analysis of a lawyer with a poor reputation for either competence or candor.
2. Because judges are human, a judge who is already convinced of the equities of your position will be more receptive to your legal arguments. This judge will *want* you to be right on the law. This human desire can help to overcome a little of the judge's natural caution.
3. Most of us are more willing to accept the analysis of someone we like and someone who has been considerate of our needs. This is true of judges as well. This does not mean that judges decide cases on the basis of social and political connections. But a lawyer who treats the judge professionally, with respect and consideration, will be a more effective advocate than the lawyer who does not.
4. As public servants with public responsibilities, judges are concerned about the policy implications of their decisions. However, trial judges and judges serving on intermediate appellate courts often see their role as requiring them to apply the law the way the jurisdiction's highest court would. Not only do judges prefer hearing that they were right, but reversals often mean having to deal with the case again. A judge's goal is to resolve cases, not prolong them.

   Therefore, trial judges and judges serving on intermediate appellate courts are most persuaded by authorities that help them predict how the higher court would decide the question. For judges at these levels, policy arguments are less persuasive than clear mandatory authority. Judges serving on the highest appellate court in the jurisdiction are much more amenable to policy arguments than are their colleagues on lower courts.
5. Because most judges plan to spend many years on the bench, they take a long-term view of each legal issue. Judges are concerned about how an individual ruling could constrain or empower them in future cases.
6. Judges as a group tend to be personally conservative (although not necessarily politically so). Because of the public nature of their job and the fact that they are seen as safeguarders of public morality, lawyers who become judges tend to be conservative in their personal lifestyle.
7. People tend to cling more tenaciously to conclusions they think they have reached by themselves than to those asserted by others. Judges are no different. Thus, when a judge notices that the writer is using a particular technique for persuasion, the technique loses its effectiveness. Heavy-handed use of a persuasive technique usually hurts more than it helps. The most effective persuasive techniques are invisible to the reader.

---

3. Girvan Peck, *Writing Persuasive Briefs* 77 (1984).

8. A reader who feels pushed will resist. An effective legal argument will not push an unwilling reader down a path. Rather, an effective legal argument will place the reader at a vantage point that allows the *reader* to see and choose the best path. Thus, as a brief writer, you must decide how far you can take the judge without losing the judge's cooperation in the process. The consequences of pushing a judge to accept an unreasonable argument go beyond the judge's rejection of the *unreasonable* parts of the argument. The judge will tend to reject the *reasonable* parts of the argument as well.
9. Judges read briefs to decide between legal positions. When such readers are presented with categories, particularly categories identified with point headings, they tend to keep score. They might not even realize they are doing it, and they often will not observe that the rhetorical effect of keeping score is to weight each category equally. Knowing this tendency can help a writer select an organizational plan and decide how to subdivide the argument.
10. As decision-makers encounter arguments one by one, they tend to label each argument as "weak" or "strong" before going on to the next argument. Decision-makers are more likely to be convinced by one strong argument than by a series of weaker ones. Also, a strong argument will lose some of its force if it follows or is followed by weak arguments on the same point.
11. The reader's perception of the strength of the first argument affects the reader's perception of the strength of the arguments that follow. As law-trained readers, judges expect to find the strongest argument first. Unless the judge knows of a reason the weak argument had to be discussed first, the judge will presume that the strongest argument is first and thus that subsequent arguments are even weaker.
12. Judges often relate to the lawyers who practice in their courts in much the way that parents relate to children. If you are a parent, you know that there is nothing quite as tiresome and irritating as constant fighting and bickering among children. Most judges have little tolerance for bickering and blustering lawyers. Judges prefer to focus on legal issues rather than personalities.
13. One final observation about judges: The judge may skim the briefs and then ask a law clerk to read and summarize them. The impact of a law clerk on the brief-reading process is a bit of a wild card, but there are two general observations that you should keep in mind. First is the relative inexperience of most law clerks as compared to most judges. Remembering this inexperience will help you to take care not to leave out steps in the analysis on the assumption that your reader is an expert on your issue. Second, although these readers are often inexperienced, they also tend to be bright. Many judicial clerks served on their school's law review and received much of their formative training in that context. Thus, they expect the details of a brief to be right. They tend to draw conclusions about the reliability of the analysis based on the lawyer's attention to these details. They may well scrutinize every aspect of your brief more thoroughly than a busy judge could.

F. Law Professors as Readers

Your primary readers for law school documents will be law professors. Undoubtedly, these professors already understand a great deal about the relevant area of law and about the particular authorities on which your analysis will be based.

Ordinarily, a writer should tailor the document to the reader's pre-existing knowledge. If the writer is certain that the reader knows some of the relevant information, the writer would refer generally to the information only when necessary to put new information in context. However, law school writing is a different matter. Unlike most readers, your professor is not reading to learn particular information. Instead, your professor is reading to evaluate what information *you* have learned and how well you can communicate it. If the information is not set out in your document, your professor will not know whether and how well you understand it.

Therefore, in law school writing, assume that you are writing to a law-trained reader who has no particular expertise in the area you are discussing. Your goal is to include the information your professor wants to evaluate without explaining more than the assignment asks.

CHAPTER 7

Large-Scale Organization: Creating an Annotated Outline

An annotated outline is the most reliable method for making your legal analysis complete and coherent. Without it or its equivalent, you may miss issues or wander off track as you write. But if you have an annotated outline, writing the analysis will flow easily. Your topic headings, thesis sentences, and case references will already be laid out. This chapter explains how to identify the structure of a legal rule and how to use that structure to create an annotated outline for your writing assignment.

I. OUTLINING A RULE: RULE STRUCTURES

Rules of law adopt particular structures. Recognizing a rule structure is a method for quickly deepening your understanding of the rule. This study tool will work well for virtually all of your law school classes. If you are preparing a course outline for contracts, for instance, your outline will be more effective if you consciously outline the legal rules you are studying. Also, the rule's structure will become the basis for the large-scale organization (the outline) of your memo or brief, or even the relevant part of your contracts final exam.

Therefore, when you formulate a legal rule from a case opinion, try to express it in an outline format. Use any version of traditional outline form, with roman numerals, uppercase letters, Arabic numerals, and lowercase letters, as necessary. This outline of the relevant rule will focus your analysis on each part in an orderly way.

As you gain experience in outlining legal rules you will notice certain common rule structures.[1]

1. Some rules use more than one rule structure. Such a rule will use a larger structure like one of the examples set out in this section. However, the rule's subparts might use another rule structure. An example of such a rule is found at www.AspenPublishing.com/Edwards-LWAnalysis6.

A Conjunctive Test. This kind of rule sets out a test with a list of mandatory *elements*. For example, consider this rule: To revoke a will, a testator must have the intention to revoke the will and must take some action that demonstrates that intent. The outline for this rule would set out each of the required elements like this:

To revoke a will, a testator must
1. have the intention to revoke and
2. take some action that demonstrates that intent.

A Disjunctive Test. This kind of rule sets out an "either/or" test. It identifies two or more subparts and establishes a certain result if the facts fall within any *one* subpart. For example, consider this rule: A lawyer shall not collect a contingent fee in a criminal matter or a divorce. You might outline the rule like this:

A lawyer shall not collect a contingent fee in either of the following kinds of cases:
1. a criminal matter or
2. a divorce.

Notice that the difference between the first two rule structures lies in the introductory language specifying whether all subparts are required or whether any single subpart is sufficient.

A Factors (Aggregative) Test. This kind of rule sets out a flexible standard guided by certain criteria or factors.[2] Some rules condition the legal result on a more or less objective standard. A burglary statute, for instance, defines burglary using a number of fairly objective criteria. Was it a dwelling? Did it belong to another? Did the defendant enter it? However, some rules condition the legal result on a much more flexible standard, giving more discretion to the decision-maker. To keep judges from being totally arbitrary and to help them exercise their discretion wisely and uniformly, rules using flexible standards often identify factors or criteria to guide the decision-maker. Here is an example of such a rule:

> Child custody shall be decided in accordance with the best interests of the child. Factors to consider in deciding the best interests of the child are: the fitness of each possible custodian; the appropriateness for parenting of the lifestyle of each possible custodian; the relationship between the child and each possible custodian; the placement of the child's siblings, if any; living accommodations; the district lines of the child's school; the proximity of extended family and friends; religious issues; any other factors relevant to the child's best interests.

2. Some scholars use the term "rule" to refer only to fairly objective, concrete legal tests and use the word "standard" to refer to more flexible tests like a factors test or a balancing test. To avoid confusion, however, we will use the term "rule" to refer to both kinds of legal tests.

Placed in outline form, the rule would look like this:

Child custody shall be decided in accordance with the best interests of the child. Factors to consider in deciding the best interests of the child are:

1. the fitness of each possible custodian
2. the appropriateness for parenting of the lifestyle of each possible custodian
3. the relationship between the child and each possible custodian
4. the placement of the child's siblings, if any
5. living accommodations
6. the district lines of the child's school
7. the proximity of extended family and friends
8. religious issues
9. any other factors relevant to the child's best interests

Notice the critical difference between this rule structure and a conjunctive test (a rule with mandatory elements). In a conjunctive test, all of the subparts must be met, but here the subparts are just factors to consider rather than separate individual requirements. One or more can be absent from a particular case without necessarily changing the result. The decision-maker has the discretion to gauge the relative importance of each factor.

A Balancing Test. This kind of rule balances countervailing considerations against each other. A rule setting out a balancing test is also inherently flexible, so such a rule often includes factors or guidelines to assist the decision-maker in weighing each side of the balance.

For example, consider this dispute over legal procedure. Prior to trial, parties in civil litigation try to obtain information from each other by using interrogatories (written questions directed to another party and calling for answers under oath). Sometimes, the party receiving a set of interrogatories will object to certain interrogatories, arguing that answering would be unduly burdensome. To decide whether the party must answer the interrogatories, the judge applies the following rule:

A party must respond to properly propounded interrogatories unless the burden of responding substantially outweighs the questioning party's legitimate need for the information.

To measure "burden," the judge might consider a number of factors, such as the time and effort necessary to answer; the cost of compiling the information; any privacy concerns of the objecting party; and any other circumstances particular to the objecting party's situation. To measure "legitimate need," the judge might consider a number of other factors, such as how important the information would be to the issues of the trial, whether the information would be available from some other source or in some other form, and any other circumstances relating to the party's need for the information. Placed in outline form, the rule would look like this:

A party must respond to properly propounded interrogatories unless the burden of responding substantially outweighs the questioning party's legitimate need for the information.

A. The burden of answering:
   1. the time and effort necessary to answer
   2. the cost of compiling the information
   3. any privacy concerns of the objecting party
   4. any other circumstances raised by that particular party's situation
B. The questioning party's need for the information:
   1. how important the information would be to the issues of the trial
   2. whether the information would be available from some other source or in some other form
   3. any other circumstances relating to the party's need for the information

Compare this rule structure with the factors test. In a factors test, the decision-maker gauges a single interest, for example, "the best interest of the child." In a balancing test, the decision-maker balances two competing and different interests, using factors to compare the strength of each interest against the other. In the discovery rule above, these two interests are the burden of answering and the need for the information.

A Defeasible Rule. A defeasible rule is a rule with one or more exceptions. Here is an example of a rule with an exception:

A lawyer shall not prepare any document giving the lawyer a gift from a client except where the gift is insubstantial or where the client is related to the lawyer.

Placed in outline form, the rule would look like this:

A lawyer shall not prepare any document giving the lawyer a gift from a client except

A. where the gift is insubstantial or
B. where the client is related to the lawyer.

Again, notice that the critical distinction between this structure and the others lies in the introductory language defining the subparts as exceptions to a general principle. Notice also that you can accurately articulate some rules using different structures. For instance, do you see how you could easily articulate this rule using a disjunctive rule structure?

A Simple Declarative Rule. A simple declarative rule contains no elements, factors, or other subparts. For example, if you are analyzing the validity of an unsigned will, you might be dealing with a rule like this:

> To be valid, a will must be signed.

If you have looked carefully and found no subparts, factors, or other criteria for applying the rule, you can assume that your rule is a simple declarative rule. In such a case, your structure will be a simple one-point structure. However, take care to assure yourself that your rule has no lurking elements or other subparts. Overlooking elements or other subparts is a common mistake for beginning legal writers.

EXERCISE 7-1
Outlining a Rule

For each of the following excerpts from case opinions, formulate a rule and write it out in outline form using one or more of the rule structures described above.

1. *Issue: When can an otherwise legally insufficient contract still be enforced?*

   "[W]here one party has by his words or conduct made to the other a promise or assurance which was intended to . . . be acted on accordingly, then, once the other party has taken him at his word and acted on it, the party who gave the promise cannot afterward be allowed to revert to the previous relationship as if no such promise had been made." *Wheeler v. White*, 398 S.W.2d 93, 96 (Tex. 1965).

2. *Co-owners of property can ask the court to partition their property if they no longer wish to own it jointly and if they cannot agree on a manner of division. Normally, the court partitions the property by dividing it and awarding part to one co-owner and part to the other ("partition in kind"). Issue: When can a court order the sale of the property (and the division of the proceeds) rather than dividing the property itself?*

   "[P]artition by sale should be ordered only when two conditions are satisfied: (1) the physical attributes of the land are such that a partition in kind is impracticable or inequitable; and (2) the interests of the owners would better be promoted by a partition by sale. . . . [In considering the practicability of partition in kind, the court can consider such matters as] the situation and location of the parcel of land, the size and area of the property, the physical structure and appurtenances on the property, and other factors." *Delfino v. Vealencis*, 436 A.2d 27, 30–31 (Conn. 1980) (citations omitted).

Rules Combining Several Structures. Some rules use more than one rule structure. Such a rule will use a larger structure like one of the examples set out above. However, the rule's subparts might use another rule structure. For instance, consider this rule governing attacks on the credibility of criminal defendants who testify at trial:[3]

3. At a trial, the judge decides what testimony or documents can be admitted into evidence by applying the rules of evidence in effect for that court. If the judge refuses to admit a document into evidence, that information cannot be considered when deciding the case.

> Evidence that the accused previously was convicted of a crime shall be admitted if the crime involved dishonesty or false statement by the accused or if the crime was punishable by death or imprisonment in excess of one year and the conviction's probative value outweighs its prejudicial effect.[4]

This rule uses the disjunctive (either/or) structure for its larger structure, like so:

> Evidence of a prior conviction may be admitted if it falls within either of the following categories:
> **A.** if it involved dishonesty or false statement, or
> **B.** if it was punishable by death or imprisonment in excess of one year and its probative value outweighs its prejudicial effect.

Notice, however, that subpart B contains two requirements (the punishment requirement and the comparison of probative value to prejudicial effect). Notice also that the inquiry about probative value and prejudicial effect is a balancing test. What's more, the cases interpreting this rule probably describe the factors to be considered in gauging "probative value" and "prejudicial effect." Thus, a more detailed outline of the rule might look like this:

> Evidence of a prior conviction may be admitted if it falls within either category A or category B:
> **A.** if the conviction involved dishonesty or false statement; or
> **B.** if both of the following are true:
>   **1.** the conviction was punishable by death or imprisonment in excess of one year; and
>   **2.** its probative value outweighs its prejudicial effect
>   **a.** probative value is gauged by: [List factors set out in the cases.]
>   **b.** prejudicial effect is gauged by: [List factors set out in the cases.]

Finally, note that subpart A has two subparts (dishonesty or false statement), either of which is enough to answer the question.

II. CREATING AN ANNOTATED OUTLINE

As you know, outlines divide material into topics and organize them, using levels to show how the topics relate to each other. The first level of distinction

4. *See* Fed. R. Evid. 609(a) (paraphrased).

is reserved for the broadest categories. The second level represents the largest distinctions within each of the broad categories. Those second-level topics can be subdivided even further. We begin with the first level of distinction for a legal analysis: the legal question(s) you have been asked to address.

A. The First Level: The Legal Questions You Have Been Asked to Address

Your writing assignment probably identified the legal question or questions you are to address. If you have been asked to analyze whether William Levitt's actions constituted burglary, you have been asked to address only one legal question. But if your assignment also asks you to address whether his statement to Delores Corbitt, his alleged common-law wife, will be admissible at trial, you have been asked two legal questions. The first question will be governed by the rule identifying the elements of burglary. The second question will be governed by a different rule—a rule of evidence.

Use your outline's first level of distinction (roman numerals) to identify the separate legal questions you have been asked to address. At the outline stage, you can phrase these issues as questions or, if you are ready, as your answers to the question. In the example above, the outline's first level of distinction would be:

I. Do William Levitt's acts constitute burglary?
II. Will Levitt's statements to Delores Corbitt be admissible at trial?

If you have been asked only one question, use a roman numeral "I" for that question, and do not be concerned that you will not have more than one roman numeral. Let the use of the roman numeral assure you and your reader that this is the issue you were given and, therefore, that this is the point of connection between that question and your own analysis.

B. The Second Level: Governing Rules

Whether or not your assignment identifies separate legal questions, your research might reveal that the answer will depend on two different legal issues governed by two different legal rules. Your assignment might ask, "Can our client succeed in a claim for negligence against the other driver?" This is one legal question. However, you might discover that its answer will depend on the answers to two separate legal questions governed by two separate legal rules: (1) whether your client can establish the elements of a negligence claim; and (2) whether the applicable statute of limitations has expired.[5] If your answer to the question will require analysis under two different and

5. Statutes of limitation prescribe the time limits within which a claim can be brought.

unrelated legal rules, use the next level of distinction (uppercase letters) to represent the discussions of these two different rules.

For instance, in our prior example, assume that the second question (admissibility of Levitt's statements) will require analysis using two different governing rules: the rule defining a valid common-law marriage and that jurisdictions rule of evidence that prohibits admission of statements made to a common-law spouse. Our outline now looks like this:

- **I.** Do William Levitt's actions constitute burglary?
- **II.** Will Levitt's statements to Delores Corbitt be admissible at trial?
  - **A.** Are Levitt and Corbitt married according to common law?
  - **B.** Are statements to a common law spouse admissible at trial?

C. The Next Levels: Filling in the Rules

Use your outline of the governing rule(s) to form the next levels of your discussion's outline. For instance, in our example, the next levels under the roman numerals might produce the following outline:

- **I.** Do William Levitt's actions constitute burglary?
  - **A.** breaking
  - **B.** entering
  - **C.** dwelling
  - **D.** of another
  - **E.** in the nighttime
  - **F.** intent to commit felony therein
- **II.** Will Levitt's statements to Delores Corbitt be admissible at trial?
  - **A.** Are Levitt and Corbitt married according to common law?
    - **1.** intent of both parties to be married, and
    - **2.** actions holding themselves out to the community as husband and wife.
  - **B.** Are statements to a common-law spouse admissible at trial?
    [Statements made to a common-law spouse are privileged and therefore not admissible unless the privilege is waived.]
  - **C.** Has Levitt waived the privilege?

Notice that your research on the admissibility of statements to a common-law spouse has yielded a defeasible rule (a rule with an exception). The rule is a simple declarative statement with one exception: "The statements are inadmissible unless the defendant has waived the privilege." Therefore, you have discovered another subissue: whether Levitt waived the privilege. You must return to your research to learn what kinds of acts would constitute a waiver. When you find the rule that governs waiver, you will use it to structure section C in the outline.

Thus, the outlines of the relevant rules provide the organization for your working analysis of each issue. Using this outline, your analysis of the burglary question would discuss each element separately, completing the discussion of one element before proceeding to the next. Then you would proceed to the admissibility question and follow the same process there.

D. Omitting Issues Not in Dispute

You might already know that some of the categories on your outline will not be issues in your assignment. For instance, in the burglary example, the "nighttime" issue probably would not be disputed if the entry of the building occurred at 2:00 A.M. You can revise your outline now to delete the "nighttime" category, but you cannot forget the issue just yet. You will need to explain to your reader your reasons for not addressing that element. Chapter 10 will describe how and where to give your reader this information.

To be sure you do not forget the element, you can leave it in its place on your working draft outline and simply skip it when you start to write. After you have written out the other parts of your analysis, you will use your working draft to create the document designed for your reader. At that point, you will be doing some rearranging of the sections anyway, so revising the outline then would be convenient. For example, as Chapter 10 will explain, it probably will be appropriate to place the most dispositive element first in your discussion, and you might not know which element will be most dispositive until you have written out your analysis.

Leaving the category in its place temporarily can be a good idea for another reason. Legal conclusions often turn out to be less obvious than they first appeared. Only after you have researched both law and facts will you be ready to predict how the rule will apply to your client. Only then will you know for certain whether you can treat any parts of the rule as undisputed.

E. Uncertainty About Which Rule Your Jurisdiction Will Adopt

You might find that your jurisdiction has not yet adopted a rule governing your particular issue. Or perhaps your jurisdiction's rule reflects an unwise approach to the issue, and your client's interests would be served best by the adoption of a different rule. If you are writing an office memo, you will have to predict what rule the court probably would adopt. Then you can analyze the disposition of your client's particular issue, assuming that your prediction is correct. You might also need to analyze the result if the decision-maker adopts the other rule. Your working draft outline might look like this:

A. If the court adopts rule *A*, what will be the result?
B. If the court adopts rule *B*, what will be the result?
C. Which rule is the court most likely to adopt?

In section C, in an office memo, you will need to compare the two rules to predict which rule the court is likely to adopt. In a persuasive brief to the court, you will be arguing which rule the court should adopt. In either case, you will need to address the relative strength of the authority supporting each rule.

F. Annotating Your Outline

Your working outline now provides the structure for your discussion of the authorities. The next step is deciding which authorities you will discuss under each point in the outline and for what purpose. Chapter 6 described this process. Remember that you should write a complete sentence expressing each relevant point you have learned about the rules of law. *Do not select the authorities you will use until you have identified the points you will make.* This way you will find yourself organizing according to the relevant substantive points and not simply listing and describing cases without using them to make a relevant point.

EXERCISE 7-2
Outlining the Discussion of a Legal Issue

Draft an outline for a discussion of this legal issue. Assume that the rules set out below are the rules you have formulated from the applicable authorities.

Facts. Joe Barrymore and Reynold Manitoba, fans of different hockey teams, came to blows in a discussion of the relative merits of their teams. Barrymore came out the loser, with four broken ribs. The fight ended when Manitoba pushed Barrymore into a cleaning closet and padlocked the door. Barrymore has come to your firm to find out whether he can sue Manitoba for battery and for false imprisonment.

Rules

- Battery is the intentional infliction of a harmful or offensive bodily contact.
- A contact is harmful if it causes pain or bodily damage.
- A contact is offensive if it would be damaging to a reasonable sense of dignity.
- To meet the requirement of intent for a battery claim, the defendant need only have intended to make the contact; intent to harm is not necessary.
- A defendant has committed a false imprisonment if he intentionally confined the plaintiff within boundaries set by defendant.

CHAPTER 8

Small-Scale Organization: Explaining the Law

After you have a large-scale structure for your discussion, the focus shifts to small-scale organization. The next step is to write out the analysis, putting flesh on the bones of this structure. Chapters 8 and 9 will explain how to discuss a single legal issue. Chapter 10 will explain how to put the discussions of multiple issues together into one cohesive analysis.

What do we mean by a "single issue"? You will find that phrase used differently in many contexts, but for our purposes, we mean the analysis of a single part of a rule. For instance, in the burglary example, each of the elements of the crime of burglary would raise a separate issue.

This chapter begins by providing an overview of the paradigm—a commonly used organizational plan—for legal analysis. The remainder of the chapter focuses on the first half of the paradigm.

I. AN OVERVIEW OF THE PARADIGM FOR LEGAL ANALYSIS

A legal issue is analyzed by first identifying and understanding the governing rule and then applying that rule to a particular set of facts. First you must *explain* the rule; then you must *apply* that rule to the facts. Here is an overview of the basic paradigm:[1]

PARADIGM FOR A WORKING DRAFT

Rule Explanation

1. Conclusion: State your conclusion about the issue.
2. Rule: State the applicable rule of law.
3. Rule Explanation: Explain the rule.

1. You may have heard it referred to as "CREAC" (Conclusion, Rule, Explanation, Application, Conclusion) or "IRAC" (Issue, Rule, Application, Conclusion) or a similar, mysterious-sounding acronym.

Rule Application
4. Rule Application: Apply the rule to your client's facts.
5. Conclusion: Restate your conclusion.

This chapter describes the rule explanation half of this paradigm. Many new legal writers are not sure what rule explanation covers. They also might think they have explained the rule more thoroughly than they actually have. These difficulties can be eased if, after the introductory paragraph (described below), you do not allow discussion of your client's facts (the second half of the paradigm) to slip into the first half of the paradigm—your explanation of the rule itself. Mixing explanation and application leads to confusion in identifying rule explanation. If you keep application out of the spot reserved for explanation, you will learn what rule explanation is *not*, which is vital to learning what rule explanation *is*.

Separating the halves of the paradigm also will help you accurately evaluate your own writing. Often a writer states the rule and then proceeds to write several pages about the rule and how it applies to the facts. The discussion seems thorough, but how can the writer tell? An accurate self-evaluation requires checking the depth and breadth of both halves of the reasoning process, and that is difficult to do when the two halves are intermixed. As a discipline, you might want to draw a line on your working draft between the rule explanation and the rule application. The line will remind you to keep your discussion of your client's facts below the line.

Keeping the halves distinct does not mean that while you are engaged in the process of writing the paradigm you must complete rule explanation before you attempt to write any rule application. For early versions of the working draft, you can write more freely. Many writers find this unstructured prewriting helpful. Using the paradigm means simply that at the conclusion of your writing process, the document should reflect distinct sections for rule explanation and rule application.

EXERCISE 8-1
Identifying and Labeling the Parts of the Paradigm

After reading the "Facts" section of the office memo in Appendix A, read section A (a single-issue discussion). Identify each part of the paradigm.

II. STATING THE CONCLUSION

Law-trained readers want to learn your answer, so the first thing your reader will want to see is your conclusion. If you already know what your conclusion will be, put it in a sentence and use that sentence as the section heading. Then state your conclusion again, letting your reader know (1) the issue to be decided, (2) your conclusion on that issue, and (3) your basic reason for that conclusion, if you can state it succinctly. Often the governing rule will be implicit in this statement, but you need not state it directly here because you will be stating it next.

For example, assume that your firm represents Linda Pyle, who recently bought a tract of land to use as a commercial horse stable. A lawyer from another firm, Howard Gavin, represented Pyle in the land purchase transaction. After buying the land, Pyle discovered that a neighboring quarry owned an easement across her property, and the use of the easement is interfering with the stable's operation. Pyle has come to a partner in your firm, and the partner has asked you to research whether Gavin's failure to check the title for possible easements constituted legal malpractice. Here is an example of the beginning of the written discussion of this issue:

I. Linda Pyle has a strong claim for legal malpractice against Howard Gavin.

Howard Gavin committed legal malpractice in his representation of Linda Pyle because he did not meet the required standard of professional skill and diligence. The representation called for a basic task common to general practitioners, and the problem could have been prevented simply by doing thorough research.

If you are writing a brief to the court, probably you will already know what your conclusion will be. If you are writing an office memo, however, and if the issue is a close one, you might not be sure what your conclusion will be until you have progressed further in the writing process. If you are not yet sure, you can state the issue here rather than the conclusion, and proceed with writing your analysis. Once you have a solid draft, rewrite the heading and the first paragraph to provide your reader with the information above.

III. STATING THE GOVERNING RULE

Next, state the governing rule. Follow it with citations to the primary source(s) for the rule. Chapter 19 addresses proper citation form. Here is a rule statement added to our example:

I. Linda Pyle has a strong claim for legal malpractice against Howard Gavin.

Howard Gavin committed legal malpractice in his representation of Linda Pyle because he did not meet the required standard of professional skill and diligence. The representation called for a basic task common to general practitioners, and the problem could have been prevented simply by doing thorough research.

A lawyer has a duty to provide a client with representation that meets or exceeds the standard of *professional skill and diligence commonly possessed and exercised by a reasonably prudent lawyer* in this jurisdiction. **Citation**.

Usually, the rule statement should be the first paragraph after the heading. Occasionally, however, an issue is complex enough to require a little context or clarification before stating the rule. If so, *briefly* set out the necessary context or clarification, but get to the rule statement as quickly as you can. Not only will your reader be looking for the rule, but the discipline of concisely stating the rule immediately after the conclusion is an important part of your analytical process. It forces you to articulate the focal point of the first half of the analysis, and it focuses your attention on the rule you are about to explain.

After you have typed your statement of the rule, look for the key term or legal standard. The primary task of your rule explanation is to define that term or standard. Just for the working draft, you might want to use italics for these key words so you can easily refocus your attention on them.

IV. EXPLAINING THE RULE: FIVE COMPONENTS

The third step is explaining where the rule comes from and what it means. Rule explanation usually includes five components. Generally, these components are so closely interrelated that you will not be able to break them out and explain them sequentially. While you are explaining one, you will also be explaining another, so do not use this list as an organizing tool. Instead, use it to evaluate your rule explanation for its completeness:

1. Show That the Rule Is What You Say It Is. You can think of this as "rule proof." Set out the relevant content of the authorities (facts and holdings of cases or key provisions of statutes). Sometimes, if you have had to formulate the rule by synthesizing or reconciling authorities, as Chapter 3 described, you might have to explain your synthesis or reconciliation. The point is to show your reader that your rule statement is accurate.

2. Explain the Rule's Purpose or the Policies It Serves. The way the rule will apply to your client's facts will be influenced by the rule's purpose and the policies it serves, so your reader will need to understand these underlying rationales. Chapter 11 explains this part of rule explanation in greater detail.

3. Explain How the Rule Has Been Applied in the Past. Interpreting the language of a rule requires attention to how courts have and have not applied it in the past. What are some examples of cases in which the rule's requirements have been met? Have not been met? The purpose here continues to be explaining the rule and how it functions. If you are using cases to do this, you can think of this as "case illustration." You are using the cases to illustrate the rule. Don't mention your client's facts here. You'll compare the precedent cases to your client's facts later, in the application section, covered in Chapter 9.

4. Explain Any Additional Characteristics That Will Affect How the Rule May Be Applied. Is this rule to be liberally or strictly construed? Are there burdens of proof or presumptions that might affect how the rule will apply to future cases? Does the rule require an elevated level of proof, like clear and convincing evidence? Will expert testimony be required?

5. To the Extent Necessary, Discuss Any Other Possible Understanding of the Rule. If another reasonable interpretation of the rule exists, your reader will want to know it. Address any competing interpretation that is reasonably likely to arise, and explain why your interpretation is more accurate. The explanation of another possible interpretation is sometimes called "counter-analysis" or "counter-explanation."

Match the depth of your discussion to your assessment of the strength of this second interpretation. If it is possible but unlikely that a court would adopt it, cover it briefly. However, if the choice between the interpretations is a closer call, discuss the counter-analysis in more detail, and explain why it is not the best or most likely interpretation.

V. GUIDELINES FOR RULE EXPLANATION

Here are some guidelines to keep in mind as you write the rule explanation section:

Use All Relevant Tools of Statutory and Case Law Analysis. Review the tools for case law and statutory analysis described in Chapters 2–5. Remember that the value of the information they yield is not simply in reporting it but rather in *using it to make a point about the rule*.

Limit Your Explanation to Those Topics That Will Be Relevant to the Way the Rule Will Apply to Your Client's Facts. When you explain what the rule means, do not include everything one might ever want to know about the rule. Include only the information that might pertain to your client's situation. Because you have not yet written the section *applying* the rule to your client's facts, you will have to anticipate the application you have not yet written. After you write the application section, you might need to return to the rule explanation section to add or delete topics of rule explanation. Your goal is to match the coverage of the explanation section to the coverage of the application section.

Use Only Very Short Quotes of Key Language. If you force yourself to use your own words for the information you find in the sources, you will understand that information better, and you might be able to state it more clearly than the original writer did. Remember that your analysis must do more than simply retype material from the sources. Analysis begins only when you draw theses from the material in the sources and explain the reasoning that supports your theses.

Order Your Discussion of the Authorities According to Their Importance. Place the most important authorities early in the discussion. Case authorities are important to an analysis primarily by virtue of their precedential value generally or by the similarity of their particular facts to your client's facts.

Articulate Factors or Guidelines. When you discuss the cases that are similar factually, try to discern and articulate any factors or guidelines that seem to be operating when the courts apply the rule to these kinds of situations. Sometimes such information will be described explicitly by the courts; sometimes you will have to infer it from other comments the courts have made or from the way the courts have applied the rule. Either way, you are identifying factors or guidelines about how the rule works.

Do Not Use Authorities Just to Fill up Space or to Prove That You Have Read Them. Rather, demonstrate that you have the lawyerly skill of identifying the *key* authorities and analyzing them thoroughly.

Include a Description of the Rule's Historical Development. Do this if (1) the development is important for understanding the rule's current form; or (2) the rule's current form does not decisively answer your question, but the rule's history establishes a trend that can help you predict or persuade. If you choose to describe the rule's development, tell your reader why. Otherwise, a law-trained reader will become impatient with what might seem like an unnecessary history lesson.

Choose an Appropriate Option for Using Cases. You have three options for using cases to illustrate the rule: (1) using only a citation, (2) using a citation with a parenthetical summary, and (3) using a case with an in-text illustration.[2] Choose among them according to your assessment of the importance of the point you are making. Here are examples of each:

> *Citation only:*
> One who is a minor at the time of making a contract can disaffirm the contract within a reasonable time after reaching the age of majority. *Woodall v. Grant,* 9 S.E.2d 95, 95 (Ga. Ct. App. 1940).
>
> *Citation with a parenthetical summary:*
> A minor is estopped from disaffirming a contract if the minor knowingly misrepresented his age at the time he made the contract. *Woodall v. Grant,* 9 S.E.2d 95, 95 (Ga. Ct. App. 1940) (holding minor not estopped when he signed without reading a contract representing that he was an adult).
>
> *Citation with an in-text illustration:*
> A minor is estopped from disaffirming a contract if the minor knowingly misrepresented his age at the time he made the contract. *Woodall v. Grant,* 9 S.E.2d 95, 95 (Ga. Ct. App. 1940). In *Woodall,* the minor had signed a brokerage contract to purchase stock options, and the contract contained a representation that the purchaser had attained the age of majority. *Id.* at 96. However, the minor had signed the contract without reading it. *Id.* The court reasoned that the law does not require a minor to read a contract and does not enforce the same consequences on a minor as it would on an adult in the same circumstance. *Id.* The court held that the minor had not knowingly

2. Class handouts by Michael R. Smith, *Techniques for Using Authority in a Memo* (1991) (on file with the author).

misrepresented his age and, therefore, that he was not estopped from disaffirming the contract. *Id.*

You will need to decide which technique to use every time you use a case to help explain the rule. Ask yourself why you are using the case and how much information your reader will need. If the point is undisputed and requires no explanation, you can use the citation only. If the point could benefit from a short example, you can use a citation with a parenthetical summary. For important cases that you will be comparing to in the rule application, use an in-text illustration.

VI. ORGANIZING A PURE QUESTION OF LAW

Occasionally, your issue will be a pure question of law. You have a pure question of law if the assignment asks you to analyze only *what the law is* in your jurisdiction and does not ask you to apply that law to your client's facts. For example, you might be asked, "In this jurisdiction, can a husband be forced to testify against his wife?" In such a case, your analysis will consist primarily of rule explanation, culminating with your conclusion about the question of law ("A husband cannot be forced to testify against his wife").

Or perhaps the assignment might ask you to apply the law to your client's facts, but there is no real question about the result of that application. For example, you might be asked, "Can Mr. Studdard be forced to testify against Mrs. Studdard?" Once you have explained that a husband cannot be forced to testify against his wife, the application of that rule to Mr. Studdard is clear. In that case, your analysis will consist almost entirely of rule explanation. You will spend most of your time explaining the rule. At the end of the rule explanation, you can apply the rule to Mr. Studdard, but you probably will not need to do more than announce that as Mrs. Studdard's husband, Mr. Studdard will not have to testify.

Here is an example of a working draft of a rule explanation for the Pyle/Gavin issue.

A WORKING DRAFT OF RULE EXPLANATION

I. Linda Pyle has a strong claim for legal malpractice against Howard Gavin.

Howard Gavin committed legal malpractice in his representation of Linda Pyle because he did not meet the required standard of professional skill and diligence. The subject matter of the representation is common to general practitioners, and the problem could have been prevented with thorough research. **CONCLUSION**

A lawyer has a duty to provide a client with representation that meets or exceeds the standard of professional skill and diligence *commonly possessed and exercised by a reasonably prudent lawyer in this jurisdiction.* **Citation**.	**RULE**
In *Jacobson*, the lawyer failed to file a timely claim before the medical malpractice screening panel. **Citation**. By statute, a medical malpractice claim cannot be pursued unless it has been filed before the screening panel within the applicable time limit. **Citation**. Therefore the client's claim was barred. **Citation**. Because a reasonably prudent lawyer would research and comply with the statutory requirements for bringing a particular kind of claim, the court held that the lawyer was liable for the losses that resulted from the failure to file the claim. **Citation**.	**RULE EXPLANATION** **Key facts from cited case** **Holding from cited case**
One gauge of the prudent lawyer standard is whether the task is something general practitioners are familiar with doing. **Citation**. In *Jacobson*, the court had pointed out that the enactment of the screening panel requirement had been widely publicized in newspapers, electronic media, and the state bar journal. **Citation**. However, the court explained that even without publicity, a prudent lawyer would comply with filing requirements because filing lawsuits is something general practitioners are familiar with doing. **Citation**. Therefore, if the task is familiar to general practitioners, the court need not ask whether the particular lawyer should have been aware of the particular requirement. **Citation**.	**Thesis sentence (a characteristic the court found significant)** **Key facts** **Court's statement about those facts** **How court's statement supports thesis**
Another gauge of the prudent lawyer standard is whether the error could have been prevented by research. **Citation**. In *Jacobson*, the court observed that an "error in judgment" does not constitute malpractice. **Citation**. While *Jacobson* did not expressly define the difference between an error in judgment and a breach of the prudent lawyer standard, the court distinguished the *Jacobson* facts from an "error in judgment" by pointing out that in *Jacobson* the correct answer would have been apparent had the lawyer done the necessary research. **Citation**. Therefore, although a prudent lawyer can make an error in judgment, a prudent lawyer does not make errors preventable by proper research. **Citation.**	**Thesis sentence (another significant characteristic)** **Disclosure that thesis is an inference** **Reasoning from the court's observation about the facts**
The "prudent lawyer" standard is not reduced for lawyers operating outside their area of special knowledge. **Citation**. In *Jacobson*, the lawyer-defendant had been in practice only ten weeks when he accepted the medical malpractice case. **Citation**. The court held that the lawyer's lack of experience did not excuse his failure. **Citation**. Clients should be entitled to at least the minimum standard of skill and diligence, according to the court. **Citation**. Also, a contrary rule would offer no incentive to lawyers to gain necessary knowledge or experience. **Citation**.	**Thesis sentence (how rule applies to a particular situation)** **Relevant facts** **Holding on this point** **Court's two policy reasons**

The standard probably would not be affected by facts indicating that the lawyer intended to be particularly careful, that he was otherwise skilled and diligent, or that he was a well-respected partner of a well-respected firm. **Citation.**	**Thesis sentence anticipating an issue**
Although no facts like these were present in *Jacobson*,	**Disclosure of lack of similar facts**
the court's language and policy statement explained in the previous paragraph would seem to apply to this question as well. **Citation.**	**Reasoning from policy**
It is unclear whether the court would rely on expert testimony or would make its own judgment about what a prudent lawyer would do in a particular set of circumstances.	**Thesis sentence (evidence required)**
This question was not at issue in *Jacobson*. **Citation.** However, the opinion does not mention the testimony of any expert witness, and the court's statements that a prudent lawyer would research the requirements for bringing a claim seemed to be statements of the court's own opinion rather than statements based on someone's testimony. **Citation.**	**Disclosure of no express authority**
The court's repeated references to the standard as "the minimum" that "any client should be entitled to expect," **citation**, seem to indicate that the court considered itself competent to decide the standard.	**Inferring a point from the court's language**
Thus, whether certain conduct falls short of the "prudent lawyer" standard appears to be determined on a case-by-case basis, by what the judge thinks a prudent lawyer would do. **Citation.** However, two ways to gauge whether the failure falls below the standard are: (1) whether the task is something general practitioners are familiar with doing; and (2) whether the problem could have been prevented by doing proper research. **Citation.**	**Summary of points made in rule explanation**

EXERCISE 8-2
Writing the Rule Explanation

Write out the rule explanation section for the following memo assignment, using *Lucy v. Zehmer*[3] as your only authority. One of the most common errors in legal writing is rushing into rule application before writing a sufficiently thorough rule explanation. Thus, this exercise, which requires you to write the rule explanation section only, is good practice.

Facts. Virginia Ryan is the owner of an antique shop. She has come to your firm, relating the following story and asking for advice.

Ryan is acquainted with Stewart Kaplan and his older sister, Julia Kaplan. Stewart and Julia are not on good terms. Their mother recently died, bequeathing to Stewart an old quilt and to Julia their deceased father's World War II medals. During the settling of the estate, relations between Stewart

3. 84 S.E.2d 516 (Va. 1954). Opinion reprinted in Appendix F.

and Julia became even more strained when Julia gave the medals to a local historical organization without offering them first to Stewart. Stewart had a strong sentimental attachment to the medals and he believes that Julia gave them away on purpose to spite him.

Ryan knew the facts of the dispute about the war medals, and she knew that the relationship between Stewart and Julia was strained. Ryan did not get along well with Julia either, and she and Stewart felt a common bond in this respect.

Several weeks after learning of Julia's disposition of the medals, both Stewart and Julia happened to attend a community carnival. Stewart saw Ryan there, and said to her, "Let's have a little fun." Ryan said, "OK. What do you have in mind?" Stewart said, "Follow me. We'll give my dear sister a scare." He took Ryan by the arm and led her to within earshot of Julia. Stewart winked at Ryan and, in a stage voice, offered to sell her the old quilt. Ryan said she was interested and asked what price Stewart had in mind. Stewart said, "How about $150?" Ryan said, "That's pretty steep for an old quilt. How about $25?"

Both Stewart and Ryan could tell that Julia had heard the conversation from the beginning. However, Ryan believed that Stewart was serious about selling the quilt. Stewart and Ryan continued negotiating the price, through several offers and counter-offers, finally settling on a price of $75. "Done!" said Stewart, winking at Ryan. He said, "Let's do this right. Here, let me write out the terms." He wrote, "Stewart Kaplan hereby sells to Virginia Ryan the old quilt he inherited from his mother for the price of $75." They both signed it. Still enjoying the game, Stewart said, "Wait, we need today's date and the date I'll deliver the quilt to you." He inserted the date and added, "Delivery to occur next Wednesday." He also wrote, "Thanks for playing along. This was fun." Both parties initialed the additional writing, and Ryan put it in her pocket. She told Stewart that it was great doing business with him and then left.

The following Wednesday Ryan called Stewart to tell him that she had the check ready and to ask when he planned to deliver her quilt. Stewart stuttered that he had never actually intended to sell the quilt. Ryan said, "I thought that you wanted to get revenge on Julia." "Yes," said Stewart, "but just by letting her know how it feels to be ignored." "Well, that's not what I thought. I thought you wanted to get revenge by selling the quilt. I want that quilt, Stewart. It is an antique, and $75 is a fair price. Besides I already promised it to one of my customers."

Ryan wants to know whether she can enforce what she thought was Stewart's agreement to sell the quilt. An attorney in the firm has asked you to analyze Ryan's question. The attorney has instructed you to assume that a judge would find that Ryan genuinely believed that Kaplan was serious.

Issue. Can Ryan enforce a contract for the sale of the quilt?

Checklist for Rule Explanation

State the Conclusion

- Did you state your conclusion on the issue and your basic reason, if you can state it succinctly?

State the Applicable Rule of Law

- Did you place the rule statement immediately after the Conclusion?

Explain Where the Rule Comes From and What It Means

- Did you show how the authorities demonstrate that the rule is what you say it is?
- Did you explain the rule's purpose or the policies it serves?
- Did you explain how the rule has been applied in the past?
- Did you explain any additional characteristics that may affect how the rule will be applied?
- If necessary, did you explain any other interpretation of the rule?

Tools for Using Case Authority

- Setting out the facts of the case
- Explaining what the court held about the rule
- Explaining any important dicta
- Explaining how the court applied the rule
- Where appropriate, explaining how the court did *not* apply the rule
- Pointing out any facts the court emphasized
- Explaining what legal commentators have said about the case or the rule

Tools for Interpreting Statutes

- Explaining the statute's plain meaning
- Applying any relevant canons of construction
- Explaining the legislature's intent
- Explaining the policies implicated by the possible interpretation(s)
- Explaining the interpretation of any governmental agencies charged with enforcement
- Explaining the interpretations of courts and respected commentators

General Principles

- Did you cite a source for each statement of a rule, a holding, the court's reasoning, or the facts from a case?
- Did you refrain from discussing your client's facts in this section?
- Did you order your discussion of the authorities according to their importance?
- Did you articulate any relevant factors or guidelines?
- Did you identify the *key* authorities and analyze them thoroughly, including historical development if helpful for prediction or persuasion?
- Did you choose wisely among the options for using cases?

CHAPTER 9

Small-Scale Organization: Applying the Law

Now that you have explained the rule, you are ready to draft the rule application. In this second half of the paradigm you will apply the rule to your client's facts and restate your conclusion. Remember that this half of the paradigm uses the deductive format of syllogistic reasoning—that is, applying a general, often abstract principle to a particular situation and arriving at a conclusion.

General principle (from rule explanation section)	Covenants not to compete are enforceable if the duration, the geographical scope, and the nature of the activity restrained are reasonable.
Application to particular facts	These three terms of the Watson/Carrolton covenant are reasonable.
Conclusion	Therefore, the Watson/Carrolton covenant is enforceable.

Although rule-based reasoning is still important, factual inferences, narrative, analogical reasoning, policy- and principle-based reasoning, and custom-based reasoning are at least as important here to rule application.

I. TWO APPROACHES TO WRITING THE APPLICATION SECTION

The point of the paradigm is to apply the rule you just explained, so the rule application section should track the explanation section. Each aspect of the rule you explained should now be applied to your client's facts. Some writers use the explanation section as their outline as they write the application section. If you use this approach, simply work your way through the application section by applying each point you discussed in the explanation section. This way you are sure to apply the rule you just explained instead of allowing your application section to wander.

You might find, however, that a slightly different approach works better for you. Although a written legal analysis ultimately should be framed in tightly reasoned logic, you might find that rigid adherence to the structure of the explanation section stifles your own writing process. You might choose to open your early drafts to a broader writing process. You can begin writing the application section by focusing on the narrative (the facts) without looking back to the explanation section. You will have the rule in mind, but more impressionistically so. This strategy frees you to think like a storyteller, focusing more on narrative themes and the policies and principles they implicate. Be sure to compare your client's facts to the facts of precedent cases, pointing out relevant similarities and differences.

When you have a draft of each section, revise them both so the rule explained in the first half matches the rule applied in the second half. Perhaps you will need to add application of a point you discussed in rule explanation but forgot to mention in the application section. Just as often, you will need to return to the explanation section to add or edit the discussion of a point you had not noticed until you began to write about your client's facts. No matter which way you approach the writing process, the end result should be the same—a logical analysis built on a narrative theme.

II. CONTENT OF RULE APPLICATION

Although the organization of each rule application section will be unique, here are some general principles to keep in mind:

1. Where appropriate, *begin with a sentence or two stating your factual conclusion*; for example: "A judge would probably find that a reasonably prudent lawyer in Howard Gavin's situation would have checked the title for easements."
2. Then *apply each point from the rule explanation section*, keeping the most important points early in the discussion.
3. For each point you made about the rule in the rule explanation, *write a thesis sentence* stating how that point will apply to your client's case.
4. In one or more paragraphs following each thesis sentence, *use your client's facts to explain why your thesis sentence is accurate*. If your role is predictive, explain the inferences and factual conclusions you think a judge or jury would draw from these facts. If your task is persuasive, use the facts to set out and support the inferences you want the court to draw.

   Use common sense. Imagine the situation your client has described to you. What would it have looked like? Seemed like? What other things might have been true if these are the facts? What additional unconfirmed facts might you be assuming? How might the scenario look to a judge or a jury? What facts would be important to a judge or a jury? Could someone else use the same facts to paint a different picture?
5. When engaging in analogical reasoning, *support your thesis with direct fact-to-fact comparisons*. Identify the factual similarities between your

client's situation and relevant cases, explaining how these similarities demonstrate your points. Also, identify any significant factual *differences*, and explain the point they demonstrate. These case comparisons are analogies and disanalogies. Chapter 11 explains this important reasoning skill more thoroughly.

6. If helpful, *apply the rule's underlying policies to your client's situation*. Your client's facts might raise the precise concerns the rule was designed to address. If so, a court will be more likely to apply the rule strictly and resolve doubts of application in your client's favor. Reread the sample office memo in Appendix A, this time noticing particularly the uses of policy to help predict a result. A similar use of policy can persuade as well.
7. In an office memo, *identify any unknown facts that would be important to a resolution of the legal issue*. The assigning attorney will need to know if potentially important facts are missing from the analysis.[1]
8. Where necessary, *refute any alternative rule applications*. In Chapter 8, we saw that you sometimes need to address and refute alternative interpretations of the rule. Just so, there might be alternative views of how the rule might apply to your client's facts. This process is sometimes called "counter-application" or simply "counter-analysis." In predictive writing, your reader will need to understand these alternative views. In persuasive writing, you will need to address and refute your opponent's position.

   Note the difference between counter-analysis in the two stages: In the rule explanation stage, the disagreement is over what the rule means. Here, the disagreement is over how the rule should apply to the facts. In either case, however, do not let your analysis become lost in your focus on counter-analysis. Keep your own explanation and application at the center of the conversation.
9. *Restate your conclusion*. At the end of the application section, restate the conclusion. If the analysis has been long or complex and your document will not have a separate "Conclusion" section, summarize the key reasons supporting the conclusion.

III. COMMON TROUBLE SPOTS IN RULE APPLICATION SECTIONS

The three most common weaknesses in rule application sections are failing to (1) apply the rule as the first half of the paradigm explained it, (2) sufficiently explain the reasoning that supports the prediction, and (3) recognize other possible interpretations of the facts.

1. In a law office setting, if you realize that facts are missing, it is best to inform the assigning attorney immediately in case the facts can be obtained readily and, therefore, included in the memo's analysis.

We have already discussed in some detail the first common weakness: failing to apply the rule as it was explained. Yet this is such a common difficulty that it merits a reminder. Be sure to match the coverage and approach of the explanation section. Equally important, be sure to revise the rule explanation section to reflect the deepened and sharpened rule understanding you gained by writing out the factual analysis. This double-checking of rule-based and narrative reasoning against each other is an example of why both are critical to good legal writing.

The second common weakness may result from believing that the application is so obvious that no explanation of the supporting reasoning is necessary. This belief is rarely true. Even in cases where the application seems obvious, *some factual analysis* is necessary.

The third common weakness is failing to realize the diverse possible interpretations of the facts. Think independently and realistically about the facts. Don't assume the inferences that someone else—like the client or the requesting attorney—has drawn from the facts. Most facts support diverse inferences and interpretations.

Perhaps an analogy will show how hard this can be. Look at Figure 9-1. You might have seen a graphic like this before. Do you see the old woman in this graphic? Do you see a young woman as well? Your brain can organize the black and white shapes of the graphic into a picture of either, but most of us can see only one image at a time. More pointed for our purposes, once your brain has organized the sections to display one figure, it is difficult to find the other figure at all. Imagining diverse interpretations of facts is just as hard as imagining diverse interpretations of these black and white lines.

Not "seeing" these diverse interpretations of the facts is difficult to diagnose and cure. Just remember that you bring your own experiences and

Figure 9.1
How old is this woman?

biases to the table and you need to be open to alternative interpretations of the facts. If your assignment permits, ask others to help you. Present a friend or colleague with a simple chronology or other sanitized version of the facts rather than with your written description of them.[2] Your goal is to learn what story someone else might see in the facts, especially someone who has not first seen the story through your or your client's eyes.

If you must work alone, you must think both critically and creatively about the facts. Try to imagine how the various other parties to the situation would describe it. How would you describe it if you were representing those parties? How might the facts appear to someone who disliked your client and was therefore looking for a negative interpretation? This task will never be easy, but each year of law practice will improve your ability to see diverse interpretations of a set of facts.

Here is an example of rule application for the Pyle/Gavin issue.

PYLE/GAVIN EXAMPLE—RULE APPLICATION ADDED

I. Did Howard Gavin commit legal malpractice in his representation of Linda Pyle? — **Issue**

CONCLUSION

Howard Gavin committed legal malpractice in his representation of Linda Pyle because he did not meet the required standard of professional skill and diligence. The subject matter of the representation is common to general practitioners, and the problem could have been prevented with thorough research.

RULE

A lawyer has a duty to provide a client with representation that meets or exceeds the standard of professional skill and diligence commonly possessed and exercised by a reasonably prudent lawyer in this jurisdiction. **Citation**. . . .

RULE EXPLANATION

[*See* Chapter 8 for the rest of the rule explanation.]

RULE APPLICATION

Thesis sentence stating factual conclusion

A judge would probably find that a reasonably prudent lawyer representing any purchaser in a real estate transaction would check the title for easements.

Reasoning from general facts

Receipt of title is, after all, the heart of the transaction, and carefully checking the title would be critical to evaluating the title the purchaser would receive from the seller.

Thesis sentence applying Gavin's particular facts

The duty to check the title carefully would be particularly clear in a situation like Gavin's where the client has asked specifically whether there would be any problem with using the land for a particular purpose.

Reasoning from factual comparisons

A prudent lawyer would know that the use of real property can be limited either by law (such as by a zoning regulation) or by private agreement (such as an easement or a restrictive

2. Take care not to breach client confidentiality. *See* Model R. Pro. Conduct r. 1.6 (Am. Bar Ass'n 2013).

covenant recorded against the title). The client's specific question should have flagged the issue for Gavin, making Gavin's error even less excusable than the error in *Jacobson*. In *Jacobson*, the client did not ask a question that should have reminded the lawyer of the possible problem; yet the lawyer's error constituted professional malpractice anyway. **Citation**.

Further, both of the *Jacobson* gauges point toward Gavin's liability. Representing a party to a real estate transaction probably falls within the group of tasks a general practitioner is familiar with doing. Basic real estate transactions are as common in the general practice of law as filing lawsuits. Nor was Gavin's omission a mere error in the exercise of professional judgment. The need to look for an easement would have been apparent if Gavin had done adequate *legal* research, and the easement itself would have been apparent if he had done adequate *factual* research. Just as in *Jacobson*, Gavin's error could have been prevented by proper research.

Thesis sentence applying points from rule explanation

Comparing facts

Applying second point and comparing facts

Since the standard is not reduced by virtue of facts particular to the lawyer's experience, Gavin's relative inexperience and his lack of real estate expertise will not affect the legal result. Nor will his status in the bar or his usual skill and diligence. However, these facts do add to the equities of his case, especially since a judge in this jurisdiction would probably be aware of them. Although those facts should not change the ultimate result, they probably mean that the judge will not be happy about having to rule against Gavin. The evidence at trial will have to establish the cause of action clearly.

Thesis sentences dealing with other facts

Flagging the human impact

Finally, this evaluation that Gavin's representation fell below the prudent lawyer standard is based on an assumption that the standard can be judged without expert testimony. Additional research would be necessary to check this assumption. If the standard must be evaluated by reference to expert testimony, it will be necessary to consult with an expert.

Pointing out a necessary qualification

The claim that Gavin breached the applicable standard of care is strong. The subject matter of the representation is common to general practitioners. The problem could have been prevented with proper research. If Pyle is interested in pursuing the matter further, our next step should be the completion of our research on the need for expert testimony.

CONCLUSION

Summary of most important points

IV. EVALUATING YOUR DRAFT

Try to complete your working draft in time to put it away and let your mind clear. Then go through this procedure:

1. *Check the paradigm.* Mark off and label each subpart of the paradigm—Conclusion, Rule, Rule Explanation, Rule Application, and Conclusion. Check to be sure that each part is there and in its proper order. Be sure that rule explanation and rule application are not intermixed.
2. *Evaluate the depth of rule explanation.* Ask yourself how well settled the rule is and how much explanation is necessary to clarify the rule's meaning.
3. *Evaluate the depth of rule application.* Have you written out a complete discussion of how the rule would apply to your client's facts and what inferences a judge or jury might draw from them? Watch particularly for rules that include an element pertaining to someone's state of mind or rules that set out a flexible standard (such as "a reasonable person" or "the best interests of the child"). For those rules, you probably will need to do significant factual analysis in the application section.
4. *Evaluate the content and internal organization of rule explanation and rule application.* First, confirm that the rule you explained is the rule you applied. Now, examine each section in smaller chunks. Identify the blocks of text devoted to particular substantive points, using labels in the side margin as do the sample drafts in this chapter and in Chapter 8. Is your organization logical? Does it communicate good ideas clearly?
5. *Check your perspective.* Remember the difference between predicting and persuading. If you are writing a predictive document, maintaining an objective perspective can be difficult. Many writers find themselves slipping into advocating their prediction rather than objectively evaluating it. Be sure you have not slipped into writing as an advocate.

EXERCISE 9-1
Recognizing Analogical Reasoning

In the sample office memo in Appendix A, identify each instance of analogical reasoning (analogizing and distinguishing cases).

EXERCISE 9-2
Writing the Rule Application

Write a working draft of your analysis of the issue set out in Exercise 8-2. If you already wrote out a rule explanation section, simply complete the working draft by adding the rule application. Pay special attention to using analogical reasoning (analogizing and distinguishing cases) in your rule application.

Checklist for Rule Application[3]

Apply the Rule to Your Client's Facts

- Be sure the content of the rule explanation and rule application sections are consistent and that you applied the rule you explained.
- When engaging in analogical reasoning, compare the key facts from the case authorities to the key facts of your client's situation, noting the legally significant similarities and differences.
- Explain the inferences and factual conclusions a judge or jury could draw from your client's facts.
- In the draft of an office memo, identify any unknown facts that would be important to a resolution of the legal issue.
- Evaluate the appropriateness of the factual discussion's depth.

State Your Conclusion

- Restate your factual conclusion in one sentence.
- If the analysis has been long and complex or if your document will not have a separate Conclusion section, include a brief summary of the primary reasons supporting the conclusion.

---

3. See the end of Chapter 8 for a checklist for the rule explanation half of the paradigm.

CHAPTER 10

Discussing Multiple Issues: Putting It All Together

Chapter 7 explained how to use the question(s) you have been asked and the relevant governing rules to create the outline for your analysis. Chapters 8 and 9 explained how to write the analysis of each single issue identified on your outline. This chapter explains how to finish writing the analysis, connecting these single-issue discussions and putting them in the order your reader will prefer. With very little revision, this completed analysis will become the "Discussion" section of your office memo or the "Argument" section of your brief to the court. Here is an overview of an analysis of multiple issues:

THE MULTI-ISSUE PARADIGM

I. Heading stating your overall conclusion on a legal question

[An "umbrella section" introducing the subsections to follow.]

A. Heading stating your conclusion on the first issue

- Conclusion
- Rule
- Rule explanation
- Rule application
- Conclusion on this issue

B. Heading stating your conclusion on the second issue

- Conclusion
- Rule
- Rule explanation
- Rule application
- Conclusion on this issue

[Add discussions of any other issues.]

Overall conclusion

I. ORDERING FOR YOUR READER

A. Accounting for Elements Not at Issue

Recall from Chapter 7 that your outline did not have to cull out the elements not at issue. Now that you have completed your study of the authorities and how they apply to your client's facts, you can finalize the selection of elements requiring discussion. Remove from your draft the headings for any elements needing no discussion, but make a note of them. You will need to explain to your reader why you are not discussing them. Section II explains where and how to give your reader this information.

B. Selecting an Order for the Remaining Issues

Now that your analysis is complete, you have the information you need to select the order your reader will prefer. The three most common choices for the order when writing the analysis of a single rule with subsections are (1) important issues, (2) threshold issues, and (3) familiar order.

1. Important Issues. The important-issues approach places subissues in the order of importance to the reader and to the analysis.[1] An issue can be important because it is likely to be dispositive. For instance, any burglary element the state cannot prove would be dispositive since the state must prove all elements to win a conviction. The issues most likely to be dispositive usually should be discussed first.

A subissue can be important even if it would not be dispositive alone. For instance, in a factors test, usually no one factor is dispositive; yet the particular circumstances of a case can make some factors more important to the analysis than others. A child custody dispute is a good example. The court will consider many factors in deciding custody. Rarely will one factor be dispositive alone, but several might be especially important. All other things being equal, discuss these first.

Organizing according to importance is an effective tool to help your reader manage a number of issues or subissues. The most important issues are placed where the reader's attention is greatest. The time a busy reader must invest is minimized. The reader can choose how far into the analysis to read and with what degree of care. It assures the reader that the writer's analysis is complete enough to identify the most important issues.

2. Threshold Issues. A threshold issue is one that determines the direction of the analysis from that point on. For instance, assume that a rule of law tells you that if a business is a lending institution, it may not do certain things.

1. The importance to the reader and the importance to the analysis should be the same unless the writer and the reader have differing views of the analysis. If the writer suspects a difference, the writer should either (1) use the introductory paragraphs to convert the reader to the writer's view of the analysis or (2) order the subpoints by their importance to the *reader's* analysis.

The issue of whether your client is a lending institution within the meaning of that rule determines the direction of the analysis from that point on. If your client is *not* a lending institution, the rule prohibiting certain conduct does not apply to your client, and the analysis can move on to any other rules that might apply to your client. But if your client *is* a lending institution, the rule does apply, and the analysis must continue to determine whether your client's proposed conduct falls within the category of conduct prohibited by the rule. Thus, the issue of whether your client is a lending institution is a threshold issue.

When you are analyzing a legal question that includes a threshold issue, consider placing the threshold issue first. The reader probably will expect the analysis to begin with the threshold issue. Also, if you conclude that the threshold step in the analysis is not met, the reader need not devote as much attention to later steps.

Occasionally, however, you might be working with a rule where the analysis of the threshold issue is complex and your answer to a remaining issue makes the complex analysis of the threshold issue unnecessary. For instance, perhaps the issue of whether your client is a lending institution—and therefore whether the statute would apply to your client at all—is a close and complex question. However, even if the statute applies to your client, the statute rather clearly would not prohibit your client's proposed conduct. If this second conclusion is relatively clear and easily explained, your reader might prefer that you organize by importance. Simply explain your organizational choice in the umbrella section, explained in Section II below. Your reader will appreciate your organizational choice if she understands your reasons.

3. Familiar Order. Many rules of law are familiar to law-trained readers, and the elements of those rules are often listed in a certain familiar order. Often the familiar order is the order the rule uses. Common-law burglary is a good example. The definition of burglary is traditionally stated as "the breaking and entering of the dwelling house of another in the nighttime with the intent to commit a felony therein." On a burglary issue, a law-trained reader will be accustomed to thinking of the elements in the order recited in that sentence.

Even if no rule establishes a familiar order of elements, the custom of ordering issues chronologically might establish a familiar order. If the subissues pertain to events occurring in a chronology, a law-trained reader probably will expect to analyze the issues in that order. For instance, contracts issues are often ordered by the chronology of events constituting the formation and performance of the contract: offer, acceptance, modification, and performance. Unless the reader's other needs require a different choice, order your discussion in the way the reader is expecting.

II. UMBRELLA SECTIONS

All the subsections are in place now, but you need introductions so your reader will understand what will follow and why. We will call these introductions "umbrella sections." Umbrella sections are appropriate wherever the analysis is broken down into subsections. Take a moment to read an example of an umbrella section between "I" and "A" in Appendix A.

The umbrella section can serve four main functions. First, it provides a place to *state the governing rule(s)* so the reader has a road map of the analysis to follow. If you use it for this purpose, provide a citation to the main authority establishing the rule, and include any other information important to how the rule functions. For instance, one party will carry the burden of proof. The rule might require a higher-than-normal level of proof (for example, clear and convincing).[2] Some rules come with a presumption of one variety or another.[3] Some come with policy "leanings" (for instance, case law stating that doubts are to be resolved in favor of the criminal defendant). The procedural posture of a case, such as a motion for summary judgment, a motion to dismiss, or an appeal from a jury verdict, might impose a particular standard more favorable to one party. A canon of statutory construction might call for a strict reading of a particular kind of statute. If the authorities have mentioned any such information, you can include it here.

Second, an umbrella section can *identify elements not at issue*. For each undisputed element, ask yourself whether your conclusion will be readily apparent to your reader or whether the reader will require some (although perhaps simple) analysis to be satisfied on the point. Make this decision based on your assessment of (1) your reader's existing knowledge, (2) the degree of your reader's faith in you as a legal thinker, and (3) your reader's need for certainty. Make these assessments conservatively. If you are in doubt, err on the side of treating an issue as disputed.

If you conclude that an issue is not genuinely disputed, say so. And if your reasons might not be obvious to your reader, provide a cursory explanation of the basis for your conclusion—just enough to reassure the reader that your reasons for this conclusion are consistent with the reader's understanding.

Third, the umbrella section *identifies the remaining issues and explains the order in which you will address them*. Explaining your choice of structures is particularly important if your structure is different from the one the reader expects.

Finally, if necessary to prevent confusion, *identify any related legal issues not covered by the analysis*. If a reader might assume that your analysis includes all relevant legal issues pertaining to the question but it does not, be sure to say so. For example, the requesting attorney might have asked you to analyze claims under only one statute, but claims might exist under other statutes as

---

2. The most common standard for a burden of proof in a civil case is proof by the preponderance of the evidence. That means that the party bearing the burden need only present stronger evidence than that of the opposing party to win. However, in a criminal trial, the prosecution must meet a higher standard of proof—proof beyond a reasonable doubt. In some circumstances, a party might be required to prove certain facts by a higher standard than a mere preponderance, but not beyond a reasonable doubt. Courts often refer to this intermediate standard as "clear and convincing evidence."

3. In the determination of most legal and factual issues, the decision-maker starts from a neutral posture. However, sometimes, as a matter of policy, the law will impose a "presumption" supporting a certain result. For instance, the law imposes a presumption that service of process in a judicial proceeding has been accomplished lawfully. In such a case, the decision-maker presumes the truth of the presumption until sufficient evidence to the contrary has been offered.

well. In such a case, clarify that your memo covers only possible claims under the identified statute. Your reader will appreciate this clarity, and you will be protected from later misunderstandings.

Often the umbrella section is fairly simple. For instance, in the burglary example, the umbrella section would state the rule defining burglary and cite to the statute establishing it. One item of rule explanation applies to all elements: the burden of proof. If several of the elements are not disputed, the umbrella section would explain their omission and explain organizational decisions. The umbrella section need contain nothing else. It would look like this:

I. Jamison's actions probably do not establish the elements of burglary.

To obtain a burglary conviction, the state must prove that Jamison's conduct constituted a breaking and entering of the dwelling house of another in the nighttime with the intent to commit a felony therein. **Citation**. The state must prove each of these elements beyond a reasonable doubt. **Citation**. The only elements in dispute are the nighttime element and the intent element. Since the nighttime element is most likely to be dispositive, this memo discusses it first.

A. Jamison probably did not enter the building in the nighttime.

- Conclusion
- Rule
- Rule explanation
- Rule application
- Conclusion on nighttime element

B. The state probably can prove that Jamison intended to commit a felony inside the dwelling.

- Conclusion
- Rule
- Rule explanation
- Rule application
- Conclusion on intent element

Here is an umbrella section for a discussion governed by several separate rules.

I. The Foster car sale probably included a warranty.

In [name of jurisdiction], warranties governing U.C.C. transactions are set out in **citation**. Non-U.C.C. warranties are set out in **citation**. Because these warranty provisions differ in critical ways, the first question this memo will discuss is whether U.C.C. warranties would apply to the Foster transaction.

The first section concludes that U.C.C. warranties probably will govern the Foster transaction, so the second section discusses the application of those provisions to that transaction. However, because the application of U.C.C. warranties is a close question, the final section of the memo discusses the possible application of non-U.C.C. warranties to that transaction.

A. The U.C.C. warranty provisions probably govern this transaction.
- Conclusion
- Rule
- Rule explanation
- Rule application
- Conclusion

B. Assuming the U.C.C. warranty provisions apply, the provisions impose a warranty on this kind of transaction.
- Conclusion
- Rule
- Rule explanation
- Rule application
- Conclusion

C. If the non-U.C.C. law controls, it is unlikely that a warranty will be imposed on this transaction.
- Conclusion
- Rule
- Rule explanation
- Rule application
- Conclusion

Notice that this umbrella section does not attempt to state the warranty rules. Both rules are complex, and each will be the subject of its own subsection. What the reader needs in this umbrella section is a road map of the organization to follow. With this map, the reader will know exactly where to look for the rule statements.

An effective umbrella section provides the reader with the context for the analysis, and it clears away the underbrush—the issues that the reader need not consider. It provides a road map for the remaining issues and explains the organizational choice to follow. In other words, the introduction meets the reader where she is, deals with her immediate needs, and leads her to the starting point of the analysis.

III. THE CONCLUSION

If the format of your document permits, write a conclusion pulling together the results of each separate analysis and setting out the ultimate conclusion on the issues addressed. Include a summary of the primary reasons for the overall conclusion. Chapter 12 explains the Conclusion section of an office memo, and Chapter 14 explains the Conclusion section of a brief to the court. Chapter 13 explains the format for professional correspondence.

IV. EDITING SUBSECTION LENGTHS

Now that you have your organization in place, check the length and complexity of each of the subsections. If a subsection strikes you as particularly long and complex, consider further subdivisions with headings. These subdivisions can reflect different lines of authority, different tests set out in case law, rule explanation versus rule application, or any other points of division that would be helpful to the reader. For length, use three pages as a rough outside limit. Headings and subheadings will constitute your reader's road map. Most busy readers want to orient themselves in the text at least every three pages or so. Also remember that reader attention wanes between subheadings and can be renewed with a new subheading.

Finally, check your headings and subheadings to be sure they communicate your conclusions. Headings are important to readers because they make the large-scale organization visible at a glance. They mark the reader's progress through the analysis, so the reader always knows where she has been and where she is headed. They mark the spots where the reader might choose to invest a bit more attention. They assist the reader in evaluating the analysis itself, and through it the writer's ability and credibility. They enable the reader to consider preliminary issues with the assurance that anticipated sections are coming. They allow busy readers to jump immediately to the particular sections they want to review.

V. VARIATIONS OF THE MULTI-ISSUE PARADIGM

Like the paradigm for a single-issue analysis described in Chapters 8 and 9, the multi-issue paradigm provides a format you can adapt to fit each assignment. The most common adaptation of the paradigm is stating and explaining the rules for *all* elements before applying any of them to the facts. An outline for such a discussion would look like this:

I. Conclusion statement
[Umbrella section]
- **A.** Rule statements and explanations
  - **1.** First element
  - **2.** Second element
- **B.** Rule applications
  - **1.** First element
  - **2.** Second element

Conclusion

In some situations, you can explain all elements before applying any of them, as this outline does. The rules and rule explanations for each element may be particularly interrelated in the authorities. The distinctions among them might be minor, and separating the rule explanation sections might require you to repeat material. If the courts seem to take a more unified view of the elements, separating the rule explanation sections could even sacrifice some precision in the analysis. If your careful evaluation of the rule convinces you that these descriptions apply to your assignment, you can opt for this variation of the multi-issue paradigm. Remember, though, that the key virtue of the basic paradigm is that its structure forces you to think precisely about each element. Do not discard the advantages of that structure lightly.

EXERCISE 10-1
Identifying the Parts of a Multi-Issue Discussion

Read the Discussion section of the office memo in Appendix A (a multi-issue discussion). Identify and label each part of the multi-issue discussion. Include the parts of the basic paradigm within each subsection of the discussion.

EXERCISE 10-2
Writing a Multi-Issue Discussion

Write a working draft of an answer to the question presented below, using as your only authority the case summaries in Exercise 3-2.

Facts. Mr. and Mrs. Carillo, each sixty-four years old, live in a neighborhood that includes older people, middle-aged people who have teenaged or young-adult children, and people with young children. The elementary school is about two blocks away, although most children walk to school down the next street over. The closest neighbors who have children living at home are the Lupinos, three houses away from the Carillos.

About a year ago, the Carillos bought a trampoline for the use of their four grandchildren, who visit from time to time. The trampoline is located in the Carillos' backyard. The yard is not fenced, but it is surrounded by a hedge and other shrubbery that effectively shield the backyard from view. Nonetheless, the neighborhood children know that the trampoline is there because they sometimes play with the Carillos' grandchildren. All of the children know that they are not permitted to jump on the trampoline unless an adult is present.

One day last spring, nine-year-old Jimmy Lupino was playing outside with a group of friends. One of the friends remembered the trampoline and suggested to the group that they ask the Carillos if they could play on the trampoline. They knocked, but the Carillos were not home. They huddled about what to do and decided they would each take just one turn on the trampoline. They went around the back and began to take their turns. When Jimmy Lupino's turn came, he climbed on. On his fourth jump he got too close to the edge, hit the metal side of the trampoline, and broke his spine. He is now partially paralyzed.

The Lupinos have asked if your firm will represent them on a contingency basis in a lawsuit against the Carillos. To decide whether to accept the case on this basis, you need an idea of what claims the Lupinos might be able to bring. One of the possible claims you need to evaluate is an attractive nuisance claim.

Issue. Do the Lupinos have a reasonable chance of recovery on an attractive nuisance claim?

CHAPTER 11

Deepening Your Analysis

Now that you have an overview of the basic structure and content of rule explanation and application, we will explore some ways to deepen and strengthen your analysis.

I. USING POLICIES AND PRINCIPLES IN RULE EXPLANATION

The main forms of legal reasoning used in rule explanation and their common uses are:

Rule-Based	Clarifying the precise language, structure, and meaning of the rule
Policy-Based	Identifying underlying rationales intended to encourage desirable results for the society at large and affecting either the rule's original purpose or the ways the rule might be interpreted now
Principle-Based	Identifying any principles that the rule is intended to serve or that might constrain the rule's interpretation
Custom-Based	Identifying social norms or business customs that the rule supports or formalizes

Once you have formulated the rule, supported your formulation with citations to authority, and shown how the courts have applied the rule in the past, you have given the basic explanation of the rule. But you should also explain the purpose of the rule to understand and eventually apply the rule with some degree of confidence. In most cases, policy- and principle-based reasoning will be your most valuable tools in explaining the rule's purpose. Does the rule embody a broad principle valued by our society, or might its interpretation and application be constrained by such a principle? What did the creator of the rule, be it a legislature or a court, intend to accomplish? To answer these questions, you need policy- and principle-based reasoning.

Policies and principles cover many kinds of concerns. Professor Ellie Margolis has identified four common categories:[1]

Policies affecting judicial administration pertain to the practical administration of the rule by the courts.[2] For example, a court's reasons for choosing a flexible factors test might include the ability to fashion a particularized fair result in each future circumstance. The choice of a more rigid rule, however, might be designed partly to maximize people's ability to predict legal outcomes and to bring their conduct into line with that prediction, thus reducing the need for litigation.[3]

Normative policies promote shared societal values. These policies can include moral considerations such as the promotion of honesty and fair dealing, social considerations such as the promotion of stability within families, and corrective justice considerations such as the placement of liability on the most culpable party.[4]

Institutional competence policies recognize the value of relying on the decision-maker who is most capable of resolving the dispute wisely.[5] Perhaps the rule is designed to encourage an appellate court to defer to the trial court because the trial judge is able to see the witnesses and evaluate their demeanor. Perhaps the rule relies on the expertise of an administrative agency staffed by presumably neutral experts in a complex field. Perhaps the rule defers to the legislature because the legislative process allows for more public input and accountability.

Economic policy rationales seek to maximize efficient resource allocation, keep economic costs in line with resulting benefits, and maintain a free market.[6] Economic rationales include such considerations as placing the liability on the party most able to obtain insurance for such losses. They also can include larger scale economic considerations such as balancing the desire to refrain from government interference against the need for protection against practices that, in the long term, would reduce desirable competition.

As we saw in Chapter 5, these policies and principles can help you predict how a court might apply the rule to a particular set of facts, especially in a close case. Most assuredly, policy- and principle-based rationales can help you persuade a court to apply the rule in your client's favor. A court will try to apply the rule in a way that advances the policies and principles the rule is designed to advance. Conversely, the court will try to avoid applying the rule in a way that impedes those policies and principles.

The first and best place to look for policy- and principle-based rationales is in the authorities themselves. Often a statute or its legislative history will contain a statement of the purposes for the legislation. Often courts

1. *See generally* Ellie Margolis, *Closing the Floodgates: Making Persuasive Policy Arguments in Appellate Briefs*, 62 Mont. L. Rev. 59 (2001).

2. *Id.* at 72.

3. *See also* Carol M. Rose, *Crystals and Mud in Property Law*, 40 Stan. L. Rev. 577 (1988).

4. Margolis, *supra* note 1, at 74. This category is closely related to principle-based reasoning as described in Chapter 5.

5. *Id.* at 77.

6. *Id.* at 78–79.

will articulate the rationales their rulings are designed to address. Secondary sources like treatises and law review articles are instructive as well. And you can use your own common sense. What are the most likely goals the legislature or the courts had in mind when they were developing the rule? What long-term results would follow if courts ruled one way rather than the other on your issue? What advantages would be produced? What dangers? To jumpstart your thinking, here are examples of some common policy rationales:

- As between two parties, the law should place the risk of liability on the party most able to prevent a loss.
- As between two parties, the law should place the risk on the party who already bears similar risks and therefore whose legal and practical situation will be least affected by the risk.
- Where the bargaining positions of certain kinds of parties are grossly disparate, the governing rule should protect the weaker party.
- The law should not impose a liability that might limit the ability of people to engage in a particular business in the future, especially if the business provides a socially desirable service.
- The rule should place the burden of proof on the party with the easiest access to the evidence.
- The governing rule should be workable in light of the practical realities of day-to-day life. It should incorporate a realistic view of human psychology and business custom.
- The governing rule should not create a legal standard that is easily subverted by knowledgeable and crafty individuals and businesses.
- Stability in the law is desirable. The law should not change unless the need for the change is clear.
- The realities of modern life have changed significantly (explain how). The law must be willing and able to change and adapt to changing circumstances.
- The law should resist the temptation to rush to the rescue when a refusal to intervene will encourage people to be diligent and responsible in handling their economic and legal affairs.
- The rule should not create additional costs for a person or an industry unless the harm to be prevented justifies the imposition of those costs.
- The governing rule should not add impediments to the free transfer of assets and the ease of doing business.
- The governing rule should be flexible enough to allow future courts to achieve a fair result in individual future circumstances.
- The governing rule should be concrete enough to ensure that future adjudications will be based on objective criteria rather than on prejudices of the decision-maker.
- It is appropriate for the law to require a higher standard of conduct from a commercial party than from an individual not engaged in a particular business.
- The court should adopt a rule that is as consistent with established custom as possible since customs become established because, over time, people have discovered that they work well.

II. USING ANALOGICAL REASONING IN RULE APPLICATION

In the rule application section, the focus shifts to your client's facts. Each of the forms of reasoning described in Chapter 5 can be brought into play here. You need not use all forms of reasoning in all cases, but you should not neglect to consider how each of them might serve your purpose. The structure, the specific words, and the form of the rule must be related to the situation at hand (rule-based reasoning). But the law is more than words, so you should look behind the words to consider the principles or social policies the rule serves. Consider how those principles and policies could bear on your client's story (policy- and principle-based reasoning). Look for any customs, practices, or normal behavior of people in your client's situation, and consider that most rules of law probably intend to codify normative conduct, not prohibit it (custom-based reasoning). Look also for the narrative themes of your client's story, particularly those that might affect the way the rule should be applied (narrative).

All of these forms of reasoning can be helpful in the rule application section, but analogical reasoning is one of the most important forms of reasoning here. It can provide the critical connection between your client's facts and the way the rule has been interpreted in prior cases. Chapters 5 and 9 introduced analogical reasoning; now we explore it in greater depth. Analogical reasoning compares two things. A lawyer uses analogical reasoning when she compares the facts of a prior case with her client's facts, pointing out similarities that can help her predict or advocate a similar result. This process is sometimes called *analogizing* cases. A lawyer can also compare two cases to find differences that might call for a different result. This process is called *distinguishing* cases.

A. Deciding Which Similarities and Differences Are Significant

The first step in mastering the skill of analogizing and distinguishing cases is to understand what kinds of similarities and differences could be legally significant. If you have a sense of how you might use a similarity or difference, you will have a better idea of what you are looking for. A similarity or difference is legally significant if it relates to

- a key term in the governing rule of law, or
- a policy or principle implicated by the rule or its application in this case.

Comparisons relating to a key term of the governing rule are the most important. The governing rule is the starting point for all legal analysis. No matter how compelling a party's case, the judge must be able to reconcile the result with the governing rule. If a factual similarity or difference would help a court decide how the rule might apply to that party's situation, the comparison will be important.

For example, in most jurisdictions, a seller of real property who knows or should know of material defects in the property must disclose those defects to a potential buyer. Notice that this rule has two elements:

A seller must disclose if:
1. the seller knows or should know of the defect, and
2. the defect is material.

Therefore, factual similarities or differences will be most important if they help the judge decide either of these two elements—what kind of "knowledge" is enough to raise the duty and how to gauge whether a defect is "material."

Similarities or differences that do not relate directly to an element of the rule but do relate to the purpose or policy behind the rule can be important as well. If applying the governing rule in your client's case would not serve the policies the rule was meant to further, a court might be willing to create an outright exception for situations like that of your client.

B. Choosing a Format for Your Case Comparison

Now that you have identified the comparisons you want to make, you can decide how much depth you need. Professor Michael Smith has identified two formats for case comparisons: the short form and the long form.[7] Use the long form for important comparisons, for complicated comparisons, or for multiple points of comparison. In all other circumstances, you can use the short form. In either format, however, be sure to give direct, fact-to-fact comparisons. Notice how the examples below directly compare facts.

1. Short-Form Case Comparison

Begin with a thesis sentence stating the point of the comparison. Then, give a factual overview of the cited case, unless your reader is already familiar with its facts. Next state the specific facts that will form the basis of your factual comparison, and state the result reached in the cited case.[8] Then use a thesis sentence to state the nature of the similarities or differences you are pointing out. Identify the specific facts from your client's situation to which you are comparing the cited case, and use that comparison to explain why the result in your client's situation should or should not be the same. Here are two examples of a short-form case comparison, one showing differences and the other showing similarities:[9]

7. Class handouts by Michael R. Smith, *Techniques for Using Case Authority to Discuss 'Points' in a Memo* (1992–1994) (on file with the author).

8. Note that the factual overview, specific facts, and result of the cited case are frequently set forth in the rule explanation. In that case, it is not necessary to repeat in the rule application.

9. Citations have been omitted.

Differences

Buckley's representation that she was old enough to buy a car is significantly different from the representations in *Carney*. There, a minor entered into a contract to purchase a car. The minor affirmatively stated to the sales agent that he was twenty-two, and the agent recorded that information on the loan application, which the minor then signed. The court affirmed the holding that the minor had fraudulently misrepresented his age and was therefore estopped from disaffirming the contract. *Id.* at 807–08.

Buckley, however, never stated her age at all. Further, her answer, taken to mean what she intended it to mean, was not even false. The sales agent had asked her whether she was old enough to buy a car. Buckley misunderstood the question, thinking the agent was asking whether she was old enough to drive. She truthfully answered the question she thought the agent was asking. She said "yes," meaning that she was old enough to have a driver's license. Thus Buckley's facts do not constitute misrepresentations according to the *Carney* standard.

Similarities

Buckley's statement is much closer to the situation in *Woodall*, in which the minor made the representation "unknowingly." In *Woodall*, the minor did not realize that he was making a representation of majority because he did not read the form contract he was signing. *Id.* at 97. Similarly, Buckley did not realize that she might be making a representation of majority because she misunderstood the agent's question. In both cases, the requisite intent to deceive is absent. Therefore, the result in Buckley's situation should be the same as the result in *Woodall*—an order permitting disaffirmance.

2. Long-Form Case Comparison

The long-form case comparison uses an extensive in-text discussion of the case to give the reader more information about the cited case and about the relevant comparisons.[11] Here is an example of a long-form case comparison[10] that demonstrates many factual similarities and also a factual difference:[12]

> *Fahmie v. Wulster*, 408 A.2d 789 (N.J. 1979), provides the closest analogy to Frimberger's situation. In *Fahmie*, a corporation that originally owned a parcel of property requested permission from the Bureau of Water to place a nine-foot diameter culvert on the property to enclose a stream. The Bureau required instead that a sixteen-foot diameter culvert should be installed. The corporation, however, went ahead with its original plan and installed the nine-foot culvert.
>
> The property was later conveyed to Wulster, the CEO of the corporation, who had no knowledge of the installation of the nine-foot culvert. Nine years later, Wulster conveyed the property, by warranty deed, to Fahmie.
>
> In anticipation of the subsequent resale of the property, Fahmie made application to the Economic Development Commission to make additional improvements to the stream and its banks. It was then that the inadequate nine-foot culvert was discovered, and the plaintiff was required to replace it with a sixteen-foot diameter pipe.

---

10. Again, this extensive in-text discussion is frequently set forth in the rule explanation.
11. Adapted from *Frimberger v. Anzellotti*, 594 A.2d 1029 (Conn. App. Ct. 1991).
12. Citations have been omitted.

Fahmie sued Wulster for the cost to correct the violation, claiming a breach of the deed's warranty against encumbrances. The New Jersey Supreme Court concluded that a claim for breach of a covenant against encumbrances cannot be predicated on the necessity to repair or alter the property to conform with land use regulations.

Similarities

The *Fahmie* case is remarkably similar to Frimberger's situation. Like the plaintiff in *Fahmie,* Frimberger is also alleging a breach of the covenant against encumbrances based on the necessity of bringing the property into compliance with a state environmental land use regulation. Just as in *Fahmie,* neither the current owner nor his immediate predecessor knew of the violation of the regulation. In both cases, the violation was created by a remote owner. In both cases, this remote owner knew or should have known that he was creating a violation of the regulation. In neither case did the current owner's deed contain an exception for violations of land use statutes. In both cases, the current owner discovered the violation upon filing an application with the relevant regulatory agency to make further improvements to the property.

Difference

The only relevant difference between the two situations results in an even weaker case for Frimberger. In *Fahmie,* the state agency actually required the plaintiff to replace the inadequate culvert with the larger culvert, thus causing the plaintiff significant expense. In Frimberger's situation, however, the state agency has taken no action to require abatement of the violation. As a matter of fact, the agency has invited Frimberger to apply for an exception to the relevant requirement, a procedure which Frimberger has thus far declined to pursue. Therefore, it is even less likely that Frimberger's facts establish a breach of the covenant than did the facts in *Fahmie.*

This example has three key characteristics: Notice how specific is the discussion of the facts from each case. Notice how many factual similarities and differences are identified (find them and count them). And notice how the theses sentences provide the structure and explain the points of the comparisons they introduce. (Find the theses sentences and underline them.) Emulate these three characteristics in your own case comparisons.

EXERCISE 11-1
Analogical Reasoning

Formulate the rule of law from *Goldman v. Kane,* reprinted in Appendix F. Then read Karen Berry's facts set out in Exercise 12-3. Make a list of the similarities between Berry's facts and the facts in *Goldman v. Kane.* Make a list of the differences. Identify the similarities and differences that are legally significant for Berry's case and explain why.

EXERCISE 11-2
Policy Analogies

Assume that several months after closing, a buyer of real property discovered a major structural defect on the premises. The buyer has sued the seller, alleging that the seller knew of the defect and failed to disclose it to the buyer. You represent the seller. Assume that your jurisdiction has historically followed the older rule on this issue (a seller has no duty to disclose defects), but the state's highest court has signaled a willingness to consider imposing such a duty. The buyer's attorney will argue, among other things, that in recent years the law has imposed such a duty on sellers of personal property (goods) and that the law governing the sale of real property should be the same. What analogies can you expect the buyer's lawyer to make between the sale of personal property and the sale of real property? What arguments will the buyer's lawyer make based on those analogies? What differences might you point out, and what arguments might you make based on those differences?

III. USING FACTUAL INFERENCES IN RULE APPLICATION

As we saw in Chapter 5, inferential reasoning (abduction) does not provide irrefutable evidence of a conclusion, but it can show that a particular conclusion is consistent with the provable facts. Better yet, it can show that this conclusion is more likely than any other. In Chapter 5 we used this example: Assume that a patient had normal blood pressure during all prior phases of treatment and then the doctor changed one of the patient's medications. Immediately after taking the first dose, the patient developed high blood pressure. No other changes in treatment or lifestyle occurred. One could infer from this set of facts that the new medication caused the high blood pressure.

Inferential reasoning (drawing factual inferences) is important in analyzing many legal issues. It is especially important when the legal rule calls for a conclusion that cannot be directly observed—questions like causation (as in our prior example), knowledge (whether a person was aware of a certain fact or situation), or motive or intent (whether a person intended to cause a certain result). Many rule application sections deal with such legal questions that cannot be answered definitively. Without an undisputed answer, we must rely on inferences.

For much of this book, we have been studying the meaning of "legal analysis" and we have seen a recurring theme: We cannot simply state a conclusion and expect a reader to be satisfied. Merely "telling" the reader the answer is not enough. We must both "show" and "tell." Nowhere is this truer than in the rule application section, where many new legal writers are tempted to state the rule and then simply assert that it is or is not met by the client's facts. Inferential reasoning can be the vital link between the facts and the conclusion.

You might think that the application is obvious and that there is no need to talk about the facts. Talk about them anyway. Explain to the reader exactly why the test is or is not met. The facts will not be as obvious to the reader as they seem to you. Also, as you write out why the facts lead to a certain result, you will think of other reasons that had not occurred to you before, and you might even notice some other facts that call your conclusion into question.

For inferential reasoning, your primary goal is to bolster your conclusion by showing how a particular cluster of facts is consistent with the conclusion you are asserting. If possible, you want to do even more. You want to challenge other possible conclusions by showing that the facts are not consistent with other conclusions. You might even be able to point out missing facts—facts that one would expect to see if the other conclusion were true.

In our blood pressure example, for instance, we are showing that the new medication was the only change relevant to blood pressure and that the high blood pressure occurred immediately after that change. If the change had been caused by something else, we would expect to see facts consistent with that other cause, such as the gradual development of the problem over time, or a sudden increase in salt, a sudden decrease in exercise, or a sudden new anxiety-producing situation in the client's life. If those facts are *not* present, you can draw inferences from their very absence.

To notice the factual inferences you can draw, your imagination is your best friend. If the medication caused the high blood pressure, what facts would you imagine in that scenario? Do the client's facts match your imagination? Do the same for competing conclusions. If the cause were age, nutrition, lack of exercise, or situational anxiety, what facts would you imagine? Are those facts present? Then write out your thought processes, so your reader can see exactly why you think that the facts do or do not establish a certain factual conclusion.

EXERCISE 11-3
Factual Inferences

Read the case of *Lucy v. Zehmer* in Appendix F. You'll notice at least three factual issues there. The court wants to show (1) that Zehmer was not too drunk to make a valid contract; (2) that Zehmer was serious about selling his farm; and (3) that irrespective of Zehmer's actual intention, it was reasonable for Lucy to believe that Zehmer was serious about selling the farm. How did the court use the facts to "show" (not just "tell") these three conclusions?

PART FOUR

Predictive Writing

CHAPTER 12

Writing an Office Memo

Chapters 6–11 focused on Step 3 of the writing process, writing the discussion of a legal question. In Step 4, the writer converts the analysis into a document designed for a reader. As introduced in Chapter 1, readers perform three types of writing: predictive, persuasive, and preventive. We will begin by discussing predictive writing here in Part Four and move on to persuasive writing in Part Five.

The traditional way to provide a colleague with a predictive analysis is by using an office memo. Now, however, many situations call for an e-memo, an e-mail version of the traditional memo. This chapter covers both.

I. THE FUNCTION OF AN OFFICE MEMO

An office memo is an internal working document. It is not designed for outside readers, although clients and others might receive a copy if the need arises. The function of an office memo is to answer a legal question, usually for a particular client in a particular situation. Often, it will be the primary basis for making a decision with both legal and nonlegal consequences. Also, the firm might keep office memos for future use when a similar question arises again. Therefore, your document could have a long life, affect many clients, and create impressions about you in the minds of many future readers.

When you write an office memo, your role is predictive rather than persuasive. You must take an objective view of the question you are asked. The client and the requesting attorney need an accurate understanding of the situation. Learning bad news later could be costly for the client, for the firm, and for you. Making an accurate prediction, then, is the function of an office memo.

II. AN OVERVIEW OF THE OFFICE MEMO FORMAT

The format of a memo is designed to fit its function and its reader's needs. Because a memo is an internal document, law firms are likely to have a preferred memo format. The firm's format may use various words for the section titles, it may place the sections in an order different from that described here, or it may include other sections. If your reader (your teacher or law firm) has a particular format preference, use it. If not, you can use the standard memo format this chapter describes. Variations in format are much less important than the accuracy and thoroughness of the analysis. The components of a standard office memo are

1. Heading
2. Question Presented
3. Brief Answer
4. Fact Statement
5. Discussion
6. Conclusion (when appropriate)

Look at the sample memo in Appendix A to locate and review each component.

Heading. The function of the Heading is to identify the requesting attorney, the writer, the date, the client, and the particular legal matter.

Question Presented. The Question Presented identifies the question(s) you have been asked to analyze. It allows your reader to confirm that you have understood the question(s). It also might remind a busy reader of the question(s) he or she asked you to analyze.

Brief Answer. The Brief Answer provides your answer quickly and up front. The reader then can decide how much attention to invest in the explanation that follows.

Fact Statement. This section sets out the facts on which your answer is based. You probably obtained the facts from your reader (the requesting attorney) in the first place, but your memo must repeat them. Your reader will want to be sure you have not misunderstood any important facts. Also, your reader, who has been busy working on other cases, might need a review of the facts, and other attorneys working on this case or future cases might need access to your analysis. Finally, reading your fact statement in conjunction with your legal analysis could cause your reader to realize that she has neglected to give you a critical fact.

As the writer, you have an interest in reciting the facts as well. Your legal analysis will be based on the facts as you understand them. If the facts were to change, the result might change. If you memorialize the facts you have been given—the facts on which your answer is based—you ensure that your work will be evaluated with reference to those facts. No future reader will think you had access to other, different facts and therefore expect you to have reached a different answer.

Discussion. The Discussion section explains to your reader the analysis that led to your answer. Chapters 7–11 that addressed Step 3 of the writing process, writing the discussion of a legal question, explained how to write this section using the rule explanation and rule application paradigm.

Conclusion. You may choose to end with a Conclusion section, a summary of the main points of your analysis. A Conclusion section can be helpful in two ways. First, if the analysis has been complex, a Conclusion section can tie together and summarize the Discussion section. Sometimes, this summary can add clarity that the Discussion alone might not be able to achieve. Also, a Conclusion can increase your reader's options for deciding how much attention to invest in understanding the details of your analysis. A Conclusion would be a summary with more detail than the Brief Answer but not as much as the Discussion. Therefore, a law-trained reader could read your Brief Answer first, then proceed to your Conclusion for somewhat more depth, and finally read your Discussion for even more depth. After reading each section, your reader can decide how far and how deeply to read on.

III. DRAFTING THE HEADING

Draft a heading in the format of standard business interoffice communications. Here is an example of a heading:

MEMORANDUM

TO:	Ramon Caldez
FROM:	Marcia Willingham
DATE:	March 17, 2020
RE:	Sharon Watson (file #19-24795); covenant-not-to-compete against Carrolton; enforceability of the covenant

Since the law is subject to change, the memo's date tells future readers whether and for what period of time your analysis must be updated. The "Re" section identifies the client, the file number of the legal matter you are working on, and the particular issue you have been asked to analyze. Your firm might be handling a number of matters for this particular client and your reader will want to know at a glance which issue your memo analyzes.

IV. DRAFTING THE QUESTION PRESENTED

The Question Presented,[1] sometimes called the Issue Statement, states the question(s) you have been asked to analyze. If you have been asked only to research the state of the governing law on a particular question, without reference to a particular client, the Question Presented simply states the legal question:

1. The acronym "QP" is often used to refer to the Question Presented.

> Under what circumstances does Iowa law allow recovery on a claim for the wrongful death of a fetus?

If you have been asked to apply a rule to a set of facts and predict a result—the more common scenario—drafting a readable Question Presented can be more of a challenge. The Question Presented should include the question, the most important facts, and perhaps the governing rule as well. Here are several format options.

Format Option 1
Organize the content of the Question Presented in two sections: a statement of the legal question and a concise statement of the major relevant fact(s).[2]

Can . . . [state the legal question] . . . when . . . [state the major relevant facts]?

This format does not state the rule of law as part of the Question Presented. Here is an example:

> Can Carrolton enforce the Watson covenant-not-to-compete when the covenant prohibits Watson from making sales contacts for three years and applies to the three counties closest to Carrolton's headquarters?

Common verbs for beginning a Question Presented in this format are: "Can . . . ?" "Did . . . ?" "Was . . . ?" "May . . . ?" and "Is . . . ?" Common transitions into the factual description are: "when . . . " and "where. . . . "

Format Option 2
An even simpler version of a Question Presented is the format beginning with "whether" and constituting a clause rather than a complete sentence. This format still begins with the legal question and ends with the major relevant facts:

> Whether Carrolton can enforce the Watson covenant-not-to-compete when the covenant prohibits Watson from making sales contacts for three years and applies to the three counties closest to Carrolton's headquarters.

When the Question Presented uses the "whether" format, the clause can be followed by a period and treated as a complete sentence although it is not.

Format Option 3
A third format option is the "under/does/when" format. This format usually results in the longest and most complex Question Presented, although it allows for a shorter Brief Answer (the succeeding section). The Question

2. The term "relevant facts" refers to the legally determinative facts—facts that affect the analysis.

Presented is longer and the Brief Answer shorter because this format puts the statement of the law in the Question Presented rather than in the Brief Answer. Here is an example:

> Under the Georgia common law rule that allows covenants-not-to-compete only when the area restrained, the activities restrained, and the duration of the restraint are reasonable, can a covenant-not-to-compete be enforced when the covenant prohibits the covenantor from making sales contacts for three years, and applies to the three counties closest to the headquarters of the covenant's beneficiary?

The middle verb can vary, using the same common verbs identified above: "can," "did," "was," "may," or "is."

Format Option 4
Any of these formats can be expanded to include the key facts on both sides of the question. Because a memo's analysis should be as objective as possible, an explicitly balanced description of the key facts can be helpful both to your reader and to you. It gives the reader a quick overview of the most important facts on both sides of the question, and it can remind you to recognize what is compelling about each side's arguments. This format is particularly appropriate when each side would want to emphasize different facts rather than simply construct legal arguments about the same facts. For instance, assume that the question is whether an airline passenger attempted to intimidate a flight crew member. Here is an example of a Question Presented that identifies key facts on both sides of the question:

> Under [statute], did Mitchell Sheffield attempt to intimidate the flight crew when he left his seat, approached the door to the control cabin, and shouted at the co-pilot but never articulated any threat or attempted any violent act?

Notice that the key facts tending to show intimidation are grouped together, followed by the key contrasting facts. This structure provides an immediate overview of the facts and points toward the key factual arguments on both sides.

Generic Versus Specific References. No matter which format you choose, you will need to decide whether to use a general or a specific Question Presented. For example, Format Options 1 and 2 above refer specifically to Watson and Carrolton, whereas Format Option 3 does not. Here is an example of a generic Question Presented drafted in Format Option 1:

> Can a covenant-not-to-compete be enforced where the covenant prohibits the covenantor from making sales contacts for three years and applies to the three counties closest to the headquarters of the covenant's beneficiary?

You will find proponents of both the generic and the specific Question Presented. The specific Question Presented directly states the question the requesting attorney wants to know. The senior attorney who requested the memo is not asking an academic legal question; rather he wants to know the fate of a particular client—Sharon Watson. Although this memo might someday be placed in the firm's memo file and be examined by a future reader for purposes of another case, the primary function of this memo is to answer a question about the *present* client.

The abstract version of the Question Presented refers to the parties involved by characterizing them rather than by naming them. When the requesting attorney reads this characterization, he probably will have to stop as he reads it to substitute in his mind the names of the parties in place of the characterizations. He also will have to ask himself whether the characterizations accurately refer to the parties in this particular case because if they do not, then the answer set out in the memo might not apply to these parties. But the question of whether the law set out in the memo applies to these parties is part of what the senior attorney wants *you* to analyze *for* him.

Finally, as a practical matter, a Question Presented that uses the parties' names generally uses fewer words and is easier to read. Notice how this is true for the examples above. Because some Questions Presented must include a great deal of information, finding ways to reduce the number of words and simplify the sentences can be helpful.

On the other hand, a busy attorney with a heavy caseload might not remember the names of the parties as easily as the characterizations (the landlord, the contractor, the lender). If you suspect that your reader is not familiar enough with the case to remember the names, either use generic references or use names with characterizations in parentheses, like this:

> Can Carrolton (the beneficiary) enforce the Watson covenant-not-to-compete when the covenant prohibits Watson (the former employee) from making sales contacts for three years and applies to the three counties closest to Carrolton's headquarters?

Again, use the phrasing you think your teacher or requesting attorney will prefer. As with most other writing decisions, your assessment of your reader's starting point should be the most important factor.

Degree of Detail. Try to limit the Question Presented to one readable sentence. Packing both the legal issue and the major facts into one readable sentence can be quite a challenge. If your draft of the Question Presented is unwieldy, first use the editing techniques described in Chapter 20. If those techniques do not allow you to achieve a readable sentence, consider shortening the facts you include. If all else fails, use two sentences. Two clear sentences are better than one confusing sentence.

Assuming the Answer in the Question Presented. Avoid stating the Question Presented in a way that assumes the answer. For instance, in the Watson/Carrolton case, the following Question Presented assumes the answer:

> Can Carrolton enforce the Watson covenant-not-to-compete when the covenant prohibits Watson from making sales contacts for an unreasonable length of time and applies to an unreasonable geographic area?

According to the governing rule, a covenant with unreasonable terms is not enforceable. But the requesting attorney did not ask merely what rule governs the issue. The requesting attorney has asked how the rule applies to Watson's facts. She has asked whether the Watson terms are unreasonable, so do not phrase the Question Presented so as to assume the very question you are to answer.

EXERCISE 12-1
Drafting a Question Presented

For each of the following Questions Presented, use a different format. Use specific references for one and generic references for the other.

a. Draft a Question Presented for an office memo addressing Ms. Ryan's question in Exercise 8-2.
b. Draft a Question Presented for an office memo addressing Ms. Pyle's question introduced in the hypothetical on page 91 and continuing with the working draft of the analysis on pages 95-97 and 105-106.

V. DRAFTING THE BRIEF ANSWER

The Brief Answer gives your busy reader the answer quickly and right up front. If you have more than one Question Presented, you will need a Brief Answer for each one. Unlike in the Discussion section, citations to supporting authorities are not necessary.

Because Questions Presented come in several formats, their Brief Answers do as well. A Brief Answer responding to a Question Presented that does not articulate the rule of law (those described in Formats 1 and 2) should state the answer forthrightly ("yes," "probably yes," "no," or "probably not"). The remainder of the Brief Answer should set out, either directly or indirectly, the rule of law governing the issue and a summary of the reasoning leading to the answer. Assume that you have decided that Carrolton will be able to enforce the Watson covenant. Your Brief Answer might be:

> Probably yes **[forthright statement of the answer]**. A covenant-not-to-compete is enforceable under Georgia law if the activity restrained, the geographic area of the restraint, and the duration of the restraint are all reasonable **[statement of the governing rule of law]**. Several Georgia courts have held that covenants restraining sales contacts are nearly always reasonable as to the activity restrained. Georgia

courts have also held covenants reasonable when the duration of the restraint was up to three years and when the area restrained included up to ten counties **[summary of reasoning]**.

Brief Answers that respond to Questions Presented in Format Option 3 (Questions Presented that have already stated the rule of law) can be shorter. When you are using this format, state the answer in the first few words. Then state, in several complete sentences, the reasons for your answer, like so:

Probably yes **[forthright statement of the answer]**. Several Georgia courts have held that covenants restraining sales contacts are nearly always reasonable as to the activity restrained. Georgia courts have also held covenants reasonable when the duration of the restraint was up to three years and when the area restrained included up to ten counties **[summary of reasoning]**.

Generic Versus Specific References. Use references that match those in the Question Presented. If you used the parties' names in the Question, use them in the Brief Answer. If you used characterizations in the Question Presented, use those characterizations in the Brief Answer as well.

Degree of Detail. An average length for a Brief Answer is one moderate paragraph (about one-third to one-half of a double-spaced page). The function of the Brief Answer is compromised when the Answer is much longer than that. Occasionally, you will be dealing with a rule that is so complex that even a Brief Answer will take more space, but usually not. Try to limit this section to a maximum of five sentences, like the example above.

Degree of Certainty. For many memo assignments, deciding your degree of certainty is daunting. Perhaps the answer seems clear and certain. Have you simply received an easy, straightforward assignment? Or have you missed something important? Perhaps you think the answer could go either way, and you cannot decide which is more likely; yet you know that the requesting attorney wants an answer, not a coin toss.

There is no easy solution to this discomfort. You are just beginning the lifelong project of developing the legal judgment to gauge the certainty of a predicted result. With experience, you will get better at making these judgments. For the time being, you must research and analyze thoroughly and then make the best judgment you can.

When you are struggling with the question of the degree of certainty of your answer, keep in mind the possible spectrum:

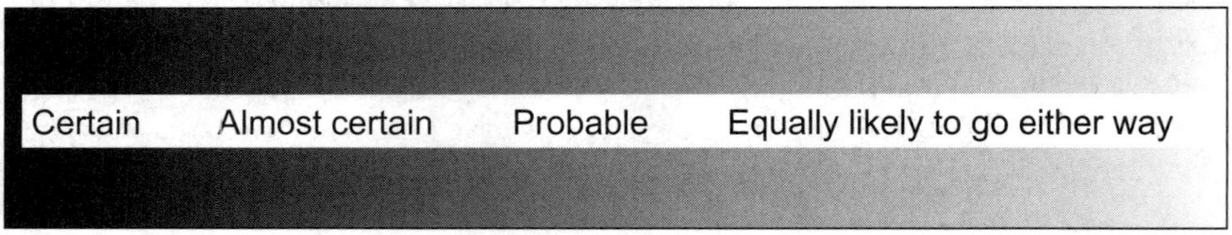

Think carefully before you choose an answer on either end of the spectrum. Some issues actually have certain answers, but before you conclude that yours is one of them, be sure you have done a complete and accurate legal and factual analysis. Some issues actually will be a coin toss, but before you conclude that yours is one of them, ask yourself whether you are simply resisting the discomfort of having to make a prediction in an uncertain area.

Here is how the office memo looks so far:

MEMORANDUM

TO: Ramon Caldez
FROM: Marcia Willingham
DATE: August 17, 2020
RE: Sharon Watson (file #19-24795); covenant-not-to-compete against Carrolton; enforceability of the covenant

QUESTION PRESENTED

Can Carrolton enforce the Watson covenant-not-to-compete where the covenant prohibits Watson from making sales contacts for three years and applies to the three counties closest to Carrolton's headquarters?

BRIEF ANSWER

Probably yes. Carrolton should be able to enforce the Watson covenant. A covenant-not-to-compete is enforceable under Georgia law if the activity restrained, the geographic area of the restraint, and the duration of the restraint are all reasonable. Several Georgia courts have held that covenants restraining sales contacts are nearly always reasonable as to the activity restrained. Georgia courts have also held covenants reasonable when the duration of the restraint was up to three years and when the area restrained included up to ten counties.

EXERCISE 12-2
Drafting a Brief Answer

For each of the Questions Presented you drafted for Exercise 12-1, draft a corresponding Brief Answer.

VI. DRAFTING THE FACT STATEMENT

In drafting the Fact Statement, your primary tasks are (1) selecting which facts to include, (2) organizing those facts in an effective way, and (3) remembering your predictive role.

A. Fact Selection

Often you will know many facts about a particular client's situation. However, your busy reader will want to know only two kinds of facts: (1) facts relevant to the Question Presented and (2) background facts necessary to provide context for these legally relevant facts. Contextual facts will come to you naturally as you write, so we will focus on identifying the legally relevant facts.

Relevant—or legally determinative—facts are those that help you decide how the rule of law will apply to your client's situation. Writing your working draft of the analysis has already given you a good sense of the facts that will be relevant to the issues. Especially as you wrote the rule application section of your analysis, you considered how the legal rule would apply to your client's situation. Review your Discussion section to make a list of these relevant facts. Your list certainly should include all facts you discussed in your analysis, but do not limit your list to those facts. Let the process of reexamining each part of your legal discussion be an occasion for double-checking your fact application. You might be surprised at how often you will see a fact in a significant new way when you are working on the fact statement.

Also, include any facts that could have a powerful emotional impact on the decision-maker, even if those facts are not technically relevant to the legal issues. Remember that judges and other decision-makers are human. Few of us can separate completely our objective legal analysis from our reaction to compelling parts of a story. Although legally irrelevant facts theoretically should not affect a result, judges might be more swayed by these inevitable responses than theory contemplates. For instance, in a divorce case, the judge deciding property issues might be influenced by knowing that one spouse has assaulted the other spouse, even if the applicable law does not make fault relevant to property division. If your case includes an emotionally powerful fact, do not ignore it, especially if the legal rule you are working with gives the decision-maker some discretion.

Any fact that appears in the Discussion section must also appear in the Fact Statement. Accordingly, make sure to review the Fact Statement once the Discussion section is complete. That being said, all of the facts that appear in the Fact Statement do not need to be in the Discussion.

Finally, include facts only. Save the coverage of legal authorities and arguments until the Discussion section. For cases already in litigation, include the current procedural posture of the case and, if relevant, a summary of the procedural history.

As you compile your list of known relevant facts, ask yourself what other facts you would like to know: What unknown facts might affect your prediction? Even if the requesting attorney has not asked you to identify important unknown facts, she almost certainly will appreciate ideas about factual investigation. Also, you will find that legal analysis and fact investigation are inextricably intertwined. Often the process of identifying important unknown facts will yield new insights about rule application, rule explanation, or both. Fact identification is yet another opportunity to deepen your analysis of the Question Presented.

B. Organizing the Fact Statement

Once you have identified the facts, think about how you want to organize them. Normally, your first paragraph should identify your client and briefly describe the client's problem or goal. This paragraph will give your reader a context for the facts that follow. The first or the last paragraph should describe the current status of the situation, including the procedural posture of any litigation. You can organize the material in between chronologically, topically, or both.

Chronological Organization. If the legal analysis has not identified complex and distinct factual topics, if the order of events is particularly important, or if there are a number of factual developments in the story, a simple chronology might be best. For instance, turn back to the description of the Ryan/Kaplan facts in Exercise 8-2. Notice how those facts are organized. The legal issue there is whether a reasonable person would have thought that Kaplan was serious. The story has a number of factual developments, and the chronology is particularly important. Therefore, a chronological organization works well.

Topical Organization. When the facts are complex and cover a number of topics, or when they include more description than plot, a topical organization might work best. For example, consider these facts:

Janet Harbin represented Marcel Myers in a divorce proceeding. Myers made some statements to Harbin that caused Harbin to fear that Myers might physically injure his estranged wife. Harbin disclosed these statements to a police officer. Subsequently, Myers filed a disciplinary complaint against Harbin. Assume that under the applicable ethical rule, a lawyer may reveal information if the lawyer reasonably believes that disclosure is necessary to prevent the client from committing a criminal act that is likely to result in imminent death or substantial bodily harm.

Here, chronology might not be important. The facts might simply describe topics: Myers' statement, the circumstances surrounding it, the possible consequences of it, and Harbin's reaction to it. If we had more detailed facts about each of those topics, perhaps each topic might become one or more paragraphs. This would be an example of a topical organization.

Combination of Chronological and Topical Organization. If the facts have characteristics of both patterns, you can use a combination. Turn back to the Carillo facts in Exercise 10-2. Some of those facts have chronological importance, but many are descriptive. Notice how they fall roughly into four topics: (1) an introduction of the Carillos and a description of their neighborhood; (2) facts surrounding the purchase of the trampoline, its purpose, its placement in their yard, and the rules for its use; (3) the events on the day of the accident; and (4) the present status of the matter. The overall organization of that fact statement is topical, devoting a paragraph to each factual topic. However, the topics appear chronologically, and the facts within the third topic are presented chronologically.

Identifying format choices will be helpful as you organize your first few Fact Statements. Many writers find it best to write a preliminary draft, letting the story unfold according to the writer's intuition. Then they can identify the format that emerged, evaluate where it works and where it does not, and edit it in a second draft. Your goal is to use the format that will best meet your reader's needs for clarity and logical presentation.

C. Remembering Your Role

As you begin to write the Fact Statement, be particularly attentive to your role. Remember that both your legal analysis and your factual description must be as objective as possible. Watch for the tendency to try to prove something by the way you tell the story. Here are three techniques to help you avoid this role confusion:

1. Use neutral language and objective characterizations when possible. Rather than writing, "the defendant was speeding through the school zone," write instead "the defendant was traveling 40 MPH through the school zone." Rather than writing, "Wade brutally beat the victim," write instead, "Wade struck Baker on the head several times, resulting in multiple lacerations and a concussion."
2. Include the unfavorable facts. You may have to remind yourself to identify and include these unfavorable or conflicting facts, but the discipline will help you stay in role.[3]
3. Where appropriate, identify one or two important unknown facts. Pointing out a potentially important but currently unknown fact will help counteract the unconscious tendency to slip into describing the facts with more certainty than you can justify.[4]

EXERCISE 12-3
Critiquing a Fact Statement

Critique the following Fact Statement, using the criteria described above and any others you choose. Then write an improved version.

Fact Statement. On March 1, 2019, our client Karen Berry, a lawyer, loaned $50,000 to her client, Morgan Cox. Cox was to use the money to purchase a lot to construct a warehouse for his wholesale distribution company, ABC Distributing. The loan was to be repaid over ten years. As security for the loan, Berry took a mortgage on the lot and assumed a fifty-one percent partnership status in ABC. The partnership documents give Berry both control over ABC and joint ownership with Cox of all company assets.

ABC had been operating out of leased space, but the lease would soon expire, and the owner had served notice that the lease would not be renewed. ABC had only four months to vacate the leased premises. Berry had learned of this fact during the course of her representation of Cox and ABC in the

3. For example, note that the Fact Statement in Appendix A includes Buckley's potentially problematic answer to the agent's question.

4. The last line of the Fact Statement in Appendix A provides an example of this.

negotiations to renew the lease. Upon learning that the owner had decided not to renew the lease, Berry suggested to Cox that he buy a particular lot in the heart of the industrial district and build a warehouse on the lot. Cox responded that he did not think he could come up with the necessary funds. Berry offered to loan him $50,000 at 8 percent per annum. She said that as security she would take a mortgage on the lot, and she would assume fifty-one percent partnership status in ABC.

The law requires that Berry refrain from misrepresenting or concealing any material fact. Berry knew that the lot was close to one of the routes proposed for a planned interstate connector. She knew that the value of the lot would increase if that route was chosen for the highway. Berry says that she told Cox about this possibility. Whether Cox will confirm Berry on this point is presently unknown.

On the matter of the $50,000 loan, Berry says that she explained the transaction to Cox. However, she says that Cox already understood the proposed transaction clearly because he has over twenty years of business experience. Cox has a master's degree in business administration, and he was at one time a licensed real estate broker. Clearly, with this kind of background, Cox should have been aware of the nature and effect of the proposed transaction. Being sure that the client is aware of the nature and effect of the proposed transaction is one of the key elements required by *Goldman v. Kane.*

Shortly after completing the transaction Berry discovered that Cox had a gambling problem and was draining ABC of its cash. The business was in serious trouble. Fortunately for Berry, she was able to dissolve the partnership agreement before she incurred significant liabilities. Because Cox was in default on the loan payments, Berry foreclosed on the lot. She did not claim interest in any other company asset.

Within a month after Berry took title to the lot, the proposed connector route nearest the lot was selected for the new highway. Two months later Berry sold the lot for $80,000. Cox has filed a disciplinary grievance against Berry, alleging that Berry violated the ethical rule governing a lawyer's business transactions with a client.

VII. DRAFTING THE CONCLUSION

If your Discussion section is relatively short and clear and if your teacher or requesting attorney does not have a preference, you need not add a separate Conclusion section. A Conclusion section should not simply repeat the Brief Answer. However, if your analysis has been complex or multifaceted, a Conclusion section can tie together and summarize the Discussion and provide strategic recommendations or identify additional information that needs to be obtained. A Conclusion should include more detail than the Brief Answer but not as much as the Discussion.

Checklist for an Office Memo

Heading

- Have you included MEMORANDUM at the top of the page and then the name of the requesting attorney; your name; the date; and the client's name, the file number, and a phrase identifying the particular legal matter and issue?

Question Presented

- Have you made an appropriate choice of format?
- If you chose the "legal issue/major facts" format, did you state the legal question in the first half of the sentence and the significant facts in the second half?
- If you chose the "whether" format, did you state the legal question first and the significant facts second, all in a clause and ending with a period?
- If you chose the "under/does/when" format, did you state the rule, then the legal question, and then the significant facts?
- Have you made an appropriate choice of generic or specific references?
- Have you edited to achieve one readable sentence, if possible?
- Have you maintained an objective perspective?

Brief Answer

- Have you stated the answer in the first several words?
- Have you included a statement of the rule if the Question Presented did not already state it?
- Have you stated a summary of the reasoning leading to the answer?
- Have you chosen either generic or specific references to match the Question Presented?
- Have you kept the Brief Answer to a maximum of one-third to one-half a double-spaced page?
- Have you taken a position, even if you are not sure?
- Have you avoided sending your reader mixed signals about how sure you are of your answer?

Fact Statement

Fact Selection

- Have you included all legally significant facts?
- Have you included sufficient factual context?
- Have you included any major emotional facts?
- Have you avoided including discussion of legal authority?
- Have you avoided "arguing" the facts and drawing legal or factual conclusions?

Organization

- Have you identified the client and the client's situation at the beginning of the Fact Statement?
- Have you selected an appropriate organization (chronological, topical, combination) for the facts?
- Does your last paragraph give the facts closure and lead into the Discussion section by explaining the procedural posture of the legal issue or by some other device?

Remembering Your Role

- Have you maintained neutral language and objective characterizations?
- Have you included both favorable and unfavorable facts?

Discussion

Umbrella Section

- Have you summarized the rule, setting out all subparts and clarifying how they relate to each other?
- Have you included any important information about how the rule functions generally, such as a burden of proof or a relevant presumption?
- Have you identified any genuinely undisputed issues and, if necessary, provided a cursory explanation for why they are not in dispute?
- Have you stated the order in which the remaining issues will be discussed, explaining the reason for this organizational choice?
- If necessary to prevent confusion, have you identified any related legal issues not covered by the memo?

Analysis

- Have you selected an appropriate order for the issues?
- Have you checked section lengths, combining or dividing subsections where appropriate?
- Are your headings complete thesis sentences?
- Have you also used the checklists at the ends of Chapters 8 and 9?

Conclusion

- Have you added a Conclusion section only if your reader prefers or the Discussion has been long and complex?
- Is your Conclusion more detailed than the Brief Answer but significantly less detailed than the Discussion?

VIII. WRITING AN E-MEMO

In practice, one of a lawyer's primary means of communicating legal analysis is via e-mail. The shift from traditional paper communication to e-memos is partly due to the cost and inefficiencies of the traditional office memorandum. But don't be fooled into thinking that e-memos do not require the same rigorous analysis and excellent legal writing skills. An e-memo demands a careful balance of clarity and brevity because the writer has less space to make a point. Even when issues are complex, an e-mail summary can accompany a more traditional hard-copy memo, serving many of the same functions as the Brief Answer or Conclusion sections of the memo format.

The content of an e-memo will vary, but the most common form will include very short versions of the same components typically included in a traditional memo. The heading of the e-mail will mimic the heading of the traditional form. After the salutation, the body of the e-memo will set forth the issue being addressed, a brief answer, and key points of the legal analysis—applying the law to the facts, where appropriate. E-memos should be approximately one to two pages in length. Accordingly, for the sake of brevity, e-memos tend to rely on parenthetical explanations of cases rather than in-text illustrations.[5] Often the e-mail will end with some reference to the next appropriate steps. In this example of an e-memo for the Pyle/Gavin facts from Chapter 8, identify the components that resemble a more traditional office memo:

FROM: mcairn@AcosataKraine.com
TO: Raquel Acosta
SENT: Thursday, Feb. 16, 2020
RE: Linda Pyle's Possible Attorney Malpractice Claim against Howard Gavin

Raquel,

I've looked into the question of whether Linda Pyle might have a viable malpractice claim against Howard Gavin for his failure to notice the access easement across the land Ms. Pyle bought for a commercial horse stable. My research shows that she has a strong claim.

A lawyer has a duty to provide the standard of skill and diligence commonly exercised by a reasonably prudent lawyer. **Citation.** Courts have found that duty breached when lawyers fail to do sufficient research or when they make mistakes on matters commonly handled by general practitioners. **Citation.** Representing a buyer in a land purchase is commonly included within the general practice of law, and the easement would have been easily located had Gavin performed a title search. A title search is routine in all land transactions, but here Gavin knew of Pyle's proposed use for the land, so he knew she had a special need for sole control of the property. This special knowledge seems to make Ms. Pyle's case even stronger.

I understand that you'll be meeting with Ms. Pyle next week. Let me know if you would like me to summarize my analysis in an office memo for the file.

Best,
Matt

Acosta & Kraine
43 Rice Street
Tempe, AZ 85282
480.665.8724

Be especially careful to use appropriate professional tone and etiquette in an e-memo. Don't let e-mail habits used in social settings creep into your professional e-mails. The next chapter contains a section on voice, tone, and style in professional e-mails.

Look at the sample e-memo in Appendix B. Find and review each part. Note that subheadings can be used to assist the reader. Moreover, note the

5. *See* Chapter 8, Section V.

format of the e-memo. Unlike traditional memorandums in print, the best practice for e-mails is to use a sans serif font,[6] not indent the paragraphs, and place a space between paragraphs.

If e-memos are now the principal mode of communicating legal analysis, why is so much time spent addressing how to write traditional office memoranda? The skills that you are learning are transferable. Drafting a traditional office memorandum requires you to support your position step by step, not leaving it to the reader to fill in the gaps, which is vitally important when drafting e-memos as well.

6. Sans serif fonts do not have serifs, the small ornaments at the top and bottom of letters. Examples include Arial and Calibri.

CHAPTER 13

Writing Professional Correspondence

Professional correspondence—letters, e-mail messages, and more recently texts—are critical to a lawyer's reputation. Lawyers write far more letters, e-mails, and texts than office memos or briefs, and these less formal communications are seen by many people—people with whom the lawyer must maintain a key professional relationship and people the lawyer will never meet. Unlike oral communications, letters, e-mails, and texts can have a long life. They often are copied and distributed well beyond the original audience, and they are read and reread long after a human voice would have died away.

Perhaps even more important, self-disclosure is nearly impossible to avoid when you write a letter, e-mail, or text. The genre is by far the most personal kind of writing lawyers do, and inevitably, the reader of correspondence forms opinions about the character and personality of the writer. These opinions might not be true, but they become part of the lawyer's reputation anyway.

Of course, letters and e-mail messages are important substantively as well. Key information is conveyed in both media. Clients make decisions based on their lawyer's letters and e-mails, and lawyers are exposed to malpractice liability when a letter or e-mail is inaccurate or misleading.

This chapter introduces professional letter writing, with the term "letter" referring to both paper and electronic communications. The first section discusses the general characteristics of professional letters. The next section introduces an important client letter: the advice letter. We conclude with a section on writing professional texts and e-mails.[1]

I. GENERAL CHARACTERISTICS OF PROFESSIONAL CORRESPONDENCE

Readers. Because letters are more personal than office memos or briefs, it is especially important to consider the needs and characteristics of a reader. Lawyers write letters to diverse people in diverse circumstances. These

1. The website for this book, www.AspenPublishing.com/Edwards-LWA6, covers retainer letters, status reports, demand letters, confirming letters, and transmittal letters.

circumstances often are highly charged emotionally, and the lawyer might have a number of delicate purposes for the communication. Therefore, a letter writer must fine-tune her understanding of her reader.

The writer must consider three kinds of facts about her reader. First, what does this reader already know and understand? This question includes both general knowledge and legal knowledge. The reader could be a well-educated and experienced business person who knows nearly as much about the legal environment of her business as does the lawyer. The reader might be another lawyer or a judge. The reader might be uneducated or developmentally disabled or not fluent in English. The writer would communicate the same information to all of these readers in very different ways.

Second, what is this reader's current mental and emotional status? All emotions, especially anxiety, fear, grief, and anger, affect the way people receive and process information. A writer must be sensitive not only to which emotions the reader might be feeling, but also to the causes of those emotions. The content of the letter might touch on some of those causes, and the writer will need to decide how to handle those subjects appropriately.

Third, what is this reader's personality? If the reader is a client, does this client prefer to be treated formally or informally? Does he want a calm, wise counselor or an impassioned advocate? Does he want an empathetic lawyer or one who is businesslike and efficient? The purpose of asking these questions is not to enable the writer to be someone she is not. Every good lawyer possesses all of these traits and more. Nor will the writer always choose to present a persona consistent with the reader's preferences. The lawyer must decide which traits will serve the client best in the present situation, and knowledge of the reader is the first step toward making that decision.

Substantive Purposes. Every letter has at least one substantive purpose. Letters are used primarily (1) to convey information or advice objectively; (2) to document information for the protection of the client and the lawyer; and (3) to persuade someone to do something. For these substantive purposes, you will need the same analytical skills you have already been learning: accurate content, good organization, and clarity of expression.

Relational Purposes. Every letter also has at least one relational purpose. Relationally, letters are used primarily (1) to establish and maintain a good relationship; (2) to communicate the writer's competence; and (3) to establish professional boundaries. For these relational purposes, you will need the analytical skills set out above plus one more important writing skill—the careful use of tone.

Tone. The letter's tone is the primary way the writer communicates two important kinds of information: the writer's personality and character traits and the writer's opinion of the reader. A letter's tone usually reflects particular character and personality traits of the writer. Some traits like trustworthiness, knowledge, skill, experience, reliability, and diligence are appropriate in nearly all situations. Other traits are appropriate in some but not all situations; these are traits like warmth, empathy, passionate advocacy, detachment, coolness, efficiency, and measured rationality. A lawyer should never appear sarcastic or contemptuous and should never appear to act out of anger.

Tone is created primarily by content choices, attention to detail, word choices, placement choices, and sentence formats. Content choices and attention to detail help establish many of the most important traits of the lawyer: trustworthiness, knowledge, experience, skill, reliability, and diligence. Traits relating to more personal aspects of the relationship often are more subtle. Here are some examples of methods for creating a warm tone (friendly, kind, empathetic, encouraging) or a cool tone (detached, efficient, rational, stern).

WARMER TONE	COOLER TONE
Beginning and ending the letter with content establishing a personal connection.	No content establishing a personal connection.
Word choices without connotations of blame, fault, criticism.	Word choices that are sharp, blunt, biting.
Words with more syllables and soft initial sounds; sentences with longer phrases.	Shorter words with hard consonant sounds; shorter sentences with powerful verbs and vivid nouns but fewer adjectives and adverbs.
Contractions (only when informality is appropriate).	No contractions.
Mutual references using the pronoun "we" to underline the relationship.	Liberal use of the pronoun "you" to underline the distinction between the writer and the reader.
Tempering any uncomfortable subjects with offsetting indirect assurances that the writer likes and respects the reader.	Discussing uncomfortable subjects without any reassurances.
Using passive voice for uncomfortable subjects.	Using the active voice for uncomfortable subjects.
Placing uncomfortable subjects in the middle of the letter or in the middle of a paragraph.	Placing uncomfortable subjects early in the letter and at the beginning of a paragraph.

Professional Letter Writing Formalities. The general form of business letters and e-mails should be used for professional legal correspondence. For traditional letters in print, use letterhead that provides your contact information. In addition, provide the date, the name and address of the recipient, and a reference to the matter being addressed—the "Re:" line. With an e-mail, the message header will provide the date, recipient's name and e-mail address, and subject line. The signature block at the end of the e-mail should set forth your contact information. When an e-mail is long, you may want to attach a PDF version of the letter on letterhead. Begin the correspondence with a salutation and end with an appropriate closing.

Letters as Public Documents. One word of caution is helpful. Because letters are addressed to particular readers and are not usually filed in court, it is easy to think of them as private documents. But any document that goes outside your office is or might one day become a public document. You could find your letter appended as "Exhibit A" to a court document or presented against you or your client in a future dispute or settlement negotiation. Remember that e-mails cannot be completely deleted. Never write a letter that you would cringe to see again in another context. If you are angry, do not mail a letter until you either have calmed down or had another lawyer review what you have written. Do not click on your e-mail program's Send button in the heat of the moment.

II. ADVICE LETTERS

Lawyers write two kinds of advice letters: formal advice letters (usually called "opinion letters") and informal advice letters. Opinion letters are formal documents communicating a lawyer's legal opinion. They are commonly required for particular kinds of transactions, as a form of assurance to the parties of their legal situation. The requirements for these opinion letters often are highly specialized and beyond the coverage of this course.

Informal advice letters, however, are common, important, and well within your present ability. Use your understanding of your reader to help you decide the appropriate level of formality for the letter. Here is a summary of the content and organization of an informal advice letter, which is similar to that of an office memo. Refer to the advice letter in Appendix E for an example of each of the following components.

Opening Paragraphs. After the salutation, begin with any personal material that is appropriate for your relationship with this client in this particular matter. For instance, assume that you are probating the estate of your client's deceased wife and that during your last conversation with your client, he told you that his children were having difficulty adjusting to their mother's death. You might begin with an expression of hope that the children are doing better. Do not manufacture a stilted opener, however. Simply respond genuinely to your client, as one human being to another.

Then set out a summary of the question you have analyzed. This is similar to the Question Presented discussed in Chapter 12. Usually you can summarize the question in one paragraph or less, although a complex question might take more space. If you think your reader is ready, provide a summary of your conclusion here as well, similar to the Brief Answer. If you think your reader will be more receptive to your conclusion after reading your reasoning, postpone your conclusion.

Fact Summary. Usually you should include a fact summary to be sure that your client understands the facts on which you base your conclusion. If your understanding of the facts is incorrect or incomplete, the client can advise you. Your responsibility for the accuracy of your conclusions is limited to the circumstances of which you were aware. If different circumstances develop in the future, you will not be held accountable for a conclusion not meant to apply to those other circumstances.

Legal Analysis. Explain the results of your research and the legal conclusions you have reached. Use your understanding of your reader to help you decide the appropriate level of detail for this explanation and the degree to which you can use legal terms. Follow roughly the paradigm for legal analysis; that is, explain the governing rule and then apply it to your client's situation. If the analysis must cover several separate topics, feel free to use headings to help you mark the transition from one topic to the next. Clear organizational markers help readers manage new, frightening, or complex material.

Advice. You might have been asked simply to provide a legal conclusion, such as whether certain conduct would be legal. If so, your analysis in the prior section will have answered the question adequately. However, you might have been asked a broader question, such as "Should I sue my employer for salary discrimination?" The answer to that question certainly includes one or more legal questions aimed at learning whether the client has a legally viable claim. But the question also asks you to help the client think about the personal and professional consequences of bringing a claim against a current employer. If the answer to the broader question is complex or sensitive, you might prefer to discuss it in a personal meeting with your client, perhaps summarizing your advice after the meeting. If the answer to the broader question is more straightforward, however, you can communicate it here, at the end of your legal analysis. Feel free to organize the components of your advice according to simple topics, such as advantages, disadvantages, likelihood of success, and time frame.

III. SPECIAL CONSIDERATIONS FOR E-MAILS AND TEXTS

In light of advances in technology, e-mails and texts are frequently used in place of traditional paper correspondence. Used well, e-mails and texts are a boon both to efficiency and relationship-building. Used poorly or carelessly, electronic means of communication can damage critical relationships and significantly limit careers. This section introduces you to the practice of professional e-mailing and texting.

A. E-mails

Part of the difficulty with learning to use email skillfully is that it is a hybrid form of communication—occupying relatively uncharted terrain between writing and speaking. What's more, learning a good email style can be tricky because most of us are accustomed to using email primarily for personal and social purposes. This section will introduce you to the practice of professional emailing, starting first, as always, with readers.

Readers. In the practice of law, e-mail readers largely fall into three groups: clients, lawyers inside your firm, and lawyers representing other clients. To some degree, however, all of these readers are likely to share some characteristic responses to e-mail.

First, many e-mail readers are overwhelmed with incoming e-mail of various kinds. Much of that e-mail flood is of little value or relevance to the reader, and some of it can be downright harmful. In the face of this e-mail onslaught, readers may tend to skim their inboxes and hit the Delete button quickly. They also may be annoyed by the sheer volume of what feels like an assault, so your e-mail may find them in a grumpy mood, less likely to give you the benefit of any doubt about either competency or attitude.

Second, and speaking of attitude, e-mail is a cold medium. A short, concise e-mail can seem abrupt and hostile when the writer intended simply to get to the point efficiently and take up as little of the reader's time as possible. An e-mail cannot rely on vocal inflection or facial expression to warm its tone or assure the reader of a friendly or respectful attitude. That deficiency is why so many e-mail writers resort to emoticons, but emoticons are inconsistent with professional style. They make the e-mail and its writer seem juvenile or frivolous, and most readers react negatively to their use in a professional setting. Deprived of that easy solution to the problem, a professional e-mail writer must take special care to monitor an e-mail's tone and to find other ways to prevent a misinterpretation of the writer's attitude.

Third, readers of a long e-mail string are unlikely to remember with much clarity what was said earlier in the string. Since the direction of the thread can get lost and the context can shift, current additions to the string often need to summarize prior e-mails rather than assuming either that the reader will remember or will reread the string. Summarizing can be tricky, though, because a reader may become impatient to get to the new point and the summary may refocus the string in unintended ways.

Professional Uses. The first question is whether to choose e-mail as the medium for your message. Usually you have six choices: a face-to-face conversation, a telephone conversation, a hard-copy letter, an e-mail, a text, or a combination of media. If the message is significant and difficult—such as bad news to the client—the best choice may be a face-to-face conversation. If the message is complicated, you may need the length and physicality of a hard-copy letter. Even for a simple message, you may need to document the file with a hard-copy letter. If you need to ease your recipient into hearing the news, you might want to begin with a phone call, text, or e-mail that prepares the way but does not yet communicate the entire scope of the message. Then, after an in-person meeting or telephone call, you might need to document the file.

Before composing an e-mail, consider any client confidentiality issues that could arise. Whenever an e-mail is sent, there is a risk that an unintended third party will intercept the message or that the message will be disclosed to unintended third parties. If this disclosure is viewed as a waiver of attorney-client privilege, the attorney-client privilege will not protect the information that is revealed. Your employer will most likely have some form of confidentiality statement. For example:

> NOTICE: This message was sent from Huang Briggs PC and is intended only for the designated recipient(s). It may contain confidential or proprietary information and may be subject to the attorney-client privilege or other confidentiality protections. If you are not the designated recipient, you may not review, copy, or distribute this message. If you receive this in error, please notify the sender by reply e-mail and delete this message. Thank you.

Confidential material should not be sent via e-mail—even between colleagues at work—without first asking the supervising attorney. If permission is granted to send confidential material, be sure to include the confidentiality warning.

As you can see, choosing the medium can require almost as much thought as choosing your words. The most important point, however, is to choose intentionally rather than defaulting to the easiest or least threatening medium.

Content.[2] Clarity, concision, and organization are important for any kind of writing, but especially critical when e-mailing. Here are some tips:

1. Use the subject line to catch your reader's attention. Clearly state the e-mail's subject and purpose in terms that will be specific enough to communicate well but not too detailed to be read at a quick glance ("Re: Research on scope of Watson covenant not to compete").
2. Use a salutation rather than abruptly plunging into the message. Choose between a first name ("Amy") or a last name ("Ms. Diemling") according to the situation.
3. After the salutation, use the first sentence to summarize the situation. If your e-mail is a response to a partner's request for research or factual investigation, use the first sentence to identify the question ("You asked me to research the enforceability of Watson's covenant not to compete with Carrolton."). If the e-mail thread has gotten long or complicated, use the first sentence or two to summarize the status of the discussion.
4. Move quickly to the e-mail's main message. Don't test the reader's patience by taking too long to get to the point. Your reader is expecting to see the e-mail's point within the first two or three sentences. See the example in Section VIII of Chapter 12 and Appendix B.
5. After stating the e-mail's main point or the answer to the question you've been asked, add a succinct summary of your supporting analysis. The analysis you provide in an e-mail will necessarily be shorter and more concise than the analysis you would provide in a traditional office memo, though you may choose to follow up with a more formal and complete memo. In the e-mail, give your reader only the main points with a very brief summary of your sources, if appropriate.

2. For e-memos, consider this section together with Section VIII in Chapter 12.

6. Keep the paragraphs in the e-mail short and concise. Distribute white space evenly to make it easier for the reader to process and understand the content.
7. Usually an e-mail shouldn't be longer than one screen on a traditional computer monitor. Keep in mind that many e-mail recipients read their e-mails on smartphones or tablets, so an e-mail longer than one computer monitor screen is especially difficult to manage on these smaller devices. If you need more space, consider sending only a manageable summary by e-mail, accompanied by a longer hard-copy memo. Tell your e-mail readers that they will receive more detailed information by hard copy. If you make that promise, however, be sure to keep it, providing the hard-copy memo promptly.
8. Tabulate multiple points. E-mails are often read in places like restaurants and elevators. Readers may have a harder time than usual organizing the material in their minds. Also, they often reply to the last point and forget to reply to earlier points. If you are making more than one point or asking more than one question, use numbers enclosed in parentheses to identify the points. Since formatting will differ on various devices, don't rely on formatting the points as a list. Either keep them all in the same paragraph or begin a new paragraph for each item.

Dear Ann,

Today we received discovery documents from the defendants. They have requested information from three sources: (1) your office files; (2) your medical files; and (3) your contractor's files....

9. Use an appropriate closing, such as "Best," "Cordially," "Regards," "Yours," or "Sincerely yours." Use a casual version of your first name ("Ben") if your relationship with the recipient calls for that kind of informality, but then follow with a standardized closing that includes your full name, your firm's name, and all of your contact information. You may want to create an automatic signature, but avoid including quotes, pictures, or similar "extras" in your signature that could come across as unprofessional.

Voice and Style. E-mails usually should be slightly less formal than traditional professional writing but more formal than a social message. Striking that professional middle ground can be an adjustment. Here are some tips:

1. Remember that an e-mail is a professional communication, just like a hard-copy letter, a pleading, or a brief. Maintain a professional voice and tone. Avoid using sarcasm and humor in e-mails, as they can be easily misunderstood. Maintain the sort of professional tone you would use in any other context, using the kind of language a client would expect to hear from her lawyer or another lawyer would expect to hear from a competent professional.

2. Use normal punctuation and capitalization. While e-mail provides a faster way to communicate, it is not an excuse for typos, spelling errors, or grammatical mistakes.
3. Don't use all caps, the electronic version of shouting. Find other ways to emphasize a point or to format your message, but keep in mind that italics or boldface type might not appear on your reader's screen.
4. Don't use "e-speak" phrases like "BTW," "OMG," or "IMHO." Instead use normal English words.
5. Use contractions. Contractions often make the message easier to read, and e-mail's slightly reduced formality allows contractions where more formal writing might not. In fact, avoiding contractions in an e-mail can make the message seem stilted, awkward, or arrogant.
6. Be alert to the need to use a slightly warmer tone than you otherwise might. E-mails can sound hostile or cold when the writer did not intend to project that attitude. Preventing misunderstanding is a much better choice than repairing relationship damage after the fact. Review the information on tone in Section I of this chapter.
7. E-mails don't give you permission to say things you wouldn't normally say or to say them more rudely than you would ever say in person. Some writers seem to turn into different people when they are operating behind e-mail's electronic curtain. Never type something in an e-mail that you wouldn't say to the recipient in person.
9. If the e-mail string turns into a confrontation, stop the e-mail cycle and switch to another medium. Schedule an in-person meeting. Pick up the telephone. In a worst-case scenario, switch to hard-copy correspondence. The immediacy and abstractness of e-mail makes it a problematic form of communication for tense, emotional, or hostile situations. Do not reply when you are angry.

Troubleshooting. By its very nature, e-mailing happens quickly, in the press of a busy day. That situation calls for some special care. Here are some tips to avoid common e-mail problems.

1. Before sending an e-mail, confirm that you have correctly set forth to whom the e-mail should be sent. The auto-complete feature might input the incorrect e-mail address.
2. Don't forward an e-mail you have received unless you're certain that forwarding is appropriate, either because of the context (an e-mail of the kind you'd be expected to share with your client) or because the e-mail's author has given permission to forward.
3. On the other hand, always assume that your own e-mails may be forwarded, usually to the person you'd least want to see them. An e-mail makes its way out into cyberspace, and after you've hit the Send button, you have no control over its path.
4. To avoid accidentally sending an e-mail before you've had a chance to reread it, checking its content, style, and tone, leave the "To" line blank until you are sure you are ready to send it.
5. Never use the Reply All function without carefully checking all the names included, but remember to use the Reply All function to avoid unintentionally cutting others out of the conversation.

6. Be especially careful when replying to a message sent originally from a listserv. Some listserv settings send replies to the whole list, even when the writer has used Reply rather than Reply All.
7. Before clicking Send, check to be sure you've attached the documents you meant to attach and not one you didn't mean to attach.
8. Use folders to store important e-mails you've received. Your e-mail system will have some kind of system for saving e-mails. Use it. An alternative is to save the e-mail to a server-based electronic file system.

B. Texts

Texting is another mode of communication that lawyers use, and it is consistent with a lawyer's responsibility "to stay on top of changes related to law and the practice of law," which includes "the benefits and risks associated with relevant technology."[3] The key is to understand the benefits and to avoid the risks of lawyer texting.

When employed properly and used in the appropriate circumstances, texting allows for a more client-centered experience in light of the ability to communicate more quickly and more frequently. Moreover, clients are more likely to read and reply to a text. Thus, a quick text can help to meet a lawyer's obligation to keep clients well-informed on the status of a case and "promptly comply with reasonable requests for information."[4]

Lawyers engage in two main types of texting. The first is automated texting—a one-way text that sends out a simple communication. Examples include a text notifying a client about a meeting or providing a client with directions. The second type of text is a two-way text where attorney and client communicate with each other directly. The earlier discussion of tone applies here. With texting, make sure to use professional language and refrain from being too casual.

While providing a more client-centered experience, texting as a means of communication is not appropriate in all situations. Learn your jurisdiction's bar association guidelines regarding texting and your office's protocol before selecting texting as a mode of communication with clients. If texting is allowed, you will also need to discuss texting with your clients to establish its appropriate use. In general, texting can be appropriate for short messages regarding things like scheduling meetings, court date notifications and times, and case status updates. For longer exchanges use traditional letters or e-mails. Moreover, do not use texts to discuss complex legal issues or personal problems or to send documents and sensitive information.

When using texts to communicate, there are a few dangers that you will need to keep in mind. The first has to do with security. Lawyers have an obligation to keep client information confidential. To that end, consider using

---

3. Model Rules of Pro. Conduct r. 1.1 cmt. 8 (Am. Bar Ass'n 2012).
4. *Id.* at r. 1.4(a) (Am. Bar Ass'n 2009).

a work phone to text, disabling message previews, and using an encrypted text messaging service. Second, although texting might feel more casual, the texts are still considered client communications. Therefore, copies of all texts must be retained, similar to what is required for written correspondence and e-mails. Screenshots and third-party platforms that automatically archive text messages can be used to document texts. Be sure to learn what the office protocols are regarding texting.

PART FIVE

The Shift to Advocacy

CHAPTER 14

Introduction to Brief Writing

The briefs you write will be vital to your clients. The outcome of most cases depends on the judge's rulings on numerous legal questions arising during the litigation. Most of those questions will be decided after you have filed a brief. A brief is a document that a party to a case submits to court, setting forth the reasons why she should triumph over the opposing party or parties to a lawsuit. Briefs are also referred to as "legal memorandums" or 'memorandums of law." Judges tend to be influenced more by your brief than by any other form of argument you make. Therefore, for your client's sake, your brief must be thorough, well written, accurate, honest, free of technical errors, and in compliance with the court's rules.

Your brief writing will be important to you as well. Your reputation as a lawyer will be built, in significant part, by the care you take in brief writing. And reputation is more than just a personal matter; it is an integral part of your professional effectiveness. Over the course of her career, a lawyer with a reputation for honest and careful work will be able to accomplish much more for her clients than a lawyer with a reputation for dishonesty or slipshod work. Thus, every brief you write is a document with persuasive impact, for good or for ill, not only for your current client but also for all your future clients. So write as if your practice depends on it, because it does.

We begin our study of briefs with some important general principles. First, we examine more closely the ethics of brief writing. Then the chapter considers the characteristics of judges as readers. Finally, the chapter describes the common components of trial-level and appellate briefs and how to format these documents.

I. ETHICS AND THE ADVOCATE'S CRAFT

Language and justice are distinctive attributes of humanity. Instead of growling and gesticulating out of naked aggression or craving, human beings reason with language toward resolutions that are just, compassionate, and practical. This connection between language and justice made rhetoric an honored study and practice in classical antiquity, a study and practice whose foundations were formed, in part, by ancients such as Socrates, Aristotle, and Cicero. In writing a brief, today's lawyer takes her place within that honorable tradition. Reasoned argument in the quest for justice is not a mere trade performed for pay, but a craft in the Aristotelian sense, and its right practice helps sustain and advance our common humanity.

Many of the ethical principles that govern the right practice of brief writing are codified in the professional rules governing lawyers. Chapter 1 covered many of these duties, but a reminder and some additional explanation is in order here.

1. A Brief Writer Must Not Knowingly Make a False Statement of Law.[1] This means, for example, that the writer must not assert that a particular case stands for a proposition of law when no reasonable interpretation of the case would yield that proposition. It also means that the writer cannot fail to disclose that a case has been reversed or overruled. Many law-trained readers maintain that citing an authority is an implicit representation that the writer has read the authority itself (not just the headnotes—brief summaries of legal issues in a case written by a commercial publisher). Citing an authority you have not read and updated is unprofessional and extraordinarily risky. Never do it.

2. A Brief Writer Must Not Knowingly Fail to Disclose Directly Adverse Legal Authority in the Controlling Jurisdiction.[2] The writer is not required to disclose the adverse authority if it has been disclosed already by other counsel. However, omitting the authority from an opening brief cannot be justified by the argument that the lawyer was simply waiting to see if opposing counsel would raise it in reply.[3]

Disclosure is not only ethically required, but it is strategically wise as well. If you wait for the opposing lawyer to raise the adverse authority, you forgo the chance to be the first to interpret the authority and explain its impact. Allowing opposing counsel the first shot at interpreting the authority means that you start out behind and must make up that lost analytical ground.

The scope of the duty to disclose can be articulated in several ways, most often focusing either on the question of whether the case is one that the judge should consider or on the more subjective reactions of a "reasonable judge." In a pre–Model Rules Formal Opinion, the ABA Ethics Committee adopted both articulations:

> The test in every case should be: Is the decision which opposing counsel has overlooked one which the court should clearly consider in deciding the case? Would a reasonable judge properly feel that a lawyer who advanced, as the law, a proposition adverse to the undisclosed decision, was lacking in candor and fairness to him? Might the judge consider himself misled by an implied representation that the lawyer knew of no adverse authority?[4]

---

1. Model R. Pro. Conduct r. 3.3(a)(1) (Am. Bar Ass'n 2013).
2. *Id.* r. 3.3(a)(2).
3. *Jorgenson v. County of Volusia*, 846 F.2d 1350 (11th Cir. 1988) (applying Fed. R. Civ. P. 11).
4. ABA Comm. on Ethics & Pro. Resp., Formal Op. 280 (1949).

The ABA Model Rule expressly requires disclosure only if the authority is in the controlling jurisdiction, but some jurisdictions broaden the requirement. For instance, the New Jersey Supreme Court has required, on federal questions, disclosure of adverse decisions of any federal court.[5]

3. A Brief Writer Must Not Knowingly Make a False Statement of Fact.[6] Moreover, if you unknowingly make a false statement of fact, you must correct the statement as soon as you learn that it was false.[7] The duty to refrain from false statements of fact applies throughout the brief, not merely to the section of the brief labeled "Statement of Facts" or "Statement of the Case."[8]

4. A Brief Writer Must Not Assert a Frivolous Legal Argument. In defining what is frivolous, let's begin with what is not. A position that argues for an extension, modification, or reversal of existing law is not frivolous. When defending the accused in a criminal matter, it is not frivolous to require that every element of the case be established.[9]

A claim is not frivolous merely because the lawyer believes that probably it will fail.[10] But when a lawyer cannot "make a good faith argument on the merits of the action" the claim is frivolous.[11] The attorney's subjective belief is not sufficient to meet the standard. The test is whether a reasonable, competent attorney would believe that the argument could have merit.[12]

The meaning of "frivolous" in this context often is subject to debate, even among experienced lawyers. In the early years of law study, while you are still observing the kinds of arguments that do and do not have persuasive value for judges, you might feel particularly lost at sea with this standard. When you suspect that you might be approaching the line, consider doing two things: (1) Ask a more experienced lawyer whether the argument might be frivolous,[13] and (2) ask yourself (and the more experienced lawyer) whether making such a marginal argument is good strategy, even if the argument is permissible. If you are wondering whether the argument is so weak that it might be considered frivolous, your position might be stronger without it.[14]

5. A Brief Writer Must Not Communicate Ex Parte[15] ***with a Judge About the Merits of a Pending Case, Unless the Law Specifically Permits the Particular Ex Parte Communication.***[16] In the context of brief writing, this means that you must provide each party (through counsel, if any) with a copy of your brief. Court rules may require certification that you have done so.[17]

---

5. *In re Greenberg*, 104 A.2d 46 (N.J. 1954).
6. Model R. Pro. Conduct r. 3.3(a)(1).
7. *Id.*
8. See Chapter 16.
9. Model R. Pro. Conduct r. 3.1.
10. *Id.* r. 3.1 cmt. 2.
11. *Id.*
12. *See, e.g.*, *Beeman v. Fiester*, 852 F.2d 206, 211 (7th Cir. 1988).
13. Take care not to violate any honor code regulations pertaining to your law school assignment or your duty of confidentiality to a client.
14. *See* Chapter 6, Section IIE.
15. Ex parte, in this context, means without notice to other parties in the litigation.
16. Model R. Pro. Conduct r. 3.5.
17. *See* Fed. R. Civ. P. 5.

6. A Brief Writer Must Not Intentionally Disregard Filing Requirements or Other Obligations Imposed by Court Rules.[18] Virtually all courts operate under rules of procedure that set out the applicable time deadlines and format requirements for your brief. Many courts impose page limits, and some prescribe the margins and number of permissible characters per inch. You can guess the purpose behind these rules. It might be tempting to change the font or ignore the margin requirements so that you can file a longer brief, but it is neither ethical nor wise to do so. In response to these creative attempts, courts have refused to accept briefs and imposed sanctions on attorneys.[19] Resist the temptation, both in practice *and* in your legal writing course.

II. JUDGES, BRIEFS, AND PERSUASION

In your brief writing, judges are your primary readers, so keep in mind their needs and expectations. Review the description of judges in Section IIE of Chapter 6. Judges serve an important and difficult role, and respect for their position requires a respectful tone and the formality befitting the position and the task at hand. Do not use contractions, colloquialisms, slash constructions ("and/or"), or note-taking abbreviations. Do not use humor, for the job you are doing is serious work.

The judge should find your brief clear and in control of the material, respectful of the court, and focused on issues rather than personalities. Here are some editing strategies to help you send these important messages.

Tabulate. When your document deals with several items (such as elements of a rule, factors, guidelines, categories of facts), consider tabulating the items.

> A lawyer has a responsibility to undertake legal service in the public interest. Among the possible avenues of service are (1) free or reduced-fee representation of the poor, (2) free or reduced-fee representation of public service organizations, (3) participation in activities designed to improve the legal system, or (4) financially supporting legal services programs.

Tabulating not only helps your reader navigate through the substance of your text; it also demonstrates to your reader that you are in control of the material. Your reader will be more willing to follow you along your line of reasoning if the reader finds you an effective leader.

Use Short Forms of Reference. Where helpful, create shortened forms of reference for people and things your text refers to often. This is another technique for sending the message that you are in control of the material.

---

18. Model R. Pro. Conduct r. 3.4.

19. *See N/S Corp. v. Liberty Mut. Ins. Co.*, 127 F.3d 1145, 1148 (9th Cir. 1997) (dismissing case for breach of multiple rules, including word limit); *Kano v. National Consumer Co-op Bank*, 22 F.3d 899, 899-900 (9th Cir. 1994) (levying $1,500 in sanctions for circumventing page limit by submitting brief with lines typed one-and-one-half spaces apart instead of double-spaced).

Introduce the shortened reference at the earliest feasible occasion, and maintain consistency of reference from then on. If you will use several shortened references, consider a paragraph or footnote early in the text introducing all of them.

> This brief will refer to Defendants Carter, Colham, Tellerhoff, and Winston, in combination, as "the owners" and to Defendants Allen, Rakestraw, and Vernon, in combination, as "the managers." The brief also refers to 42 U.S.C. § 2000e-17 by its popular name, "Title VII," and to 42 U.S.C. § 1983 by its popular reference, "Section 1983."

Where possible, select a shortened reference that will facilitate your theory of the case. Avoid references that will work at odds with your theory of the case.

Add Explanatory Parentheticals to Citations. Before finalizing your brief, review your citations to identify any authorities that could use an explanatory parenthetical.[20] A citation might profit from a parenthetical if you are not discussing its facts and reasoning in the text. Look for cases you are citing cursorily, either as support for a minor and uncontested proposition or as additional authority for a proposition principally supported in some other way. You can use the parenthetical to quote a nugget of language or to provide relevant facts that serve as examples of your point. Here is an example of each:

> *See also Furman v. Georgia*, 408 U.S. 238, 309 (1972) (Stewart, J., concurring) ("These death sentences are cruel and unusual in the same way that being struck by lightning is cruel and unusual.").

> Courts have held that a defendant who resides out-of-state cannot be lured into the state by fraud or trickery and then served with process. *McClellan v. Rowell*, 99 So. 2d 653, 656–57 (Miss. 1958) (noting petitioner told his ex-wife that his mother was dying and wanted to see the couple's child one last time); *Zenker v. Zenker*, 72 N.W.2d 809, 813 (Neb. 1955) (asserting plaintiff told defendant that his presence was needed to convey certain real estate).

Purge Your Document of Vague References. Avoid references like these:

this matter	with regard to
it involves	it deals with
it pertains to	it concerns

Writing peppered with these phrases forces the reader to struggle to understand the reference and to wonder whether the writer is in control of the material.

Don't Tell a Court What It "Must" Do or What It "Cannot" Do. Use less confrontational language when referring to limits on the court's authority or power. For instance, avoid:

> The Court must reverse the trial court's order . . .
> The Court cannot grant the Defendant's motion . . .
> The Court is not permitted to consider subsequent negotiations . . .

20. See Chapter 8, Section V.

Here are some better options:

a. Shift the focus to a tactful statement of another court's error:

> The lower court erred in ordering that . . .

b. Substitute "should" for "cannot" and switch to a permissive statement (what the court *should* do) rather than a prohibitory statement (what the court *should not* do):

> The Court should deny the Defendant's motion . . .

c. Focus on the rule that governs the issue rather than on the entity that must follow the rule:

> The rule allows consideration of subsequent negotiations only where . . .

Edit Out Signs of Negative Emotion. Cool reason is much more persuasive than sarcasm or anger. Cool reason says to your reader, "The law and the facts are on my side, so I do not have to be disturbed by the opposing side's position."

Focus on the Judge Rather Than on the Opposing Party or the Opposing Lawyer. A brief writer's focus can be distracted by seeing the litigation as a battle. Do not let your day-to-day contact with the parties and their lawyers cause you to forget that the primary focus of your brief must be the *reader* (the judge).

Moderate Any Exaggerations of the Law, the Facts, or the Inferences. A necessary part of the advocacy process is the shift from an objective perspective to a partisan perspective. But a brief writer still must evaluate the final draft of the brief with an objective eye, being careful not to overstate the law or the facts. Remember that a reader who suspects that the advocate has exaggerated one point will doubt all of the writer's other points as well.

III. THE COMPONENTS OF A TRIAL-LEVEL BRIEF

Although formats for trial-level briefs vary with the customs of the court and the law firm, the variations are seldom substantively significant. This chapter describes a standard format for a trial-level brief. Refer to the sample trial-level brief in Appendix C for examples of the components described here. Later chapters will provide more detail about drafting the major components.

Case Caption and Title of Document. The function of the Caption is simply to identify the court, the case, and the document. For example:

IN THE UNITED STATES DISTRICT COURT FOR THE
SOUTHERN DISTRICT OF TEXAS

CAROLINE MacDONNELL and BARBARA JAMES, Plaintiffs, v. ELLIS PEST CONTROL, INC., and FORREST MICHIE, Defendants.	Civ. No. 99-8636

BRIEF[21] IN SUPPORT OF PLAINTIFFS' MOTION TO COMPEL
THE PRODUCTION OF DOCUMENTS

The Caption must include the docket number (the case number assigned by the court)[22] and the name of the document. In many courts, the captions of cases with multiple parties need list only the first plaintiff and the first defendant followed by "et al."[23] Court rules might require additional information such as the name and address of the attorney or the name of the assigned judge. The Caption can appear on a separate cover sheet or simply at the top of the first page of the brief.

Introduction. The Introduction (sometimes called a "preliminary Statement") introduces the judge to (1) the nature of the case, (2) the parties, (3) the motion or other procedural event that has led to filing of the brief, (4) the party's requested relief, and (5) the primary legal points justifying that relief. All of this information must be conveyed concisely, usually in one or two paragraphs that appear immediately after the title of the document, without a separate heading to introduce it. Here is an example of an Introduction:

This is a sexual harassment action brought against Ellis Pest Control, Inc., and its President, Forrest Michie, by Caroline MacDonnell and Barbara James, former employees of the corporate defendant. The action alleges violations of Title VII of the Civil Rights Act of 1964, 42 U.S.C. § 2000(e) *et seq.*, and related contract claims.

Plaintiffs file this brief in support of their Motion to Compel Defendants' response to Plaintiffs' Requests for Production of Documents, properly filed and served on May 14, 2020. The requests seek production of Plaintiffs' employment files and all documents referring to any evaluations of the Plaintiffs' job performance. Defendants refuse to provide any of these documents, despite the reasonableness and clearly permissible scope of the requests.

21. The title may also read "Memorandum of Law in Support of . . . ".

22. *See* Fed. R. Civ. P. 10(a).

23. *Et al.* is an abbreviation for *et alii,* meaning literally "and others." *See* Fed. R. Civ. P. 10(a) & 7(b)(2).

Statement of Facts. This section sets out the facts relevant to the legal issues addressed by the brief, as well as the context necessary for understanding those facts. The Statement of Facts is an important opportunity for advocacy, requiring skillful and careful drafting. Chapter 18 explains how to draft a Statement of Facts.

Question(s) Presented. The Question(s) Presented section states the legal issues addressed by the brief and the factual context in which they have arisen. The questions are phrased favorably to your client's position, suggesting a decision in your favor. Some lawyers include Questions Presented in trial-level briefs and some do not. Chapter 15 of this book explains how to draft Questions Presented.

Argument. The Argument section contains your fully articulated argument on the legal issues. In drafting the argument, you will be drawing on the analytical material in Chapters 3–5 and the organizational material and writing process information in Chapters 6–11. Chapter 16 provides some suggestions and important reminders for drafting this section.

Remember one special characteristic of trial judges, however. Trial judges are constrained by mandatory precedent. They primarily want to know what those precedents are and how they apply to your case. Authorities from other jurisdictions hold less interest for trial judges, most of whom do not see themselves as free to change the law. Therefore, right up front, the trial judge wants to know whether there are mandatory authorities on your issue, and if so, what they are. Use authorities from other jurisdictions only to fill in any gaps in your jurisdiction's mandatory authority and only after you have explained to the judge why you are presenting these outside authorities.

Conclusion. The Conclusion refers to the arguments set out in the body of the brief and states that the requested relief should be granted. It is followed with a courtesy closing like "Respectfully submitted," a signature line, and the typed name, address, and telephone number of the signing attorney. Two schools of thought exist on the content of conclusions. The more traditional approach is a pro forma statement of the precise relief sought:

> For the foregoing reasons, the Court should grant the Defendant's Motion to Dismiss.

However, if court rules and local customs permit, consider a Conclusion that gives you one last opportunity for advocacy. This sort of Conclusion should still be short—no more than half a double-spaced page—but it could gather together the most compelling arguments in support of the result you seek. Here is an example:

Therefore, as this brief has demonstrated, the circumstances of this case render the covenant's terms unreasonable. The covenant would protect Carrolton to a degree far greater than necessary, while devastating both Ms. Watson's fledgling business and her personal finances. Further, it would significantly infringe the public's interest in reasonably priced health care equipment, merchandise vital to the community's well-being. For these reasons, the Court should deny Carrolton's Motion for Summary Judgment.

Certificate of Service. Ethical rules prohibit ex parte contact with the judge about the merits of a legal matter.[24] Court rules require copies of all filings to be served upon all parties, via their attorneys.[25] The Certificate of Service demonstrates compliance with these rules.

If the brief is filed by mail or delivery to the court, a Certificate of Service is required on the brief, either after the Conclusion or on a separate page at the end of the brief. It certifies that copies of the brief have been mailed or delivered to the attorneys for all parties. For an example of a Certificate of Service, see the last page of the sample trial brief in Appendix C.

That being said, courts now allow, and sometimes require, that attorneys file briefs via the court's electronic filing system.[26] When filing via an electronic filing system, a Certificate of Service may or may not be required.[27] Consult the applicable court rules in the jurisdiction.

IV. THE COMPONENTS OF AN APPELLATE BRIEF

An appellate brief is a working document for the court, so its sections and format are designed to make it a useful and efficient tool for the judges and law clerks who will work on the case. Requirements for appellate briefs largely are determined by court rules, which vary from court to court. This section describes a standard set of sections and formatting practices. Follow these instructions unless your assignment requires different sections or formats.

Cover Page. The cover page of an appellate brief usually is printed on colored paper of a heavier stock than the rest of the brief. Court rules determine the color of the cover page according to the kind of brief. For instance, the cover sheet on the appellant's[28] brief might be blue and the cover sheet on the appellee's[29] brief might be red. These colors allow the court and the law clerks to distinguish the briefs easily and quickly. On the cover sheet, place

24. Model R. Pro. Conduct r. 3.5(b).
25. *See, e.g.*, Fed. R. Civ. P. 5(a).
26. *See, e.g.*, Fed. R. Civ. P. 5(d)(1)(B).
27. *Compare id. with* Mass. Sup. Jud. Ct. R. 1.25(7).
28. An appellant is a party appealing the decision of a lower court to a higher court.
29. An appellee is the respondent in a case appealed to a higher court.

the case caption, the docket number, the document's title, and the lawyer's name and contact information. See the sample appellate brief in Appendix D as an example.

Table of Contents. Include all subsequent sections of your brief in the Table of Contents along with the page numbers on which they appear. These section titles (such as "Table of Authorities") should appear in initial caps here, although they will appear in all caps in the body of the brief. The Table of Contents also includes the point headings and subpoint headings, allowing a busy judge to skim the Table of Contents for a quick summary of the major points of the argument. Point headings and subheadings should appear in the Table of Contents in the same typeface as they appear in the text of the Argument. The first page of the Table of Contents should be numbered as page one.

You can create the Table of Contents manually, but this is not the most efficient approach. Keep in mind that with the correct formatting in Microsoft Word you can insert a Table of Contents that will update automatically.

Table of Authorities. Here, provide the titles and citations for all authorities on which you rely in the brief as well as the page number(s) on which they appear in the Argument. If an authority appears on numerous pages, use the term "passim" in place of a page number. Organize the authorities according to categories with labels, such as Cases, Constitutional Provisions, Statutes, Administrative Regulations, Law Review Articles, and Miscellaneous. Beneath each category, the authorities should appear in alphabetical order in proper citation form. As with the Table of Contents, Microsoft Word also has formatting options for a Table of Authorities.

Question(s) Presented. The Question(s) Presented section states the legal issues addressed by the brief and the factual context in which they have arisen. The questions are phrased favorably to your client's position, suggesting a decision in your favor. Chapter 15 will explain in detail how to draft Questions Presented.

Additional Sections. Some courts might require other sections, such as the following: Opinion Below (a complete sentence providing the court with the citation to the opinion from which the appeal is taken); Jurisdictional Statement (a complete sentence providing the citation to the statute on which appellate jurisdiction is based); Constitutional and Statutory Provisions Involved (a section setting out the text of and the citation to any constitutional provision or statute important to the resolution of the issues); and Standard of Review[30] (a section setting out the appropriate standard(s) for the court's review of the legal issue(s) raised by the brief). See Appendix D for examples of some of these sections.

Statement of the Case. The Statement of the Case is the customary title for the fact statement of an appellate brief. Chapter 18 will explain how to draft a fact statement.

---

30. See Chapter 17 for a discussion of the Standard of Review.

Summary of the Argument. Summarize your argument here, allotting approximately one paragraph per issue. Often the judge will read the Summary of the Argument either first or immediately after reading the Question Presented, so this section provides an early opportunity for advocacy. Phrase your summary as persuasively as possible, pulling together your most important points. Citations to authority are not required in the Summary of the Argument.

Argument. The Argument section sets out your argument in its complete form. Draw on the analytical material from Chapters 3–5, the organizational and writing process material from Chapters 6–11, and the brief-writing material in Chapters 14–19. Most court rules require an appellate brief to identify the appropriate standard of review for each legal issue. Chapter 16 will provide some important suggestions and reminders about writing this section.

Conclusion. The Conclusion of an appellate brief is a one-line, pro forma request for the relief you seek, for instance: "For the foregoing reasons, the Court should reverse the judgment of the District Court and remand the case to the District Court for a new trial.

Certificate of Service. As with trial briefs, a Certificate of Service may be required. See Section III, above.

Certificate of Compliance. The rules of appellate procedure that pertain to the filing of appellate briefs in your jurisdiction may require a Certificate of Compliance certifying that you have complied with the format and content requirements set forth in the rules of appellate procedure. These rules may relate to, among other things, proper font, word limit, and line limit.[31]

31. *See, e.g.*, Fed. R. App. P. 32(g); Mass. R. App. P. 16(a)(14) & (k).

CHAPTER 15

Questions Presented and Persuasive Headings

Two of the potentially most persuasive parts of a brief are the Questions Presented—also known as Issue Statements—and the Persuasive Headings. This chapter explains their function and tells you how to draft them effectively.

I. WRITING THE QUESTION PRESENTED

A Question Presented should both apprise the judge of the legal issue to be decided and begin persuading the judge to decide that issue in your client's favor. To draft a Question Presented that accomplishes both purposes, the writer must walk a fine line between neutrality and overzealous advocacy. The goal is to draft a Question Presented that accurately states the issue *and* suggests a favorable answer. For example, here are examples of Questions Presented from opposing briefs:

QUESTION PRESENTED

Is a covenant-not-to-compete enforceable where the covenant was a bargained-for term of the sale of a business, where the term was negotiated as part of the agreement to allow the seller to continue working for the business, and where the sale specifically included the company's customer lists and good will?

QUESTION PRESENTED

May a large, established business enforce a covenant-not-to-compete where the covenant would eliminate all competition within the market area and where the prohibited activity would affect only four percent of the covenant-holder's profits?

Notice how each accurately recites the legal issue and several key facts while suggesting an answer favorable to the client for whom the brief is written.

Drafting a Question Presented is like creating a haiku. Each of these literary forms requires meticulous attention to word selection and placement, sentence structure, and theme. Unlike poetry, however, no one would argue that obscurity of message is desirable for a Question Presented. Rather, a Question Presented should be a powerful sentence that is easily understandable on first reading.

Keep reworking the Question Presented for readability and subtle persuasiveness. Use the techniques presented in Chapter 20. Try to achieve a concise, clear, and direct style, and a persuasive framing of the Question. Here are some particular suggestions:

Format for a Pure Question of Law. A Question Presented for a pure question of law is a straightforward statement of the legal issue. It should identify the particular legal issue, rather than simply asking whether one side's position is correct. For instance, the first of the following Questions Presented simply asks whether one party's position is correct, without identifying the legal issue. The second actually poses a legal question.

> Can Dole bring a claim for malicious prosecution?
>
> Can a criminal defendant bring a civil action for malicious prosecution prior to the resolution of the criminal proceedings that give rise to the claim?

Traditional Formats for a Question Requiring the Application of Law to Facts. If your legal issue requires applying law to facts, your Question Presented should include both law and facts. You can think of the Question Presented in two parts, the first part stating the legal issue and the second part stating the key facts.

> Can . . . [state the legal question] . . . where . . . [state the major facts] . . . ?

Both of the examples on the preceding page use this format. Common verbs beginning the Question Presented are: "May . . . ?" "Does . . . ?" "Is . . . ?" and "Did . . . ?" Common words used for the transition to the second part of the Question, referring to facts, are "when" and "where."

A Question Presented also can be phrased as a clause beginning with "whether" and ending with a period:

QUESTION PRESENTED

Whether a large, established business can enforce a covenant-not-to-compete where the covenant would eliminate all competition within the market area and where the prohibited activity would affect only four percent of the covenant-holder's profits.

References to Parties. To refer to the parties, a Question Presented can use (1) the parties' names, (2) generic descriptions (property owner, retailer, buyer, lessor), or (3) procedural titles (plaintiff, defendant, appellant, respondent). Procedural titles require the judge to remember who the parties are in this particular case. Thus, they make the Question Presented less readily understandable and, for this reason, some court rules instruct the lawyers to avoid procedural titles.[1] You can use procedural titles, however, when they are actually the generic description of the kind of person to whom the question would pertain, for example:

> Can a criminal defendant bring a civil action for malicious prosecution prior to the resolution of the criminal proceedings that give rise to the claim?

In other cases, the better choices are generic descriptions or the parties' names. Choose the clearest and most persuasive alternative. Sometimes, using the parties' names can serve the strategic function of humanizing the parties and the legal issues in dispute. Using names can serve a practical function as well, allowing the drafter to use fewer words. For instance, in the third example above, the generic description "an established business" is longer than the name "Carrolton" would have been.

On the other hand, using generic descriptions could allow the writer to give additional helpful information about the party. For instance, in the Carrolton example, the generic description allowed Watson's lawyer the chance to convey some helpful information about Carrolton—that it is an established business. In such a situation, the additional information might be worth the added length. Experiment with both alternatives and select the one that works best for your particular case.

Do Not Avoid the Actual Question the Judge Must Decide. Some writers are tempted to assume the answer to the question the judge must decide, like so:

> May Carrolton enforce the terms of the covenant-not-to-compete where the terms are unreasonable?

Neither party argues that Carrolton can enforce a covenant with unreasonable terms. The governing case law clearly states that Carrolton cannot, and neither party is asking the court to change that rule. Rather, the question the judge must decide is *whether the terms are reasonable*. Perhaps the drafter of this Question Presented was hoping that the assumption would slip past the judge, but it will not. Write a Question Presented that addresses the actual legal issue.

Phrase the Question in a Way That Suggests a Favorable Answer. Generally, a question that suggests an affirmative answer is more persuasive than a question that suggests a negative answer. Sometimes, however, other rhetorical factors can outweigh that advantage. For instance, a structure that

1. *See* Fed. R. App. P. (28)(d).

asks, "Can *X* force *Y* to do *Z*?" implies that *X* is being oppressive to *Y*, simply by virtue of the structure of the question. The structure invites the reader to respond with a resounding "No." For example, consider this Question Presented:

> Can an employer, in order to collect urine samples, force employees to urinate in the plain view of a supervisor?

Don't Overdo the Advocacy. Some court rules require that Questions Presented not be argumentative, but even in the absence of court rules, overzealous advocacy is counterproductive. It causes the skeptical reader to discount the material because the writer's agenda is too obvious. The goal is to state the question in a way that allows the *facts* to speak for themselves. Facts persuade more effectively than bluster and puffery ever can. Here is a Question Presented that has crossed the line into argumentativeness:

> Can a reckless defendant, whose callous conduct caused the death of a precious new life, escape liability for wrongful death just because the baby's guardians had not yet completed an adoption proceeding?

To avoid argumentative Questions Presented, limit adjectives and adverbs, using facts instead of such descriptors. Edit out language that smacks of name-calling. Stick to facts the opposing party cannot dispute.

> Can legal guardians recover for the wrongful death of a child when the guardians had raised the child as their own for four years, had instituted adoption proceedings two years prior to the child's death, and had believed, reasonably and in good faith, that a final adoption decree had been issued?

Drafting More Than One Question. A brief can raise several questions and thus have several Questions Presented. In such a case, draft a separately numbered Question Presented for each legal question. Place these Questions Presented in the order in which the issues will appear in the Argument section.

Using a "Deep Issue"[2] Format. If court rules permit some variation, you might not be limited to the traditional one-sentence or one-phrase format. If so, consider using two or even three sentences so you can add context while maintaining clarity. The Question Presented should still be short—usually no

2. *See generally* Bryan A. Garner, *The Deep Issue: A New Approach to Framing Legal Questions,* 5 Scribes J. Legal Writing 1 (1994–1995).

more than about seventy to eighty words—but the multiple-sentence structure will allow you to tell a tiny story, to clarify the legal standard, or to frame the issue more effectively. Here is an example of a "deep" issue:

> To maintain a cause of action for fraud under California law, a plaintiff must show that the defendant made a false representation. In his deposition, Jones concedes that neither Continental nor its agents or employees made a false representation. Is Continental entitled to summary judgment on Jones's fraud claim? [forty-nine words.][3]

This issue statement uses three sentences. The first clarifies the applicable legal standard, providing the legal context. The second presents the key facts. With both the legal standard and the applicable facts clearly stated, the third sentence asks the question.

A "deep" issue format can state the facts first, essentially telling a mini-story. Here is an example of that strategy:

> At 7:30 one morning last spring, Father Michael Prynne, a Roman Catholic priest, was on his way to buy food for himself at the grocery store when his car collided with Ed Grimley's truck. The Catholic Church neither owned Michael Prynne's car nor required its priests to buy groceries as part of their priestly functions. Was Michael Prynne acting as an agent for the Church at the time of the accident? [seventy-one words][4]

Once in a while you might even use more sentences while keeping them short enough to remain within the seventy- to eighty-word range. Here is such an example:

> Fiver's insurance policy required it to give Barndt Insurance notice of a claim "immediately." In May 1994, one of Fiver's offices was damaged by smoke from a fire in another tenant's space. Ten months later, Fiver gave notice. Barndt investigated the claim for six months before denying coverage and did not raise a late-notice claim until eighteen months after the claim was filed. Can Barndt now deny coverage because of late notice? [seventy-three words][5]

Notice how all of these examples are both easily readable and narrative in form. If you are having trouble drafting an effective Question Presented using the traditional format and if court rules or your professor will allow, consider using this less stylized format.

3. *Id.* at 4.
4. *Id.* at 13.
5. *Id.* at 35.

EXERCISE 15-1
Critiquing Questions Presented

Review the Carillo facts in Exercise 10-2. Assume that the matter is now in litigation. Critique these two versions of the Question Presented drafted by the lawyer for the Lupinos. Then write a better version.

Version 1 Can the Carillos maintain an attractive nuisance in their backyard?
Version 2 Does a trampoline constitute an attractive nuisance?

II. PERSUASIVE HEADINGS

In trial and appellate briefs, headings serve as a persuasive tool. Point headings and subheadings persuade if they state your position in a compelling way. The judge is likely to read the point headings and subheadings first, either in the Table of Contents or by paging through the body of the Argument. If so, the headings provide a quick, persuasive summary of your entire argument.

A. Identifying Point Headings

Usually, *a point heading* is the statement of your argument on a *dispositive* legal issue—that is, an independent and freestanding ground that entitles your client to the relief you seek. Here is an example of a point heading:

> I. THE COURT SHOULD ENFORCE THE WATSON COVENANT BECAUSE ITS RESTRICTIONS ON DURATION, NATURE, AND SCOPE ARE REASONABLE.

To tell if your argument on an element or set of elements is an independent ground for the relief you seek, ask this: If the judge agrees with me on *only* this component of the rule, is that enough? If yes—if the judge would not need to consider other legal issues before granting the ruling you seek—then your argument on that component of the rule is an independent ground. A heading that states your conclusion on that component is a point heading.

This definition will be clearer if we look at an example. In a burglary case, the state must prove *all* of the elements to win a conviction. Thus, a defense attorney's brief need only show that any one of these elements is missing to show that the state cannot prove the burglary charge. In that brief, each challenged element will constitute an independent ground for the desired result. If the attorney challenges the state's proof on three elements ("nighttime," "intent," and "of another"), the defense attorney will have three independent, freestanding ways to win. The defense attorney can prevail by persuading the judge on any *one* of these elements. Therefore, the argument on each element will constitute a *point*, and the defense attorney's brief will contain three point headings.

However, the prosecution's brief must argue that the state can prove all of the elements of burglary. The state cannot obtain the ruling it seeks (submission of the case to the jury) simply by showing that the facts will prove any *one* element; the prosecutor's brief must show that the facts can prove *all* of the challenged elements. In the prosecutor's brief, then, each challenged element will be a subpoint. The prosecutor's brief will have only one *point* heading—a point arguing that all elements are provable. As in an office memo, having only one roman numeral is fine. The roman numerals will identify for the judge the freestanding arguments that entitle your client to the result you seek.

As we said, a point heading is generally a freestanding ground that will entitle your client to the relief she seeks. In brief writing, this is not a rigid rule, but rather a custom and a general principle of persuasion. In most cases, your reader will expect you to follow this method, and your case usually will be more persuasively presented if you do. Rarely will you have three free-standing grounds for relief that would be more persuasively argued under a single point heading. Instead, you will want to emphasize each by giving each its own point heading. You will want the judge to know at a glance that you are correct for three independent reasons, not just one.

Occasionally, however, you might choose to treat an issue as a point heading even if it is not a freestanding ground for relief. You might consider this organizational variation if your case falls into one of the following categories:

- When you have a major threshold issue;
- When you are responding to a brief that has given that issue its own point heading;
- When you must win on two weighty issues that are very different from each other.

Arguing an Important Threshold Issue. Recall that a threshold issue is one that determines the direction of the analysis from that point on.[6] For instance, the question of which standard of review is appropriate would be a threshold issue. The court must decide how much deference to give to the trial court's opinion before the court can consider what decision it will make on the issues you raise.

The question of which law will govern your legal issue would be a threshold issue. Perhaps the court will have to decide whether the law of state *A* or the law of state *B* will govern the situation. Or perhaps your client's legal duty would be different depending on whether a particular statute applies to your client. For instance, under Title VII, an "employer" must not discriminate on the basis of religion.[7] The question of whether your client is an "employer" as defined by the act would constitute a threshold question.

An evidentiary or procedural issue may be a threshold issue. The court might have to decide an evidentiary or other procedural issue before it can consider your argument on the merits. The court might have to consider whether a particular document was properly admitted into evidence before

6. See Chapter 10, Section IB.
7. 42 U.S.C. § 2000e-2(a).

that court can consider whether the trial evidence was sufficient to support the trial court's opinion.

If you have a threshold issue such as one of these, and if you do not have much to say about it, you can simply include it in the umbrella section of another point heading. But if you have a great deal to say about it, you might want to give it a point heading of its own.

Mirroring the Organization of the Opening Brief. If you are filing a brief in response to another brief, you might find that the judge's understanding of your arguments will be improved if you adopt the organizational structure of the opening brief. If the judge will have read your opponent's brief, which uses three point headings, you can consider whether to respond by giving each of those three issues its own point heading in your brief as well. Be careful, though, not to concede structural decisions to your opponent too easily. Sometimes structural decisions carry important implications for persuasion.

Arguing Two Major Issues. Occasionally you will have to win on two weighty issues, and the analysis of each of those weighty issues will be quite different in nature. For instance, you might have to argue that a particular statute is constitutional and also that your opponent breached its terms. Although you will have to win on both of those issues, you might find that each is a very large issue, that you have a great deal to say about each, and that the nature of your argument for one is quite different from the other (constitutional principles in one case and statutory construction principles in the other). In such a case, you might want to give each of those weighty issues its own point heading. However, do not rush into the decision to separate them. Quite often, your argument on each will be strengthened by a closer association with the other, an association you can emphasize by positioning them as subpoints under a common point heading.

B. Drafting Point Headings

Headings and subheadings provide the structure of your Argument. They also serve as a tool of persuasion. They can persuade because they assert your position in compelling language; they make visible the persuasive structure you have selected for your rule and your argument; and they allow the judge to find a quick summary of your entire argument by reading only the point headings and subheadings, either in a Table of Contents or by paging through the body of the Argument itself.

Ideally, a point heading should identify, expressly or implicitly, three things: (1) the result you seek, (2) the part of the rule that justifies that result, and (3) the key facts supporting that result.[8] The heading should phrase these items of information as assertions of their correctness. One way to learn to draft point headings is to think of them in halves. The first half asserts the correctness of the result you seek. The second half identifies, at least implicitly, the part of the rule that justifies that result and adds the key facts:

---

8. If the issue is a pure question of law, not requiring fact application, then you have no facts to add. However, the heading should still state the supporting rationale.

DRAFTING A POINT HEADING

____

[Identify the ruling you seek, asserting its correctness.]

because

____

[Identify the part of the rule justifying the result and the key facts.]

Here is an example of a burglary point heading. Notice how the second half of the point heading implicitly identifies the part of the rule that determines the desired result and asserts a conclusion about it:

A BURGLARY POINT HEADING

The Court should dismiss the burglary charge

[Identify the ruling you seek, asserting its correctness.]

because

the testimony of the bartender and other bar patrons establishes that Mr. Shaffer arrived at the house earlier than thirty minutes past sunset.

[Identify the key facts and state how they establish the correctness of the ruling.]

When the point heading must cover more than one element, placing the key facts for all those elements in one sentence could result in an unwieldy heading. In that situation, move the facts for each element into the subheading dealing with that element. For example, here are the prosecutor's headings for a brief responding to the defendant's challenge of three elements. Because the prosecutor must win on all three challenged elements to prevail, the point heading must cover all three elements, but there are separate subheadings for each. Notice that the subheadings expressly identify the components of the rule to be addressed in that subsection and add the key facts.

I. THE COURT SHOULD NOT DISMISS THE BURGLARY CHARGE AGAINST THE DEFENDANT BECAUSE THE EVIDENCE AT TRIAL WILL ESTABLISH ALL ELEMENTS OF BURGLARY.

- **A.** The evidence will show that the crime occurred in the nighttime because it occurred at 6:45 P.M., more than thirty minutes past sunset.
- **B.** The evidence will show that the Defendant intended to commit a felony when he entered the house because he alluded to his intent to batter Mrs. Shaffer before he left the bar for her home.
- **C.** The evidence will show that the dwelling was not the Defendant's own because he had waived his claim to the premises and did not retain any right of access.

As you write out the body of the Argument, you will develop even more clarity about which facts are compelling. Revise your point headings to reflect these new insights.

One last point: This section began by stating that point headings "ideally" should include key facts. A situation is less than ideal, however, when the key facts, stated in isolation from other facts and from your explanation of them, are not persuasive. Sometimes the facts of a particular case are persuasive only in a particular context. Or perhaps they require some explanation before their significance will be apparent to the judge. In either case, including the key facts in the point heading probably will hurt rather than help. In either case, then, leave the facts out of your point heading.

Similarly, a point heading for a pure question of law[9] usually would not include your client's facts. For a question of law, the court will only be deciding what the law is, not how that law applies to your client's facts. In place of facts, however, the point heading should assert the key argument(s) supporting your position on the question of law before the court. Here is an example of a point heading for a pure question of law:

> I. THE STATUTORY PROCEDURE FOR DECIDING ZONING AMENDMENT APPLICATIONS COMPLIES WITH DUE PROCESS REQUIREMENTS BECAUSE IT PROVIDES FOR A PETITION FOR RECONSIDERATION AND A SUBSEQUENT APPEAL TO DISTRICT COURT.

EXERCISE 15-2
Evaluating the Content of Point Headings

Facts. Several years ago Clifford Foodman defended Raymond Carson on hit-and-run charges. Now Foodman is defending a new client, Alice Janoff, on a contract dispute. Carson is the plaintiff in this new case. Before accepting Janoff's case, Foodman wrote to Carson explaining that there appeared to be no relationship between the two representations and inviting Carson to raise any concerns he had about Foodman's acceptance of Janoff's case. Carson did not respond. Carson has now filed a motion to disqualify Foodman from representing Janoff. One of the issues raised by this motion is whether Carson's failure to respond to Foodman's letter constituted consent to Foodman's representation of Janoff.

Read the following versions of the "consent" point heading for Foodman's brief. Identify the point heading that best includes the information a point heading should contain. For the others, identify which part is missing.

1. Carson consented to Foodman's representation of Janoff when he did not respond to Foodman's letter.
2. The Court should deny the Motion to Disqualify because Carson did not respond to Foodman's letter.

9. See Chapter 16, Section IA.

3. The Court should deny the Motion to Disqualify because Carson consented to the representation.
4. The Court should deny the Motion to Disqualify because Carson's failure to respond to Foodman's letter constituted consent to the representation of Janoff.

C. Editing Point Headings for Readability and Persuasion

1. Editing for Readability

Often the inclusion of all desirable information in a point heading results in a long, complex, and confusing sentence. Yet a point heading cannot persuade a judge of something she cannot decipher. And readability is especially important for point headings because the traditional format for point headings—all capital letters—already hinders readability. If you have some flexibility, avoid all caps.

If you are struggling with readability, use all relevant editing techniques in Chapter 20 to help simplify and clarify the heading. As a quick checklist, here are some of the techniques most likely to help tame a point heading.

1. *Keep the subject and the verb close together.* In other words, avoid intrusive phrases and clauses.
2. *Avoid nominalizations.* Nominalizations are noun forms of verbs. "Investigate" is a verb; "investigation" is a nominalization. Nominalizations require more words and make sentences harder to understand.
3. *Avoid unnecessary passive-voiced verbs.* Passive verbs make the sentence's subject something other than the actor. These verbs generally require more supporting words and make sentences harder to understand.
4. *Keep the facts and reasoning at the end of the sentence.* Placing the desired result first and the facts and reasoning second often results in a more readable point heading.
5. *Avoid vague words.* Vague words cause the reader to puzzle over the writer's meaning. Purge your point headings of words like these:

this matter with	regard to
it involves	it deals with
it pertains to	it concerns

6. *Avoid negatives.* Negatives, especially multiple negatives, can make a sentence harder to understand.

If you have tried all available editing techniques and still cannot produce a readable point heading, the best solution is to remove one of the items of information. Decide which one, based on persuasiveness and on your assessment of your reader's needs. If the key facts are particularly persuasive, remove the relief requested or the part of the rule at issue. The facts might sufficiently imply the part of the rule at issue, or perhaps the judge is already well aware of the nature of the relief you seek. Regardless, an easily readable point heading that asserts the party's legal argument but lacks supporting facts is more persuasive than a point heading that includes the facts but cannot be understood.

EXERCISE 15-3
Editing Point Headings for Readability

Edit the following headings to make them more easily readable. Use the techniques identified in the prior section and in Chapter 20.

1. It is clear that Crawford's actions of sitting peacefully in the parking lot of an open store, entering the store and leaving therefrom without incident, and driving lawfully out of the parking lot do not give rise to a reasonable, articulable suspicion of criminal activity to make a valid stop of said defendant.
2. The Defendant's Motion to Dismiss should be granted in as much as the contract involved provided that the escrow account under consideration could be closed by the escrow agent at the point in time when at least three days have passed from the date the notice of default was issued by the lender.
3. The Motion to Attach Assets should be denied because the Court should take into consideration the Defendant's reduced line of credit and the unavailability of other sources for cash for the purpose of operating the business during the litigation in this matter.
4. The Motion for Summary Judgment filed by the Defendants, Mr. and Mrs. Carillo, should not be denied due to the fact that the evidence will show that the injured child understood the danger involved in a trampoline.
5. There is no reasonable, articulable suspicion to justify a stop of Salavar where the testimony of the officer is contradicted on virtually every point, where the officer has no facts to support a claim of criminal activity, and where the officer only witnessed Salavar's car in an area of criminal activity and therefore the Defendant's Motion to Dismiss should be granted.
6. The leased premises, which are subject to the constant threat of very disruptive demonstrations, are not suitable with regard to the purpose for which they were leased, and therefore the lessees have been constructively evicted.
7. A minor who induces another to enter into a contract with him by making a false representation of his age is estopped from a disaffirmance of the contract if the other party demonstrated reasonable and justifiable reliance on the minor's representation.

2. Editing for Persuasion

Editing for persuasion is the final step in the process of drafting point headings. Here are three rhetorical strategies particularly applicable to point headings.

*1. **Affirmative Language Versus Negative Language.*** Most briefs focus on certain conduct: Is the conduct lawful? Proper? Desirable? Sometimes the writer can articulate the client's position either by using affirmative language or negative language. In addition to being more readable, affirmative language generally is more forceful and appealing than negative language. Here are examples of two point headings, one using affirmative language and one using negative language.

Negative language	The Court should grant Carrolton's Motion for Summary Judgment because Watson is unable to show that the terms are unreasonable or that she has not breached those terms.
Affirmative language	The Court should grant Carrolton's Motion for Summary Judgment because the terms of the covenant-not-to-compete are reasonable and the uncontested facts establish Watson's breach.

2. Varying the Structure of the Point Heading. The point heading structure described in this chapter is the easiest structure for learning to draft a readable point heading. It begins with the relief you want and follows with the facts and law supporting that relief. After you have a little practice with drafting point headings, however, you can vary the formula and sometimes achieve a more persuasive version. For instance, consider these versions of a burglary heading. What differences in effectiveness do you notice?

Version 1 The Court should dismiss the burglary charge against Mr. Shaffer because the alleged breaking and entering occurred at 6:15 P.M., which was earlier than thirty minutes after sunset.

Version 2 Because the alleged breaking and entering occurred at 6:15 P.M., which was earlier than thirty minutes after sunset, the Court should dismiss the burglary charge against Mr. Shaffer.

Version 3 The alleged breaking and entering occurred at 6:15 P.M., which was less than thirty minutes after sunset, and therefore the burglary charge against Mr. Shaffer should be dismissed.

Tinker with the structure of the point heading until you are satisfied that it is as persuasive as it can be.

3. Phrasing Alternative Arguments. When you have more than a single point heading, one or more of the headings may be an alternative argument, presented in case the judge does not agree with the first argument. The challenge here is to avoid seeming to reduce the credibility of the first argument by making an alternative argument. The following example demonstrates this flaw:

I. THE LAW OF THIS JURISDICTION DOES NOT ALLOW RECOVERY FOR THE WRONGFUL DEATH OF A FETUS, EVEN IF THE FETUS IS VIABLE AT THE TIME OF THE INJURY.

II. THE LAW OF THIS JURISDICTION ALLOWS RECOVERY FOR THE WRONGFUL DEATH OF ONLY A *VIABLE* FETUS, AND THE LAWRENCE FETUS WAS NOT VIABLE AT THE TIME OF THE INJURY.

In this pair of headings, a strong first argument is followed by a second argument that seems to undercut the first. Rather than undercutting your own best argument, phrase alternative arguments *in terms that assume the correctness of the first argument.* One way to do this is to restate the first argument expressly, like this:[10]

I. THE NEGLIGENCE CLAIM IS BARRED BY THE STATUTE OF LIMITATIONS BECAUSE THE PLAINTIFF DID NOT FILE THE COMPLAINT UNTIL FOUR YEARS AFTER THE ALLEGED NEGLIGENT ACT.

II. NOT ONLY IS THE CLAIM BARRED BY THE STATUTE OF LIMITATIONS, BUT THE PLAINTIFF'S ASSURANCE THAT HE WOULD NOT PURSUE AN ACTION BARS THE CLAIM UNDER THE EQUITABLE DOCTRINES OF ESTOPPEL AND WAIVER.

Reiterating the first point in the course of making the second can make the second heading unwieldy, however. Another way to avoid seeming to disavow the first point heading is to use, in the second heading, a verb tense that communicates that any assumption of a flaw in the first point is contrary to fact:

I. THE LAW OF THIS JURISDICTION DOES NOT ALLOW RECOVERY FOR THE WRONGFUL DEATH OF A FETUS, EVEN IF THE FETUS IS VIABLE AT THE TIME OF THE INJURY.

II. EVEN IF THE LAW DID ALLOW RECOVERY FOR THE WRONGFUL DEATH OF A VIABLE FETUS, THE LAWRENCE FETUS WAS ONLY IN THE FOURTH MONTH OF GESTATION, AND THEREFORE WAS NOT VIABLE.

Notice the use of the subjunctive verb "did." The subjunctive is used when stating something contrary to fact. Therefore, the first clause of the alternative heading affirms your assertion of the first heading rather than disavowing it.

D. Identifying Subheadings

In addition to express persuasion, subheadings have three main functions. First, subheadings provide the judge with an easily identifiable road map. Second, they invite increased attention levels because they let the judge pause for a moment. And third, they make the persuasive rule structure visible.

Use the rule's structure and your annotated outline[11] to create any additional subheadings you desire. Look at the rule's structure first. For example, if the rule is a factors test such as the child custody rule on page 80, you can allocate subheadings to each of the factors your brief will discuss.

If the rule does not identify subheadings like factors, you can create your own subheadings based on your major arguments on the point. For instance, if your point heading is a question of statutory interpretation, you can allocate subheadings to the major canons of construction you use or the major policy rationales you assert. Here is an example:

10. Modified from Girvan Peck, *Writing Persuasive Briefs* 135–36 (1984).

11. See Chapter 7.

I. THE COURT SHOULD DISMISS THE COMPLAINT BECAUSE THE PLAINTIFF LIED ON HER EMPLOYMENT APPLICATION AND UNDER 42 U.S.C. § 2000e, A PLAINTIFF CANNOT RECOVER IF SHE OBTAINED HER JOB UNDER FALSE PRETENSES.
 A. The plain meaning of the statute establishes that only an employee who has acted in good faith can recover.
 B. The legislature did not intend to allow a windfall to an employee who lied on the application.
 C. Construing the statute to allow recovery would encourage applicants to lie and would undermine employers' efforts to employ trustworthy employees.

As discussed above in regard to point headings, be sure to edit the subheadings for readability and persuasion. As Chapter 10 explained,[12] use three pages as a rough maximum for a section or subsection. Readers prefer to orient themselves every three pages or so, and new section headings will revive waning attention levels.

E. Formatting of Headings

The first place to look for rules regarding formatting are the court rules and your law firm's or professor's instructions. To whatever extent they don't contradict your other instructions, follow these guidelines for your headings. As mentioned above, when drafting point headings, avoid using all caps if permitted. Moreover, single-space the point headings. While some writers center point headings, that can make a long point heading even harder to read. Instead, use the full width of the line. Subheadings should be indented one tab space, single-spaced, and underlined, in regular type.

12. See Chapter 10, Section IV.

CHAPTER 16

Writing the Argument Section

I. ARGUMENTS FOR DIFFERENT KINDS OF LEGAL ISSUES

Legal issues, including legal writing assignments, come in several varieties. Drawing on the material in earlier chapters, this section will identify the major kinds of legal issues and provide suggestions for how to handle each. Some of these categories overlap, so be sure to read each section to learn if your assignment falls into more than one category.

A. A Pure Question of Law

You have a pure question of law when the only issue meaningfully before the court is *what the law is*—when there is no meaningful issue before the court about *how that law will apply to the facts*. The application of the law to the facts either is not before the court or is essentially uncontested. You can have a pure question of law before either a trial court or an appellate court.

For instance, assume you are representing a plaintiff in a wrongful death action arising from an automobile accident in which your client's wife was killed. At the time of the accident, your client's wife was pregnant with the couple's second child, and the unborn child also died. The defendant might file a motion to dismiss part of your client's claim, arguing that the law in your jurisdiction does not allow recovery for the death of an unborn child. You would file a brief arguing that the law does allow recovery. Both briefs deal with a pure question of *law*. The question of how that law will apply to the *facts* of the case is not yet before the court. That will be a question for the jury to decide.

The same issue also could come before the court on uncontested facts. For instance, the defendant might move for summary judgment in this same wrongful death claim, arguing that the law in your state allows recovery for the death of an unborn child only if the fetus was viable at the time of the injury. If your client's unborn child clearly was not viable at the time of the injury, your only response to the defendant's motion can be to argue that the law does (or should) allow recovery for a fetus not yet viable. You will be arguing a pure question of law—whether the law in your jurisdiction allows recovery for a fetus not viable at the time of the accident. The way the law will apply to your client's facts is not in dispute. For a pure question of law, your introduction or umbrella section will explain to your reader, if necessary, why the facts are not at issue. Then you will proceed with rule explanation. The core of your issue is *what* the law requires—what the governing rule is in this jurisdiction. Once your rule explanation section has proven and explained this governing rule, your work is done. You need not add a rule application section in the usual sense.

You still might be able to use your client's facts to help you persuade the judge on the question of law, however. Consider using your client's facts in your rule explanation section to demonstrate any policy rationales or important principles on which you rely. You might be able to strengthen these policy- or principle-based rationales by showing the results of each possible interpretation of the law in situations like your client's. This strategy would be an exception to the normal practice of avoiding discussion of your client's facts in the rule explanation section.

B. An Issue of Statutory Interpretation

You have an issue of statutory interpretation when the primary question before the court is what a particular statutory provision means and especially when little case law has arisen defining the provision. In such a situation, the court must interpret the statute itself rather than relying on interpretations other courts have given. The issue might arise because the statute does not directly address your client's legal question or because the statute addresses the question in ambiguous language.

For issues of statutory interpretation, you should use all the relevant tools from Chapter 4. Start with the statutory text—the language and punctuation of the provision itself and other related provisions; any definitions of terms; the titles of the provisions; and the name of the act itself. Consider any arguments you can make from the legislative history or from other indicia of the legislature's intent. Discuss any favorable interpretations by other courts, by an enforcing agency, or by law review authors or other commentators. Argue from any helpful canons of construction. Do not forget to rely on policy- and principle-based reasoning. In matters of statutory construction, these arguments can be particularly persuasive.

C. An Issue of Common Law Case Synthesis

You have an issue of common law case synthesis when you must combine holdings of several cases to formulate the governing rule, to discern the factors courts consider when deciding an issue under the rule, or to discern any exceptions to the rule. For issues of case synthesis, find arguments by using all of the tools in Chapters 2, 3, and 7. Consider the following:

- Which cases are most similar to your client's case;
- Whether any of the opinions have subsequently been followed, overruled, or questioned;
- Distinctions between a holding and dicta;
- The breadth of the holdings;
- Differences in the precedential values of the cases;
- Differences in the procedural histories of the cases;
- The depth of the courts' analyses and the quality of the courts' reasoning processes;
- The age of the various opinions;
- The weight of authority in your own jurisdiction and in others;
- The evaluations of commentators;
- The comparison between the rule the court announced and the way the court ruled on the facts before it;
- The facts the courts emphasized;
- Any rulings the court declined to make, either expressly or by implication;
- Whether any of the opinions are concurring or dissenting opinions; and
- Whether cases, reviewed chronologically, establish a trend.

For issues of case synthesis, sensitivity to the varying precedential values of cases is critical. The judge will want you to focus on the mandatory authorities and on the cases from the highest courts in your jurisdiction.

Again, do not forget to consider policy- and principle-based reasoning. Not only will judges consider the policies and principles implicated by various understandings of the rule of law, but some of the cases whose holdings you must synthesize might raise policy and principle concerns that are different from or closely similar to your client's situation. Those policy- and principle-based comparisons can help you justify placing more reliance on some cases than on others.

D. A Case of First Impression in Your Jurisdiction

You have a case of first impression if the courts of your jurisdiction have not addressed the legal question you must brief. Usually, the issue has been decided in other jurisdictions, although perhaps inconsistently. For federal issues, this situation is sometimes called a "circuit split," meaning that the circuit courts have issued inconsistent opinions on the question and the United States Supreme Court has yet to rule on the issue.

For an issue of first impression, research the holdings of the other jurisdictions to identify the approach most favorable to your client, and argue that this approach is the best. Use all the tools set out in subsection C above to show why your proposed approach is best and why the other approaches are inferior. If more jurisdictions have adopted the approach you prefer, be sure to point out that the "weight of authority" supports your position. Where possible, use analogies to align your case with similar cases from favorable jurisdictions. Rely on any secondary authorities that have compared the diverse approaches and supported the approach you prefer. You can include interdisciplinary sources that support your position. Also, use policy- and principle-based reasoning. When a court must rule on a case of first impression, policy and principle considerations are among the most important parts of your analysis.

E. Seeking a Change in the Law

You have an issue asking for a change in the law when the existing law in your jurisdiction is not favorable for your client and you must ask the court to change the rule or to create an exception to it. The strategies for handling such an issue are similar to those used for a pure question of law (subsection A above) and a circuit split (subsection D above). You must honestly disclose the existing state of the law but show the court why a change is appropriate. Therefore, your job is to point out the infirmities of the existing rule, propose the change you desire, and explain why your proposal is better. Courts hesitate to change the law without careful thought because the law should be stable and because citizens plan their lives and businesses in reliance on the law. Therefore, address these concerns directly if you can. Also, state clearly the change you propose. A court cannot effectively consider changing the law without understanding the exact nature of the change you request.

Again, policy- and principle-based rationales are persuasive. You might draw on persuasive authority from other jurisdictions, the opinions of legal scholars in secondary sources, and available interdisciplinary sources. If you can, use your client's facts as an example of the infirmities of the old rule and the advantages of the rule you propose.

F. An Issue Applying Law to Fact

You have an issue applying law to fact when the issue will be resolved primarily by how the court views your client's facts. Issues of application of law to fact often arise when the governing rule is a factors test or a balancing test or when the language of the governing rule is vague enough to invite speculation about how it might apply. A classic example is the standard for defining negligent conduct: the "reasonable person." If you have taken torts, you probably have had many debates about what conduct would be reasonable in particular circumstances. These debates raise issues of application of law to fact.

Analogical reasoning (analogizing and distinguishing cases) is by far the most important tool for issues such as these. Your analysis should provide the judge with examples of cases in which courts have applied the governing rule to situations like your client's and ruled as you hope your judge will rule. Focus primarily on opinions from courts in your jurisdiction. Use opinions from other jurisdictions in a supporting role if necessary to bolster your jurisdiction's case law.

Explicitly state the similarities between your client's facts and the facts of the favorable cases. Distinguish unfavorable cases by showing relevant factual differences. Show similarities or differences of policy and principle as well, thus further aligning your client's case with the favorable cases and distinguishing it from the unfavorable cases. Custom-based reasoning can be effective to show that your client's actions were consistent with customary practices and that the actions of other parties strayed beyond those bounds.

II. HONING YOUR ARGUMENT FOR THE COURT'S ROLE

The roles of trial court judges and appellate court judges differ significantly. Effective arguments target precisely the role of the judge who will be reading the brief. Let's review the most important differences.

A. The Trial Judge

Most trial judges share the characteristics described in Chapter 6, Section IIE. They are busy, skeptical, and impatient with squabbling. They want to make good decisions that accurately apply the law in their jurisdiction and achieve a fair result. More than any other characteristics in a brief, they want clarity, brevity, and accuracy.

Because trial judges have heavy caseloads, they usually are not familiar with individual cases in the pretrial stages, when most of your briefs will be filed. They might or might not be familiar with the law on your legal issue, depending on how often that issue has arisen in prior cases. Therefore, do not assume that your judge knows the facts and circumstances of your case or even that the judge knows the law on your issue. Your brief must give the judge the factual and legal background necessary to decide your issue.

Finally, trial judges are constrained by mandatory precedent. They primarily want to know what those precedents are and how they apply to your case. Authorities from other jurisdictions hold less interest for trial judges, most of whom do not see themselves as free to change the law. Therefore, right up front, the trial judge wants to know whether there are mandatory authorities on your issue and, if so, what they are. Use authorities from other jurisdictions only to fill in any gaps in your jurisdiction's mandatory authority and only after you have explained to the judge why you are presenting these otherwise extraneous authorities.

B. Appellate Judges and the Appellate Process

Both a trial-level brief and an appellate brief are written to persuade a judge to rule favorably on one or more legal issues. But on appeal, the lawyer's job is more complicated and more difficult. First, the appellate court will not review the entire proceeding below. The court will review only the issues the appellant's lawyer has identified for appeal and see only the portions of the trial record the lawyers have designated to be included in the record on appeal.[1] Therefore, the appellant's lawyer must first comb the record of the proceedings below to identify issues that might have been decided wrongly.

It might not be enough, however, that the appellate court would have decided the case differently had it been sitting in the trial judge's place.

1. The appellee's lawyer can cross appeal, identifying additional issues for review. For easier reference here, we will refer only to the role of the appellant's lawyer.

Rather, as Chapter 17 explains in greater detail, reversal of some kinds of cases would require a finding that (1) the trial judge applied the wrong law, or (2) the record below cannot reasonably be read to support the decision below, even if all inferences are interpreted in the appellee's favor. Further, not every clear error of law or fact will result in appellate relief, but only those that might have made a difference in outcome ("reversible" error). Nor can any additional evidence be submitted,[2] although the appellate court might rely on extrinsic information in making policy judgments.[3] The appellate court will be evaluating whether the record below adequately supported the lower court's decision, so the relevant facts are those that were before the lower court.

Not only does the decision-making process differ on appeal, but the roles and perspectives of the judges differ as well. Appellate judges, especially those sitting on the highest appellate level of their jurisdiction, see themselves as responsible for the law's development. They are more willing to reevaluate the wisdom of a governing rule and therefore more willing to consider policy- and principle-based reasoning. Still, they understand the value of stability and the legitimate need of citizens to rely on legal rules. Therefore, they find analogical reasoning (analogizing and distinguishing cases) persuasive because they want their rulings to be consistent with similar prior rulings, if possible. Although they are just as persuaded by stories as are trial judges, they are seeing only the "cold" record, not the actual witnesses, and so will tend to defer to the lower court's subjective interpretations.

Important similarities remain, however. All of the characteristics attributed to trial court judges above apply to appellate judges as well. They are busy with heavy caseloads. They want to issue good, just rulings. More than anything else in a brief, they want clarity, brevity, and accuracy.

III. REMINDERS ABOUT ORGANIZATION

Umbrella Section. If your brief will analyze several rules or several elements of a rule, begin with an umbrella section.[4] An umbrella section should be concise—generally limited to one or two short paragraphs. Its primary function is to introduce the components of the analysis that follows. You can use an umbrella section at the beginning of the Argument section (before the first roman numeral) to introduce the roman numerals or after a point heading to introduce subparts within that point heading.

The content of an umbrella section depends on the particular situation and on your own writing decisions. Among the uses for an umbrella section

---

2. There are some exceptions to this rule, but none that need concern us here.

3. *See generally* Ellie Margolis, *Beyond Brandeis: Exploring the Use of Non-legal Materials in Appellate Briefs*, 34 U.S.F. L. Rev. 197 (2000).

4. Chapter 10, Section II, explains umbrella sections in more detail.

are the following: (1) stating the overall conclusion that you would like to the court to reach, particularly when the umbrella section precedes the first roman numeral; (2) summarizing the rule and citing the controlling authority defining the rule; (3) providing any favorable principles affecting the application of the rule, such as presumptions, burdens of proof, elevated levels of proof (such as clear and convincing evidence), or policy leanings;[5] (4) explaining the status of any elements not discussed in the brief; (5) providing a one- or two-sentence summary of your argument on each element; and (6) resolving any potential resistance to the order in which you will discuss the issues.

The Standard Paradigm. Because a brief is an advocacy document, it asserts positions (conclusions) at numerous points. The argument begins with a statement of the conclusion the writer hopes the judge will reach. This conclusion, in one form or another, appears in the heading for that issue, as Chapter 15 explains. It also may appear in the first paragraph of text beneath the heading. Finally, the conclusion appears at the end of the argument on that issue. This repetition contributes to an orderly route through rule-based reasoning. Also, subtle repetition is an effective technique for emphasis.[6] Here is an overview of the paradigm for the persuasive analysis of a single issue:

RULE EXPLANATION

Conclusion

- State the conclusion you want the judge to reach on this issue (your thesis).
- Place it in the point heading and sometimes in the first paragraph.
- Succinctly state the most important reasons supporting your conclusion.

Rule Statement

- State the applicable legal rule.
- State it in the form and structure most favorable to your client's position.

Rule Explanation

- Explain where the rule comes from so the judge is satisfied that your rule statement is accurate.
- Explain what the rule means .
- Explain these characteristics of the rule in the terms most favorable to your client's position.
- Rebut any counterexplanation you can weaken by a preemptive discussion.

5. See Chapter 10.

6. Mary Barnard Ray & Barbara J. Cox, *Beyond the Basics: A Text for Advanced Legal Writing* 212 (3d ed. 2013).

RULE APPLICATION

Rule Application

- Discuss how the rule applies to your client's facts.
- Emphasize the favorable facts and deemphasize or justify the problematic facts.
- Rebut any counter-application you can weaken by a preemptive discussion.

Conclusion

- Restate your conclusion.
- Unless the discussion has been short, summarize the key points supporting the conclusion.

Separating Rule Explanation and Rule Application. Remember that rule explanation generally should remain distinct from rule application, with rule explanation coming first. All the reasons we saw earlier for keeping these sections separate still apply, but in persuasive writing another important reason applies as well. Presenting the reader with rule explanation first and separate from rule applications capitalizes on a principle of persuasion: Readers are more persuaded by ideas they have first thought of themselves than by an idea first asserted by another.[7] This is especially true when the reader knows that the person doing the asserting is an advocate with an admitted persuasive agenda.

The strategy goes like this. The reader first reads the brief's fact statement and has those facts in mind when reading the rule explanation. During the rule statement and explanation, the reader will be thinking of those facts and anticipating rule application. The reader's Commentator[8] will be applying each point the writer is explaining about the rule to those facts. Presenting rule explanation first, without explicit application to the facts, allows the rule explanation to lead the reader to the desired conclusions about rule application, *before the writer asserts those conclusions.* Then, when the writer reaches the rule application phase, she is only asserting the conclusions the reader has already reached on his own.

Variations on the Paradigm. Occasionally, later drafts can alter the normal paradigm by combining the rule explanation section for each element into one comprehensive explanation of the rule and then combining the rule application section for each element into a comprehensive application of the rule. If you think that your situation might call for this approach, review the description of this variation in Chapter 10, Section V. However, resist using this variation for the first draft. Let the discipline of separately writing out the rule explanation and rule application for each individual element help you deepen your understanding of that element. After you have mined the depths of possible arguments for each individual element, you can decide whether a combined discussion is appropriate.

7. See Chapter 6, Section IIE.
8. See Chapter 6, Section IID.

Writing the Fact Statement First. You might find it helpful to write out a draft of the Statement of Facts[9] before writing a draft of the Argument section. If you are having trouble getting started, this strategy could help. Also, you might find that immersing yourself in your client's story is excellent preparation for the more linear reasoning required in the Argument section.

EXERCISE 16-1
Labeling the Components of the Paradigm

Make a photocopy of the Argument section of the brief in Appendix C. Locate and label the parts of the umbrella paragraph and, for each issue, the sections of the standard paradigm.

IV. USING CASE COMPARISONS TO SUPPORT YOUR ARGUMENT

When you learned to write an office memo predicting the answer to a legal question, you used analogical reasoning to explain your conclusion. Look again at Chapter 5, Section II and Chapter 11, Section II. What you have already learned will be our starting point here, but now you are ready to hone your skills even further.

Know Exactly Why You Are Making the Comparison. Don't discuss the case simply to show that you have read it. Here are the most common reasons for making a case comparison: (1) If the cited case's outcome supports your position, you want to show that your client's case is similar, or better yet, that your client's case is different in a way that makes the desired result even clearer in your case. (2) If the cited case's outcome was different from your position, you want to show that your client's case is different in a way that really matters.

State Your Point in a Clear Thesis Sentence Right up Front. Now that you know exactly why you are making the comparison, lead with it. Don't make the judge read a long description of the cited case without knowing what your point will be. For instance, in the Buckley short-form example in Chapter 11, the case comparison began like this: "Buckley's representation that she was old enough to buy a car is significantly different from the representations in *Carney*." Now the judge knows exactly what to be looking for as you begin to explain what happened in *Carney*.

Use Parallel Structure to Make the Similarities and Differences Clear. The parallel structure will let you put the key facts right beside each other so the judge can compare them up close. For instance, in the Frimberger example in

---

9. See Chapter 18.

Chapter 11, the comparison begins with the key thesis (that the *Fahmie* case is remarkably similar to Frimberger's situation) and then lays out the comparisons like this:

> Just as in *Fahmie*, [states a similarity]. In both cases, [states another similarity]. In both cases, [states a third similarity]. In neither case [states a fourth similarity]. In both cases, [states a fifth similarity].

Use as many key similarities (but only *key* similarities) as the opportunity presents. You can make a list or you can present one single point of comparison as being the crucial one. Either way, you can persuade the judge of your point.

Use Mostly Your Own Words. If There Is Key Language in the Cited Case, Quote Only Those Key Words. If the judge wanted to read long passages from the cited case, the judge would read that case (and probably will). Your purpose in the brief is to write primarily about your own case and make the comparison easy to read. The best way to do that is to minimize quoting. That way, when you *do* quote a word or a phrase, it takes on added importance. For instance, notice how the Buckley example in Chapter 11 uses a single quoted word to bring the key comparison into focus:

> Buckley's statement is much closer to the situation in *Woodall*, in which the minor made the representation "unknowingly." In *Woodall*, the minor did not realize he was making a representation of majority because he did not read the contract he was signing. *Id.* at 97. Similarly, Buckley did not realize that she might be making a representation of majority because she misunderstood the agent's question. In both cases, the requisite intent to deceive is absent. Therefore, the result in Buckley's situation should be the same as the result in *Woodall*—an order permitting disaffirmance.

Don't Be Afraid to Say Your Case Is Different from a Cited Case with a Result You Like. What you are looking for is a key difference that makes your client's case even more compelling than the cited case. For instance, in the Frimberger example in Chapter 11, after pointing out a number of relevant similarities, the comparison points out a key difference:

> The only relevant difference between the two situations results in an even weaker case for Frimberger. In *Fahmie*, the state agency actually required the plaintiff to replace the inadequate culvert. . . . In Frimberger's situation, however, the state agency has taken no action to require abatement of the violation. As a matter of fact, the agency has invited Frimberger to apply for an exception to the relevant requirement, a procedure which Frimberger has thus far declined to pursue. Therefore, it is even less likely that Frimberger's facts establish a breach of the covenant than did the facts in *Fahmie*.

Consider Other Effective Formats. If you have mastered the basic formats explained in Chapter 11 and if your professor agrees, you can adapt the basic formats to suit your particular purpose and situation. Remember, though, that effective comparisons nearly always begin with a clear thesis sentence stating the point you want to make and nearly always put the points to be compared up close to each other.

V. REBUTTING YOUR OPPONENT'S ARGUMENTS

As we saw in Chapter 1, lawyers write both opening briefs and briefs responding to the briefs filed by others. Lawyers often need to rebut their opponent's arguments, both in their own opening brief, where they anticipate opposing arguments, and in responsive and reply briefs filed after those opposing arguments have been made. Often lawyers must rebut both an opposing *explanation* of the law and an opposing *application* of the law to the current situation.

Lawyers struggle with how to treat counter-argument in an opening brief. On the one hand, the writer wants to respond to the arguments she anticipates. On the other hand, she does not want to raise arguments the opposing party might not have thought of or articulate them better than the opposing brief would have.[10] Nor does she want to sacrifice her affirmative stance—the primary advantage of the opening brief—by turning her own brief into a defensive document. Resolving these strategic questions is always a case-by-case task, but here are some helpful guidelines:

1. Include counter-argument in an opening brief when you are relatively sure that the opposing brief or the court itself will raise the argument and when you can weaken it by a preemptive discussion. More often than not, a well-crafted preemptive discussion will weaken an opponent's argument.
2. The most effective forms of counter-argument might not draw attention to opposing argument by labeling it as such ("The defendant may argue that. . . . However, . . . "). Instead, the counter-argument disproves opposing arguments primarily by affirmative proof of the writer's own position ("The Defendant's actions constituted negligence [explain why]. The unreasonableness of the behavior is not justified by . . . or by . . . [explain why].")
3. Articulate your position on that argument in more detail than you use to articulate the opposing party's argument. Detail is a technique for emphasis, and lack of detail is a technique for deemphasis.[11]
4. Do not place an identified counter-argument ahead of your own affirmative argument. Address it after you have made all of your own

10. This concern applies to adverse *arguments*, but not to directly adverse *authorities*. As you know, the lawyer has a duty to disclose directly adverse authorities in the controlling jurisdiction.

11. Mary Barnard Ray & Barbara J. Cox, *supra* note 6, at 210.

points. Otherwise, your brief will take on a defensive tone and will lose much of its rhetorical power.

5. After you have a draft of the argument, compare the space devoted to counter-argument with the space devoted to affirmative argument. The great majority of the draft should be devoted to your own affirmative argument.
6. If your opponent has used rhetoric that is either excessive or particularly effective, consider ways to defuse that opposing rhetoric. Confront excessive rhetoric if you think that, left unconfronted, it could influence the judge. Confront particularly effective rhetoric if you can devise a way to remove the rhetoric's power. Usually the best way to remove the power of rhetoric is by using the law or the facts or both. For example:

> Defendant's brief contains broad general conclusions such as "preemptive effect . . . is firmly established in the case law," a "comprehensive network of agency regulations," "pervasive nature of the regulations," and the agency's "specifically stated intent." Def. brief 4 [sic]. The support and analysis of these grandiose phrases and broad-brush conclusions consists simply of three agency source materials, plus an extensive reliance on one district court opinion, *Simon*. We now show these authorities do not support these statements.[12]

VI. USING LEGAL THEORY TO SHARPEN YOUR ARGUMENTS

Forms of legal reasoning draw their persuasive force from underlying assumptions about the nature and function of law—about how cases are and should be decided. These are the questions of legal theory (jurisprudence). Jurisprudence ponders such topics as what law is; where it comes from; whether it is internally consistent; whether it is or can be neutral; how we should decide new or hard cases; and whether and how law relates to morality, social values, economics, or politics.

The more you know about jurisprudence, the more it will show you practical arguments and lawyering strategies. Your own grasp of the jurisprudential basis of a form of argument and your sensitivity to the jurisprudential approach of the judge will strengthen your ability to use these forms of argument to represent your clients well. For helpful material on the major schools of American jurisprudence and how they can help you make effective arguments, see www.AspenPublishing.com/Edwards-LWAnalysis6.

---

12. Irwin Alterman, *Plain and Accurate Style in Court Papers* 26 (1987).

CHAPTER 17

Standards of Review

Effective appellate advocacy requires careful attention to the standard of review. The standard of review is a vitally important threshold issue shaping how other issues will be decided. Also, it determines the language in which you frame the issues, especially in your point headings.

The standard of review defines the level of deference the appellate court must give to the trial court's decision. Can the appellate court freely decide the question on its own, without any regard for the decision of the trial court? This standard would be good news for the appellant, who objects to the trial court's decision. It would be like starting over, as if the trial court had never decided the question. Or must the appellate court give some level of deference to the trial court's decision? That would be good news for the appellee, who agrees with the trial court's decision. It increases the odds that the trial court's decision will prevail. The question of which party will have the good news, and just how good the news will be, depends on the kind of trial court decision being appealed.

I. CATEGORIES OF TRIAL COURT DECISIONS

In a trial before a judge (a bench trial), the judge must decide both the law and the facts. A trial judge also must decide many discretionary questions, often procedural in nature. Errors in making any of these decisions—decisions of law, decisions of fact, or decisions left to the court's discretion—can lead to an appeal. The following sections describe these categories of decisions and the standard of review and policy rationale applicable to each.

Questions of Law. A pure question of law can be decided without reference to the facts of the case. Does this jurisdiction recognize a claim for the wrongful death of a fetus? Within what time period must a notice of appeal be filed? Must a will be signed? These are all purely questions of law. They can be researched and answered without reference to any particular set of facts.

A trial court's decision on a pure question of law is subject to de novo review. The appellate court need grant no deference to the trial court's opinion. The appellate court is free to substitute its own opinion on the question of what the jurisdiction's law provides.[1] The principle of stare decisis encourages the appellate court to pay some deference to existing common law, but this deference is unrelated to whether the lower court adopted and applied that law. Therefore, an appellate court need not give any deference even to a trial court ruling that is *correct*—correct in the sense that it accurately states the rule of law at the time of the lower court's decision. Depending on the level of the appellate court and on the nature of the issue being appealed, the appellate court might decide that the trial judge was right in concluding what the law *was*, but that the law *ought* to be something else. The appellate court might take the opportunity presented by this case to announce a change in the law.[2] As a matter of fact, the primary rationale for the "de novo" standard is the recognized function of appellate courts to make new law.

Questions of Fact. A pure question of fact is a question that can be decided on the basis of only the evidence in the record. What the law is has absolutely nothing to do with the question. What speed limit was posted? Did the defendant enter the building? Is the signature on the contract that of the plaintiff? These are all purely questions of fact. They can be decided without reference to any rule of law. You could have decided such questions long before you came to law school.

A trial *judge's* decision of a pure question of fact usually is subject to review using a "clearly erroneous" standard.[3] To overturn the trial judge's decision, an appellate court would have to decide that, although *some* evidence supporting the decision might exist in the trial court record, the appellate court "is left with the definite and firm conviction that a mistake has been committed."[4] It is not enough that the appellate court would have made a different decision. As long as the lower court's decision is plausible, given the record as a whole, the opinion must be upheld.[5]

The most common policy rationales for the clearly erroneous standard are (1) the better opportunity of trial courts to judge the credibility of witnesses and the weight to be accorded to testimony, (2) the function assigned to trial courts as the primary fact finders, (3) the inadvisability of expending judicial resources on duplicating functions and responsibilities, (4) the unfairness of requiring the parties to convince two different courts of their facts, (5) the concern for crowded appellate dockets, and (6) the advantage of a trial judge's expertise in fact-finding.

A *jury's* decision on a pure question of fact usually is subject to an even more limited standard of review—a "competent evidence" standard. If the jury was properly instructed and if the record contains some modicum of competent evidence supporting the jury's decision, the appellate court must allow the jury's decision to stand.[6] In other words, the appellate court's only function in reviewing a jury verdict is to be sure that the jury's verdict is not

1. *See, e.g., Watzek v. Walker*, 485 P.2d 3, 6 (Ariz. Ct. App. 1971).
2. Whether that change in the law will apply to the case then before the court is a separate legal issue that is the subject of a separate body of law.
3. *See* Fed. R. Civ. P. 52(a)(6).
4. *Anderson v. City of Bessemer*, 470 U.S. 564, 73 (1985).
5. *Id.* at 573–74.
6. *See, e.g., I.M.A., Inc. v. Rocky Mountain Airways, Inc.*, 713 P.2d 882, 887 (Colo. 1986).

irrational, given the trial evidence.[7] In addition to some of the same policies supporting the limited review of a judge's fact-finding, the primary rationale for this competent evidence standard, the most limited of reviews, is the parties' constitutional right to a trial by jury.

Mixed Questions of Law and Fact. Identifying purely factual or purely legal questions and the corresponding standards of review is fairly straightforward. The matter becomes more complex, however, when the question involves a mixture of law and fact. For example, consider the following example drawn from a car accident case. Here are some questions of *fact* and the trial court's decisions on them:

Question of Fact	***Trial Court's Answers***
What speed limit was posted?	55 MPH
What speed was the defendant traveling?	65 MPH
Was it raining?	Yes
Did the driver signal before changing lanes?	No

Here is a question of *law* and the trial court's decision on it:

Question of Law	***Trial Court's Answers***
What is the duty of care owed by an automobile driver to other drivers?	A driver must exercise the degree of care that would be exercised by a reasonable person under those same circumstances.

Having decided both the *facts* and the relevant *law*, the trial court now decides *how that law applies to those facts.*

Mixed Question of Law and Fact	***Trial Court's Answers***
Is driving sixty-five miles an hour in the rain when the speed limit is fifty-five and not signaling the intention to turn [facts] consistent with the degree of care that would be exercised by a reasonable person under those same circumstances? [law]	No

Now, assume that the defendant appeals. She does not disagree with the trial court's answers deciding the speed limit, her speed at the time of the accident, whether it was raining, and whether she signaled. Assume also that she does not disagree with the trial court's answer defining the duty of care owed to other drivers. Rather, she disagrees with the trial court's decision

7. Robert J. Martineau, *Fundamentals of Modern Appellate Advocacy* 133–34 (1985).

that driving at that speed under those conditions and changing lanes without signaling *was inconsistent with* the way a reasonable person would drive. In other words, she disagrees with the way the trial court applied the law to the facts. This is a disagreement about a mixed question of law and fact.

For a mixed question of law and fact, the reviewing court must decide whether to use a de novo standard (the standard for questions of law) or a clearly erroneous standard (the standard for questions of fact). Usually the court chooses the standard on a case-by-case determination of whether factual questions or legal questions predominate in the particular issue before the court. The majority of mixed questions are subjected to de novo review, and mixed questions of constitutional law are nearly always subject to de novo review.[8] Questions of negligence generally are subjected to clearly erroneous review.[9]

Questions Within the Trial Court's Discretion. A trial judge has no discretion about whether to apply the relevant rule of law. However, during a case, a trial judge must decide many other questions, questions that the applicable rule of law leaves within the judge's discretion.

The governing rule and relevant authorities might identify factors or guidelines to help the judge know *how* to make the decision, but the governing rule and relevant authorities do not tell the judge *what* to decide. Instead, the rule recognizes that the best answer to that particular question will differ from situation to situation and will depend on circumstances that no single rule of law could anticipate, describe, and evaluate.

Questions left in the trial court's discretion are usually either matters of equity or matters of procedure and case management. For instance, in some circumstances, a party who has filed an answer must obtain the judge's permission before she can amend that answer.[10] Case law might give the judge some guidelines about when to give permission, but under most court rules, the decision is left to the judge's discretion. The trial judge's duty in making such decisions is to refrain from acting unreasonably or arbitrarily.

This scope of authority gives a trial judge broad latitude, and, correspondingly, it gives appellate courts a narrow role in reviewing these decisions. An appellate court is not free to overturn a trial judge's decision merely because the appellate court would have made a different decision. To overturn a decision left to the trial court's discretion, the appellate court must hold that the decision was an abuse of discretion.[11] As long as the trial court's decision was not unreasonable or arbitrary, the appellate court must affirm it. Policy rationales justifying the "abuse of discretion" standard include (1) the need for flexibility in case management; (2) judicial economy and the crowded appellate docket; (3) judicial comity, that is, a judge's respect for the decisions of other judges; (4) the ability of the trial judge to assess the circumstances firsthand; (5) the need for flexible rules of law to address satisfactorily all possible

8. *See, e.g., United States v. McConney*, 728 F.2d 1195, 1203 (9th Cir. 1984) (en banc).

9. *Id.* at 1204.

10. *See, e.g.*, Fed. R. Civ. P. 15(a).

11. *See, e.g., Kern v. TXO Prod. Corp.*, 738 F.2d 968, 970 (8th Cir. 1984); *Napolitano v. Compania Sud Americana De Vapores*, 421 F.2d 382, 385 (2d Cir. 1970).

circumstances; and (6) the need to support the trial judge's authority and control of her own courtroom.

II. ADVOCATING FOR A MORE FAVORABLE STANDARD OF REVIEW

The first and best way to identify the appropriate standard of review for your case is to look for opinions issued by the court deciding your case. Search for cases deciding issues similar to yours, and see what standard of review the court used. If you are relying on appellate cases from your own jurisdiction for some of your argument on the merits of your case, those cases probably also mention the appropriate standard of review. If not, look for cases on your issue from other appellate courts, and look for opinions from your own jurisdiction on similar issues.

It should go without saying that an advocate should look for authority, including policy arguments, supporting the most favorable standard of review possible. Where doubt exists as to the proper standard, an appellant should argue for the *least* restrictive standard—a standard that maximizes the appellate court's authority to overturn the challenged decision. An appellee should argue for the *most* restrictive standard—a standard that limits the appellate court's authority to overturn the trial court's ruling. On pure questions of law, the de novo standard of review is well settled, and few, if any, distinctions will affect it. On pure questions of fact, the clearly erroneous or competent evidence standards are fairly well settled, too. However, an advocate might still be able to influence, subtly, an appellate court's application of the standard for reviewing fact-finding. For instance, in an appropriate case the lawyer might point out that the evidence was entirely documentary (requiring no assessment of witness credibility) or that the evidence was uncontested. In either situation, the policy rationales listed above would be less relevant.

However, the standards applicable both to mixed questions of law and fact and to questions left to the trial court's discretion might leave some room for advocacy. For questions that might be categorized as mixed law and fact, a lawyer might influence the appellate court's decision on whether the particular question *is* a mixed question and, if so, what standard should apply. Does the *factual* aspect or the *legal* aspect predominate? Were the facts contested? Was the law well settled and construed by many cases? Were the facts established by a judge or by a jury? Does the case involve an important issue of constitutional rights?

For questions that might be left to the trial court's discretion, the advocate can sometimes influence the appellate court's decision on (1) whether the applicable rule *does* leave the question to the trial court's discretion and, if so, (2) just how much discretion the appellate court should allow the trial court to exercise

Compare the policy rationales for the abuse of discretion standard to the circumstances of your case, and use your common sense. What small points can you make to subtly convince the appellate court to narrow or widen the deference it will give to the trial court? For instance, do the authorities announce standards or factors that are to guide the trial court's discretion? Did the trial court have to make factual findings as part of the decision of the question left to its discretion? How important are the rights at stake? How desirable is it to increase the uniformity of approach among trial courts on this issue? Has the trial court deviated from a common custom or practice? Is this a relatively new question that could benefit from a period of experimentation at the trial court level before an appellate court takes a position on it? The answers to these sorts of questions can provide the raw material for influencing the way the appellate court applies the standard.

III. CONFORMING HEADINGS TO THE STANDARD OF REVIEW

The brief's point headings ordinarily should be consistent with the applicable standard of review.[12] Here are examples of headings phrased according to the appropriate standard:

No competent evidence	The Court should reverse the burglary conviction because the record contains no competent evidence that the breaking and entering occurred later than thirty minutes after sunset.
Clearly erroneous	The Court should reverse the judgment because the trial court's finding of intent to discriminate was clearly erroneous.
De novo	The Court should reverse the judgment entered on the Defendant's Motion to Dismiss because this jurisdiction allows recovery for the wrongful death of a fetus.
Abuse of discretion	The trial court abused its discretion when it issued a preliminary injunction prohibiting the Defendant from concealing or disposing of his assets.

Notice that the de novo standard does not change the phrasing of the argument because that standard puts no gloss whatsoever on the question. That standard imposes no limitations on the appellate court's decision.

A brief is far more effective when it establishes the most favorable standard of review and makes a few points about how that standard should be applied to the pending case. Consider the policy rationales that underlie each standard of review. As you write the argument, make whatever points you can in favor of applying the standard most favorable to your position. As Senior United States Circuit Judge Ruggero J. Aldisert explained,

12. If the standard of review is unfavorable, you might not wish to reiterate it in each point heading. A simple acknowledgment of the standard early in the brief might be sufficient.

"[S]tandards of review are critically important in appellate decision making."[13] Yet many lawyers forget to research the proper standard and to couch their arguments according to its terms. As a matter of fact, Judge Aldisert described his experience of observing the "psychological block" that seems to prevent some lawyers from recognizing and dealing with the standard of review.[14] If, from the beginning of your practice, you pay careful attention to the standard of review, you will never be one of the lawyers Judge Aldisert described.

EXERCISE 17-1
Identifying Categories of Trial Court Decisions

You are a staff attorney in the local legal aid office, which represents people who do not have sufficient income to pay an attorney. One of your clients is Sophia Guzman. Guzman has five children. Her husband died three years ago, and she had to resort to public assistance to support her family. She and her children rent a two-bedroom apartment in a dilapidated building owned by A-1 Realty Co. She lives there because she cannot afford to pay higher rent elsewhere, nor can she afford the costs of moving. The building is in terrible shape. The water and sewer system work sporadically, the power surges and wanes, and the rat population is increasing. After many complaints to the landlord, Guzman has sued the landlord, alleging constructive eviction. You are her lawyer.

Believing that the facts about the property's condition are compelling, you decided to move for summary judgment. For each of the following issues on appeal, decide whether the issue is a question of law, a question of fact, a mixed question, or a question of the trial court's exercise of discretion.

1. Assume that the trial court ruled against Guzman. The trial court held that, to prevail on a claim for constructive eviction, the plaintiff must prove that the property was unsuitable for occupancy for the purposes for which the occupancy was intended. The court decided that the apartment had been leased as a residence and that the condition of the apartment was suitable for occupancy as a residence. You have appealed the court's decision that the apartment was suitable for occupancy as a residence.
2. Assume that the trial court ruled against Guzman and in favor of A-1 Realty. The trial court held that, to prevail on a claim for constructive eviction, the plaintiff must prove that the property was unsuitable for occupancy for the purposes for which the occupancy was intended. The court's opinion stated that a dwelling with rats would be unsuitable for occupancy but that this building does not contain rats. You have appealed the court's finding that the building does not contain rats.
3. Assume that the trial court ruled against Guzman and in favor of A-1 Realty. The trial court decided that, to prevail on a claim for constructive eviction, the landlord must have intended to force the tenant to move. You have appealed the trial court's decision that a successful claim for constructive eviction must prove intent to evict.

---

13. Ruggero J. Aldisert, *Opinion Writing* 53 (1990).
14. *Id.*

4. In pretrial discovery, A-1 Realty refused to answer ten of Guzman's interrogatories. Guzman moved for an order requiring A-1 to answer the ten interrogatories. The trial court decided that five of the interrogatories were proper and five were objectionable. The court ordered A-1 to answer the five proper interrogatories and refused to order A-1 to answer the other five. You have appealed the trial court's order.
5. The applicable rule of procedure provides that when a motion to compel discovery is granted in part and denied in part, the court "may" apportion the expenses of bringing and resisting the motion among the parties.[15] In the *Guzman* case, the trial court ordered that each party bear its own expenses on the motion. Both parties appealed the court's order apportioning expenses, each arguing that the court should have required the other party to reimburse that party's expenses. Your research on this question will yield case opinions that tell you the applicable standard of review on this issue, but what is your best guess about what standard these opinions will identify?

15. *See, e.g.*, Fed. R. Civ. P. 37(a)(5)(C).

CHAPTER 18

Writing a Statement of Facts

There is an adage among trial lawyers: If you have to choose between the law and the facts, take the facts. The adage reflects the experience of many lawyers that a judge or jury convinced of the justice of your cause will find a way around unfavorable law. Conversely, if the judge or jury perceives that justice is on the other side, favorable law might not be enough.

The Statement of Facts (sometimes called the "Statement of the Case") is the primary place where your reader's sense of justice about the case will be formed. As a general rule, narrative is more effective at creating attitudes than is intellectual analysis. *The Jungle* persuaded countless readers of the inhumanity of the meat-packing industry. *Cry, the Beloved Country* convinced people around the world of the injustice of apartheid.

Consider your own reactions. Imagine reading a well-reasoned analysis arguing that Hitler should not have imprisoned and killed European Jews. The analysis explains and applies certain abstract moral principles. Imagine your response. Now compare it to your response to *The Diary of Anne Frank* or *Schindler's List* or *Sophie's Choice.* Which would you find more powerful: the rational analysis or the stories of the people who lived the facts? Which would you remember longer? Which would persuade you more?

Stories grab us, persuade us, and motivate us. Your client's story can persuade a judge, just as a movie or book can persuade you. But to be persuasive, your client's story must be told skillfully. Many lawyers believe that the brief that tells the most effective story is the most likely to prevail. But writing this key part of the brief is more challenging than writing a short story or novel. It is harder because you cannot make up desirable facts or imagine away undesirable facts, and because you must use the facts to persuade without *appearing* to do so. You must recite the facts objectively enough to be fair and yet persuasively enough to be compelling. As Professors Ray and Cox put it:

> If briefs to the court were gymnastics events, their statements of facts would be performed on the balance beam. Writing a persuasive statement is accomplished not by following one set of rules, but by balancing your use of various techniques to maintain credibility while achieving the stance needed to highlight favorable facts. It does not require the brute force of emphatic language so much as a subtle blend of strength and control of structure and detail. It involves much thought, consideration of alternatives, and monitoring the interactions of various techniques. Yet an excellent statement of

facts looks natural and effortless, just like a complex routine looks easy when performed by a skilled gymnast.[1]

I. FACT ETHICS AND THE CONVENTIONS OF A STATEMENT OF FACTS

A. Fact Ethics

Remember from Chapter 14 that a lawyer must not misrepresent facts.[2] Misrepresentation includes both stating facts untruthfully and omitting material facts when the result of the omission is to create a false inference. The rule further requires lawyers to disclose material facts when disclosure is necessary to avoid assisting the client in a criminal or fraudulent act.

In virtually every case, you will find some facts you wish were not there. The more material the facts are, the more you wish they would go away. But they exist nonetheless, and leaving them out of your Statement of Facts will not make them disappear, for they will certainly appear in the opposing brief. Omitting them from your brief will only damage your credibility before the judge, causing the judge to wonder how much she can rely on the other facts you assert and on the legal analysis you propose. Few things make a judge angrier than feeling misled by a lawyer.

The omission of important facts also forces the judge to use the opposing party's Statement of Facts, rather than yours, as the court's primary factual reference. These consequences are serious for both lawyer and client. Therefore, both good ethics and good strategy require inclusion of all material facts, favorable or not.[3]

B. The Conventions of a Statement of Facts

Certain formal requirements and generally accepted conventions apply to the Statement of Facts. Refer to the Statement of Facts in the briefs in Appendices C and D for examples of how a Statement of Facts employs the following conventions:

1. When it comes to the client's facts, a trial and appellate brief must refer only to facts that are a part of the court record. For trial-level briefs, this includes the pleadings and information from discovery. For appellate briefs, the record includes all relevant proceedings at the trial court. Facts cannot be added to the record on appeal.[4] Because the point of an appeal is to decide

---

1. Mary Barnard Ray & Barbara J. Cox, *Beyond the Basics: A Text for Advanced Legal Writing* 195 (3d ed. 2013) (footnotes omitted).

2. Model R. Pro. Conduct r. 3.3(a)(1) & (3)(b) (Am. Bar Ass'n 2013).

3. Later sections in this chapter identify ways to neutralize or deemphasize unfavorable facts.

4. There are rare exceptions to this rule, but none that we need to worry about here.

whether the lower court's decision on a certain point was supported by the facts and the law *before that court*, the appellate court may consider only the factual record that was before the lower court at the time of the decision from which the appeal has been taken.

The Statement of Facts must cite the location of the facts in the information gleaned from discovery (for trial briefs) or in the record (for appellate briefs).[5] The citation allows the judge to verify that the fact actually appears in the record and to check that the writer's descriptions of the fact and its context are not misleading. Judges *do* check the facts. For trial briefs, a citation to a court or litigation document includes the name of the document, abbreviated where appropriate, the local or pinpoint cite, and the date of the document, when required.[6]

Complaint	Compl. ¶ 4
Deposition	Liu Dep. 56:5-9
Hearing Transcript	TRO Hr'g Tr. 45:12, April 4, 2022

For an appellate brief, the most common form for these citations to the record is "R. at [page number]." Moreover, briefs filed electronically frequently include direct links to documents, photos, or other parts of the record.[7]

2. A Statement of Facts is a part of a legal document and retains the formal style of the rest of the brief. Although a Statement of Facts tells the story of the legal dispute, its style is not like a short story. You do not want the style of the Statement of Facts to cause the judge to wonder if she is reading fiction. Therefore, present the facts in an objective style, avoiding obvious appeals to emotion, grand description, dramatic literary devices, and other obvious attempts to manipulate the reader. The style should be dignified and courteous, never sarcastic or angry.

3. A Statement of Facts generally does not discuss law. It sets out all of the facts the rule makes important, but it customarily does not explain the rule or make legal arguments. Rule explanation and application come in the Argument section. An exception to this convention is that the last paragraph of the Statement of Facts may segue into the legal argument by stating the legal issue the Argument will address.[8]

4. A Statement of Facts should not contain overt argument, whether legal or factual. The goal of the Statement of Facts is to persuade, of course, but the facts should be presented in an objective style rather than in a style that makes the attempt to persuade too obvious. Also, the Statement of Facts doesn't expressly assert factual conclusions. For instance, for a case involving medical malpractice, the Statement of Facts might relate the patient's vital

5. Fed. R. App. P. 28(a)(6).

6. See Carolyn V. Williams, ALWD, *ALWD Guide to Legal Citation* R. 25 (7th ed. 2021); *The Bluebook: A Uniform System of Citatio*n B17 (Columbia L. Rev. Ass'n et al. eds., 21st ed. 2020). When citing to court documents with a case management system, you also need to include the Electronic Cast Filing number that PACER assigned to it.

7. In similar fashion, attorneys often embed hyperlinks to definitions for complex terminology in an effort to eliminate an extra step that the judge would have to take.

8. See Section IVB.

signs, the medical test results, the patient's medical history, and the nurse's observations, but the writer would not argue that the doctor breached the applicable standard of care.

Note that this restriction applies to conclusions drawn by the *writer*, but the writer *is* permitted to relate the conclusion of someone else. For instance, the writer can report the testimony of an expert witness who asserted that the doctor breached the applicable standard of care. The testimony of the witness is a *fact* that occurred at a deposition or at trial. Reporting the conclusions of others is sometimes called "masked editorializing."[9] Quotations, used in moderation, are appropriate in a Statement of Facts, and often are effective, as Section IV explains.

A Statement of Facts also can point out the *absence* of certain facts from the record. The absence of a fact from the record is itself a fact. Thus it is fair game to include in the Statement of Facts the following:

> At trial, three officers testified that they were stationed at the building's entrance between 5:00 and 6:00 P.M. However, no witness testified to seeing the janitor enter or leave the building.

Pointing out a fact's absence can allow the writer to make a point about the evidence while remaining within the legitimate bounds of fact reporting. One of the most common and most unfortunate errors lawyers make is neglecting to notice important *absent* facts.

II. DEVELOPING A THEORY OF THE CASE AND SELECTING FACTS

Although some facts must be included no matter what theory of the case or theme the lawyer selects, other fact-selection decisions are tied directly to the theme the lawyer will develop. This section explores these two interrelated lawyering tasks.

A. Developing a Theory of the Case

Lawyers use the term "theory of the case" to refer to the theme they will weave throughout the facts, the theme that will explain the facts from their client's perspective. The theme should be sympathetic to the client. It should help the judge understand who the client is, why the client acted in the way he did, feels the way he does, and needs the things he needs. At the least, a good theory of the case assures the judge that a ruling in favor of your client will not be unjust. At best, the theory convinces the judge that justice requires a ruling for your client.

Of course, a theory of the case must be consistent with the key facts. Creating a theory is easy when the facts are generally favorable and much

9. *See* Louis J. Sirico & Nancy Schultz, *Persuasive Writing for Lawyers and the Legal Profession* 81 (2d ed. 2001).

more difficult when they are not. For troublesome facts, you must work even harder to see and *feel* the story from your client's perspective. Look at the sample Questions Presented for Carrolton and for Watson in Chapter 15, Section I. Can you see what Carrolton's theory of the case will be? How about Watson's?

To find an effective theory of the case, try to look at the facts from your client's perspective and look for narrative themes. Professors Brian Foley and Ruth Anne Robbins have pointed out seven common kinds of narrative themes: (1) a person against another person, (2) a person against herself, (3) a person against nature, (4) a person against society, (5) a person against a machine, (6) a person against God, and (7) a person against everybody else.[10] Might one of these stock themes describe your client's struggle? If so, explore possible theories of the case that would communicate that narrative theme.

You might find that several of these themes could describe your client's story. People are complex, after all, and seldom are we motivated by only one need, feeling, or goal. For presentation of the facts in a legal proceeding, however, beware of trying to present several themes at once. The medium of a brief generally is better suited to handle one consistent theme rather than several themes intermixed. The effort to combine several themes might leave the reader with no coherent theory at all; so pick the theme that is most compelling and best supported by the facts.

The best way to find an effective theory of the case is by talking with your client. However, your client might not be good at communicating the heart of his position and might not even be consciously aware of it himself, so you will need also to use your imagination. Try to put yourself in his position. Imagine what it must have been like, what it must be like now. Try to understand who this person is and who the other key characters are. Mull it over in the shower, on your morning run, or on your way to the grocery store. Try to fill in the blanks of the following statement: "This is a story about a (man) (woman) who (is) (was) . . . [describe client] . . . and who is struggling to. . . ." If you can do so without breaching client confidentiality, try telling the story orally. Go to lunch with another lawyer from your firm and tell her your client's story. Telling the story and then talking about it with another person often gives you a fresh perspective. After you have developed a clearer sense of your client and the situation, what helps you understand your client's behavior? What moves you about the story? What might move the judge?

Once you have an idea, try articulating it in a few sentences, like so:

> Carrolton bought Watson's company, the only provider of health care products in the area, and immediately began to take advantage of the company's customers by raising prices, limiting product lines, and allowing long delays for special-order items. Because the customers had nowhere else to go for their health care products, they had no choice but to pay the prices and put up with the limited service. Watson, who had continued to work at the business, had to sit by and watch as Carrolton took advantage of her

---

10. Brian Foley & Ruth Anne Robbins, *Fiction 101: A Primer for Lawyers on How to Use Fiction Writing Techniques to Write Persuasive Fact Sections*, 32 Rutgers L.J. 459, 469 (2001) (citing Josip Novakovich, *Fiction Writer's Workshop* 74–75 (1995)).

> neighbors and longtime customers. Many of them even thought that Watson was intentionally profiting at their expense, as she was still the customer contact person in the office—the only face her old customers saw. This situation was personally distressing to Watson. She also became increasingly convinced that it just wasn't right.

A good theory of the case should be consistent with the facts and with a common-sense notion of fairness. It should explain as many of the unfavorable facts as possible, and it should cast your client in a sympathetic light.

B. Selecting and Citing to Facts

Once you have developed your theory of the case, select the facts you will include in the Statement of Facts. Include these facts:

1. Facts that fit the theory of the case
2. Facts mentioned in the Argument section of the brief
3. All legally determinative or analytically significant facts, whether favorable or unfavorable
4. Significant background facts
5. Emotionally significant facts

Note the location of each fact in the record. In the final draft of a trial-level brief, the citations should appear like so:

> On January 20, 2019, Carrolton filed a complaint in state court alleging that Watson was violating the terms of the covenant-not-to-compete. Compl. ¶ 27. Carrolton's Vice President, Justin Bakker, stated that the Complaint was filed within one month of Carrolton's discovery of Watson's business activity. Bakker Aff. ¶ 14.

III. ORGANIZATION

A. Formats

The most common organizational formats for Statement of Factss are organizing chronologically, by topics, or by theories of the case.

Chronological. For simple facts, a chronological presentation is often best. For instance, in a simple collection matter, the facts will usually set out the events giving rise to the debt, the default, the plaintiff's demand that the defendant cure the default, and the amount owed. These simple facts are best presented chronologically.

Topical. For more complex facts, the topical format might work best. Set out the facts according to relevant topics. For example, in an employment discrimination case, the plaintiff's facts might be organized according to these topics: the nature of the defendant's business, the defendant's usual hiring process, the defendant's usual employee evaluation procedure, the procedures used in selecting employees for layoffs, the hiring process for the plaintiff's position, the terms of the plaintiff's employment, the plaintiff's employee evaluations, the business conditions that necessitated layoffs, the selection of plaintiff for layoff, and the defendant's efforts to assist laid-off employees to find other jobs. The topics should be ordered logically, perhaps chronologically.

Theory of the Case. This format might be effective when the opposing party has some powerful facts that seem to support her position, but you have some key facts or a compelling theory of the case that will explain away those opposing facts. The format first sets out the powerful facts that seem to support your opponent's theory of the case, and then neutralizes them by setting out the facts that explain or justify the opposition's facts.

Organizing by theory of the case is a more daring choice for several reasons. First, the odds are good that the reader will be paying close attention at the beginning of the Statement of Facts. Second, a busy judge might be interrupted and not finish reading the Statement of Facts. Third, the writer who selects this organization is betting a large stake that the supporting facts will defeat the opposing facts. Because the format sets up such a direct and express juxtaposition of these facts, the writer had better be right.

When this organizational format works, however, it is extraordinarily effective. Having heard the worst facts and having decided that they do not necessarily mean what they first seemed to mean, the reader is far less likely to be impressed on reading them in the opposing brief or on hearing them at oral argument or at trial. So be aware that this organizational format is an option, but choose it only after careful evaluation.

B. Subheadings

Regardless of the organizational format you choose, consider using subheadings. For lengthy Statement of Facts, subheadings can help the judge understand the facts. Subheadings are particularly effective for topical or combination formats.

C. Procedural History

No matter which format you choose, you will need to decide where to place the procedural history. Court rules or the instructions for your assignment might make this decision for you.[11] Or the rules or instructions might require a Preliminary Statement or Introduction, in which case the procedural history goes there, in its own section.

If court rules or your instructions have not identified the location for the procedural history, the two most common places for it are at the beginning or the end of the Statement of Facts. At the beginning, it can help to establish

11. *See, e.g.*, Fed. R. App. P. 28(a)(6).

the context for the facts that follow. At the end, it can serve as a natural segue into the Argument section. Either way, consider using subheadings to divide the Statement of the Case into at least two subsections: the "Factual History" and the "Procedural History." Because the procedural history will seldom comprise a compelling part of the theory of the case, using subheadings can put the dull procedural facts out of the way of the theme you hope to deliver with the facts.

IV. TECHNIQUES FOR PERSUASION

As you draft the Statement of Facts, keep in mind the following techniques for writing the facts persuasively. Note that many of these techniques apply equally to the other components of a trial or appellate brief.

A. General Principles

1. Clarity is more important than using sophisticated techniques for persuasion. Judges will not be persuaded by a Statement of Facts they cannot understand. If a technique impedes the clarity of favorable facts, don't use it.

2. Don't use a technique that the reader will notice. An effective technique must be invisible or nearly so. Once a reader recognizes a technique, it has lost its power because the reader's attention is on the technique and not the fact. For instance, assume that you have used the technique of repetition to emphasize a favorable fact. You hoped that it would encourage the reader to realize the significance of the fact, to let it sink in. If, instead, your reader's Commentator[12] observes, "Ah, look, the writer is repeating this fact to try to get me to notice it," the reader will be thinking about the technique and the writer's goals rather than the fact. Your Statement of Facts would have been more persuasive if you had not used the technique at all.

3. Don't overuse any technique. Overuse creates monotony, decreases the technique's power, and increases the chances that the reader will notice the technique rather than the facts.

4. Any technique for emphasizing one fact or group of facts deemphasizes the remaining facts. To the extent you try to use techniques of emphasis for nearly all of the facts, your strategy will fail. Pick the few facts you want most to emphasize and allow the others to serve as the background.

5. Some of the techniques described below are inconsistent with each other. The inconsistency doesn't mean that one is right and the other wrong, but only that each has its advantages and disadvantages. The writer's job is to select the technique that will work best for the needs of a particular Statement of Facts.

---

12. See Chapter 6, Section IID.

B. Large-Scale Organization

The Beginning

6. Unless you know differently, assume that the judge is not already familiar with the case. The beginning of the Statement of Facts should establish the context for the facts that follow. Otherwise, the judge might find herself reading a chronological account of a series of events without knowing why these events are important. Context can be provided by a procedural history or by a short summary of what the case is about, written to be consistent with your theory of the case. Here is an example written on behalf of Carrolton:

> This is an action to enforce the terms of a covenant-not-to-compete. As part of the sale of her business to Carrolton Company, the Defendant promised that for the three years immediately following the sale she would not compete with Carrolton in the three counties closest to Carrolton's headquarters. Eighteen months after the sale was completed, the Defendant opened a competing business just one mile from Carrolton's office. She has been competing directly with Carrolton in the three prohibited counties ever since. This action seeks to enjoin her continued breach of the covenant-not-to-compete.

7. The reader's attention level is high in the first few paragraphs. When you can find a way to do so logically, capitalize on this increased attention level by selecting an organization that allows you to place in the first few paragraphs the material you want to emphasize. This strategy can be consistent with a summary of the case drafted from your client's perspective, like the one above.

8. Aim for a beginning that will spark the reader's interest. Journalists call this "the lead." The conventions of a legal document do not allow for some of the more dramatic forms of grabbing attention, but you do want the reader to be drawn into the story and want to read on. For example, a prosecutor's brief might begin with the facts of the crime rather than with the procedural history of the appeal.

The Middle

9. Here is the place for the facts you want to deemphasize. Normally, a reader's attention level is at its lowest about three-fourths of the way through the section.[13]

The End

10. Readers might pay more attention to the material at the beginning, but they remember longest the material at the end. Readers tend to take a mental break to let the story sink in, and when they do, the last sentence lingers in their minds. Try to select an organization that allows you to place at the end material you most want the reader to remember.

---

13. Ray & Cox, *supra* note 1, 200 (2d ed. 2013).

11. The last paragraph should have the "feel" of a concluding paragraph. One way to accomplish this is to close with a transition into the legal argument to follow by identifying the legal positions staked out by the parties. Be careful not to include overt legal argument. Limit yourself to identifying the positions each side will take on the legal dispute. Avoid stating the opposing position any more favorably than you have to. Keeping in mind that the last sentence lingers in the reader's mind, end with your legal position rather than your opponent's. Here is an example of such a transition:

> The bank has admitted that it did not disclose the effective interest rate to the Turners. However, it claims that disclosure was not required, arguing that the transaction was not a "consumer loan" under the Consumer Protection Act. This brief will show that the transaction was, indeed, a "consumer loan" and that the bank's failure to disclose to the Turners the effective interest rate was a violation of the Act.

C. Paragraph Organization

12. A reader devotes more attention to the beginning and the end of a paragraph than to the middle. Put facts you want to emphasize in the first sentence or in the last clause or phrase of the last sentence. Deemphasize unfavorable facts by placing them in the middle.

13. Be conscious of paragraph length. In sections where you want to emphasize the facts, keep paragraphs relatively short. Where you want to deemphasize facts, let the paragraphs get longer, and put the facts you particularly want to deemphasize deep in the paragraph.

D. Techniques with Sentences

14. As a general rule, reduce clutter by using the techniques in Chapter 20 to eliminate surplus verbiage. Clutter reduces clarity, irritates the reader, and deemphasizes the important facts. Occasionally, you can allow just a bit of clutter to surround an unfavorable fact. The clutter will reduce emphasis by lengthening the sentence and by making it less striking. Use this technique sparingly.

15. Use active verbs for emphasis and passive verbs for deemphasis or to avoid focus on the identity of the person who took the action.

a. *To encourage focus on the person taking the action:*

> Shaffer kicked in the front door of the house and attacked his estranged wife, breaking her forearm.
>
> ***[Here the prosecutor wants all attention on Shaffer as he takes these violent actions.]***

b. *To avoid focus on the person taking the action:*

> Acme Health Equipment was formed and began operation on April 22, 2021.
>
> ***[Here the writer seeks to deflect attention away from the person who formed and ran Acme—Watson.]***

c. *To focus on a person other than the one taking the action:*

In the early morning of January 1, 2022, after attending several New Year's Eve parties, the Defendant was stopped for a routine sobriety test.

[Here the writer is not so much trying to keep attention away from the police officer who stopped the defendant as to keep the focus on the defendant who was stopped.]

16. Place favorable facts in main clauses and unfavorable facts in dependent clauses. Consider this sentence in a brief for Watson:

Although Acme's business does compete with Carrolton [dependent clause], the competition only extends to three small product lines and could only impact, at the most, four percent of Carrolton's profits [main clause].

17. If an unfavorable fact *must* go in the first or last sentence of a paragraph, place the dependent clause carrying the unfavorable fact toward the interior of the paragraph. Thus, for the first sentence of the paragraph, a dependent clause carrying an unfavorable fact should go at the end of the sentence. Which party's brief would contain this sentence?

Acme competes directly with Carrolton in the three prohibited counties [main clause], although the competition presently extends only to three product lines [dependent clause] . . . [paragraph continues by setting out the facts of the competition].

For the last sentence of the paragraph, try putting the dependent clause at the beginning:

[The paragraph has set out the facts establishing the competition.] Thus, while the competition extends only to three product lines [dependent clause], Acme directly and openly competes presently with Carrolton in the three prohibited counties [main clause].

18. Occasionally, when you want the reader to slow down and take in the significance of the material in all parts of the sentence, place a phrase or dependent clause in the middle of the sentence, interrupting the reader's usual path from the subject directly to the verb.

Watson, who admits that she is intentionally violating the terms of her covenant, asks this Court to use its equitable powers to relieve her of the consequences of her own actions.

Use this technique sparingly because it makes sentences less readable.

19. Use shorter sentences for material you want to emphasize and longer sentences for material you want to deemphasize.

Longer Sentences for Less Emphasis

On July 1, while Mr. and Mrs. Emilio and their daughter Ashley were driving south on Interstate 75 toward Valdosta, a car swerved across the median and hit the Emilio car. Mr. and Mrs. Emilio survived, although they were seriously injured. Their daughter, who had been riding in the back seat, died as a result of the injuries she sustained in the accident.

Shorter Sentences for Greater Emphasis

On July 1, Mr. and Mrs. Emilio were driving south on Interstate 75 toward Valdosta. Their daughter Ashley was riding in the back seat. A car swerved across the median and hit the Emilio car. Mr. and Mrs. Emilio survived, though seriously injured. Ashley, however, died.

E. Other Small-Scale Techniques

20. Compress the space you devote to unfavorable facts, and expand the space you devote to favorable facts. The more material you provide about the favorable facts, the more emphasis they garner.

21. Use detail to describe the material you want to emphasize. Conversely, limit the detail of your discussion of the unfavorable facts, although of course you cannot omit any significant facts.

22. Use *visual* facts and images to describe favorable facts; avoid them for unfavorable facts. Visual images carry particular power for placing the reader, mentally, at the scene.

> On July 1, Mr. and Mrs. Emilio were driving south on Interstate 75 toward Valdosta. Their daughter Ashley was riding in the back seat. A car swerved across the median and crashed into the Emilios. The front of the other car hit the Emilio car at the left rear door, precisely where Ashley was sitting, strapped in by her seat belt.
>
> The force of the impact carried the other car's engine well into the passenger cabin of the Emilio car. It ripped Ashley from her seat belt, pinned her against the opposite door, and crushed her thoracic cavity.
>
> Mr. and Mrs. Emilio survived, though seriously injured. Ashley, however, died at the scene.

23. Short quotations (a sentence or two) or snippet quotations (just a word or a phrase) can be powerful facts. If the words of the witness or document are particularly helpful, quote them.

> Shaffer left the bar, declaring, "I'm going to go talk to my wife, and she'll need a doctor before I'm through."

Avoid overquoting, however. Overquoting will result in a disjointed story and will cause the most effective quotes to fade into the pack with the rest of the quotes.

24. When you can repeat key facts *unobtrusively*, the repetition serves to emphasize those facts or concepts. For instance, the first sentence of the paragraph might summarize the facts, and the remaining sentences could set out the facts in more detail. Or the beginning of a sentence might refer to the facts of the prior sentence as a transition.

> Marie Claxton, the expert witness who testified on behalf of Pyle, concluded that a reasonable and prudent lawyer would have checked the deed for easements. Claxton explained that deeds often contain restrictions that significantly affect the use of the property. She testified that any prudent lawyer would know that such restrictions are common. According to Claxton, Gavin's failure to check the deed fell below the standard of professional skill and diligence of a reasonable and prudent lawyer.

Do not just repeat particular facts, seemingly for no reason, however. It will bore and irritate your reader. Remember that the Argument section gives you a natural opportunity to repeat the key facts.

25. Place unfavorable facts in a favorable or mitigating context. You can juxtapose the unfavorable fact with favorable facts or you can place the unfavorable fact in a context that negates some of the unfavorable inferences the fact might otherwise invite.

Juxtaposing an Unfavorable Fact with Favorable Facts

> Although Acme's business does compete with Carrolton, the competition only extends to three small product lines and could only impact, at the most, four percent of Carrolton's profits.

Placing the Unfavorable Fact in a More Favorable Context

> While the demonstrations against the abortion clinic are disruptive to the other tenants, the landlords cannot prevent the demonstrations; nor can they force the clinic to move until the clinic's lease term expires.

26. Humanize your client. The most important way to do this is by telling the story from the client's perspective, as your theory of the case will already accomplish. Include, where possible, a description of the client's feelings, responses, and motivations. It is also helpful to refer to your client by name and use titles that communicate respect, like "Mr.," "Ms.," "Mx.," "Dr.," or "Officer."

It is especially important to humanize corporate clients. Remember that every story involving a corporation is really a story about people. Identify the people who took the actions, and humanize those people. Portray them in a sympathetic light by setting out the context for their actions.

27. Generally, do not humanize opposing parties. Where there is no need to use the names of opposing individuals, consider using generic descriptions instead ("the officer," "the insurance agent," "the electrician"). Generic descriptions can be especially helpful where the description has unsympathetic connotations, such as "the finance company," "the insurance company," or "the corporation." However, humanize when your theory of the case depends on showing the judge not only the sympathetic facts about your client, but also the outrageously bad behavior of one or more of the opposing parties. In such a case, you might need to humanize the opposing party so you can show the outrageousness of his or her behavior.

28. Use graphic words, especially verbs, for facts you want to emphasize.

> The van *crashed into* [instead of "hit"] the taxi, and the force of the impact *shattered* [instead of "broke"] the driver's spine.

29. Refrain from name-calling. Name-calling tells your reader that you do not have good facts, so you are compelled to resort to derogatory characterizations.

30. Where possible, delete adverbs in favor of additional facts and more vivid verbs. Vivid verbs, alone, are much more powerful than a ho-hum verb with an adverb. Avoid such artificial intensifiers as "very" or "extremely."

31. Pay careful attention to common connotations of words. Choose words with helpful connotations and avoid those with unhelpful connotations.

A Word with Potentially Troubling Connotations

> Mr. and Mrs. McMann were *anxiously* awaiting the birth of their first child. ["Anxiously" carries the connotation of worry. Use it if the connotation helps your theory, but avoid it if the connotation either impedes the theory or might distract the reader into wondering what they were worried about.]

An Option with a Better Connotation

> Mr. and Mrs. McMann were *anticipating* the birth of their first child.

32. Finally, put the draft down for a few hours and then read it afresh. Try not to look for the techniques you used, but rather read openly, as you hope your reader will. Notice your reactions and fix anything that troubles you.

EXERCISE 18-1
Critiquing a Statement of Facts

Here are two Statement of Factss for the Watson covenant-not-to-compete issue. Each Statement of Facts has strengths. Neither is perfect. Evaluate each, identifying what works well and what could be improved. One formulation of the governing rule of law is:

> A covenant-not-to-compete is enforceable if all of the following elements are reasonable:
>
> A. the kind of activity restrained;
> B. the geographic area of the restraint; and
> C. the time period of the restraint.

Another possible formulation of the rule is:

> To be enforceable, a covenant-not-to-compete must be reasonable. Factors for deciding reasonableness are:
>
> A. the needs of the restraining party;
> B. the needs of the public;
> C. the needs of the restrained party; and
> D. any other relevant circumstances.

Which rule formulation does the drafter of each Statement of Facts seem to have in mind?

Statement of Facts on Behalf of Carrolton

STATEMENT OF FACTS

This is an action to enforce the terms of a covenant-not-to-compete. On Dec. 1, 2015, the Defendant sold Carrolton Company to Richard Meyers, Andrea McPhane, and James Rey ("Purchasers") for $420,000. (Compl. ¶ 10.) The sale included not only Carrolton's inventory and accounts receivable, but also the company's good will in the community. (Compl. ¶ 11.) As part of the contract of sale, the Defendant promised that she would not compete with Carrolton for the three years immediately following the sale. (Compl. ¶ 13.) The covenant covers only Quincy, Herring, and Gawin Counties, the three counties closest to Carrolton's office. (Compl. ¶ 13.)

The covenant-not-to-compete was an integral part of the Defendant's sale of Carrolton to the Purchasers. (McPhane Aff. ¶ 8.) Carrolton retails in-home health care products in the Kinston, Georgia area. (Compl. ¶ 13.) Through her ownership of Carrolton, the Defendant had been engaged in the retail sales of health care products in the Kinston area for fifteen years. (McPhane Aff. ¶ 8.) On behalf of Carrolton, she had made and maintained the sales contacts necessary to be a successful retailer of those products. (McPhane Aff. ¶ 9.) Her contacts and ongoing relationships with physicians and customers were part of the good will for which the Purchasers paid. (McPhane Aff. ¶ 10.) Thus, these contacts and relationships were a critical part of the sale of the business. (Compl. ¶ 14.) The covenant prohibits the Defendant from making sales contacts for in-home health care products in the three counties that comprise the heart of Carrolton's marketing area. (Compl. ¶ 15.)

After the Defendant sold Carrolton to the Purchasers, the Defendant remained with the company, employed as Carrolton's General Manager. She held that position of trust for fourteen months after the sale. (Compl. ¶ 16.) On February 21, 2017, the Defendant left her position as Carrolton's General Manager and immediately opened a competing business one mile from Carrolton's office. (Compl. ¶ 17.) Since that date, the Defendant has been making sales contacts for health care products in the three prohibited counties, in direct competition with Carrolton. (Compl. ¶ 18.) The Purchasers have filed this action seeking to enjoin the Defendant's continued breach of the covenant not to compete.

Statement of Facts on Behalf of Watson

STATEMENT OF FACTS

In 2000, Sharon Watson founded Carrolton Company, a retailer of in-home health care equipment in Kinston, Georgia. (Watson Aff. ¶ 3.) Before Carrolton opened, residents of Kinston and the surrounding area had to travel seventy-five miles to the nearest retailer of health care equipment. (Williams Aff. ¶ 2.) The lack of a nearby health care equipment retailer was particularly problematic for the Kinston community because people needing in-home health care equipment are among those least able to make a seventy-five-mile trip to purchase that equipment. (Williams Aff. ¶ 3-6.) With Carrolton's opening, area residents had local access to the health care equipment they needed. (Williams Aff. ¶ 8.)

As the only retailer of in-home health care equipment in the area, Carrolton did a large volume of business. (Watson Aff. ¶ 7.) Ms. Watson believed that Carrolton's virtual monopoly brought with it an obligation not to take advantage of her customers. (Watson Aff. ¶ 9.) Thus, she used a markup of only thirty-five percent to ensure that her customers paid fair prices. (Watson Aff. ¶ 10.) She kept the business responsive to customer needs, making diligent efforts to fill special orders, and maintaining close communication with local physicians. (Williams Aff. ¶ 8; Watson Aff. ¶ 11.) She made certain that Carrolton was a concerned and responsible commercial citizen of the community. (Tharpe Aff. ¶ 6; William Aff. ¶ 9.)

In early 2015, a group of Atlanta investors approached Ms. Watson about the possibility of buying Carrolton. (Compl. ¶ 5.) Over the next few months, the parties discussed the terms of a possible sale. (Compl. ¶ 7.) During these conversations, Ms. Watson expressed concern about how the business, still a virtual monopoly, would be run. (Watson Aff. ¶ 12.)

In response to these concerns, the investors suggested that Ms. Watson remain with the company as General Manager and continue to manage the operation. (Watson Aff. ¶ 14.) The investors explained that they would not want Carrolton's fundamental operating policies to change, and Ms. Watson's continued management would be a way to continue the company's successful marketing approach. (Watson Aff. ¶ 15.) They explained that Ms. Watson's approach was so important to them that they would like the transaction to include the covenant that Ms. Watson would not leave Carrolton to compete in the local market for at least three years. (Watson Aff. ¶ 15.) Ms. Watson agreed, and on Dec. 1, 2015, after fifteen years of building the business, Ms. Watson sold Carrolton to its present owners. (Compl. ¶ 10.)

The terms of the sale placed Ms. Watson in the position of General Manager. (Compl. ¶ 12.) While the contract did not expressly state the reason for the terms, the parties had always discussed Ms. Watson's continued service and noncompetition covenant as a method to maintain continuity of management philosophy. (Watson Aff. ¶ 14.) The covenant prohibited Ms. Watson from competing with Carrolton's new owners in the three counties that make up Carrolton's virtual monopoly. (Compl. ¶ 11.)

Within a month after the sale, Carrolton's new owners began implementing management changes. (Williams Aff. ¶ 11; Watson Aff. ¶ 16; Tharpe Aff. ¶ 8.) They issued new pricing policies, raising the company's markup on its product lines. (Watson Aff. ¶ 16.) They ordered Ms. Watson to lay off one of Carrolton's only two other employees, and they eliminated most special orders. (Watson Aff. ¶ 17.) Eliminating these special orders effectively blocked the access of area customers to any health care products not a part of Carrolton's regular inventory. (Tharpe Aff. ¶ 9.)

In response to Ms. Watson's protests, the owners argued that these new policies maximized efficiency and company profits. (Watson Aff. ¶ 19.) They maintained that customer complaints were not important since without Carrolton, customers would have no local access to health care equipment at all. (Watson Aff. ¶ 20.)

On Feb. 21, 2017, after repeated attempts to persuade Carrolton's new owners to rescind their new policies, Ms. Watson left her position at Carrolton. (Watson Aff. ¶ 22.) Believing that Carrolton's owners had breached their assurances that Carrolton would continue being responsive to its customer's needs, Ms. Watson formed Acme Health Care. (Watson Aff. ¶ 22.) Ms. Watson incurred $150,000 in personal debt to open Acme, mortgaging her home to secure the loan. (Watson Aff. ¶ 23.) In the first two years of business Acme will do well to break even. During that time, Ms. Watson will have to make loan payments from her personal savings. (Watson Aff. ¶ 24.)

Although Ms. Watson hopes that one day Acme will represent a viable customer alternative to Carrolton (Watson Aff. ¶ 27), presently Acme competes with Carrolton in only three product lines: respiratory equipment, diabetic monitoring equipment, and wheelchairs. (Watson Aff. ¶ 25.) Even in these lines, Acme's business is just beginning. Presently, Acme carries only the products of the two leading manufacturers in these product lines. (Watson Aff. ¶ 26.) During the next nineteen months (the remaining term of the covenant-not-to-compete), Acme cannot expect to attract more than thirty percent of Carrolton's business in these product lines. Acme will have no impact on Carrolton's virtual monopoly over the twenty-two other product lines Carrolton sells. (Watson Aff. ¶ 29.)

Even if Acme meets with phenomenal success during the next nineteen months, Carrolton will still make healthy profits. (Watson Aff. ¶ 32.) During the remaining covenant term, Acme poses no realistic threat to Carrolton's business. (Watson Aff. ¶ 34.) Acme's potential threat to Carrolton is the potential end to Carrolton's virtual monopoly over the in-home health care market in the Kinston area. (Watson Aff. ¶ 35; Williams Aff. ¶ 17; Tharpe Aff. ¶ 15.) That threat to Carrolton's market position would arise, if at all, long after the covenant has expired. (Watson Aff. ¶ 36.)

Checklist for Statement of Facts

Large-Scale Organization

- Does the organization present the facts clearly? Is it easy to follow?
- Does the organizational format allow you to put most of the unfavorable facts in the middle and put some of the favorable facts at the beginning and some at the end?[14]
- Does the material at the beginning catch the reader's interest?
- If your reader needs context, does the material at the beginning provide it?
- Does the draft communicate your theory of the case?
- Does the draft include all significant facts and all facts mentioned in your Argument?
- Does the draft include enough context to allow the reader to understand the dispute and your theory of the case, but no more?
- Does the draft place the procedural history at an appropriate location?
- Does the last paragraph have the "feel" of an ending?
- Does the draft end with a sentence that you want the reader to remember?

Paragraph Organization

- Are your best facts on the outside ends of the paragraph, while your least favorable facts are in the middle?
- Does the last phrase or clause of the paragraph contain favorable information?
- Are the paragraphs with facts you want to emphasize relatively short?
- Are those with facts you want to neutralize longer?

Techniques with Sentences

- Are the sentences (except one or two carrying unfavorable facts) free of clutter?
- Do the passive-voiced verbs serve a purpose? Are there any actions you would like to deemphasize by changing to passive?

---

14. The "theory of the case" format is an intentional exception to this principle.

- Where appropriate, are unfavorable facts in dependent clauses juxtaposed with more favorable facts or explanatory context?
- Do the shorter sentences carry favorable facts? Where appropriate, are the unfavorable facts in longer sentences?
- Using brackets in the margins of the draft, identify the text that deals with favorable topics and the text that deals with unfavorable topics. How does the total allocation of space to each compare?
- Notice where you have used detail and visual images. Notice where you have not.
- Do the quotations really help?
- If you have used the technique of repetition, is it too obvious?
- How have you referred to your client? To the opposing parties?
- At spots where you are presenting favorable material, are there any verbs you can switch for more powerful or graphic synonyms?

PART SIX

Style and Formalities

CHAPTER 19

Citations and Quotations

After you have a completed draft, it's time to edit cites and quotes.

I. CITATION IN LEGAL WRITING

In legal writing, as in other writing, you must cite to the sources for both ideas and quoted words. Citing to authority has twin purposes:

- to show your reader the authority that supports what *you* say, and
- to identify the ideas and words that *someone else* said.

In legal writing, it's essential to show support for your points. Your cites should prove that the law is what you say it is and means what you say it means.

A cite is also your attribution to another writer, recognizing that the ideas (and the words, if you are quoting) came from that writer. Remember the discussion of plagiarism in the Introduction to this book. Because a reader will assume that you are the source for uncited material, a cite is your way of disclaiming credit for the words and ideas you didn't create. So, cite when you quote and when you paraphrase someone else's point.

Use Citations

1. When you state a legal principle.
   Example: Intent is a required element of a plaintiff's claim. **Citation.**
2. When you refer to or describe the content of an authority.
   Example: In an earlier opinion, the court had held that intent was irrelevant. **Citation.**
3. When you quote.
   Example: The court reasoned that "the state of mind of the defendant had no impact on the extent of damages suffered." **Citation.**

EXERCISE 19-1
Recognizing Ideas That Need Citations

Read the following passage.[1] Identify the statements for which a citation is either necessary or desirable. Be prepared to explain your answers.

The lawyer has a fiduciary relationship with his or her client. The fiduciary aspect of the relationship is said to arise after the formation of the attorney-client relationship, and it applies to a fee agreement reached after the attorney-client relationship has been entered.

There are at least three reasons for imposing fiduciary obligations on a lawyer. First, once the relationship is established, the client will likely have begun to depend on the attorney's integrity, fairness, and judgment. Second, the attorney might have acquired information about the client that gives the attorney an unfair advantage in negotiations between them. Finally, the client will generally not be in a position where he or she is free to change attorneys, but will rather be economically or personally dependent on the attorney's continued representation.

Accordingly, an attorney breaches his fiduciary duty when he abuses his client's trust. For example, in *Benson v. State Bar*, the attorney borrowed money from a current client. He "was heavily in debt, and insolvent, at the time he approached [the client] for these loans." In return for the loans, he gave the client unsecured promissory notes. In disbarring the lawyer, the court described the client's trust in the lawyer's judgment and wrote:

> The gravamen of the charge is abuse of that trust, and regardless of petitioner's contention that he never specifically recommended the unsecured loans to [the client], it is undisputed that in soliciting them he failed to reveal the extent of his preexisting indebtedness and financial distress.

In addition, in *People v. Smith*, James Smith, an attorney, was under investigation for drug use. He offered to cooperate with the Colorado police as an undercover informant. He secretly recorded a telephone conversation with a former client in which he asked the former client to sell him cocaine. He then met with the former client wearing a body microphone. The recorded conversations were ultimately used to convict the former client of three felony charges. The Colorado Supreme Court held that although Smith

> no longer represented the [former client], the conduct in all probability would not have occurred had [Smith] not relied upon the trust and confidence placed in him by the [former client] as a result of the recently completed attorney-client relationship between the two. The undisclosed use of a recording device necessarily involves elements of deception and trickery which do not comport with the high standards of candor and fairness to which all attorneys are bound.

For these and other offenses, Smith was suspended from the practice of law.

---

1. Modified from Stephen Gillers, *Regulation of Lawyers: Problems of Law and Ethics* 61–62 (4th ed. 1995).

II. CITATION FORM

A citation is your promise to your reader that the cited material says what you say it says. It also helps your reader find the source and gives some basic information about precedential weight. Several commercially published citation authorities exist, and some courts have adopted their own citation rules. The two most often used citation guides are the *ALWD* (pronounced "ALL-wid") *Guide to Legal Citation*[2] ("*ALWD Guide*") and *The Bluebook: A Uniform System of Citation* ("*Bluebook*").[3] These citation guides focus on different audiences. The focus of the *ALWD Guide* is a practicing attorney citing in documents such as office memos and persuasive briefs to the court. Conversely, the focus of the *Bluebook* is authors citing in scholarly works such as law review articles. That being said, practitioners and scholars can use both citation guides as they both provide guidance for both audiences and the citations produced are identical, reflecting the national preference.

Learning to use one of the citation systems is unavoidable. As much as you might like to, you can't just copy the citations you find in the authorities. Many of those citations don't conform to current citation requirements. Moreover, online programs that purport to correct all citations are frequently inaccurate. This chapter covers both the *ALWD Guide* and the *Bluebook*. We'll begin by becoming familiar with the overall layout of each book.

A. Using the *ALWD Guide*

As mentioned above, while the *ALWD Guide* is geared toward writing in practice, it also provides guidance for scholarly writing. Where needed, the *ALWD Guide* identifies the necessary scholarly modifications to the citation format.

1. Sections of the *ALWD Guide*

The *ALWD Guide* contains the following sections and features:

1. *Introductory material and inside covers.* The *ALWD Guide* begins with a short section expressly designed to introduce you to the purposes and uses of citation and how to use the book. This section explains the book's organization and helps you find quick answers to common questions. A particularly helpful feature of this section is the discussion of how word processing software can affect citation formats. The section gives suggestions for handling spacing, default settings, and quick-correct features, all of which can alter your citations in ways you didn't expect or intend. Reading these six pages will help you understand how to use the *ALWD Guide* and how to manage your word processor.

---

2. Carolyn V. Williams, ALWD, *ALWD Guide to Legal Citation* (7th ed. 2021) [hereinafter *ALWD Guide*].

3. *The Bluebook: A Uniform System of Citation* (Columbia L. Rev. Ass'n et al. eds., 21st ed. 2020) [hereinafter *Bluebook*].

2. *Part 1—Citation Basics:* This section gives you key general information, such as when to italicize or underline; how to abbreviate; what to capitalize; how to decide spacing; when to represent numbers as numerals or words; how to indicate page numbers, sections, and paragraphs; and when to use full and short citation formats. Familiarize yourself with the foundational points in this section before you look up citation rules in later sections.
3. *Part 2—Citing Specific Sources.* The citation rules specific to all printed legal authorities are found in Part 2. The most commonly used are cases (Rule 12), statutes (Rule 14), books (Rule 20), and periodicals (Rule 21). One of the best features of the *ALWD Guide* is the Fast Formats at the beginning of each rule covering how to cite to a source. The Fast Format gives you, on a single page, examples of how to cite to that type of authority in the most common circumstances.
4. *Part 3—Online Sources.* This part tells you how to cite to electronic legal sources such as an Internet site, e-mail, and cases from a commercial database like Westlaw and Lexis.
5. *Part 4—Incorporating Citations into Documents.* You'll find more basic information here about how to use citations, covering such common questions as how many and which citations to include, where to put them, in what order, how to use signals, and how to use explanatory parentheticals.
6. *Part 5—Quotations.* Pesky questions about handling quotations are answered here. This section covers use of quotations as they appear in the original source, alteration of quotations, and trimming quotations down to size.
7. *Part 6—Appendices.* The appendices contain a wealth of important information. Appendix 1 tells you exactly how to cite all the primary authorities (like statutes and cases) from your particular jurisdiction. Appendix 2 gives you all the local court citation rules from each jurisdiction. Appendices 3 through 5 show you how to abbreviate almost all the words you'll need to abbreviate as you cite. Appendix 5, which contains the abbreviations for the titles of periodicals and words commonly used in titles of looseleaf services, is fully online. Appendix 5 provides instructions on how to access the online Appendix. Subsequently, Appendices 6 and 7 provide guidance on citing Federal Taxation Materials and Federal Administrative Agency materials. Finally, Appendix 8, new in the seventh edition, sets forth cross-references to the rules in the *Bluebook* for law review members to use if a reference to the *Bluebook* rule is required.

2. How to Locate the Rules You Need

Finding the rules you need in the *ALWD Guide* isn't hard. Here are the best strategies for locating rules and finding out how to cite a certain kind of source:

Ways to Find the Rules You Need

1. For the quickest way to check basic form, *use the "Fast Formats" Locator* on the inside front cover. This handy list will take you immediately to the Fast Formats

for the source you're citing. For example, if you want to see how to cite to a case, the Locator will refer you to the Fast Format found at the beginning of Rule 12, the rule covering cases. There, on a single page, you'll find examples of how to use all the major varieties of case cites. Then, if you need more, you're already at the beginning of the section covering cases, so you can simply go further into the following pages to find a more specific answer.

2. If you can't find what you need by using a Fast Format, use the index, which is excellent.
3. To find larger sections of the *ALWD Guide*, such as the whole section covering electronic sources, use the Table of Contents.

B. Using the *Bluebook*

The *Bluebook* will intimidate you if you let it. The best way to approach the *Bluebook* is to cut it down to size mentally by identifying the primary parts you'll use. Notice the larger sections of the *Bluebook* as they are set out in the Table of Contents.

1. Sections of the *Bluebook*

1. *Introduction and inside covers*. The *Bluebook* begins with an Introduction expressly designed for new users. The Introduction describes the parts of the *Bluebook*. Also, notice the reference guides on the inside front and back covers. The front cover provides a Quick Reference Guide for law review footnotes and the back cover provides one for court documents and legal memoranda.
2. *The* Bluepages *("B")*. This section is necessary because the rest of the *Bluebook* focuses on citation form for law review publishing. The Bluepages section adapts the rules in the rest of the *Bluebook* to practitioner writing—the kind you'll be doing in your legal writing class and in practice. Here, you will find references to related rules and tables contained in the other parts of the *Bluebook*. This section also includes a table for suggested abbreviations to use in court documents and a table identifying jurisdiction-specific citation rules.
3. *Rules ("R")*. The rules themselves come next in the *white pages*. (If you stand the *Bluebook* up you will see the Bluepages at the beginning followed by the Rules in the white pages.) Rules 1–9 are general rules that apply broadly to many situations. These rules cover how to structure and use citations; what typeface to use; how to quote; how to use abbreviations, numerals, and symbols; and what to capitalize. They are followed by rules dealing with citing kinds of sources. You'll use Rules 10, 12, 15, and 16 (cases, statutes, books, and periodicals) most often.
4. *Tables*. After the rules comes a second set of tables. These are reference sources for basic information about court and reporter systems and statutory compilations for each jurisdiction as well as standard abbreviations for courts, case names, publications, and other commonly used terms.

2. How to Find the Rules You Need

Here are the best strategies for finding information in the rules:

Ways to Find the Rules You Need

1. Use the *Bluebook*'s index, which is quite good.
2. Use the Table of Contents.
3. When reading a rule, look at the listed cross-references.
4. Use the Quick Reference [for] Court Documents and Legal Memoranda found on the last page and the *back* inside cover. (The one on the front inside cover and first page is for law review citations.)

C. Several Key Concepts

Before you dive into either citation guide, you'll want to know these two general concepts:

Typeface Requirements. The *ALWD Guide* follows the commonly accepted approach for practitioner writing, so selecting the correct typeface is easy. Most material in a citation is presented in ordinary type, italics, or underlined type. The *ALWD Guide* rule covering a certain kind of source will tell you (and show you) which information, if any, to either italicize or underline.

The *Bluebook*'s rules (the white pages) are designed primarily for law review writing, not practitioner writing. For law review writing, the *Bluebook* requires, on different occasions, large and small capitals, regular typeface, and italics. The examples and explanations in the rules section (the white pages) use those typeface distinctions. Practitioner writing is simpler, using only regular type such as courier and *either* italics or underscoring. Simply type everything else in regular typeface, and don't worry about the more complicated distinctions in the rules section of the *Bluebook*.

Notice, though, that for practitioner writing, both the *ALWD Guide* and the *Bluebook* use the word "italics" to include either slanted type or underscoring.[4] You can use either, but don't use both in the same document.

Citing in Text Versus Citing in a Footnote. Law review articles are notorious for footnotes, and the rules section of the *Bluebook* provides special requirements for citations in law review footnotes. But footnotes should be the exception rather than the rule for practitioner writing. When practitioners do use a footnote, they usually use the same citation principles they have been using in the text.

4. *ALWD Guide*, *supra*, R. 1.3(a); *Bluebook*, *supra*, B2.

D. Introduction to Citation Form

Although the applicable rules are more detailed, an overview will help you put the more detailed rules into context. Here are the basic components of a citation to a case, a statute, a book, and a law review article:

BASIC COMPONENTS OF A CITATION TO A CASE[5]

1. Case name
2. Case's location:
   a. Volume
   b. Abbreviation for name of reporter
   c. Page where the case begins
   d. Page where the cited material appears ("pinpoint" or "local" cite)
3. Court and date parenthetical
   a. Court abbreviation (sometimes)
   b. Year

State Court Example

Watzek v. Walker, 485 P.2d 3, 6 (Ariz. Ct. App. 1971)

1 2a 2b 2c 2d 3a 3b

Federal Court Example

1 2a 2b 2c 2d 3a 3b

Staron v. McDonalds Corp., 51 F.3d 353, 357 (2d Cir. 1995)

Pursuant to *Bluebook* B6, practitioners now have the option to close up the abbreviations in reporter names to address word limit constraints in court documents. Nevertheless, maintaining the spacing is recommended, as this was a new rule beginning in 2020.

BASIC COMPONENTS OF A CITATION TO A FEDERAL STATUTE[6]

1. Official name of statute, if there is one
2. Title number
3. Abbreviation for name of code
4. Section number
5. Publisher if citing unofficial code
6. Year the code was published *or*, if citing to a statute in a commercial database, "database [through] currency information," *if desired.*

5. *ALWD Guide*, *supra* note 2, at R. 1.3(a); *Bluebook*, *supra* note 3, at B2.
6. *ALWD Guide*, *supra* note 2, at R. 14.2; *Bluebook*, *supra* note 3, at B12.1.1 & R. 12.

Examples

2 3 4 5 6

42 U.S.C.A § 1983 (West 2018) *or*

2 3 4 5

42 U.S.C.A § 1983 (West)

BASIC COMPONENTS OF A CITATION TO A STATE OR TRIBAL STATUTE[7]

1. Abbreviation for name of code
2. Title, chapter, or volume number, if applicable
3. Section number
4. Publisher if citing unofficial code
5. Year the code was published *or*, if citing to statute in a commercial database, "database |through| currency information"

Examples

1 3 4 5

Ga. Code Ann. § 51-7-60 (West 2019) *or*

1 3 4 5

Ga. Code Ann. § 51-7-60 (West, Westlaw through L. 2020, Act 469)

1 2 3 5

Navajo Nation Code Ann. tit. 21, § 1 (2019)

BASIC COMPONENTS OF A CITATION TO A BOOK[8]

1. Volume number if a multivolume work
2. Name of author(s)
3. Title of book
4. Section, paragraph, or page number
5. Name of editor(s), if applicable
6. Edition number, if more than one
7. Year of publication

7. *ALWD Guide*, *supra* note 2, at R. 14.4; *Bluebook*, *supra* note 3, at B12.1.2 & R. 12.
8. *ALWD Guide*, *supra* note 2, at R. 20; *Bluebook*, *supra* note 3, at B15 & R. 15.

Example

2 — Richard H. Chused, 3 — *A Property Anthology* 4 — 149 6 — (2d ed. 7 — 1997)

Richard H. Chused, *A Property Anthology* 149 (2d ed. 1997)

BASIC COMPONENTS OF A CITATION TO A LAW REVIEW ARTICLE[9]

1. Name of author(s)[10]
2. Title of article
3. Location of article:
   a. Volume number
   b. Abbreviation for name of law review
   c. Page where article begins
   d. Page where cited material appears
4. Year

Example

Murray M. Schwartz, *The Exercise of Supervisory Power By the Third Circuit Court of Appeals,* 27 Vill. L. Rev. 506, 508 (1982)

1 — Murray M. Schwartz; 2 — *The Exercise of Supervisory Power By the Third Circuit Court of Appeals*; 3a — 27; 3b — Vill. L. Rev.; 3c — 506; 3d — 508; 4 — (1982)

E. Matching the Citation to the Text[11]

A writer tells a reader which point the cite supports by where she puts the cite. If the cite is put outside the textual sentence, the reader knows that the cite supports all the material in the preceding sentence. For example:

> To prove a claim for sexual harassment without showing an adverse employment action, a plaintiff must show that the harassment created a "hostile or abusive work environment" and that the plaintiff indicated that the harassment was unwelcome. *Meritor Sav. Bank v. Vinson,* 477 U.S. 57, 66 (1986).

This sentence says two things: that the plaintiff must show a hostile environment and that the plaintiff must show that he or she communicated that the conduct was unwelcome. The placement of the citation to *Meritor* outside the textual sentence (as a *citation sentence* of its own ending with a period) tells the reader that *Meritor* establishes both points.

9. *ALWD Guide, supra* note 2, at R. 21; *Bluebook, supra* note 3, at B16 & R. 16.

10. If the law review article was written by a law student, the word "Note" would need to appear after the author's name and before the title, separated by commas. That being said, for weight of authority purposes, you want to be cautious about citing to student work.

11. *ALWD Guide, supra* note 2, at R. 34.1; *Bluebook, supra* note 3, at B1.1 & R. 1.1.

But if *Meritor* supported only the first of these points, the cite would go inside the textual sentence, immediately after the point it supports (as a *citation clause*). The writer would cite another authority for the other proposition, like this:

> To prove a claim for sexual harassment without showing an adverse employment action, a plaintiff must show that the harassment created a "hostile or abusive work environment," *Meritor Sav. Bank v. Vinson*, 477 U.S. 57, 66 (1986), and that the plaintiff indicated that the harassment was unwelcome, *Beard v. Flying J, Inc.*, 266 F.3d 792, 797 (8th Cir. 2001).

If the writer has authority for one part of the sentence but no authority for the other part, the cite still goes immediately after the proposition it supports, like this:

> Though a plaintiff can prove a claim by showing that the harassment created a "hostile or abusive work environment," *Meritor Sav. Bank v. Vinson*, 477 U.S. 57, 66 (1986), Willingham has made no such showing in this case.

Sometimes a writer points out an aspect of an authority and then uses that aspect of the authority to reason her way to another point about that authority. The first point came from the authority but the second point didn't, so the cite goes immediately after the point that came from the authority, like this:

> The court has allowed recovery on an attractive nuisance claim by a child who came into the defendants' yard to hide from her friends and fell into a swimming pool while there. [The citation to *Newcomb v. Roberts* goes here.] Though *Newcomb* made no mention of the issue, the court's allowance of recovery on these facts shows that recovery no longer requires that the child be drawn to the property by the artificial condition. [The citation to *Newcomb* does *not* go here because *Newcomb* doesn't say that actual attraction is no longer required.]

EXERCISE 19-2
Identifying the Text the Citation Supports

Identify the proposition(s) each of the following citations supports in the following excerpt of an office memo.

The Bernsteins' possession and use of the Disputed Property was continuous between 1999 and 2018. A claimant's use of property is continuous if it is of the type and duration that an average owner would make of the property, *Jarvis v. Gillespie*, 587 A.2d 981, 985 (Vt. 1991), taking into consideration the nature of the land, *Williams v. Johnson*, 139 A. 182, 182 (Vt. 1928).

To demonstrate continuous use, the adverse use must be that of an average owner, considering the nature of the property and the predominant usage of property in the surrounding area. *Williams*, 139 A. at 182. For example, in *Williams*, the court considered whether the claimant's use of a parcel of land that contained three or four apple trees and twenty maple trees to gather apples was that of an average owner. *Id.* Holding that the use was not open and notorious, the court compared the claimant's use of the parcel to that of neighboring owners, many of whom were maple syrup producers, to determine the predominant usage in the area, and suggested that an average owner might have used the land for maple syrup production and not merely sporadic apple gathering. *Id.* at 183. Comparatively, the *Jarvis* court held the claimant's use of land to keep animals, cut firewood, grow and cut Christmas trees, and tap trees for maple syrup production in an agricultural area was continuous because it was consistent with the agricultural nature of the land. 587 A.2d at 984.

While use of land must be more than fragmentary and occasional, *Zuanich v. Quero*, 376 A.2d 763, 765 (Vt. 1977), use only during certain seasons of the year is continuous, as long as the use is consistent with the nature of the land. *Jarvis*, 587 A.2d at 986.

F. Citing with Style and Grace

Citations can make the text hard to read. A reader must jump over all the names, numbers, and parentheticals; find the spot where the text begins again; and then pick back up on the message. Granted, law-trained readers become good at these mental and visual gymnastics, but even law-trained readers can use all the help a writer can give them. Here are some suggestions for minimizing the disruption caused by citations:

1. Move the Cite out of the Middle of the Sentence. Cites in the middle of the sentence make it hard to find the key parts of the sentence and combine them into a coherent thought. For example, notice how you have to hop through the embedded citation in this sentence:

> A majority of the Court in *General Electric Co. v. Gilbert*, 429 U.S. 125, 136 (1976), followed *Geduldig v. Aiello*, 417 U.S. 484 (1974), and held that pregnancy classifications were not gender classifications.

These techniques can help clear the reader's path from subject to verb to object:

a. Move the cite outside the sentence and into its own citation sentence.
b. Move the cite to the beginning of the sentence, in an introductory phrase.
c. When the sentence contains two propositions, each requiring its own authority, consider dividing the sentence into two sentences. Then each citation can be moved outside the textual sentences.
d. Consider moving less important material into a parenthetical in the citation.

Notice how techniques a and d have made the sentence more readable:

> In 1974, a majority of the Court held that pregnancy classifications were not gender classifications. *General Elec. Co. v. Gilbert*, 429 U.S. 125, 136 (1976) (following *Geduldig v. Aiello*, 417 U.S. 484 (1974)).

2. Avoid Beginning a Sentence with a Hard-to-Read Cite. Here is an example of a sentence with this problem and a better version:

Change	Public Law 95-555, 92 Stat. 2076, October 31, 1978, included a new § 701(k).
To	Congress added a new version of § 701(k) when it enacted Public Law 95-555, 92 Stat. 2076, October 31, 1978.

3. Don't Overuse String Citations. A *string citation* "strings" together many authorities to support the same point. Lawyers often cite several authorities for an important proposition, but the longer the "string," the more the citations impair readability and frustrate a reader. And since citations alone are devoid of discussion, the long list seldom adds much to the analysis. When using a string cite, limit it to four sources, use a signal[12] to start the string, and incorporate a parenthetical proof (see Chapter 9) that informs the reader how the source supports the text.[13]

EXERCISE 19-3
Editing the Placement of Citations

Use the techniques described in Section D to make the following passage more readable and to be sure that the placement of the citation accurately identifies the textual material it supports:

> 42 U.S.C. § 2000e-2(a) prohibits employers from discriminating against applicants or employees based on the individual's race or sex. The act, titled the "Civil Rights Act of 1964," protects individuals of all races and both genders, not just minorities and women. *McDonald v. Santa Fe Trail Transp. Co.*, 427 U.S. 273, 280 (1976); *Hannon v. Chater*, 887 F. Supp. 1303, 1312 (N.D. Cal. 1995); *Hall v. City of Brawley*, 887 F. Supp. 1333, 1342 (S.D. Cal. 1995); *Curler v. City of Fort Wayne*, 591 F. Supp. 327, 333 (N.D. Ind. 1984).
>
> The Court, however, has never been comfortable with the issues raised by the application of Title VII to the racial majority or to men. In *United Steelworkers of America v. Weber*, 443 U.S. 193, 215 (1979), the Supreme Court upheld a voluntary race-conscious affirmative action plan, but several years later the Court held that, to be permissible, a voluntary affirmative action plan had to benefit only "actual victims of the discriminatory practice." *Firefighters Local 1784 v. Stotts*, 467 U.S. 561, 579 (1984).
>
> Just three years later, the Court, in *Johnson v. Transportation Agency of Santa Clara County*, 480 U.S. 616 (1987), seemed to reaffirm its holding in *Weber* when it expressly followed the *Weber* holding. The Court wrote that the *Johnson* issues "must be guided by our decision in *Weber*." *Id.* at 627.[14] *Johnson* dealt with a voluntary affirmative action plan designed to improve the representation of racial minorities and of women in traditionally male jobs. *Id.*

---

12. *ALWD Guide*, *supra* note 2, at R. 35; *Bluebook*, *supra* note 3, at B1.2 & R. 1.2.

13. Longer string cites can be helpful when your reader needs every relevant authority or in the unusual situation when you want to demonstrate, graphically on the page, the overwhelming strength of support for the point. If you do cite to multiple authorities, review *ALWD Guide* Rule 36 or *Bluebook* Rules 1.3 and 1.4.

14. The first time a source is cited in a document it is necessary to provide a full citation. Once you have provided a full citation, it is permissible to use a short citation to cite to the source thereafter. *Id.* is a permissible short form when citing the immediately preceding authority and the immediately preceding citation only cites to one authority. *ALWD Guide*, *supra* note 2, at R. 11.3; *Bluebook*, *supra* note 3, at B4 & R. 4.1. Here, the writer is citing to page 627 of the *Johnson* case, the only case cited in the immediately preceding citation.

G. Editing Citation Form

This section assumes that you've looked up the relevant citation rules in your citation manual. What follows is an editing checklist to help you find the most common citation errors.

Checklist for Editing Citations

General Principles	***ALWD***	***BB***
1. Where possible, have you cited legal authority for each point you have made about the law or the authority?	pp. 2–3	B1
2. Have you placed each citation immediately after the proposition it supports?	35.1	1.1
3. Have you placed your citations at the end or the beginning of your sentences whenever possible?	34.1	1.1(b)
4. Have you avoided unnecessary string citations?	34.3	1.3
5. Have you minimized the number of sentences beginning with a citation?	34.2	1.1
6. Have you italicized or underscored using an unbroken line: a. Case names, titles of books, and articles? b. Signals (such as *e.g.* or *see*)? c. Phrases giving prior or subsequent history (such as *aff'd* or *cert. denied*)? d. Terms used in short citation forms to indicate a cross-reference (such as *id.*)?	1.3	B2
7. For citing all authorities other than names of periodicals, have you closed up all adjacent single capitals, individual numerals, and ordinals (for example, "3d"), and initials in personal names?	2.2 4.3	6.1(a)
8. Have you left a space between single capitals and multiple-letter abbreviations (for example "F. Supp.")?	2.2(a)	6.1(a)
9. When you put the citation outside the sentence, have you placed a period at the end of the citation?	34.1(a)	B1
10. When you put the citation inside a sentence, have you set off the citation with commas?	34.1(b)	B1
11. When you have cited to several authorities together, have you separated them with semicolons?	36.1	B1
12. In a title, have you capitalized according to the relevant rule?	3.2	8
13. Have you placed multiple authorities in the order set out by the relevant rule?	36	1.4

Cases

Long Form	***ALWD***	***BB***
14. Have you used only the last names of the individual parties?	12.2(d)	10.2.1(g) B10.1.1(ii)
15. Have you omitted all parties other than the first party listed on each side of the v.?	12.2(c)	10.2.1(a) B10.1.1(i)
16. Have you avoided using "et al." to signal that you have omitted the names of additional parties?	12.2(c)	10.2.1(a) B10.1.1(iii)
17. Have you used "v." (rather than "vs." or "v" or "V")?	12.2(c)	B10.1.1(i)
18. Have you abbreviated case names in citations according to the relevant rule?	12.2(d) & (e) App.[15] 3(E)	10.2.1 & 2 T.6[16]
19. Have you placed a comma after the case name and refrained from underlining or italicizing the comma?	1.3	10 B10.1
20. For federal district court and circuit court cases, have you closed up the spaces in "F.3d" but left a space in "F. Supp."?	2.2(a)	6.1(a)
21. Have you included a pinpoint cite to the page(s) of the opinion where the referenced material is located?	5.2	3.2 B10.1.2
22. Have you refrained from placing any punctuation between the page number of the case and the parenthetical?	12.2(a)	10
23. Have you included the opinion's date in parentheses?	12.7	10.5
24. For cases from a state's highest court, where the state is not unambiguously conveyed by the reporter title, have you included the abbreviated name of the state in the parentheses?	12.6	10.4(b)
25. For state cases where the court deciding the case is not the highest court of the state and you are citing to the case in a regional reporter, have you included the court's abbreviation in the court and date parenthetical?	12.4(b)	10.4(b)
26. For cases from federal circuit courts, have you identified the circuit in the parenthetical and used the correct abbreviation for it (1st Cir., 2d Cir., 3d Cir., 4th Cir., 5th Cir., 6th Cir., 7th Cir., 8th Cir., 9th Cir., 10th Cir., 11th Cir., D.C. Cir., Fed. Cir.)?	12.6(c)(1)	10.4(a) T.7

---

15. App. refers to the Appendices in the *ALWD Guide*.
16. T. refers to the Tables in the *Bluebook*.

	ALWD	*BB*
27. For federal district courts, have you identified the district in the court and date parenthetical (for example, "S.D. Cal.")?	12.6(c)(1)	10.4(a)
28. Have you refrained from putting a comma between the date and any other information within the court and date parenthetical?	12.7	10
29. For the circumstances set out in the relevant rule, have you included the subsequent history in a full citation to a case?	12.8	10.7 B10.1.6
30. Have you used a comma to separate the subsequent history of the case?	12.8(c)	10.7.1 B10.1.6
31. Have you included an explanatory phrase in a second parenthetical (and before any subsequent history) when additional information would be helpful for evaluating the weight properly given to the authority?	12.8(g)	10.7.1 B10.1.5
32. Where a phrase of information would help the reader understand the significance of the cited authority, have you included that information in an explanatory parenthetical?	12.10	1.5 B10.1.5
33. Have you complied with the relevant rule by using the appropriate signal to introduce cited authorities that: a. represent one example of many authorities standing for the same proposition? (*E.g.*) b. support the stated proposition implicitly (rather than explicitly) or in dicta? (*See*) c. support the stated proposition by analogy only? (*Cf.*) d. are compared to each other to show different results? (*Compare . . . with*) e. directly contradict the stated proposition? (*Contra*) f. contradict the stated proposition by analogy? (*But cf.*) g. provide background information? (*See generally*)	35	1.2
34. Have you underscored or italicized all signals?	35.4	1.2 B2
35. Have you refrained from using a signal when the authority directly supports the stated proposition?	35.2	1.2(a)

	ALWD	BB
36. When you are citing to a concurring or dissenting opinion, have you disclosed in a parenthetical this potential limitation on the weight of the cited material?	12.10(a)	10.6
37. Have you indicated by parenthetical any other limitations on the weight of the cited material (for example, that the cited language is dictum or that your proposition is contained in the cited material only by implication)?	12.10(a)	10.6
38. For cases available only on an electronic database, have you followed the format provided in the relevant rule?	30.2	10.8.1
39. When more than one source is available, have you cited to the appropriate source?	12.4(b)	10.3.1 B10.1.3(v)
40. When citing U.S. Supreme Court cases, have you cited to the official reporter (U.S.) where possible?	12.6(b)	10.3.1 T.1 B10.1.3(i)

Short Forms	ALWD	BB
41. Have you used a full citation the first time you cite to a particular authority?	11.1(a)	—
42. Have you chosen to use a short citation form with the reader's needs in mind?	11.2	B4
43. When you have used *id.*, have you been referring to the case cited immediately prior to the *id.* cite?	11.3(a)	4.1 B4
44. Have you refrained from using *supra* to refer to a case?	11.4(b)	4.2 B4

Statutes and Rules	ALWD	BB
45. Have you abbreviated the statutory compilation as provided in the relevant table?	App. 1	T.1
46. If the information would be helpful, have you given the statute's name (official or popular)?	14.2(a)	12.3.1(a)
47. If possible, have you cited to the official code rather than to an unofficial code?	14.1 App. 1	12.2.1 T.1

	ALWD	*BB*
48. For state and tribal statutes, and when desired for federal statutes, have you included in parentheses the year of the code you are citing (*not* the year the statute was enacted)?	14.2(f)	12.3.2
49. Have you identified the title, chapter, or volume number, if any, according to the relevant rule?	14.2(b) App. 1	12.3.1(b) T.1
50. Have you refrained from using *"et seq.,"* but rather designated the exact sections you are citing?	14.2(d)	3.3(b)
51. Have you left a space after the section symbol?	6.2 14.2(d)	6.2(c)
52. If you have cited a privately published version of the code, have you identified the publisher in the parenthetical that contains the year?	14.6(b) 14.4 App. 1	12.3.1(d) T.1
53. For state and tribal statutes, and when desired for federal statutes, have you included the currency information when citing to the statute on a commercial database such as Lexis and Westlaw?	14.2(f)	12.5
54. If you are citing material contained in a supplement, either alone or in addition to material contained in the main volume, have you followed the format shown in the relevant rule?	14.2(f)	3.1(c) 12.3.1(e)
55. If you are citing a statute that has been repealed or superseded, have you followed the format shown in the relevant rule?	14.3	12.7
56. If you are citing rules of evidence or procedure, have you followed the format provided in the relevant rule?	16.1	12.9.3
57. Have you used a full citation the first time you cite to the statute?	11.1(a)	B12.2
58. If you used a short form of citation, have you followed the format set out in the relevant rule?	14.5	12.10 B12.2

Books	*ALWD*	*BB*
59. For the first citation to the book, have you used the author's full name followed by a comma?	20.1(b)	15.1
60. If the book has more than one author, have you followed the relevant rule?	20.1(b)(2)	15.1

	ALWD	*BB*
61. If the book has an editor or translator, have you followed the relevant rule?	20.1(e)(1)	15.2
62. Have you italicized or underlined the name of the book?	20.1(c)(1)	B15
63. Have you capitalized the name of the book as set out in the relevant rule?	3.2	15.3
64. Have you cited to the latest edition and identified the edition in the parenthetical?	20.1(e)(3)	15.4
65. In the parenthetical, have you identified the year of publication?	20.1(e)(5)	15.4
66. If the cited material appears in a supplement, have you followed the format set out in the relevant rule?	8 20.1(e)(5)	3.1
67. If you have used a short form for later citations to the same book, have you complied with the relevant rule?	20.6	15.10 15.2
68. Have you used a pinpoint cite to identify the page(s) on which the cited material appears?	5.2 20.1(d)	3.2(a) B15.1 & 2

Periodicals	*ALWD*	*BB*
69. Have you provided the author's full name (including student authors) followed by a comma?	21.2(a)	16.2
70. If you are citing to a Note by a student author, have you indicated this after the author's full name by writing "Note"?	21.2(b)	16.7.1
71. Have you italicized or underlined the title of the article and followed the title with a comma?	21.2(c)	16.3 B1
72. Have you capitalized the title in accordance with the relevant rule?	3.2	8
73. Have you abbreviated the periodical as set out in the relevant table? If your periodical is not included in the list, have you used the relevant rules as your guides for constructing the periodical's abbreviation?	21.2(e) App. 3 App. 5	T.13
74. Have you followed the relevant rule for spacing between the letters abbreviating the periodical name?	2.2	6.1(a)
75. Have you included the volume number of the periodical (before the abbreviated title of the periodical)?	21.2(d)	16.4

	ALWD	*BB*
76. Have you identified the page on which the article begins, placing it after the abbreviated title of the periodical and refraining from using a "p." or "pp."?	21.2(f)	16.4 16.5
77. Have you included a pinpoint cite to the page(s) where the cited material is found?	5.2 21.2(f)	16.4 16.5 B16.1
78. Have you refrained from putting a comma between the page number and the parenthetical?	21.2(g)	16
79. Unless the periodical uses the date for the volume number, have you included the date of the volume in the parenthetical?	21.3(d)	16.4 16.5

EXERCISE 19-4
Editing for Citation Form

Edit the following citations for correct citation form. Use the checklist in section G. If you spot an error that you cannot correct without additional information, simply note the error and identify the information you would need to correct it.

1. *Leibel vs. Raynor Manufacturing Co.*, 571 S.W. 2nd 640 (1978).
2. Brown v. New Haven Civil Service Comm., 474 F.Supp. 1256, 1263, (1979).
3. *Equal Pay Act of 1963*, 29 USC § 206(d), *et seq.*
4. Hubbard v. Chinle School District, Apache County, Arizona, 3 Navajo Nation Rptr. 167, 168 (Ct. App. 1982).
5. Harold S. Lewis, Jr., Litigating Civil rights and Employment Discrimination cases, 1996. (This is a book.)
6. *Humphrey v. McLaren*, 402 N.W.2d 535 (Minn, 1987). [cited in a brief filed before a trial court in Minnesota]
7. *Prandini v. National Tea Co., Id.* at 49.
8. Jack Lee Sammons, *The Professionalism Movement: the Problems Defined*, 7 Notre Dame Journ. of Law, Ethics & Public Pol. 269, 1993.
9. e.g., *U.S. Dept. of Labor v. Triplett*, 494 US 715, 716 (1990).
10. *Laffey v. Northwest Airlines, Inc.*, 567 F.2d 429, 431 (1978).

III. QUOTATIONS

The most common quotation problems are (1) not using quotation marks for borrowed language; (2) using too many quotes; (3) not editing a quote down to its nub; and (4) making errors in quotation mechanics. The rest of this chapter deals with these common quotation problems.

A. When Quotation Marks Are Required

Use quotation marks to show that the words themselves came from someone else.[17] Quotation marks tell a reader the source of the language, and they give the creator the credit (or blame) for the creation.

Quotation marks are necessary when you quote the words of another but unnecessary when you paraphrase. Sometimes it's hard to tell the two apart. When are the words yours and when are they "the words of another"?

Start with the proposition that usually you should rephrase the thoughts of others into your own words and sentence structures. But even if you aren't looking at the source while you write, you might find that your text turns out to be similar to your source's text. Maybe the source uses common words or sentence structures to express the idea, or maybe, without realizing it, you've been thinking of the topic in the source's words.

If the original text used the word "table" and you use it too, no one would argue that you should put quotation marks around "table" in your document. But if your draft shares a whole paragraph in common with the original text, everyone understands that the paragraph must be presented as a quotation. Somewhere between these two extremes lies the point at which the words qualify as someone else's (and quotation marks become necessary), but no bright-line test will tell you precisely where.

The absence of a clear test is particularly unfortunate in legal writing. Legal writers rely heavily on sources, and most legal writing texts advise writers to paraphrase most sources. If you follow this good advice, you'll be doing a lot of paraphrasing. How can you know whether your paraphrase is different enough from the original text that it doesn't need quotation marks?

To decide whether you need quotation marks, consider the *combined effect* of these factors:

- the length of the common unit of text;
- the number of units in common;
- whether the sentence structure is the same or similar; and
- whether the common units include particularly striking language.

Some writers use a seven-word benchmark as a starting point for measuring the length of a common unit. If seven or more words used together in your text match the text of the source, use quotation marks for those words. The benchmark recognizes the unlikelihood of a common seven-word unit appearing inadvertently in texts by different authors. So to be safe, use quotation marks *at least* for any unit of seven or more words.

But you can't avoid quotation marks just by changing every seventh word. The seven-word benchmark is only an approximate measure, and it applies only when the texts aren't similar in other ways, so consider also whether there are other common units of text and whether the sentence structure is similar. Would an objective reader think that this passage is fundamentally someone else's, with just a few surface changes?

---

17. *Ideas* that come from another author must always be attributed to the other author. This section assumes that you're already attributing the *ideas* to their source. Here we're dealing only with deciding when to attribute the *words*, too.

Finally, use quotation marks for language another author has used in a particularly vivid, creative, or unusual way. For example, in *Griggs v. Duke Power Co.*, Chief Justice Burger condemned employer practices that function as "built-in headwinds" impeding employment for minority groups.[18] In *Watson v. Fort Worth Bank & Trust*, Justice O'Connor described the positions argued by the parties as "stark and uninviting alternatives."[19] In his dissent in *Wards Cove Packing Co. v. Atonio*, Justice Stevens described the living and working conditions at the defendant's canneries as "a plantation economy."[20]

These are examples of words and phrases used in distinctive ways. In each case, the author was especially effective in selecting the words to express the idea. In each case, the author's effective use of language merits recognition, and other writers who use these phrases should give credit to the original author by using quotation marks.

Make your decisions conservatively. It's far better to use quotation marks or to paraphrase the passage more thoroughly than to risk questions about whose writing your document really reflects.

B. Choosing to Use Quotation Marks

Even if quotation marks aren't required, you might choose to use them anyway, for example, when the analysis applies a particular legal test or interprets the words of a statute. Here are examples:

PARTICULAR LEGAL TEST

A lawyer must use the degree of skill commonly exercised by a "reasonable, careful and prudent lawyer." *Cook, Flanagan & Berst v. Clausing*, 438 P.2d 865, 867 (Wash. 1968).

PARTICULAR WORDS OF STATUTE

Title VII makes it unlawful for a labor organization "to exclude or expel" an individual because of religion. 42 U.S.C. § 2000e-2(c)(1).

Quotation marks wouldn't be required for these words, but you should use them anyway to let the reader know that these are the key words at issue in the analysis.

C. Overquoting

Chapter 7 warned against using too many quotations.[21] There, in the working draft stage, the danger was confusing quoting the authorities with analyzing them. The editing stage raises two more reasons to minimize quotes.

18. 401 U.S. 424, 432 (1971).
19. 487 U.S. 977, 989 (1988).
20. 490 U.S. 642, 662 n.4 (1989).
21. *ALWD Guide* Rule 38.1 contains the same caution.

First, busy readers are tempted to skip quoted material entirely. Maybe they assume that the quoted material simply supports the points the writer has already stated. Maybe busy readers are discouraged by the single-spacing of a block quote. Whatever the reason, readers do tend to skim or skip quoted material.

Second, a quotation seldom communicates your point as clearly, directly, and succinctly as you could. After all, the original writer wasn't writing about *your* case. Your paraphrase can do what quotations can't, that is, tie the substance of the precedential source directly to the issues of *your* case.

Generally, quote only in these circumstances:

1. Quote when the issue will turn on the interpretation of key words of a statute, rule, or case, as described above. Limit the quotation to *those words* so your reader will understand the issue and your analysis of it. Here is an example:

   > A lawyer must use great care in deciding whether to undertake representation of a new client when that representation might be directly adverse to an existing client. Model R. Pro. Conduct r. 1.7(a)(1) (Am. Bar Ass'n 2013). The existing client must consent to the lawyer's representation of the new client. *Id.* r. 1.7(a)(2). However, even if the client consents, the lawyer must not undertake the new representation unless the lawyer "reasonably believes" that the new representation will not "adversely affect the relationship" with the existing client. *Id.* r. 1.7(a)(1).

   Note that when the rule comes from a statute, you will want to quote the pertinent parts of the statute when setting forth the rule. Unlike the language in cases, the precise language of a statute is the result of discussion among legislators.
2. Quote *key* language from an authority with a great deal of precedential value. This could be mandatory authority or highly respected persuasive authority such as an opinion of the United States Supreme Court, a provision of a Restatement of Law, or an opinion written by a respected judge, for example:

   > To prevail, the plaintiff must prove that the injuries would not have happened but for the defendant's unlawful actions. *June v. Union Carbide Co.*, 577 F.3d 1234, 1239 (10th Cir. 2009). That causation standard requires the court to imagine a scenario that did not, in fact, occur. *Price Waterhouse v. Hopkins*, 490 U.S. 228, 240 (1989). As Justice Brennan has observed,
   >
   >> But-for causation is a hypothetical construct. In determining whether a particular factor was a but-for cause of a given event, we begin by assuming that that factor was present at the time of the event and then ask whether, even if that factor had been absent, the event nevertheless would have transpired in the same way.
   >
   > *Id.*
3. Quote *key* language when the author has found a particularly effective way to express the idea you want to convey, for example:

   > Under Rule 60(b) the court possesses "a grand reservoir of equitable power" to accomplish justice. *Thompson v. Kerr-McGee Ref. Corp.*, 660 F.2d 1380, 1385 (10th Cir. 1981).

D. The Mechanics of Quoting

Here is an editing checklist to help you flag the most common quotation errors:

1. Indent quotations of fifty or more words from both side margins. The indentation indicates that the material is quoted, so don't use quotation marks. Indented quotations should be single-spaced. *ALWD Guide* R. 38.5; *Bluebook* R. 5.1(a).
2. Don't indent or single-space quotations shorter than fifty words. Use quotation marks. *ALWD Guide* R. 38.4; *Bluebook* R. 5.1(b).
3. Put end punctuation inside the quotation marks if it is part of the quoted material. For punctuation you add, put commas and periods inside the quotation marks, but put other added punctuation outside the quotation marks. *ALWD Guide* R. 38.4(b); *Bluebook* R. 5.1(b).

   "Discriminatory employment practices are prohibited."
   [The period is part of the quoted material.]

   The statute prohibits "discriminatory employment practices."
   [The period is not part of the quoted material.]

   Does the statute prohibit "discriminatory employment practices"?
   [The question mark is not part of the quoted material.]

4. Show changes in the quotation by using brackets. Use brackets when you replace letters or words or when you add material to the quotation:

   "[R]egulations [of employee appearance] making distinctions on the basis of sex will not support allegations of discrimination unless [the regulations] are unreasonable or unevenly enforced."

   In the first bracket, the uppercase *R* replaces a lowercase *r* because in the original the quoted language did not begin a sentence. The second and third brackets identify material added or substituted to clarify, simplify, or shorten the quoted material. *ALWD Guide* R. 39; *Bluebook* R. 5.2 & 5.3.
5. To show that you've omitted letters, use empty brackets. For instance, write "draft[]" when omitting the "ing" from "drafting." *ALWD Guide* R. 39.2; *Bluebook* R. 5.2(b).
6. To show that you've omitted words, use ellipses. An ellipsis is a series of three dots with a space before, between, and after. *ALWD Guide* R. 40.1 & 40.2; *Bluebook* R. 5.3.

   First, the court noted that "[t]he evidence included a communication . . . suggesting that the employee should wear clothing of a more feminine style."

7. Don't use an ellipsis at the beginning of a quotation. A reader will know that the original source might include material ahead of the quote. *ALWD Guide* R. 40.3(b); *Bluebook* R. 5.3(b)(i).
8. Don't use an ellipsis at the end of a quotation if the quoted material ends with a complete sentence. A reader will know that the original source might contain material after the quoted sentence. *ALWD Guide* R. 40.3(c); *Bluebook* R. 5.3(b)(iv).

9. When you use material that was a *part* of a sentence in the original but you are using it as a complete sentence in your text, show the omitted material at the end of the quotation with an ellipsis after the end of the quote and then add the period to the end of the sentence.

   > "The mere existence of a grievance procedure does not insulate an employer from liability. . . ."

   The ellipsis tells the reader that in the original, the sentence contained additional material. *ALWD Guide* R. 40.2(b); *Bluebook* R. 5.3(b)(iii). Note that you want to avoid using quoted language as a complete sentence. The reader is more likely to skip over the sentence because it may appear that the author has simply cut and pasted the material, and thus not exercising any control over the material.
10. Use a parenthetical at the end of the cite to signal that you've omitted citations or footnotes or to signal added or deleted emphasis. *ALWD Guide* R. 40.3(c); *Bluebook* R. 5.3(c). For example:

    > The court observed that a partner's interest in partnership property "is a derivative interest subject to significant limitations. [A partner] has *no right to use this property for other than partnership purposes* without the consent of the other partners." *Bellis v. United States,* 417 U.S. 85, 98 (1974) (citations omitted; emphasis added).

    Here, the original material contained citations after "limitations" and before the next sentence. The italicized phrase was not italicized in the original.
11. If you find an error in the quoted material, either alter the quotation to correct the error or signal the error by following it with "sic" enclosed in brackets. *ALWD Guide* R. 39; *Bluebook* R. 5.2(c). For example:

    > In addition, the court reasonined that "[t]he party least anxious to settle was her [sic]."

E. Editing Quotations

Edit quotations down to their key words so your reader doesn't have to sift through unnecessary material to find your point. Editing must not change the meaning, but within that constraint you have great latitude to clear away the underbrush. Often the most effective quotation has been edited down to a short phrase or even a single word. Restrained use of italics and underlining in quoted material can encourage busy readers not to skim or skip quotations.

For example, assume that you represent the defendant in a sexual harassment claim. The plaintiff alleges that her supervisor pressured her into going to dinner with him and kissing him. You are writing a brief to the trial court on the issue of what the plaintiff must prove. Compare the following examples:

Example 1

The Supreme Court has held that "the District Court in this case erroneously focused on the 'voluntariness' of respondent's participation in the claimed sexual episodes. The correct inquiry is whether respondent by her conduct indicated that the alleged sexual advances were unwelcome, not whether her actual participation in sexual intercourse was involuntary." *Meritor Sav. Bank v. Vinson*, 477 U.S. 57, 68 (1986).

Example 2

The Supreme Court has held that a plaintiff cannot prove a sexual harassment claim merely by showing that she participated in the sexual conduct involuntarily. *Meritor Sav. Bank v. Vinson*, 477 U.S. 57, 68 (1986). She must prove that "by her conduct [she] *indicated* that the alleged sexual advances were unwelcome." *Id.* (emphasis added).

Which manner of quoting distills the key distinction and highlights it for your reader? Which states the legal principle as it would apply to the procedural posture of your case? Which states the legal principle in language that would apply to the facts of your case? Which is more readable?

Now that your citations and quotations are in good shape, we're ready for the last step: editing the rest of the document.

Checklist for Editing Quotations

	ALWD	*BB*
1. Have you used a block quote for a quotation of fifty or more words?	38.5	5.1
2. When you have used a block quote, have you indented the quotation from both side margins, single-spaced the quotation, and not used quotation marks?	38.5	5.1(a)
3. Have you placed the end punctuation of a quotation in the appropriate place?	38.4(b)	5.1(b)
4. For all cites to the quotation, including parallel citations, have you included the pinpoint cite to the page where the quoted material appears?	5.2	3.2(a)
5. When you have used a block quote, have you placed the citation at the normal left margin on the line immediately following the block quote?	38.5(e)	5.1(a)(ii)
6. When the source to which you are citing has quoted the material from another source, have you used an explanatory parenthetical?	38.4(c) 38.5(b)	5.2(e)

	ALWD	*BB*
7. When you have added or deleted citations or indications of emphasis, have you used an explanatory parenthetical?	39.4 40.3(c)	5.2
8. Where you have altered a quote, such as by changing a lowercase letter to an uppercase letter, have you signaled the alteration by using brackets?	39.1	5.2(a)
9. Have you properly indicated an omission with an ellipsis?	40.1	5.3

CHAPTER 20

Paragraphs, Sentences, and Style

The revision process is comprised of multiple steps. As discussed in prior chapters, the process begins with large-scale organization of the analysis of a legal issue—beginning by setting forth the rule explanation and the rule application. The next step is smaller scale editing for style and technical correctness, including proper paragraph structure. Finally, the last step in the writing process is editing at the sentence level and polishing.

Good editing requires reading a document as if you have never seen it before. Try to arrive at the editing stage with enough time to put the document down for a day or at least for several hours. Then read as if you were a complete stranger to the document. Use the following suggestions as part of your editing process.

Watch for other errors not highlighted here and for typographical errors. Have a good composition handbook or style manual—in print or in an open tab for an online e-source—available to check grammar or punctuation questions. You also want to make sure to carefully set any editing or proofreading options available in the writing platform you are using, such as Microsoft Word. For example, you might want to make sure spellcheck applies to words in all caps, such as those in a point heading in a persuasive brief, or elect to have passive voice flagged to help keep a careful eye out for it.

In addition, editing software, some of which might be based on artificial intelligence (AI) technology,[1] designed for legal writing is available to assist in the editing process.[2] AI editing tools do not free lawyers from having strong writing skills, but these tools can increase efficiency and prompt the writer to consider the suggested changes. That being said, to grow into your full potential as a lawyer and to develop your professional judgment as a writer, avoid relying on this advanced technology. Check with your professor about using computer programs for checking grammar, punctuation, style, and cite form, but remember that no computer program can replace your own careful proofreading.

---

1. AI refers to technologies that employ computers and software to complete tasks similar to those people can perform.

2. BriefCatch and WordRake are types of editing software created specifically for legal writing. Grammarly and StyleWriter are examples of more general editing software.

I. PARAGRAPHING

Each paragraph should have a topic or a thesis sentence, which generally appears as the first sentence of the paragraph.[3] The paragraph should be limited to information about that topic or thesis, and it should fit smoothly and logically between its neighbors.

These paragraphing principles are more than just principles of writing style. Proper paragraphing will improve the substance of your analysis by helping you flesh out and order your thoughts, make appropriate decisions about the depth of your analysis for each point, and think of new points you want to include. Here are some important guidelines for paragraphing:

When Possible, Use a Thesis Sentence Rather Than a Topic Sentence. A topic sentence identifies the topic the paragraph will discuss, but that is all it does. A paragraph centered on a topic sentence is apt to discuss the topic without ever making a point. A thesis sentence, however, asserts a position. A paragraph centered on a thesis sentence will support or explain this position. It will focus on the material that "proves" the thesis. Often the thesis is the rule itself, a part of the rule, or a point about how the rule functions. Compare the following paragraphs. Which has the best thesis sentence? Notice how the thesis sentence articulates a point that advances the analysis. Notice how its discipline has led the writer to analyze rather than merely report on the authorities.

Cantwell v. Denton, **citation**, dealt with the issue of when a choice is sufficiently voluntary to constitute assumption of the risk. In that case, the defendant negligently caused a fire in an apartment building, and a father entered the burning building to save his child. **Citation**. The court held that the father's action was not sufficiently voluntary to constitute assumption of the risk. **Citation.**

A choice is not sufficiently voluntary to constitute assumption of the risk if the defendant's negligence has forced the plaintiff to choose between the threatened harm and another equal or greater harm. **Citation** to **Cantwell v. Denton**. In *Cantwell*, the defendant had negligently caused a fire in an apartment building. **Citation.** A father had to choose between entering the burning building and standing by while his child's life was in danger. **Citation.** The court held that standing by while the child was in danger would have been an equal or greater harm. **Citation.** Under such circumstances, the court held, the choice to subject one's self to danger is not "voluntary" in the sense necessary to constitute assumption of the risk. **Citation.**

3. A paragraph or even several paragraphs can refer to the thesis sentence of the prior paragraph by using a clear relational word or phrase (for example, "similarly") or when the context otherwise clearly communicates that the point of the subsequent paragraph is to provide additional evidence for the prior paragraph's thesis.

As you clarify for yourself the point of the paragraph, you may realize that the *topic* contains several different *theses*, each deserving its own supporting material. Thus, using a thesis sentence leads to a more thorough and complete analysis.

Keep the Paragraph's Content Within Its Thesis. Limiting the paragraph's content to information about the paragraph's thesis will help you find the gaps in your reasoning and in the "proof" you have found in the authorities. If you limit the paragraph to material that supports the thesis, you will notice if you have little or no support for that thesis. You will know when you need to go back to the authorities in search of stronger support.

Keep Your Paragraphs Moderately Short. Limit paragraphs to one-third to one-half of a double-spaced page. Keeping your paragraph short will keep you focused on the thesis. A long paragraph often has one of these two problems: (1) it has wandered from its thesis, or (2) the thesis is too big to be covered without dividing it into subpoints. A large thesis generally produces a large paragraph that mixes information about the subpoints more or less randomly. It also results in a discussion that is not sufficiently fleshed out. The best way to avoid these two problems is to keep your paragraph lengths at or below a half-page, double-spaced.

Use a Transitional Word, Phrase, or Sentence Each Time You Move on to a New Point. Being explicit about the relationships between the theses of succeeding paragraphs will help you ensure that your reasoning is logical. Here is a list of commonly used transitions:

TRANSITIONS[4]

	Addition	
also	in addition	not only
and	in fact	then
furthermore	moreover	
	Sequence	
first	next	finally
second		
	Comparison	
both	likewise	in comparison
	Contrast	
but	despite	nevertheless
while	still	however
instead	even though	notwithstanding
on the other hand	even so	
in contrast	though	

4. Adapted from David Angell & Brent Heslop, *The Elements of E-Mail Style* 62–64 (1994).

	Concession	
although	even though	though
	Illustration	
for instance	in particular	specifically
to illustrate	for example	
	Result	
accordingly	consequently	as a result
therefore	for	since
because	thus	
	Summary	
accordingly	thus	therefore
in summary		
	Emphasis	
above all	more important	chiefly

Thesis sentences and proper paragraphing can make a major substantive difference in your analysis. If you cannot concentrate on the material and on paragraphing at the same time, simply write your initial draft in your normal way and then, in your first revision, edit your paragraphs and add thesis sentences where necessary.

STRATEGIES FOR USING PARAGRAPHING TO IMPROVE YOUR ANALYSIS

1. *Check your thesis sentences and paragraphs.* For each paragraph, first ask yourself what your point is. Identify your thesis sentence, and underline or highlight it on your draft. Then identify the paragraph(s) that support that thesis, and be sure you know how all of the other material in that paragraph pertains to that point. Now evaluate the strength of your analysis of that point by evaluating the strength of the supporting paragraph(s). This kind of point-by-point evaluation helps you identify weak spots, leaps of logic, and misuse of sources.
2. *Check paragraph length.* Use a maximum length of about one-half of a double-spaced page. For those paragraphs that run longer, ask yourself whether the paragraph's thesis has subpoints you should separate. If you separate these subpoints and treat them in separate paragraphs, you may find that the subpoints deserve more analysis. As a matter of fact, sometimes you will find whole new issues you had overlooked.
3. *Check your transitions.* Identify each transition to a new point, and ask yourself how the new point is connected to the former point. Be sure that each transition is clearly communicated.
4. *Read all of the underlined or highlighted thesis sentences in order.* They should provide a logically ordered summary of your reasoning, point by point.

II. CHOOSE STRONG SUBJECTS AND VERBS

One of the characteristics of good style is the predominance of strong subjects and verbs. Here are some of the most effective techniques for finding and using stronger subjects and verbs.

A. Active Voice

Much legal writing is filled with unnecessary passive verbs. Learn to spot them, evaluate whether they serve a purpose, and get rid of them if they do not. You can recognize passive verbs by checking the subject of the sentence. Ask yourself whether the subject performed the action described by the verb. If it did, then you have used a verb in the active voice. If it did not, but instead was acted *upon*, you have found a passive-voiced verb.

Active	Ms. Watson signed a covenant-not-to-compete.
Passive	A covenant-not-to-compete was signed by Ms. Watson.

The subject of the first sentence is Ms. Watson. Did she do what the verb describes? Did she "sign"? Yes, she did, so the sentence uses the active voice. However, the subject of the second sentence is the covenant. Did the covenant sign? Of course not. The covenant was acted upon; the signing happened *to* the covenant. Therefore, that sentence uses the passive voice.

Why are sentences overloaded with passive verbs undesirable? First, writing in the passive voice requires more words. You can see this on a small scale in the example above, and the effect can compound in a sentence with more than one passive verb.

Passive	It was insisted by Carrolton that the covenant had been breached by Ms. Watson.
Active	Carrolton insisted that Ms. Watson had breached the covenant.

Locate the passive verbs in the first sentence, which contains fourteen words. Notice that the second sentence contains only nine words, a reduction of thirty-six percent.

Second, writing in the passive voice causes lack of clarity. Sentences in the passive voice often omit altogether the identity of the actor, for example:

A covenant-not-to-compete was signed.	[Who signed?]
It was insisted that the covenant had been breached.	[Who insisted? Who breached?]

Finally, writing in the passive voice is less forceful. A sentence in the active voice drives forward in a straight line; the subject "does" the action to the object. But a sentence in the passive voice moves in reverse, backing in stops and starts toward the subject. Like a car, a sentence driving ahead moves more smoothly and forcefully than a sentence in reverse.

Although writing in the active voice is generally preferable, an occasional passive-voiced verb can serve a particular function. For instance, a passive verb may eliminate the need for using a masculine noun or pronoun, as Section V explains. In persuasive writing, a strategic consideration might call for a passive verb; for example, if you want to hide the actor. Also, sometimes the identity of the actor is not important, and a passive verb can appropriately focus the attention on the object of the action. In court documents, a passive verb can allow you to avoid references to yourself or your firm. Sometimes using a passive verb can allow you to begin the sentence with a smooth transition from earlier material.

However, most legal writing, including the case law you spend so much time reading, relies far too much on verbs in the passive voice. Because so much of what you are reading every day is infected with passivitis, you will have to struggle against developing the habit yourself.

EXERCISE 20-1
Active Voice

Underline each passive-voiced verb and edit the sentence to eliminate those verbs. If editing would require knowing the name of a person or organization, simply create a name.

1. After a notice of appeal was filed by the defendant, the assessment of attorneys' fees was entered and payment was made a condition of probation.
2. The appropriate time to decide a motion for defense fees and costs is not set out by the statute.
3. The motion to dismiss was made by the defendant and was heard by the court on May 15.
4. Disparaging reports about Carter's performance had been made by the hospital's Credentials Committee.
5. The initial discussions by the Executive Committee of Green's abilities were prompted by Carter's testimony against Green.

B. Nominalizations

The second technique for focusing on strong subjects and verbs is avoiding nominalizations. Nominalizations are nouns that began life as a verb and should have been content with their lot. When such a verb aspires to upward social mobility (becoming a noun), it finds that it needs a crowd around it. Suddenly, your sentence has several more words than it used to.

No nominalization	The sellers decided to accept the buyer's offer.
One nominalization	The sellers *made a decision* to accept the buyer's offer.

If your sentence contains several nominalizations, the party can get really out of hand.

No unnecessary nominalizations	The sellers decided to accept the buyer's offer, so they authorized their broker to announce their decision.
Three added nominalizations	The sellers *made a decision* to accept the buyer's offer, so they *issued an authorization to* their broker to *make an announcement of* their decision.

Wordiness is not the only problem. Sentences using nominalizations lose force and clarity. Because nominalizations are still verbs at heart, they do a poor job of being nouns; they are by nature more vague than "real" nouns. Worse yet, when the hole left by the departed verb is filled, the substitute verb is usually weaker than the departed verb.[5] Here are examples of common nominalizations and the verb forms to which they should return.

Change	**To**
enter into an agreement	agree
contains a provision	provides
have a collision	collide
file a motion	move
give consideration to	consider
had knowledge that	knew
effect a termination	terminate
make an assumption	assume
make a decision	decide
places emphasis on	emphasizes
it is a requirement of the contract that	the contract requires that
commencement of discovery will occur	discovery will commence

EXERCISE 20-2
Nominalizations

Underline the nominalizations, and edit the sentences to eliminate them.

1. New York law is very protective of medical peer review procedures, so a challenge to the procedures would not be beneficial to our client.
2. The Executive Committee members made a statement to the effect that the Vice President had given them assurance that the Personnel Office had made an announcement of its decision.
3. The County Tax Assessor's Office made a number of new assessments to properties with locations in Midtown.
4. This letter serves as confirmation of our meeting last week, during which our firm agreed to provide representation to First National Bank.
5. The arbitrator made a determination that the claim for damages was reasonable.

5. Verbs like "make," "issue," "is," and "had" are much weaker than action verbs like "agree," "announce," "object," "collide," and "revise."

C. Throat-Clearing

Another major obstacle to focusing on strong subjects and verbs is the habit of "throat-clearing"—using introductory phrases that communicate little more than "I'm getting ready to say something." Here are examples:

It is interesting to note that . . .
It is important to remember that . . .
It seems that . . .
It is clear (or obvious) that . . .
It is widely understood that . . .
As noted above . . .
As to . . .
With respect (or regard) to . . .

Other examples introduce an assertion by claiming responsibility for it, such as "The defendant submits (or believes, argues, or contends) that. . . . "

We might speculate about why these phrases slip into our writing. They might reflect a natural human insecurity; they could be an attempt to elevate the tone or convey an objective perspective; or they might simply be habits born of reading poor legal writing. Whatever the reason, edit them out in revision. Let your sentences proceed directly to your point.

EXERCISE 20-3
Throat-Clearing

Edit each sentence to eliminate the throat-clearing structures.

1. The Court should note that the *Harmon* case was decided prior to the statute's adoption.
2. It could be argued that the plaintiff was not injured as a result of the other car's excessive speed but rather as a result of the plaintiff's malfunctioning brakes.
3. It appears that the defendant left the jurisdiction to avoid testifying, so it should be clear that the sanctions would apply.
4. The court's language makes it clear that the court considered whether to make the payment of fees a condition of probation.

D. Sentences Beginning with Forms of "It Is" or "There Is"

Sentence constructions beginning with forms of "it is" or "there is" always lack force and often lack clarity. Like the constructions described above, they obscure the subject and verb. Try to reword these constructions to put the "real" subject and action up front in their usual spots.

Change It is unethical to contact a party represented by another lawyer.
To Contacting a party represented by another lawyer is unethical.

Change There are four defendants seeking dismissal on jurisdictional grounds.
To Four defendants are seeking dismissal on jurisdictional grounds.

EXERCISE 20-4
"It Is" or "There Is" Structures

Edit each sentence to eliminate the "it is" or "there is" structure.

1. The cases are distinguishable because there was no notice of appeal filed in *Finkelstein*.
2. It is irrelevant in determining whether *Roberts* should control this case that the underlying trial was a criminal proceeding as opposed to a civil proceeding.
3. On September 9, 2019, Matthews filed a notice of appeal asserting that there was insufficient evidence to show that he had the requisite intent.
4. It is worth noting that the Second District has chosen not to follow the Fourth District's ruling on this issue.
5. The Florida Supreme Court recognized that there must be a line drawn to establish a clear standard for deciding which court has jurisdiction.
6. In *Finkelstein*, there was no appeal by the defendant.
7. It is irrelevant that Matthews filed a notice of appeal because the motion for a fee assessment was independent of the appeal.
8. There is a parallel between fee assessments and restitution requirements. Fee assessments and restitution requirements are parallel orders.
9. It is important for the stability of the legal system to ensure consistent decisions from the courts.
10. Furthermore, there are not enough significant differences between restitution orders and fee awards to support different results.
11. There is no claim that may be entertained by the trial court because the entire case falls within the jurisdiction of the appellate court.
12. Fees and costs cannot be assessed until there has been a determination of guilt.
13. Failure to pay the assessed fees and costs would result in incarceration even though there was no order for imprisonment as part of the sentence.
14. The Florida cases demonstrate that there is no exception in the criminal context to the rule that the filing of a notice of appeal divests a trial court of jurisdiction to assess fees.

III. AVOIDING WORDINESS

A. Revise Phrases That Can Be Replaced by a Single Word

Unnecessary phrases abound in poor legal writing. Phrases beginning with "the fact that" are nearly always culprits, but many other phrases create clutter as well. Here are examples:

Change	**To**
at the time when	when
at the point in time when	when
as a result of	because
by reason of the fact that	because
due to the fact that	because
for a period of one week	for one week
for the purpose of	to
for these reasons	therefore
inasmuch as	because
in many cases	often
in order to	to
it was formerly the case that	formerly or previously
previous to	before
that was a case where	there

Also watch for phrases that can be replaced by adjectives.

Change the contract between Wigby and Matthews
To the Wigby-Matthews contract

Change The buyer discovered six violations of code requirements. All of the violations dealt with plumbing.
To The buyer discovered six plumbing code violations.

Change . . . for the purpose for which it was intended . . .
To . . . for the intended purpose . . .

B. Avoid Legalese

For the same reasons, purge your writing of unnecessary legalese. Do not resort to the jargon of law unless it is necessary to convey your point clearly and concisely. Here are examples of unnecessary legalese:

assuming *arguendo*
the *instant* case
the *above-captioned* case
the *said* defendant
the *aforementioned* contract
the items *hereinafter* described
to wit
supra (except when properly used in a legal citation)

C. Avoid Redundancies

Redundancies can slip into language easily. Here are examples:

advance planning
final outcome
first and foremost
honest truth
old adage
past experience
point in time
reason is because
whether or not

D. Avoid Matched Pairs

Matched pairs are two words commonly used together but having the same meaning. Some examples include:

bind and obligate
by and through
cease and desist
each and every
full and complete
null and void
stipulate and agree
true and correct
will and testament

Matched pairs clutter good writing and cloud meaning. When two terms mean the same thing, choose the more familiar of the two and delete the other.

E. Avoid Intensifiers

Because generations of writers have overused words like "clearly" or "very," these and other common intensifiers have become virtually meaningless. As a matter of fact, they have begun to develop a connotation opposite their original meaning. So many writers have used those labels in place of well-reasoned analysis that some readers see these intensifiers as signaling a weak analysis. Rid your writing of these words:

clearly
extremely
obviously
quite
very

IV. OTHER CHARACTERISTICS OF GOOD STYLE

A. Keeping the Subject and Verb Close Together

The basic components of a sentence are the subject, the verb, and the object. A reader tackles a sentence by searching for those components. First, a reader looks for the subject. Once the subject is found, the reader's urge to find the verb is strong. The primary meaning of a sentence is communicated by the combination of the subject and the verb. A reader who can't find and mentally combine them quickly will be frustrated and confused.

The primary impediment to finding and mentally combining the subject and verb is the placement of long modifying phrases between them. Legal writers are especially prone to this weakness. Usually the problem is caused by trying to say too much in one sentence, for example:

> In the first month of his marriage, the defendant, who was only nineteen at the time and who had not completed high school or developed a trade and who had just lost his part-time job, was charged with robbing a convenience store at the corner of Bayside and Tenth Avenue.

This writer has a lot to say about the defendant—probably more than one sentence can bear. As a result, several modifying phrases separate the subject and the verb. Move them into sentences of their own:

> In the first month of his marriage, the defendant was charged with robbing a convenience store at the corner of Bayside and Tenth Avenue. He was only nineteen at the time. He had not completed high school or developed a trade, and he had just lost his part-time job.

Not only is the second version easier to read, it helps the reader organize the information as well.

Use these guidelines to manage long modifying phrases:

- Where clarity is not a problem, move the long phrase to one end of the sentence. This placement allows the reader to read quickly. It places the primary emphasis on the main clause, and it maximizes clarity.
- If clarity is a problem, place the modifying phrase close to the word it modifies. If the resulting sentence separates the subject and verb by too great a distance, separate the material into two or more sentences.

EXERCISE 20-5
Keeping the Subject and Verb Close Together

Edit to keep the subjects and verbs closer together.

1. The applicable rule the Florida courts have fashioned in relation to this issue states that a trial court does retain jurisdiction to assess attorney's fees and costs during the pendency of an appeal.
2. A potential counter-argument to established Florida law that the assessment of fees and costs is a collateral and independent issue from the underlying trial or appeal and should be excepted from the general rule transferring jurisdiction to the appellate court upon the filing of an appeal can be found in the case of *Woods v. State*.

B. Avoiding Long Sentences

The more complex the message, the simpler the medium must be. Long sentences bury the subject and verb and tax a reader's patience. Use twenty-five words as a benchmark for gauging maximum length.

EXERCISE 20-6
Avoiding Long Sentences

Edit to eliminate excessively long sentences.

1. The court followed the *Wyatt* ruling in *Lee v. State,* when it affirmed the trial court's imposition of § 938 fees and costs upon the defendant, who argued unsuccessfully that his notice appealing a first-degree murder conviction divested the trial court of its jurisdiction to assess fees and costs.
2. On September 16, 2021, after Defendant had filed the Notice of Appeal, the Public Defender filed a Motion for Fees and Costs, asking the trial court to assess fees and costs against Defendant, pursuant to § 938, consisting of attorney's fees and investigative costs totaling $1,040.

C. Unnecessary Variations

Clear legal writing requires consistency in terms. Once you pick a term, use the same term for each reference. Otherwise your reader will have to decide, with each new term, whether you mean something different from the prior term. Professor Wydick uses this example:

> The first case was settled for $20,000, and the second piece of litigation was disposed of out of court for $30,000, while the price of the amicable accord reached in the third suit was $50,000.[6]

The readers are left to ponder the difference between a *case,* a *piece of litigation,* and a *suit.* By the time they conclude that there is no difference, they have no patience left for *settled, disposed of out of court,* and *amicable accord,* much less for what the writer was trying to tell them in the first place.

In legal writing, consistency is important. Do not worry about seeming repetitious; it is far more important to be understood.

D. Parallelism

Sentences with repeated elements should maintain a parallel structure. A sentence has a repeated structure when it contains a list or when it contains more than one of the same kind of element. For instance, the following sentence has two dependent clauses:

6. Richard C. Wydick, *Plain English for Lawyers* 70 (5th ed. 2005).

> Acme Pest Control selected the plaintiff for lay-off because she had the least seniority and because she was consistently late to work.

Notice that the dependent clauses use a parallel structure. They each begin with "because she" followed by a verb. Here is a version of this sentence that does not maintain a parallel structure:

> Acme Pest Control selected the plaintiff for lay-off because she had the least seniority and because of her tardiness.

In this version of the sentence, the first "because" is followed by a subject and verb, but the second is followed by a prepositional phrase.

To maintain parallelism, be sure that all items in a list and all repeated structures use the same grammatical elements. If the list is complex, you can repeat the last common word so your reader will have no difficulty understanding how each item of the list relates to the rest of the sentence.

Not parallel	Problems occur when the parties conceal relevant documents or by deluging the opponent with irrelevant documents.
Parallel	Problems occur when the parties conceal relevant documents or when they deluge the opponent with irrelevant documents.

Now that the structure is parallel, extra words can go:

> Problems occur when the parties conceal relevant documents or deluge the opponent with irrelevant documents.

EXERCISE 20-7
Parallelism

Edit to achieve parallelism.

1. When Officers Dale and Hathaway found the victims, they were bruised, hungry, and suffered from exhaustion.
2. To prevail in a claim for employment discrimination, the plaintiff must prove that (1) his employer is covered by the act, (2) that he was terminated because of his age, and (3) a causal link between his termination and his damages.

V. GENDER-NEUTRAL WRITING

Gender-neutral language is language that avoids masculine nouns and pronouns for *general* reference. Using gender-neutral language smoothly is not always easy. Here are some helpful strategies.

A. Techniques for Nouns: Elimination or Substitution

1. Where possible without loss of clarity, eliminate the noun entirely. For instance, you could probably eliminate the term "bat boys" from the following sentence without altering the meaning.

   > . . . to all players, coaches, [bat boys,] ticket takers, concession workers, or other employees whose jobs are related to the sport of baseball.

2. Substitute gender-neutral synonyms where the noun is needed.

Use	Rather than
chairperson	chairman
firefighter	fireman
flight attendant	stewardess
housekeeper	maid
mail carrier	mailman
persons, individuals	men, mankind
police officer	policeman
reporter	newsman
server	waitress
staffing	manning
supervisor	foreman
worker	workman

B. Techniques for Pronouns (They, Them, Theirs, She, He, Hers, His)

1. Where showing possession is not necessary to the meaning, substitute "the" or "an" for "his" or "her."

   > . . . a plaintiff may petition the court for relief, attaching to *the* [rather than "his"] complaint a copy of . . .

2. Repeat the antecedent. The antecedent is the noun to which the pronoun refers. In the following sentence, "doctor" is the antecedent:

   > . . . to a doctor and the nurses, secretaries, and receptionists in *the doctor's* [rather than "his"] office . . .

3. Make the antecedent plural so you can use the plural (nongendered) pronoun "their."

   > The license fee applies to *taxi drivers* [rather than "a taxi driver"] driving *their* [rather than "his"] own taxis.

4. Use "they," "them," or "theirs" as a singular pronoun. As of 2019, the majority of major style guides recognize the use of the singular "they" for a person whose gender is unknown or irrelevant.[7]

7. In fact, Merriam-Webster designated "they" as the 2019 Word of the Year.

> *Anyone* who rides a roller coaster must assume the risk, and cannot recover for *their* injuries.

Although this usage is now accepted, when deciding whether to use the singular *they* in formal legal writing—in practice or for your professor—remember that this is a relatively new change to the style guides.

The other circumstance where "they," "them," or "their" could be used as a singular pronoun is where the antecedent (the person to whom the pronoun refers) identifies as gender nonbinary. The term *gender nonbinary* refers to a person who identifies as neither female nor male, as both female and male, in between the female and male genders, on or outside the gender spectrum, or beyond the gender binary scheme. Note that "they," "them," and "their" are but some of the many personal gender pronouns that a person may choose to describe themselves.[8] To ascertain what pronoun to use, simply ask.

5. Rephrase to use a clause beginning with "who."

   Change A person must assume the risk of injury if he rides a roller coaster.

   To A person who rides a roller coaster must assume the risk of injury.

6. Eliminate the pronoun by using a passive-voice verb.

   > If the examining physician knows that the person *being examined* [rather than "he is examining"] has been under treatment . . .

7. Substitute "one." This technique can seem stilted, but it might suffice from time to time.

   Change A person should always tell the truth to preserve his reputation.

   To One should always tell the truth to preserve one's reputation.

   The less formal "you" or "your" might work in less formal documents but *not* in court documents.

   > You should always tell the truth to preserve *your* reputation.

8. Rephrase the clause entirely.

   Change For each speaker, enclosed is an outline of his presentation, a copy of the exercise he has prepared, and a memorandum explaining his exercise.

   To Each speaker has prepared a presentation outline, an exercise, and an explanatory memorandum. Copies are enclosed.

8. Another example is "zie(ze)/hir" instead of she/her, he/his.

9. Where elimination, substitution, and rephrasing fail, use both pronouns separated by a conjunction, such as "or."

   A parent may enroll his or her child . . .

10. Slash constructions (his/her, he/she, s/he) are not recommended for formal professional writing.

C. Techniques for Proper Names and Titles

Refer to a client in the way that the client prefers. For example, if a person is gender nonbinary, they may prefer to use the gender-neutral honorific Mx. that Merriam-Webster introduced to their unabridged dictionary. If the client doesn't have a preference and strategic considerations do not intervene, use the following guidelines for referring to people.

1. Be consistent in the use of courtesy titles. If you do not use "Mr." for men, do not use "Miss," "Mrs.," or "Ms." for women.
2. Unless you have a good reason, use "Ms." rather than "Mrs." or "Miss." The object is to treat men and women the same. Because the courtesy title for men ("Mr.") does not indicate a marital status, the title for women should not do so either. You can decide to use "Mrs." or "Miss" when a reader prefers it, when the legal issue makes marital status relevant, when using the title will eliminate confusion, or when you have a particular strategic reason.
3. Be consistent in the use of first names and last names. You can use last names only, first and last names together, or (rarely) first names only. However, unless you have a good strategic reason, apply your decision equally to all genders.

PART SEVEN

Oral Advocacy

CHAPTER 21

Oral Argument

This chapter and your first law school oral argument provide only a glimpse of oral advocacy. Trial and appellate lawyers must know much more than this introduction can provide. Consider taking a course in trial and appellate practice and procedure. The first time you handle a case in court, you will be glad to have had that important training.

These next sections present material designed for a law school oral argument. In actual law practice, some of the details of presentation and formality expected in a particular court might differ from those expected in a law school setting. However, the fundamental concepts presented here will be equally applicable.

The sections of this chapter are designed for an appellate oral argument, but are adaptable to oral arguments in trial courts. In practice, some details of presentation and formality might differ from those expected in a law school setting, but the fundamental concepts presented here will apply equally.

I. THE PURPOSE OF ORAL ARGUMENT

Before you plunge into preparing your oral argument, consider its purpose. An oral argument is not simply an opportunity to say orally what you have already said in writing. If that were the purpose of oral argument, the judges would not waste your time or theirs. They would simply read your brief and issue a ruling.

Rather, an oral argument is *an opportunity for the judges to ask you questions.* They want to clarify their understanding of your arguments. They want to give you a chance to alleviate their concerns about adopting the position you advocate. They want to have a conversation. As your only chance to speak directly with those who will decide your case, oral argument is an important opportunity.

Oral argument also provides you a chance to return the judges' deliberation to the big picture and to emphasize the narrative themes and policy rationales that underlie your legal argument—the themes that show not just how the law *does* support your position, but also why it *should.* Direct, eye-to-eye contact often is the best way to bring home the importance of those fundamental aspects of your argument.

II. FORMALITIES AND ORGANIZATION

The first step in preparing for oral argument is to understand the formalities you will encounter and the overall organization your argument should follow. Here is an overview of the oral argument.

A. Timing

At the appellate level, each side is given a specific amount of time to make their argument to the court.[1] Parties are generally given fifteen minutes to argue. The appellant can ask to reserve some time for a rebuttal, which occurs after the appellee has argued and provides the appellant with an opportunity to respond to the appellee's arguments.

B. Preliminary Formalities

Usually you will be seated at counsel table, waiting for the judges to enter and call your case. A bailiff will announce the entry of the judges by saying something like this:

> Oyez, oyez, oyez. All rise. The First Circuit Court of . . . is now in session. All those with business before this Honorable Court may now draw near.

As soon as the bailiff begins this speech, stand up and remain standing until the judges are seated and the Chief Judge tells you to be seated. In fact, you should always stand when addressing the court. The Chief Judge will then call your case and ask if the lawyers are ready, saying something like this:

> The Court calls the case of *Jones v. Brown*. Is counsel for the appellant ready? . . . Is counsel for the appellee ready?

When the judge asks you if you are ready, stand up and say "Ready, Your Honor." The Chief Judge will then instruct counsel for the appellant to proceed.

C. The Appellant's Argument

As the lawyer for the moving party, counsel for the appellant goes first. You might be the only lawyer for the appellant, or you could have co-counsel arguing one of the issues. Use the following structure, leaving out the mention of co-counsel if you are arguing alone:

> May it please the Court. My name is Russell Stege, and along with my co-counsel, Margaret Liu, I represent the Appellant, Paul Giray. I would ask

1. Arguments are generally not timed at the trial court level.

> the Court for permission to reserve two minutes for rebuttal. [Pause to allow the Chief Justice to respond.]
>
> Thank you, your Honor. Mr. Giray respectfully asks this Court to . . . [state in one or two phrases the ruling you seek, for example, "reverse the trial court's entry of summary judgment and remand the case for trial"].
>
> The issue(s) before the Court is/are whether . . . [state each issue in one sentence, phrased favorably to your side[2]]. Ms. Liu will argue the damages issue, and I will argue the adverse possession issue.

Then give the Court a short overview of the arguments you will make.

> Your Honors, Mr. Giray will show that the undisputed facts in this case simply are not adequate to establish the elements of adverse possession. [In two or three sentences, state a summary of your argument so the judges will have a sense of the arguments you will make and the order in which you will present them. This is also a good spot to introduce your narrative theme, as described in Section III below.]

It is helpful to provide your arguments using a numbered roadmap of the points you plan to make. Then, set forth the facts.

> Your Honors, the facts are these: . . . [Inform the Court of the relevant facts, and then begin the main section of your argument, as described in Section III.]

D. Argument of Co-Counsel for the Appellant

If you are co-counsel arguing a second issue for the appellant, you will argue next. Go to the podium as soon as your co-counsel leaves it without waiting for an invitation from the judges. If the judges are still writing or conversing when you arrive at the podium, wait a moment until they are ready or until one of them tells you that you may begin. Then introduce yourself and identify your client, as the first lawyer did. You do not need to introduce your co-counsel from whom the Court has already heard. Nor do you need to repeat the request to reserve time for rebuttal. Proceed to a short overview of the arguments you will make:

> May it please the Court, my name is Margaret Liu, and I also represent Paul Giray. I will argue the issue of the adequacy of money damages in this case. Your Honors, even if the undisputed facts were sufficient to establish a claim for adverse possession, an award of money damages would be more than sufficient in this case. [In two or three sentences, state a summary of your argument. Again, a numbered roadmap is helpful.]

Your co-counsel has already stated the facts, so you do not need to repeat them. Simply begin your legal argument, perhaps starting with your narrative theme. The rest of your argument should proceed just as described above for the first advocate.

---

2. Use the same techniques you used in your brief to phrase the Questions Presented favorably. See Chapter 15, Section I.

E. The Appellee's Argument

Go to the podium as soon as counsel for the appellant leaves it. If the judges are still writing or conversing, wait a moment until they are ready or until one of them tells you that you may begin. Then introduce yourself, your co-counsel, if any, and your client, just as the first lawyer did. As counsel for the appellee, you do not have a rebuttal, so you do not need to reserve any time.

> May it please the Court, my name is Elizabeth Tunnesen, and along with Jason Kennedy, I represent Carol Cole. Ms. Cole requests the Court to affirm the trial court's order granting summary judgment. Mr. Kennedy will argue the damages issue, and I will argue the adverse possession issue. I will show that the undisputed facts are more than sufficient to establish each element of adverse possession.

Provide the court with a short overview of the arguments that you will make and introduce your theme. Counsel for the appellant has already provided the facts of the case, so you need only add or clarify any *important* fact omitted from the appellant's fact statement.

> Ms. Cole agrees with the facts as stated by the Appellant. However, the Court should also be aware that . . .

If you do not need to clarify or add an important fact, simply proceed to the rest of your argument, following the format described above.

F. Argument of Co-Counsel for the Appellee

Your argument should follow the format described for the second lawyer for the appellant.

G. Concluding the Argument

No matter whether you argue for the appellant or the appellee, you will have to reach a graceful and persuasive ending while negotiating the timing constraints. Prepare a conclusion consisting of a short summary (three to five sentences) of your best points, phrased compellingly, and a request for the relief you seek:

> [A summary of your strongest arguments]. . . . Therefore, the appellant requests that the Court reverse the trial court's entry of summary judgment and remand the case for trial on the adverse possession claim. Thank you, Your Honors.

Try to be ready to begin your conclusion at the one-minute mark. When time is up, you may finish your sentence, but then you must stop. Simply say, "Thank you, Your Honors," and sit down. If you are in the middle of answering a judge's question when time expires, stop and say to the Chief Judge:

> Your Honor, I see that my time is up. May I finish answering Judge Nottingham's question and have a moment to conclude?

The Chief Judge will probably say "Yes." If so, finish your answer and take *no more than 45 seconds* to deliver your conclusion. If the Chief Judge declines your request, simply say "Thank you, Your Honors," and sit down.

H. Rebuttal

After counsel for the appellee has finished arguing, one of the lawyers for the appellant will deliver the rebuttal. If you are that lawyer, listen carefully during the appellee's argument to identify a weak point or a point on which opposing counsel has damaged your case, especially if you can offer a strong, extremely brief rebuttal. When counsel for the appellee concludes, go to the podium and deliver your rebuttal in one to two minutes (however long you reserved). Then say, "Thank you, Your Honors," and sit down. The goal is to make your point in a compelling way and to sit down without prompting further questioning from the bench. Have one rebuttal prepared in advance, and use this prepared rebuttal in case you panic and cannot put together a compelling rebuttal based on what you have heard in the appellant's argument.

I. Oral Argument in Trial Court

There are some distinctions between appellate-level arguments and arguments at the trial court level to be aware of. Unlike appellate-level arguments that take place before a panel of judges, arguments at the trial court are generally before one judge. Moreover, oral arguments at the trial court are more fluid and not timed. Regardless, your professor may time your motion argument at the trial court. Finally, by virtue of the more fluid nature of arguments at the trial court, there is no rebuttal.

III. THE CONTENT

The following procedural facets of your case can be crucial. You must know how they apply to your case, and you must be able to phrase your arguments accurately in light of those effects.

A. The Standard of Review

The standard of review governs how much deference the appellate court must give to the decision of the judge or jury at the trial level. Review the material on the standard of review in Chapter 17. If the standard of review is favorable to your side, be especially sure to phrase your argument in its terms. No matter how much you choose to emphasize the standard, be ready to respond clearly and succinctly to a judge's question regarding the appropriate standard.

B. The Burden of Proof

Be sure you know the relevant burden of proof on the issue you are arguing. The burden of proof identifies the party who has the responsibility of proving the necessary facts and persuading the trial court. Usually, the plaintiff bears the burden of proving the elements of the cause of action, and the defendant bears the burden of proving an affirmative defense. On a procedural issue, the moving party often bears the burden. For instance, on a motion to compel discovery, the moving party would bear the burden of proof. Check the authorities on your legal issue to be sure you know which party bears the burden of proving each aspect of the case.

C. The Trial-Level Procedural Posture

Finally, your argument could be affected by the procedural posture of the ruling from which the appeal arose. The trial-level procedural posture defined the appropriate legal question in the trial court, and it is the decision on that legal question that is now on appeal. For instance, if the appeal is from a ruling granting summary judgment, the question before the trial court judge was whether the undisputed facts entitled the moving party to judgment without the necessity of a trial. Therefore, the role of the appellate court is to decide whether the trial judge ruled correctly *on that legal question*. An appellate judge doesn't decide what she would have done if she had been in the trial judge's shoes. She decides whether a reasonable judge could have made the ruling, even if the appellate judge would have ruled differently. If the appeal is from a judge's decision after a bench (not a jury) trial, the question is whether the facts in the trial record are sufficient to sustain the ruling (in other words, whether a reasonable judge, reviewing that trial record, could have decided the case in the way this judge did). Therefore, the role of the appellate court is to decide whether the trial judge ruled correctly *on that legal question*. Check the authorities to be sure of the implications of your case's trial-level procedural posture, and frame your arguments and your answers with that posture in mind.

D. Themes

Your case needs a theme, an overriding point to which you repeatedly return. Your theme should be the most persuasive big-picture point you have. Commonly, themes are based in the case's narrative (narrative reasoning), in the policies implicated by the case (policy-based reasoning), in the strength of the doctrinal law (rule-based and analogical reasoning), or in the case's procedural posture. Select a narrative theme if the most powerful part of your argument is based on your client's compelling facts:

> Your Honors, this is a case about a record title-holder who sat by and watched his neighbor build a garage, knowing that the neighbor believed the garage to be properly located on his own land. Then, just as the garage was completed, the record title-holder told his neighbor that the garage was six inches over the property line and demanded that the neighbor tear it down.

If the most compelling point of your argument is a policy implication, select a theme based on that policy:

> Even if a minor is less than completely candid about his age, the law should still require a merchant to take the remarkably simple precaution of asking to see the minor's driver's license. Such a requirement does not burden the merchant at all, and it protects against the very real danger that a merchant might find it profitable to be too easily convinced of an eager young customer's age.

If the most compelling part of your argument is the strength of the law on your side, select a theme that capitalizes on this strength:

> Despite the plaintiff's admittedly sympathetic facts, the law in this jurisdiction could not be more clear. A wrongful death action simply cannot be sustained for the death of a nonviable fetus. The legislature of this state has expressly declared this to be the law, and no fewer than five rulings of the Supreme Court have agreed.

At the appellate level, if the most compelling part of your argument is the procedural posture of the trial court decision on which the appeal is based, select a theme that keeps bringing the discussion back to that procedural posture:

> The defendant strenuously disagrees with the inferences the plaintiff asks the Court to draw from the affidavits. However, even if the affidavits did support the plaintiff's inferences, the fact remains that this case comes before the Court on appeal from a summary judgment ruling. The question is not whether the plaintiff's inferences are possible, or even whether they are the most likely, but rather whether they are the *only* possible inferences. Clearly they are not.

IV. PREPARATION

A. The Record

Thoroughly know the facts, whether it is the court and litigation documents at the trial court level or the record on appeal. For the important facts, be able to cite the page on which they appear. Do not overstate the facts, and do not state as facts the inferences you ask the court to draw from the facts. If you misstate facts, you will have lost credibility with the court, and if you misstate facts intentionally, you will have acted unethically.[3]

B. Outline Your Argument

Usually the outline of your argument should mirror the large-scale organization of your brief, as described in Chapter 7. The first level of headings should

3. See Chapter 14, Section I.

articulate your position on each relevant element of the governing rule. Under each heading, place as subheadings each argument you will make on that element, and under that subheading, place each point you will make in that part of the argument.

C. Prepare Your Folder

Prepare a folder with your notes for oral argument. You can use a file folder and small index cards. Use the front, back, and both sides of the inside of the folder for your opening and closing language (in case you panic), for important factual information to which you might need to refer (for example, dates and relevant numbers you might not remember), and for the outline of your argument.

Consider including two outlines, one for a cold bench (a bench that asks few questions) and one for a hot bench (a bench that leaves you little time for your scripted material). The outline for the cold bench is your expanded outline—the one you will use if the judges are quiet and you have time to present most of your prepared material. The outline for the hot bench is compressed into just the main points you want to make in case you have only a few minutes. You can start with the expanded outline but shift to the compressed outline as necessary during the argument.

Reserve one area of the folder for the index cards. For each important case, statute, or regulation, summarize on a card the important information from that source and quote any key language. Tape the cards on top of each other with the bottom of each card protruding a quarter of an inch from beneath the card on top of it. Tape the cards to the folder along the card's top edge, so the cards can be flipped up. In the visible space on the bottom of each card, write the name or the case, statute, or regulation. Practice finding the information on the cards and in the other parts of the folder quickly and easily.

D. Script the Entire Opening, the Conclusion, and Your Prepared Rebuttal

Although you cannot and should not try to script the body of the argument, the opening and closing should be scripted, essentially memorized, delivered with full eye contact, and spoken as if they were not memorized. This preparation will guarantee that you say what you want to say and that you say it smoothly and effectively. Your extemporaneous responses might not always be smooth, but your beginnings and endings can and should achieve a high level of poise and persuasion.

E. Practice

Practice delivering your argument to friends. Have the friends question you just as they would if they were the judges before whom you will argue. Practice at least five or six times, and more if possible. Go through the whole argument each time, and then ask for feedback. Use these practice benches to improve both your knowledge of the case and the smoothness of your delivery.

F. Visit the Courtroom

Familiarize yourself with the room where you will argue. Imagine yourself delivering your argument there, and remind yourself that you belong there, advocating for your client. Psychologically claim the space.

G. Be Prepared to Conduct an Oral Argument Virtually

Numerous changes to the practice of law were brought about by the global COVID-19 pandemic. The use of virtual conferencing technology for, among other things, client meetings, court appearances, and depositions is here to stay due to its efficiency and effectiveness. Virtual arguments bring new considerations such as lighting, sound quality, and Internet connections. Although the argument may be virtual, the same level of professionalism that is required in the courtroom is required in your office or dining room.

V. HANDLING QUESTIONS FROM THE BENCH

Because a primary purpose of oral argument is to answer the judges' questions, a big part of your preparation should consist of preparing those answers. Here are some important points to guide you.

A. Anticipate Questions

Ask yourself what you would want to know if you were a judge hearing the case. What parts of the argument would be hard to accept and why? What will your opponent argue? What key cases or statutes will the court be most concerned about? Also, pay close attention to the questions you receive in your practice rounds. Prepare answers for all of these questions.

B. Attitude

The judges will ask you questions, and they will often interrupt you to do it. This is part of the role of a judge. It is efficient and it saves you precious time. When a judge interrupts you, stop talking *immediately* and listen to what the judge is saying. Then answer the judge's question as best you can. Treat the question for what it is—a valuable opportunity to clarify a point about which the judge is concerned. Do not appear to be rushing through the answer so you can get back into your prepared argument. The judge's question is more important than your prepared argument.

The right to interrupt belongs only to the judge, however. Never interrupt a judge. No matter how badly you want to speak, wait patiently until the judge has finished speaking before you utter a sound.

C. Recognize Types of Questions

You will encounter three basic kinds of questions: friendly questions, questions genuinely seeking clarification of information, and adversarial questions.

A *friendly question* is designed to help you present your argument or make an additional point. A judge might want you to make a certain point primarily for the benefit of another judge, or a judge might simply be pleased to have thought of another point and might want to share it. Be sure to recognize a friendly question and to make use of the opportunity it gives you to agree with a judge and to articulate and validate the judge's point.

A *question genuinely seeking information* is an opportunity to be helpful to a judge who needs a point clarified. Do so willingly. Then, if you have a point to make about the subject of the inquiry, you can use this chance to make it, but only after you have answered the judge's question.

You might find that most of the questions you receive are *adversarial questions*, designed to test your arguments. Despite their threatening nature, these are the questions you should welcome most because these are the questions that allow you to resolve the concerns that could stand in the way of success. Often these questions will be politely phrased, but sometimes a judge will deliver the question in an intimidating, angry, or even rude manner. Your job is to answer politely but firmly, ignoring the packaging of the question and responding only to its content. Do not respond in anger, even if you are feeling angry. Remain calm, at least outwardly, and answer the question as best you can.

> Your Honor, I must respectfully disagree. In the *Jones* case, the Supreme Court did not hold that. . . . Rather,. . . . And this is precisely why. . . .

D. Listen Carefully to the Question

You might find that your nervousness impedes your ability to listen carefully to the question. After you hear the first part of the question, you might assume that you know what the judge will be asking, and your nervousness could cause you to stop listening and begin scrambling to formulate an answer. Yet you cannot answer a question that you have misunderstood. When a judge begins to speak, listen carefully to the whole question before you answer. Remember, it is acceptable to pause and collect your thoughts before answering.

E. Clarify the Question

Sometimes you will not understand a question even when you have listened carefully. This could happen because you are nervous or because the judge has not articulated the question clearly. Simply admit that you did not understand the question, apologize, and ask the judge to repeat it. If you think that you might have understood it but you are not sure, you can clarify your understanding: "Is Your Honor asking whether . . . ?"

F. Begin with a Clear, Direct Answer

Usually you will want to say a number of things in response to a question. However, you should always begin with a very short, direct answer to the question in the form in which the judge posed it: "Yes, Your Honor," or "No, Your Honor, I must respectfully disagree," or "Your Honor, that has sometimes been the case, but not always." After you have responded directly, you can go on to explain your answer, but the judge should know within roughly your first ten words what your answer to the question will be.

On a related note, do not put off answering the question, telling the judge "I'll get to that." This is considered rude. Moreover, the question tells you what the judge is interested in and you do not want to run the risk of not getting to it. Finally, be sure to answer the question that the judge asks, not the question you wish she had asked.

G. Returning to Your Prepared Presentation

When you have finished answering a question, return immediately to your prepared presentation. Do not wait for the judge to respond or to give you permission. Try to find a way to connect the ending of your answer to an entry point into your argument so that the answer seamlessly weaves you right back into your prepared material. However, if you cannot think of a connection on the spot, simply return to your argument.

H. Handling Questions on Your Co-Counsel's Issue

Sometimes a judge will ask you a question about the issue your co-counsel has already argued or will shortly argue. Try to answer it if you can, but qualify your answer by admitting that your co-counsel might be able to provide a better answer. This should minimize the chance that the judge will pursue the matter further.

> Your Honor, because *Home Finders* dealt with the issue of sufficiency of money damages, my co-counsel might be the best person to assist the Court on this question. However, I believe that the court there held that. . . .

I. Handling a Question for Which You Do Not Have an Answer

Your hard work should prepare you for most questions, but you might be asked a question for which you do not have an answer. A judge might ask you about a case or a statute with which you are not familiar, about how your issue compares to the comparable issue in some other area of law, or about how some particular procedural practice would affect your position. Even experienced appellate attorneys do not know all aspects of the law. If you do not know the answer to a judge's question, admit it. You can offer to find the answer and provide it to the court promptly after the argument concludes:

> Your Honor, I regret that I am not familiar with *Hatcher v. Norman*. However, if the Court allows, I will provide the Court with an answer to this question within 24 hours after today's argument concludes.

J. Agreeing When You Can

Remember that you will probably receive a friendly question here and there, so do not automatically disagree each time the judge engages you. You can even agree partially with the concerns underlying some adversarial questions as well, but go on to show why that valid concern does not defeat your position:

> Yes, Your Honor, I agree that this is a legitimate concern. However, . . .

K. Referring to Earlier Questions or Comments from the Bench

Remember the questions directed to you or to your opponent; you can refer to them when appropriate in your argument. If a judge has asked you a friendly question or made a friendly comment, you can refer to it later in the argument. You can refer also to the adversarial questions or comments directed to opposing counsel.

> As Justice Bailey pointed out, . . .

Use this technique sparingly, however. Some judges might be irritated to hear their own words used in this manner more than once or, at most, twice during an argument.

VI. PRESENTATION

A. Dress

Wear a conservative suit.

B. Body, Hands, and Eyes

Stand straight, with your weight equally placed on both feet, and remain behind the podium. Maintain eye contact with the judges, and include the whole bench in that eye contact. If conducting the argument virtually, eye contact is just as important. Do not read your argument. Rather, speak to the judges conversationally, looking down at your notes now and then. Lay your hands on the podium, and use them only moderately for occasional small gestures. Do not grip the podium. Do not put your hands in your pockets or clasp them behind your back.

C. Voice

Speak at a moderate pace. Do not allow your nervousness to cause you to speak too quickly, but do speak with a degree of energy appropriate for discussion of an important matter about which you and your client care deeply. Speak firmly and loudly enough to be heard.

D. References

Refer to the bench as "Your Honors" or "the Court." Refer to individual judges as "Your Honor" or "Justice [last name]." Refer to clients by their last name preceded by "Mr." or "Ms." or by other appropriate titles, such as "Dr." Refer to other lawyers as "counsel for Appellant/Appellee" or as "opposing counsel."

E. Nervousness

Oral argument will probably make you a little nervous, but remember that judges are human beings. Like you, they are trying to do a hard job well, and they will sometimes fall short. Although they have more experience than you do at this point in your legal career, they probably remember when they did not. All they ask of you, and all you need ask of yourself, is to do your best.

APPENDICES

Sample Office Memorandum

MEMORANDUM

To: Requesting Attorney
From: Summer Clerk
Date: November 9, 2005
Re: Beth Buckley; file # 756385; stolen car; whether Buckley can disaffirm purchase of car based on her minority

QUESTION PRESENTED

Can Buckley, a minor, disaffirm the purchase of a car when she misunderstood the sales agent's question and therefore accidentally misrepresented her age as eighteen?

BRIEF ANSWER

Probably yes. A minor can disaffirm a contract unless the minor's fraudulent misrepresentation induced the other party to rely justifiably on the representation. On Buckley's facts, a court would probably rule that an innocent misrepresentation such as Buckley's is not fraudulent and therefore would not prevent a minor from disaffirming a contract. A court might also rule that the seller did not justifiably rely on Buckley's representation.

FACTS

Our client, Beth Buckley, is seventeen and a high school senior. She will turn eighteen on December 15. Two months ago she bought a used car for $3,000 from Willis Chevrolet. She paid cash, using the money she had saved from her summer job. Buckley purchased collision insurance for the car, but she did not insure against theft. Last week the car was stolen, and Buckley has asked what she can do about her loss.

When Buckley first looked at cars on the lot, the sales agent asked if she was old enough to buy a car. Buckley did not realize that she had to be eighteen to enter into a contract, even when paying cash. She thought the sales agent was asking whether she was old enough to drive, so she said "Yes." The agent did not ask to see any identification and did not raise the subject of age again.

-1-

The next day Buckley returned to the lot, selected the car she wanted to purchase, and completed the transaction. She recalls "signing a bunch of papers," but she did not read them and does not know what they said. She says that the sales agent did not attempt to explain the documents.

He simply showed her where to sign, and she signed on those lines. She does not know if she still has copies of the documents, but she will look among her papers and let us know.

DISCUSSION

I. Beth Buckley can probably disaffirm the contract.

A minor does not have the capacity to make a binding contract, but a contract made by a minor is not automatically void. *Hood v. Duren*, 125 S.E. 787, 788 (Ga. Ct. App. 1924). Generally, one who is a minor at the time of making a contract can disaffirm the contract within a reasonable time after reaching the age of majority. Ga. Code Ann. § 13-3-20 (2007); *Merritt v. Jowers*, 193 S.E. 238, 239 (Ga. 1937). The rationale for the rule is the recognition that minors have not yet attained sufficient maturity to be responsible for the decisions they make, so the rule protects them from at least some of the consequences of bad decisions. *See generally White v. Sikes*, 59 S.E. 228 (Ga. 1907). However, a minor is estopped from disaffirming a contract if (a) the minor made a false and fraudulent representation of his or her age; (b) the contracting party justifiably relied on the minor's representation; and (c) the minor has reached the age of discretion. *Carney v. Southland Loan Co.*, 88 S.E.2d 805, 808 (Ga. 1955). Thus, if Willis Chevrolet can establish these three elements, Buckley would be estopped from disaffirming the contract. Because the first element is the most problematic in Buckley's case, the memo will discuss it first.

A. Buckley's unintentional misrepresentation of her age probably is insufficient to establish fraudulent misrepresentation.

The first element necessary for estoppel is a false and fraudulent representation. *Id.* A minor makes a false and fraudulent representation when the minor affirmatively and intentionally states a false age, intending that the seller rely on the information. *Id.* For instance, in *Carney* the minor told the car sales agent that he was twenty-two, the agent recorded that information on the loan application, and the minor signed the application and purchased the car. *Id.* The court affirmed the trial court's holding that the minor had fraudulently misrepresented his age and was estopped from disaffirming the contract. *Id.* at 807–08.

Similarly, in *Clemons v. Olshine*, 187 S.E. 711, 712 (Ga. Ct. App. 1936), the minor told the clothing sales agent that he was twenty-one and signed a contract confirming the representation. The court held that his fraudulent misrepresentation estopped him from disaffirming. *Id.*

-2-

at 713–14. In *Watters v. Arrington,* 146 S.E. 773, 773–74 (Ga. Ct. App. 1929), another car purchase case, several agents of the seller testified that the minor had twice affirmatively stated his age to be twenty-one. The court affirmed the jury's verdict for the seller, holding that a minor's fraudulent misrepresentation of age estops the minor from disaffirming the contract. *Id.* at 774.

The courts distinguish this kind of intentional, knowing misrepresentation from unintentional, even negligent misrepresentations of age. *See Carney,* 88 S.E.2d at 808; *Woodall v. Grant & Co.,* 9 S.E.2d 95, 95 (Ga. Ct. App. 1940). For instance, in *Woodall,* the minor had simply signed without reading a form contract that contained a representation that he was of age. 9 S.E.2d at 95. There the court held that the representation in the contract did not estop the minor because the minor had not read the contract. *Id.* The court reasoned that minors are not required to read contracts. *Id.* The *Carney* decision distinguished *Woodall* by pointing out that in *Woodall* "the minor's only sin, if any, was his failure to read a contract which . . . stated that he was of age, while in [*Carney*] the minor falsely gave the information put into the contract." *Carney,* 88 S.E.2d at 808.

The most recent relevant case, *Siegelstein v. Fenner & Beane,* 17 S.E.2d 907, 910 (Ga. Ct. App. 1941), reaffirmed the *Carney/Woodall* distinction. In *Siegelstein,* the jury returned a verdict for the defendant, and the appellate court reversed on other grounds. *Id.* However, the appellate court affirmed the trial court's jury instruction, stating that a minor's false representation of age "will not affect his power to disaffirm a contract unless [the representation] was made *fraudulently.*" *Id.* at 910 (emphasis supplied).

The rule holding minors responsible only for intentional affirmative misrepresentations is consistent with the policy behind allowing minors to disaffirm their contracts. Minors, by definition, are more likely than adults to make errors and other innocent misrepresentations. Given this symmetry of rationale, the courts are likely to continue allowing minors to disaffirm despite innocent, even negligent, misrepresentations.

Here, the sales agent simply asked Buckley whether she was old enough to buy a car. Buckley misunderstood the question, thinking that the agent was asking whether she was old enough to drive. Thus she innocently answered "Yes." She did not affirmatively state an age at all. This kind of misunderstanding is exactly the sort of confusion a minor is likely to experience.

Buckley's representation that she was old enough to buy a car is significantly different from the representations in the cases holding that the minor cannot disaffirm. Unlike the minors in *Carney, Clemons,* and *Watters,* Buckley never stated her age at all. Also unlike the facts in those cases, Buckley's assertion, taken to mean what she intended it to mean—that she was old enough to drive—was not even false. Further, Buckley made only this single, ambiguous statement, in comparison to the several oral and written assertions of a specific age, as in the facts of the earlier cases.

-3-

Buckley's statement is much closer to the situation in *Woodall,* in which the minor made the representation unknowingly. In *Woodall,* the minor did not know that he was making the representation because he did not read the form contract he was signing. Buckley did not know that she might be making a representation that she was eighteen because she misunderstood the agent's question. In both cases, the requisite intent to deceive is absent. Because Buckley did not intend to deceive Willis Chevrolet, a court would probably allow her to disaffirm the contract.

However, Buckley must realize that the sales agent's testimony describing their conversation may differ from hers. The agent may remember the conversation differently or may testify falsely. Others may claim to have overheard the conversation. One way or another, Buckley's testimony may be controverted. Further, the documents Buckley signed may have contained representations of age, and other witnesses may testify that Buckley read them. If we decide to proceed with Buckley's case, we will need to learn what testimony Willis Chevrolet will offer and what the documents contain. On the facts we now have, however, a court would probably conclude that Buckley did not fraudulently misrepresent her age.

B. Willis Chevrolet's reliance on Buckley's representation was probably reasonable.

The next element requires the injured party to have justifiably relied on the representation. *Carney,* 88 S.E.2d at 808. The cases that describe this element allude to the minor's physical appearance, the minor's life circumstances known to the injured party, the lack of any reason to cause the party to suspect the representation, and the lack of a ready means of confirming the representation. *Id.; Clemons,* 187 S.E. at 712–13; *Watters,* 146 S.E. at 773–74; *Hood,* 125 S.E. at 788.

For instance, in *Carney,* the court points out that the minor was married, was a father, and appeared to be of the age of majority. 88 S.E.2d at 808. In *Hood,* the court points to the minor's physical appearance and to the seller's knowledge that the minor had been married and living independently with his wife for about four years. 125 S.E. at 788. While the decisions sometimes articulate the standard as whether the defendant "failed to use all ready means" to ascertain the truth, *see, e.g., Carney,* 88 S.E.2d at 808, none of the reported decisions have found circumstances requiring the defendant to go further than the minor's representation. In fact, *Clemons* specifically held that a contracting party need not undertake an affirmative investigation beyond the representation of age when the contracting party has no reason to doubt the assertion. 187 S.E. at 713–14.

Buckley's facts do not indicate whether the sales agent knew anything about Buckley's life circumstances that would lead the agent to suspect that Buckley might not be eighteen. The facts also do not include a physical description of Buckley, although we can infer that she looks young, as the agent questioned her about her age. Although this issue would be a question of fact at trial, the facts seem similar to the facts in the reported cases. Contrary to the facts in *Hood,* Buckley is close enough to eighteen that an agent probably would not be expected to suspect her minority simply from her appearance. Also unlike the *Hood* facts, we have no reason to believe that the agent knew anything about Buckley's life, nor that he had any reason other than her appearance to suspect that she was a minor. Therefore, the facts may not be sufficient to require the agent to go further than questioning Buckley.

However, one might argue that the agent had at least one "ready means" to verify Buckley's answer, namely asking to see her driver's license. There is no discussion of requiring this simple verification in any of the prior cases, but at least for some of them, that may be because driver's licenses were not required at the time those cases were decided. Not only would this solution have been simple, but requiring it would facilitate an important policy rationale for the rule. The rule is designed to discourage sellers from being too ready to contract with minors, despite the inherent pressure to make sales. Requiring sellers to verify the ages of buyers who appear young would counteract the possible tendency of sellers to be too easily convinced of a buyer's majority.

The court's ruling on the second element probably would be a close one. However, based on the applicable case law, a court probably would find the agent's reliance reasonable.

C. Buckley had almost certainly reached the age of discretion when she made the representation of her age.

A minor cannot be held responsible for a misrepresentation unless the minor had reached the age of discretion when he or she made the misrepresentation. *Carney,* 88 S.E.2d at 808; *Clemons,* 187 S.E. at 713. A minor reaches the age of discretion when the minor has developed the capacity to conceive a fraudulent intent. *Clemons,* 187 S.E. at 713. Most minors have reached the age of discretion for criminal prosecution for fraud at least by the age of fourteen, though probably not by the age of ten. *Id. Clemons* concluded that the eighteen-year-old minor in that case was well within the age of discretion. *Id.*

Buckley was seventeen when she bought the car, just a few months away from the age of majority. She is three years older than the presumptive age of discretion for criminal prosecution, and criminal prosecution probably requires more assurance of sufficient age than simple estoppel in a contract action. A court almost certainly would conclude that Buckley had reached the age of discretion.

CONCLUSION

Buckley can disaffirm unless (1) she fraudulently misrepresented her age, (2) Willis Chevrolet justifiably relied upon the misrepresentation, and (3) Buckley had reached the age of discretion. On the facts

-5-

as we presently understand them, a court would probably rule that Buckley did not misrepresent her age. A court might also rule that Willis Chevrolet was not justified in relying on Buckley's representation. Given the probable absence of one required element and the possible absence of another, Buckley can probably disaffirm the contract.

-6-

APPENDIX B

Sample E-Memo[1]

✕ DELETE ← REPLY ⇇ REPLY ALL → FORWARD ...

Associate Kristy
Thu 6/14/2018 11:16 AM

To: Partner, Angie Renee

Angie,

You asked me to research whether Mike Dent's dog, Hopper, is a service animal under the ADA.

Hopper does not qualify as a service animal because Hopper has not been trained to specifically benefit Mike with his PTSD.

Analysis:

A service animal is "any dog that is individually trained to do work or perform tasks *for the benefit of an individual with a disability*." 28 C.F.R. § 36.104 (2017) (emphasis added). However, "tasks" do not include assisting with "emotional support, well-being, [and] comfort." *Id.*

Therefore, a service animal must have more than basic obedience training and be more than an emotional support animal that passively calms an individual with a disability. *See, e.g., Rose v. Springfield-Greene Cnty. Health Dep't*, 668 F. Supp. 2d 1206, 1215 (W.D. Mo. 2009) (finding that a monkey that the plaintiff held to lessen the plaintiff's anxiety was not a service animal); *Davis v. Ma*, 848 F. Supp. 2d 1105, 1115 (C.D. Cal. 2012) (finding a puppy with basic obedience training that did not assist with a plaintiff's disability was not a service animal).

---

1. Brad Desnoyer, *E-Memos 2.0: An Empirical Study of How Attorneys Write*, 25 Legal Writing 213 app. C-x (2021), https://www.legalwritingjournal.org/article/24785-e-memos-2-0-an-empirical-study-of-how-attorneys-write.

For a dog to qualify as a service animal, the dog must be specifically trained to perform tasks directly related to the individual's disability. *See, e.g., Cordoves v. Miami-Dade Cnty.*, 92 F. Supp. 3d 1221, 1231 (S.D. Fla. 2015) (denying summary judgment for the defendants because there was evidence a plaintiff's dog was a service animal that could detect and alert the plaintiff of oncoming panic attacks); *Alejandro v. Palm Beach State Coll.*, 843 F. Supp. 2d 1263, 1270 (S.D. Fla. 2011) (granting a plaintiff with PTSD a temporary injunction to have her dog on a college campus because the dog was trained to detect and alert the plaintiff by making eye contact, snorting, and nipping at the plaintiff's fingers).

Conclusion and Recommendation:

Hopper is not a service animal because he is not specifically trained to perform tasks that benefit Mike's PTSD. Although Hopper has general obedience training, Hopper only passively comforts Mike, thus making Hopper a mere emotional support animal.

If, however, Hopper can be trained to recognize and warn Mike before a panic attack, Hopper would qualify as a service animal. There are no specific requirements about how this training must be done. Regardless, it would be best to have the training done professionally to establish Hopper has been specifically trained to directly benefit Mike's disability.

I have attached the C.F.R. and relevant cases. Please let me know if you need more research or would like me to look into service animal training.

Sincerely,
Kristy Associate

Confidentiality Notice: *This email transmission may contain information that is privileged, confidential, and protected by the attorney-client or work-product privileges. If you are not the addressee, note that any disclosure, copying, distribution, or use of the contents of this message is strictly prohibited. If you have received this transmission in error, please destroy it and notify the sender by reply email.*

APPENDIX C

Sample Trial-Level Brief

IN THE UNITED STATES DISTRICT COURT
FOR THE DISTRICT OF COLORADO

RANDALL BROWNLEY,
Plaintiff

v.

SCOTT DUNN, d/b/a DUNN CREDIT BUREAU,

Defendant

Civ. No. 95-14867

MEMORANDUM OF LAW IN SUPPORT OF SCOTT DUNN'S MOTION TO SET ASIDE DEFAULT JUDGMENT

This is an action alleging a violation of Section 607(b) of the Fair Credit Reporting Act (FCRA), 15 U.S.C.A. § 1681e(b). The Complaint was filed and served upon Scott Dunn on October 27, 1995. Default judgment was entered six days ago, on November 17, 1995, just one day after the expiration of Mr. Dunn's time to answer the Complaint. Mr. Dunn now files a Motion to Set Aside this Default Judgment, along with a supporting affidavit and a proposed Answer to the Complaint. This brief is filed in support of Mr. Dunn's Motion.

STATEMENT OF FACTS

In September 1995, a potential lender contacted Dunn Credit Bureau requesting a credit report on the Plaintiff. Dunn Aff. ¶ 10 (Nov. 26, 1995). The Credit Bureau prepared the report, and it contained a reference to an unpaid department store account. Dunn Aff. ¶ 11. Upon the discovery of this item on his credit report, the Plaintiff contacted Mr. Dunn to demand that the item be removed, arguing that the charged merchandise had been defective and that the defect was the reason for his nonpayment. Dunn Aff. ¶ 12. Mr. Dunn asked the Plaintiff to provide this explanation in writing and promised to include it along with the store's version of the account. Dunn Aff. ¶ 13. The Plaintiff refused to provide the written explanation, but again demanded that the item be entirely removed. Dunn Aff. ¶ 14. Mr. Dunn replied by letter, declining to delete the item entirely but repeating the offer to include the Plaintiff's defense to the item. Dunn Aff. ¶ 14. The Plaintiff did not respond to Mr. Dunn's letter, and Mr. Dunn did not hear from the Plaintiff again. Dunn Aff. ¶ 15.

On October 27, 1995, copies of the Summons and Complaint in this action were served at Mr. Dunn's home by leaving them with Mr. Dunn's sixteen-year-old son, Gregory. (Ret. of Serv. Oct. 30, 1995.) On that day, Mr. Dunn and his wife had traveled to Denver, planning to return the next day. Dunn Aff. ¶ 3.

However, on the evening of October 27, Mrs. Dunn suffered a serious heart attack and was hospitalized. Dunn Aff. ¶ 4. Gregory left immediately for Denver. In the midst of the crisis surrounding his mother's heart attack, Gregory did not think to tell his father about the delivery of an envelope to the family home. Dunn Aff. ¶ 6.

Mr. Dunn remained in Denver with his wife for two weeks until Mrs. Dunn was released from the hospital to return home. Dunn Aff. ¶ 5. Upon his return, Mr. Dunn began going in to his office part time, while continuing to care for his wife. Dunn Aff. ¶ 7. Mr. Dunn did not find the envelope until November 20, 1995. On that day, Mr. Dunn moved a stack of papers on the table in the family room and found the envelope there. Dunn Aff. ¶ 8.

Mr. Dunn immediately called his attorney and began the preparations to file an Answer to the Complaint. Dunn Aff. ¶ 9. Shortly after the initial telephone conversation with his attorney, Mr. Dunn learned that a default judgment had been entered three days earlier. Dunn Aff.

¶ 9. Mr. Dunn now seeks an order, pursuant to Fed. R. Civ. P. 60(b), setting aside this default judgment.

ARGUMENT

I. THE COURT SHOULD SET ASIDE THE DEFAULT JUDGMENT BECAUSE IT WAS ENTERED AS A RESULT OF INADVERTENCE OR EXCUSABLE NEGLECT AND BECAUSE THE DEFENDANT HAS A MERITORIOUS DEFENSE TO THE PLAINTIFF'S ALLEGATIONS.

Rule 60(b) of the Federal Rules of Civil Procedure grants the Court the discretion to relieve a party from a final judgment entered as a result of inadvertence or excusable neglect. When the judgment was entered upon the moving party's default, the moving party must also demonstrate the existence of a potentially meritorious defense. *In re Stone*, 588 F.2d 1316, 1319 (10th Cir. 1978). Any doubts are to be resolved in favor of adjudication on the merits. *In re Roxford Foods, Inc.*, 12 F.3d 875, 879 (9th Cir. 1993). Rule 60(b) is to be liberally construed. *Pierce v. Cook Co.*, 518 F.2d 720, 722 (10th Cir. 1975). Doubts are to be resolved in favor of adjudication on the merits. *In re Roxford Foods, Inc.*, 12 F.3d 875, 879 (9th Cir. 1993). Mr. Dunn's facts easily establish both Rule 60(b) requirements.

A. Mr. Dunn's default resulted from excusable neglect because service was effected upon Mr. Dunn's minor son and the crisis of his mother's heart attack caused the son to forget to inform Mr. Dunn of the service.

Mr. Dunn meets the first requirement for Rule 60(b) relief because the default resulted from excusable neglect. The United States Supreme Court has defined the term "excusable neglect," in the context of bankruptcy filings, to include giving "little attention or respect" or "leav[ing] undone or unattended . . . esp[ecially] through carelessness." *Pioneer Inv. Servs. Co. v. Brunswick Assocs. Ltd. P'ship*, 507 U.S. 380, 388 (1993) (quoting *Webster's Ninth New Collegiate Dictionary* 791 (1983)). Last year the Tenth Circuit adopted this definition of excusable neglect in the context of a Rule 60(b) motion. *City of Chanute v. Williams Nat. Gas Co.*, 31 F.3d 1041, 1046 (10th Cir. 1994). The Tenth Circuit specifically held that Rule 60(b) relief is not limited to circumstances beyond the moving party's control. *Id.* The Tenth Circuit's analysis of excusable neglect considers four factors: (1) the potential prejudice to the nonmoving party; (2) the length of delay; (3) the reason for the delay; and (4) the degree of good faith of the moving party. *Id.*

The first factor, the prejudice to the nonmoving party, must amount to more than simply delaying enforcement of the judgment. *Feliciano v. Reliant Tooling Co.*, 691 F.2d 653, 656–57 (3d Cir. 1982). Usually cognizable prejudice involves some change of position in reliance on the judgment. *Id.* The second factor, the length of delay, measures both the time since the entry of judgment and the time since the party became aware of the judgment. *See Lasky v. Int'l Union*, 27 Fed. R. Serv. 2d 473, 477 (E.D. Mich. 1978), *aff'd*, 638 F.2d 954 (6th Cir. 1981) (more than one year too long). For instance, a delay of thirty-one days might be well within acceptable limits. *City of Chanute*, 31 F.3d at 1047.

The third factor examines the validity of the reason for the delay and whether the delay was willful. *Id.* at 1046. The Tenth Circuit has consistently affirmed orders setting aside default judgments entered as a result of understandable error or inadvertence as opposed to willful action by the defendant. *See, e.g., United States v. Andrews*, 790 F.2d 803, 806 (10th Cir. 1986) (finding excusable neglect where defendant filed late because of serious illness, heavy medication, and lack of legal counsel). For example, the court affirmed a decision to set aside a default judgment entered while the plaintiff believed that his new attorney was negotiating a settlement that would resolve the litigation. *Thompson v. Kerr-McGee Ref. Corp.*, 660 F.2d 1380, 1385 (10th Cir. 1981). The Tenth Circuit also affirmed an order granting Rule 60(b) relief from a judgment caused by confusion about filing a notice of appeal. *Romero v. Peterson*, 930 F.2d 1502, 1505 (10th Cir. 1991).

The excusable reasons for delay in these cases contrast with cases in which the default resulted from a willful decision by the defendant. *See, e.g., Cessna Fin. Corp. v. Bielenberg Masonry Contracting, Inc.*, 715 F.2d 1442, 1447 (10th Cir. 1983). For example, in *Cessna Fin. Corp.*, the court affirmed the trial court's decision denying relief to a corporate defendant whose representatives had decided not to answer the complaint because they believed that the corporate defendant would escape liability in bankruptcy. *Id.* at 1446–47. Similarly, in *United States v. Theodorovich*, 102 F.R.D. 587, 590 (D.D.C. 1984), the court denied relief because the default judgment had resulted from defendant's willful decisions not to attend his own properly scheduled deposition.

The final factor asks whether the defendant has acted in good faith. *City of Chanute*, 31 F.3d at 1046. This factor invites the court to consider the broad equitable question of whether the moving party has dealt in good faith with the court and with the other parties to the litigation. *Id.*

A court can also consider equitable matters. *Pioneer Inv. Servs. Co.*, 507 U.S. at 388. For instance, it may overlook the defendant's neglect if an order requiring the defendant to pay the plaintiff's costs would sufficiently alleviate any prejudice to the plaintiff. *Littlefield v. Walt Flanagan & Co.*, 498 F.2d 1133, 1136 (10th Cir. 1974).

Applying these four factors to the present case demonstrates that Rule 60(b) relief is appropriate here. First, granting Mr. Dunn's Motion would not cause the Plaintiff to suffer any cognizable prejudice. The default judgment was entered less than one week ago. The only cognizable prejudice that would result from setting aside the judgment stems from the costs the Plaintiff incurred in seeking the entry of the judgment. Mr. Dunn has offered to pay those reasonable costs Dunn Aff. ¶ 16, and an order to that effect should sufficiently relieve the Plaintiff of even this small prejudice.

-3-

The "length of delay" factor also weighs in favor of granting the motion. Only three days elapsed between the entry of the default judgment and Mr. Dunn's discovery of the litigation. Only three additional days elapsed between Mr. Dunn's discovery and the filing of the Motion and supporting documents. By comparison, the Tenth Circuit found a delay of thirty-one days "short." *City of Chanute,* 31 F.3d at 1047. A six-day delay is well within permissible bounds.

The third factor, the validity of the reason for delay, is often the most important factor. In the present case, this critical factor is the most compelling of all. Here, the delay was caused by the sudden and serious heart attack of Mr. Dunn's wife and Gregory's mother Dunn Aff. ¶¶ 4–9. That a teenager should forget to tell his father about the delivery of an unopened envelope is certainly understandable. This is precisely the sort of omission that Rule 60(b) is designed to forgive.

Mr. Dunn's good faith also argues for relieving him from judgment. Mr. Dunn has dealt with both the Court and the Plaintiff entirely in good faith. The delay was not caused by any stratagem or artifice. Mr. Dunn was entirely unaware of the litigation. Immediately upon learning of the Complaint, Mr. Dunn hurriedly contacted his attorney and began the process of responding to the litigation Dunn Aff. ¶ 9. Mr. Dunn's offer to bear the Plaintiff's costs is further evidence of his good faith.

Thus all four factors of the Rule 60(b) analysis place the Defendant's situation squarely within the parameters for Rule 60(b) relief and establish that Mr. Dunn meets the first requirement for setting aside the default judgment.

B. <u>Mr. Dunn has a meritorious defense to the complaint because the credit report accurately reflects the Plaintiff's admitted failure to pay the account.</u>

Mr. Dunn also meets the second requirement for Rule 60(b) relief, the existence of a meritorious defense. A plaintiff alleging a violation of 15 U.S.C. § 1681e(b) must establish two elements: (1) that the credit report is inaccurate; and (2) that the inaccuracy flows from the reporting agency's failure to follow reasonable procedures. *Cahlin v. Gen. Motors Corp.,* 936 F.2d 1151, 1156 (11th Cir. 1991). Establishing inaccuracy is a threshold requirement for a Section 1681e(b) claim. *Id.*

The accuracy requirement of the FCRA does not require the credit reporting agency to delete all reference to an unpaid account merely because it is disputed. *Id.* at 1158. This is true even if the consumer ultimately pays the account. *Id.* In *Cahlin,* the plaintiff's credit report included reference to a disputed account. *Id.* at 1155. Initially the account was unpaid, but after it appeared on the credit report, the consumer settled the account for partial payment. *Id.* The consumer then demanded that the credit agency delete all reference to the account. *Id.* The Eleventh Circuit held that Section 607(b) does not require a credit-reporting agency to report only favorable information. *Id.* at 1158. The court specifically held that the agency did not have to delete the

-4-

reference to the disputed account even though the dispute was settled, explaining that such an interpretation would gut the very purpose of a credit report. *Id.*

Here, the Plaintiff's credit report accurately reflects his failure to pay the balance owed on a department store charge account. Dunn Aff. ¶11. Further, unlike the account in *Cahlin,* which was partially paid, the Plaintiff's account remains unpaid. The Credit Bureau offered to include the consumer's written statement describing the dispute, as required by 15 U.S.C.A. § 1681i (b). The Plaintiff refused. This refusal is the only impediment to a more complete description of the Plaintiff's dispute with the account holder. The Plaintiff's demand that the item be removed entirely would have decreased rather than increased the report's accuracy because it would have omitted all reference to an admittedly unpaid, though disputed, debt. The FCRA simply does not require this sort of concealment of a consumer's true credit history.

Thus, the Plaintiff's credit report is accurate, and the Credit Bureau did not violate FCRA. Mr. Dunn has a meritorious defense to the Plaintiff's Complaint.

CONCLUSION

Mr. Dunn meets both requirements for Rule 60(b) relief. All four factors for evaluating inadvertence or excusable neglect strongly argue in favor of granting Mr. Dunn relief under Rule 60(b). Further, the Plaintiff's credit report met the accuracy requirement under FCRA, and thus Mr. Dunn has a meritorious defense to the complaint. Mr. Dunn respectfully requests the Court to enter an order setting aside the judgment and allowing him to file his Answer and to otherwise defend this action.

DATED: ____________________ ____________________

Attorney for the Defendant

CERTIFICATE OF SERVICE

I, ____________________, attorney for the Defendant, do hereby certify that I have served upon the Plaintiff a complete and accurate copy of this Memorandum of Law in Support of Scott Dunn's Motion to Set Aside Default Judgment, by placing the copy in the United States Mail, sufficient postage affixed and addressed as follows:

[name and address of Plaintiff's attorney]

DATED: ____________________ ____________________

Attorney for the Defendant

-5-

APPENDIX D

Sample Appellate Brief

The issue addressed in this brief is essentially a pure question of law, requiring interpretation of a rule of evidence. Therefore, the rule explanation sections focus primarily on the language of the rule, the intent of the rule's drafters, and the policies served by adhering to the rule's plain language. The writer relies on case authorities as well, but because the cases are not mandatory authority for this court, the writer presents the cases as further support for the primary arguments of plain meaning, intent of the drafters, and policy.

In both the "plain language" section and the "intent of the drafters" section, notice how closely the writer focuses on the actual words of Rule 615. If the case authority had defined the Rule's terms more fully, the writer would have relied primarily on case authority for the definitions of the words used in the Rule. Even without strong case authority defining the terms, however, a writer can use legal and other dictionaries to parse each word of a rule or statute, as the writer has done here.

In the "intent of the drafters" section, the writer casts the Rule as primarily defining what restrictions a party can force on other parties as a matter of course, without justifying the need for the restrictions. This section expressly articulates the primary theme of the brief, contrasting the trial court's powers with the powers given to parties. The section relies on a canon of statutory construction to point out not only what is included in the Rule's plain language, but also what is omitted. The writer also discusses the Rule's silence on important questions that would arise routinely if the Rule had been intended to have the scope urged by the appellant. This section ends by pointing out that the trial court, which presumably knew what it meant by its own order, did not intend that the order apply in the manner the appellant has proposed, thus harkening back to the theme of reliance on the court's trial management powers.

Then, after the rule explanation sections, the writer applies the Rule to the facts of the case before the court. The way the Rule will apply to these facts is clear, but the writer uses the rule application section as an opportunity to reinforce the points made in the rule explanation sections and to reassure the court that justice will not be infringed by a ruling in the appellee's favor.

IN THE UNITED STATES COURT OF APPEALS
FOR THE FIFTEENTH[1] CIRCUIT

DENNIS IRVING,
Appellant
v.

THE UNITED STATES
OF AMERICA,
Appellee.

Docket No. 04-1234

BRIEF OF THE APPELLEE[2]

[1]This is a hypothetical circuit.

[2]This brief is based on briefs written by students in the Spring 2005 Advanced Writing Groups at Mercer University School of Law. Professor Beth Cook of the Pennsylvania State University Dickinson School of Law graciously allowed the use of the problem that was adapted for that class.

TABLE OF CONTENTS

TABLE OF AUTHORITIES

QUESTION PRESENTED

Whether Rule 615 of the Federal Rules of Evidence should be expanded to apply to communications outside the courtroom where (1) the trial court did not intend that its routine Rule 615 order should limit outside conversation; (2) the Defendant never requested a broad sequestration order; (3) the court did not instruct witnesses to refrain from discussing their testimony; (4) a police officer spoke about his testimony to his co-worker; and (5) during the co-worker's subsequent testimony, the Defendant was able to cross-examine the co-worker about the conversation.

RULE OF EVIDENCE INVOLVED

Federal Rule of Evidence 615 provides:

> At the request of a party the court shall order witnesses excluded so that they cannot hear the testimony of other witnesses, and it may make the order of its own motion. This rule does not authorize exclusion of (1) a party who is a natural person, or (2) an officer or employee of a party which is not a natural person designated as its representative by its attorney, or (3) a person whose presence is shown by a party to be essential to the presentation of the party's cause, or (4) a person authorized by statute to be present.

STANDARD OF REVIEW

Because rulings on motions to exclude testimony raise predominately legal questions regarding the interpretation of the Federal Rules of Evidence, the appellate court reviews those evidentiary rulings de novo. *United States v. Angwin*, 271 F.3d 786, 798 (9th Cir. 2001).

STATEMENT OF THE CASE

On May 8, 2004, the Defendant, Dennis Irving, sold to Nathan Roberts more than fifty grams of methamphetamine, a Schedule II controlled substance. (R. at 1.) Officers Miller and Nelson witnessed the transaction and immediately arrested both men. (R. at 1.) Subsequently, a grand jury indicted the Defendant for offenses involving the possession and distribution of methamphetamine. (R. at 2.)

In pretrial proceedings, the district court granted the Defendant's Motion to Exclude Witnesses Pursuant to Rule 615 of the Federal Rules of Evidence and specifically ordered all prospective witnesses to leave the courtroom. (R. at 4.) The court, however, did not instruct the witnesses or counsel that witnesses were prohibited from discussing their testimony with each other. (R. at 4.)

On September 22, 2004, the trial began. That day, during the government's case-in-chief, Officer Nelson testified that he had seen the Defendant hand to Roberts the envelope containing the drugs. (R. at 5.)

Later that evening, Officer Nelson had dinner with Officer Miller, who was scheduled to testify the following day. (R. at 6.) A research assistant for the Defendant's attorney was seated nearby. (R. at 7.) According to the research assistant, as the officers ate dinner, Officer Nelson described the testimony he had given at trial that morning. (R. at 7.) In pre-trial statements, Officer Miller had described first seeing the two men at the point where the envelope was already in Roberts's hand. (R. at 7.) Allegedly, after hearing a description of Officer Nelson's testimony, Officer Miller stated that he now remembered seeing the Defendant hand the envelope to Roberts. (R. at 7.)

The next day, the Defendant moved to exclude Officer Miller's testimony, arguing that the dinner conversation between Officers Nelson and Miller the previous evening violated the court's Rule 615 order to exclude witnesses from the courtroom. (R. at 5.) The district court heard argument and denied Defendant's motion. (R. at 6.) The court reasoned that a witness's refreshed recollection of events (1) was common when talking to another person involved in the same incident; (2) was not evidence that the witness planned to perjure himself; and (3) did not violate the court's Rule 615 order, which barred witnesses only from being physically present in the courtroom. (R. at 6.)

Later that day, Officer Miller testified at trial. (R. at 7.) The Defendant's attorney cross-examined Officer Miller, confronting him with his previous statements and questioning him about his conversation with Officer Nelson the previous evening. (R. at 6.) After hearing this cross-examination and all of the other evidence in the case, the jury convicted the Defendant on all counts. (R. at 7.) The District Judge sentenced the Defendant to serve fifty-six months in a federal prison (R. at 7.), and the Defendant has now filed this appeal.

SUMMARY OF THE ARGUMENT

Federal Rule of Evidence 615 provides that upon the request of a party, the trial court "shall order witnesses excluded so that they cannot hear the testimony of other witnesses." Fed. R. Evid. 615. The Appellant asks this Court to hold that a routine Rule 615 order also prohibits witnesses from discussing their testimony with each other. Neither the plain meaning of the Rule, the intent of its drafters, nor sound public policy support the Appellant's argument.

First, the plain meaning of Rule 615 is limited to physical presence in the courtroom. The Rule provides that witnesses shall be "excluded," meaning "expelled" or "barred"—a reference to physical presence, not to communication. The Rule sets out the reason for the exclusion, "so that" they do not "hear testimony." The word "testimony" means sworn statements of a competent witness in a trial, affidavit, or deposition. Therefore, by definition, witnesses cannot "hear testimony" unless they are present when the testimony is being given. Several courts, including the First and Eighth Circuits, have so held.

Further, the plain language of the Rule indicates the drafter's intention to limit only presence in the courtroom. Because a trial court already has the power to restrict witness communication as part of its inherent authority to manage proceedings before it, the Rule's primary purpose is to define the restrictions a *party* can impose unilaterally upon other parties. By expressly delineating the power to exclude witnesses from the courtroom, the Rule impliedly withholds from parties other, broader powers. Also, the drafters did not address several key questions that would arise regularly if Rule 615 had been intended to apply beyond the courtroom, such as exactly what witnesses are prohibited from saying and whether the prohibition precludes attorneys from preparing witnesses for their testimony.

Finally, application of Rule 615 beyond its express terms would disrupt the Rule's carefully crafted balance of the rights of parties and the efficient administration of trials. Broad witness sequestration is available outside Rule 615 in those cases where restrictions on witness communication are appropriate. Blanket restrictions, however, would be burdensome to witnesses and unworkable for the trial court. Enforcement proceedings would interrupt trials and squander judicial resources. Without guidance about what sorts of communications are prohibited, outcomes of these hearings would be unpredictable. Witnesses unwilling to risk charges of contempt of court would be inclined not to testify at all.

According to its express terms, the drafter's intent, and sound policy rationales, a routine Rule 615 order is limited to excluding witnesses from physical presence in the courtroom and does not apply to conversations between witnesses. Therefore, the Rule 615 order below did not prohibit the conversation between Officers Nelson and Miller. The Government respectfully requests this Court to affirm the trial court's denial of the Defendant's Motion to Exclude Testimony.

ARGUMENT

I. THE COURT SHOULD AFFIRM THE TRIAL COURT'S DECISION BECAUSE RULE 615 PROHIBITS ONLY PHYSICAL PRESENCE IN THE COURTROOM AND THEREFORE DOES NOT APPLY TO OUTSIDE COMMUNICATIONS SUCH AS THE DINNER CONVERSATION BETWEEN OFFICERS NELSON AND MILLER.

Rule 615 provides that, upon a party's request, the trial court "shall order witnesses *excluded* so that they cannot hear the *testimony* of other witnesses." Fed. R. Evid. 615 (emphasis added). According to the Rule's plain language, a Rule 615 order bans prospective witnesses from the courtroom, but does not restrict communication outside the courtroom. The Defendant seeks to extend the scope of Rule 615 beyond its plain language, in contravention of the intent of the Rule's drafters and in derogation of the trial court's inherent discretionary authority to manage its courtroom. The district court rejected such an interpretation of the rule, and this Court should affirm the district court's ruling.

A. The plain language of Rule 615 applies only to a witness's physical presence in the courtroom.

The first step in interpreting a rule is to examine the language itself. *Thompson v. Goeztmann*, 337 F.3d 489, 495 (5th Cir. 2003). If the language is plain and unambiguous, a court should not look past this plain meaning. *Shotz v. City of Plantation*, 344 F.3d 1161, 1167 (11th Cir. 2003); *Thompson*, 337 F.3d at 495. Dictionaries often are used to confirm the plain meaning of statutory text. *United States v. Knott*, 256 F.3d 20, 28 (1st Cir. 2001).

The issue before the Court concerns only one sentence of Rule 615: "At the request of a party the court shall order witnesses excluded so that they cannot hear the testimony of other witnesses, and it may make the order of its own motion." Fed. R. Evid. 615. The phrase at issue is "*exclude*[] so that they cannot *hear . . . testimony*." *Id.* (emphasis added). "Exclude" means to "expel or ban." *Exclude, Merriam-Webster's Collegiate Dictionary* (11th ed. 2003). "Testimony" means "evidence that a competent witness under oath or affirmation gives at trial or in an affidavit or deposition." Testimony, *Black's Law Dictionary* 1485 (Bryan A. Garner ed., 7th ed., West 2000). The plain, ordinary, straightforward language of the rule, therefore, provides only that witnesses are banned from the courtroom so they do not hear other witnesses *as they testify*.

The Rule goes on to identify the reason for exclusion from the courtroom: "so that they cannot hear the testimony of other witnesses." Fed. R. Evid. 615. This phrase does not define a broad category of situations to which the Rule will apply. Rather, the phrase expressly uses the language of purpose ("so that") to set out the reason for the exclusion from the courtroom. *See id.* The plain language of Rule 615, therefore, says nothing at all about what a witness may say or do outside the courtroom. *See United States v. Scharstein*, 531 F. Supp. 460, 462–63 (E.D. Ky. 1982).

Even if the word "exclude" could be redefined to refer to something other than banning an individual from the courtroom, Rule 615, by its own terms, would apply only to hearing *testimony*. Fed. R. Evid. 615. A participant in a restaurant conversation over dinner is not "hearing testimony." In that setting, no one is under oath, no one is being questioned by an attorney, and no rules of evidence apply. The express language of Rule 615 does not apply to communications of that sort. *See* 29 Charles Alan Wright & Victor James Gold, *Federal Practice and Procedure* § 6243, at 57 (1997) ("Testimony is given only in a formal legal context such as a deposition, hearing, or trial. Thus witness communication outside that context does not enable witnesses to 'hear testimony.' ").

Several courts have held that the language of Rule 615 limits only physical presence of witnesses in the courtroom. *Sepulveda v. United States*, 15 F.3d 1161, 1176 (1st Cir. 1993); *United States v. Smith*, 578 F.2d 1227, 1235 (8th Cir. 1978). For instance, in *Sepulveda*, the First Circuit

-6-

held the Rule inapplicable to extra-courtroom communication. 15 F.3d at 1176. In that case, the defendants had been charged with offenses relating to the distribution of cocaine, and the trial court had issued a Rule 615 order before trial began. *Id.* Later in the trial, the defendants alleged that extra-courtroom witness contact had violated the Rule 615 order. *Id.* The court held that a Rule 615 order does not prohibit witness communication, stating that the Rule 615 order had "plowed a straight furrow in line with Rule 615 itself [and therefore] did not extend beyond the courtroom." *Id.*

The Eighth Circuit also has held Rule 615 inapplicable to extra-courtroom communications. *Smith,* 578 F.2d at 1235. In *Smith,* defendants were on trial for offenses associated with the distribution of heroin. *Id.* at 1229. Early in the trial, the court had issued a Rule 615 order excluding witnesses from the courtroom. *Id.* As trial progressed, a police officer took notes and relayed information to government witnesses waiting to testify. *Id.* at 1234. The trial court held that this conduct did not violate the Rule 615 order because Rule 615 only excludes witnesses from the courtroom. *Id.* The Eighth Circuit affirmed the trial court's holding, noting that the defendants had not requested additional restrictions beyond Rule 615. *Id.* at 1235. The appellate court stated that the question of whether to instruct witnesses not to communicate with other witnesses is within a trial court's discretion. *Id.* Such a discretionary instruction is not, therefore, mandated by the plain language of Rule 615. *See id.*

Similarly, the court in *Scharstein* held that the plain language of Rule 615 limits only physical presence in the courtroom. 531 F. Supp. at 463–64. In *Scharstein,* defendants had been charged with illegally manufacturing, storing, and transporting explosives. *Id.* at 461. The court declined to expand the application of Rule 615 to prohibit witnesses from conferring with each other outside the courtroom. *Id.* at 463. The court stated, "[T]his court believes that there is no reason to go beyond the plain language of the Rule," observing that the question of whether to instruct witnesses not to discuss their testimony is within the court's discretion and not required by Rule 615. *Id. ; see also Lapenna v. Upjohn Co.,* 665 F. Supp. 412, 413 (E.D. Pa. 1987) (declining to apply Rule 615 "beyond the literal meaning of the rule").

B. <u>The drafters did not intend Rule 615 to apply broadly to communication outside the courtroom.</u>

Not only does the plain language of Rule 615 call for affirmance here, but indications of the drafters' intent support that result as well. As a trial court already has inherent power to limit witness communication outside the courtroom, *Sepulveda,* 15 F.3d at 1176, the primary purpose of Rule 615 is to identify the restrictions *a party* can impose unilaterally on other trial participants. Therefore, the key inquiry is what unilateral and unrestrained powers the Rule's drafters intended to give to parties.

The drafters of the Rule rightly limited the unrestrained power the Rule would give to parties. At common law, when a court ordered sequestration, the order could include (1) preventing witnesses from hearing other witnesses testify; and (2) preventing prospective witnesses from consulting other witnesses. *Sepulveda*, 15 F.3d at 1176 (citing 6 John Wigmore, *Evidence* § 1840 at 471 n.7 (1976)). When the drafters expressly included in Rule 615 the power to "exclude" witnesses, they impliedly excluded the right to impose other more intrusive limitations. According to the canon of statutory construction *expressio unius est exclusio alterius*, the expression of one thing implies the exclusion of another. *Thompson*, 337 F.3d at 499. Rule 615, therefore, does not give parties the unilateral power to prohibit communication outside the courtroom. That power remains within the discretion of the trial court.

In fact, Rule 615 does not use the term "sequester" at all. *Black's Law Dictionary* defines "sequester" to mean "to segregate or isolate [a witness] during trial." *Sequester*, *Black's Law Dictionary* 1370 (Bryan A. Garner, ed., 7th ed., West 2000). Tellingly, the drafters did not use the term "sequester" in Rule 615. Rather, they selected only the first aspect of common law sequestration (the aspect that does not "segregate or isolate a witness") and refrained from using the term "sequester" to describe the scope of Rule 615. These drafting decisions provide further indication of an intent to withhold broad sequestration powers from the scope of Rule 615. *Scharstein*, 531 F. Supp. at 464.

Further, the drafters did not define categories of communication allegedly prohibited by the Rule—as they surely would have done had they intended to restrict communication. Violation of a trial court's order constitutes contempt of court, rendering the offending person at risk of fine or imprisonment. *United States v. Johnston*, 578 F.2d 1352, 1355 (10th Cir. 1978). A reading of Rule 615 to prohibit certain kinds of communication outside the courtroom would mean that witnesses who spoke outside the courtroom would be subject to contempt proceedings. If the drafters had intended to impose such serious individual liability for trial witnesses, they surely would have set out the prohibition clearly and defined its parameters unambiguously. The Appellant's proposed construction would render trial witnesses vulnerable to contempt proceedings without fair notice of what they must not do or what the penalties might be. The drafters cannot have intended such a result.

If the drafters had intended the construction urged by the Appellant, they also would have had to address the question of whether trial attorneys could continue preparing witnesses for their testimony. To prepare a witness to testify, any competent attorney confers with the witness about the status of the trial proceedings and about the testimony to come. *See generally United States v. DeJongh*, 937 F.2d 1, 3 (1st Cir. 1991) (A lawyer "would be foolhardy to call an important witness without attempting, first, to debrief the witness."). Because parties adjust their strategies as the trial progresses, these witness conferences are an essential part of trying a case. *Scharstein*, 531 F. Supp. at 463. In fact, the right to prepare a witness for his or her testimony is so fundamental that deprivation of this right may raise Due Process concerns. *Id.* at 463–64 (citing *Potashnic v. Port City Constr. Co.*, 609 F.2d 1001 (5th Cir. 1980)).

Had the drafters intended Rule 615 to limit extra-courtroom communication, they could have chosen either to prohibit trial attorneys from preparing witnesses or to exempt trial attorneys. Exempting trial attorneys would have rendered the proposed construction of Rule 615 pointless, however. Witnesses who have already testified would be precluded from speaking to prospective witnesses, but trial counsel could still describe prior testimony freely. In fact, because attorneys know precisely what will be most relevant in future testimony, allowing attorneys to describe prior testimony would be far more problematic than allowing other witnesses to describe their own testimony. To hold that Rule 615 prohibits witnesses from talking to each other but allows attorneys to prepare prospective witnesses for their testimony "would be an exercise in futility." *Scharstein*, 531 F. Supp. at 464.

Prohibiting trial attorneys from preparing witnesses, on the other hand, would have resulted in a sea change in standard trial preparation. Again, like the question of individual witness liability, such a drastic result would have called for express language in the Rule itself, language clearly applying the Rule to attorney conduct and identifying what attorneys could and could not say during witness preparation. Because the drafters did not address the question of whether and how Rule 615 would apply to communication with attorneys, it is most likely that the drafters did not intend to apply Rule 615 to extra-courtroom communication.

Finally, the intent of the Rule's drafters is not the only intent relevant to the question before this Court. The trial court issued its order under the authority of Rule 615, but an order limiting outside communication could have been issued as part of the court's inherent powers of trial management. *Sepulveda*, 15 F.3d at 1176. Therefore, the more important inquiry may be what the *trial court intended* by its order. A court's interpretation of its own order is given great weight. *Id.* at 1177; *Smith*, 578 F.2d at 1235 ("holding that it is within the discretion of the trial court to determine whether or not a sequestration order has been violated"). If, as here, the *trial court* did not intend its order to constrain conversation outside the courtroom, that order should not be redefined on appeal.

Both the intent of the drafters and the intent of the trial court issuing the order demonstrate that the conversation at issue did not violate the court's order. Neither the provisions of Rule 615 nor the court's own language reflect an intent to reach beyond the courtroom doors.

C. <u>Expanding Rule 615 beyond its express terms would disrupt the Rule's balance between providing truth-testing strategies and minimizing unnecessary litigation costs.</u>

The purposes of the Federal Rules of Evidence are to secure fairness in administration, eliminate unjustifiable expense and delay, ascertain the truth, and determine proceedings fairly. Fed. R. Evid. 102. The Rules aim to balance the need for legitimate truth-testing strategies with the need to minimize unnecessary expense. Expanding the scope of Rule 615 would unnecessarily disrupt the delicate balance Rule 615 has achieved.

Applying Rule 615 to out-of-court conduct is not necessary to obtain truthful testimony. Barring witnesses from the courtroom prevents them from hearing testimony directly, so their only knowledge of prior testimony will be by the general recollection of others. *Sepulveda*, 15 F.3d at 1176. In most cases, this limitation will be sufficient. *Id.* Further, a party suspecting that witness contact may have influenced testimony is free to cross-examine a witness about that contact and its content, as occurred in the case before the Court. For cases in which greater protection is appropriate, the trial court can, *sua sponte* or on proper motion, impose greater limitations, including ordering witnesses not to disclose their testimony. *See id.* In fact, this reliance on the discretion of the trial court is fundamental to the federal trial process. *Scharstein*, 531 F. Supp. at 464 ("The general approach of the Federal Rules of Evidence is to place heavy reliance on the discretion of the trial court in conducting a fair trial."). Thus, the very protection the Appellant seeks is already available without stretching Rule 615 beyond its intended application.

Not only is expansion of the Rule's scope unnecessary, but application to out-of-court communications would result in significant and often unnecessary administrative costs. First, enforcement would be extremely difficult. A court can easily enforce an order banning witnesses from the courtroom, but violations outside the judge's presence are difficult to discover. Wright & Gold, *supra*, § 6243. Further, enforcing routine orders prohibiting witness contact would require the court to undertake "an undue amount of supervision" over witnesses, distracting the court from its primary function. *Scharstein*, 531 F. Supp. at 464 n.7.

Second, extension of the Rule would result in long delays during trials. *Id.* at 464. Each time two witnesses talked, there could be grounds for a motion alleging a violation of Rule 615 and a resulting evidentiary hearing to learn the content of the conversation. *Id.* Witnesses would be called upon to disclose publically everything they had said to each other. *Id.* These hearings would occur frequently, especially in long trials with many witnesses. *Id.* Constant interruptions would impede trial management, increase litigation costs, and absorb significant judicial resources. Courts would be "bogged down in numerous inquiries . . . when there is no genuine need to do so." *Id.*

Third, the outcome of these hearings would be uncertain at best. The Rule does not define what kinds of communication would be prohibited. Neither parties nor witnesses nor the district court itself would know whether a violation had occurred if a witness stated that she had testified; that her testimony was over; that the cross-examination had been brief; that she had been nervous; that she had testified about a particular topic; or that a particular question had been asked. With no clear standard of what could and could not be said, hearings would be numerous and issues would be difficult to resolve. *Id.*; Wright & Gold, *supra*, § 6243.

Fourth, extension of the Rule would place unrealistic hardships on witnesses. An order limiting out-of-court communication between witnesses places far greater burdens on witnesses than does mere exclusion from the courtroom. Wright & Gold, *supra*, § 6243. Witnesses testifying in the same case often are spouses or co-workers. Communication between spouses or other close associates should be restricted only when absolutely necessary, not any time a party decides to invoke Rule 615.

Fifth, extending the Rule to out-of-court statements would render witnesses vulnerable to contempt proceedings. The combination of this vulnerability and the lack of clarity about what kinds of communication are prohibited would discourage witnesses from testifying. Discouraging testimony would impede the goal of obtaining truthful testimony to a far greater degree than would a decision to keep Rule 615 within its intended bounds.

Sixth, to apply Rule 615 to out-of-court conversations would be to give any party, as a matter of right, the ability to impose significant limitations on all witnesses in the case, including spouses and co-workers who must continue to have close daily contact with each other as the trial progresses. A party could use Rule 615 as another way to make the trial experience as unpleasant as possible for opposing parties and witnesses. This approach to trial management does not assist in achieving just and fair results at trial.

Only one circumstance—the reading of transcripts of actual testimony—justifies the application of Rule 615 beyond its express terms. *Miller v. Universal City Studios, Inc.*, 650 F.2d 1365, 1373 (5th Cir. 1981). In *Miller*, the trial court had entered an order excluding witnesses under Rule 615. *Id.* at 1367. During the trial, however, the defendant's expert witness was provided with daily transcripts of the trial testimony. *Id.* The district court held that providing transcripts of testimony violated the Rule 615 order, and the appellate court affirmed, explaining that the harm of *reading* testimony is potentially greater than the harm of *hearing* testimony. *Id.* Accordingly, the court held that a Rule 615 order prohibits witnesses from reading trial transcripts prior to testifying. *Id.* at 1373.

The *Miller* exception does not apply to conversation outside the courtroom, however. *Id.* The court in *Miller* compared hearing actual testimony with reading a transcript and found the key difference to be that a listener would have to rely on his or her memory of the testimony while a reader would not. *Id.* at 1372. This key distinction does not apply to conversation outside the courtroom. Unlike the reader of a transcript, who can thoroughly study the actual testimony, a participant in a conversation must rely on his or her memory of the conversation. Perhaps more significantly, the *speaker* must rely on memories of the testimony as well. By the very rationale explained in *Miller*, therefore, the danger of casual conversation outside the courtroom is considerably smaller than the danger Rule 615 is designed to prevent. Thus, the *Miller* exception does not apply to extra-courtroom conversation. In fact, *Miller's* very rationale demonstrates a key reason for limiting Rule 615 to "testimony" rather than to mere recollections of testimony.

Further, the narrow *Miller* exception is consistent with the rationales on which Rule 615 is based. The *Miller* exception does not impose the administrative costs and personal impositions on witnesses that the Appellant's construction would impose. Prohibiting the reading of transcripts creates a bright-line test, easily applied in enforcement proceedings. Witnesses need not wonder what they may and may not say. Parties need not wonder what conduct may violate the Rule 615 order. Also, a witness has access to trial transcripts only through trial attorneys, who are officers of the court and therefore more easily and effectively governed by trial court orders. Further, the prohibition on reading transcripts does not interfere with normal daily interactions between witnesses who live or work together or who encounter each other in casual interactions in the hallway.

In all other circumstances, trial judges have broad discretion to limit contact between witnesses when appropriate. *Sepulveda*, 15 F.3d at 1176. In those few cases in which a small nuance in testimony may determine the outcome, a Rule 615 exclusion of witnesses may be insufficient. *Scharstein*, 531 F. Supp. at 464. In such cases, the trial court can use its broad case management powers to determine whether "extra-courtroom prophylaxis" is necessary and what means best accomplishes the goal in that case. *Sepulveda*, 15 F.3d at 1176 (citing *United States v. Arias-Santana*, 964 F.2d 1262, 1266 (1st Cir. 1992)). Since trial courts already have the power to restrict communication when appropriate, the only effect of broadening Rule 615 to include such restrictions would be to shift the power from the trial court's discretion and place it instead in the unrestrained hands of a party. Nothing in the language or history of Rule 615 indicates that the drafters intended such a result.

D. <u>The casual dinner conversation of Officers Nelson, and Miller did not violate the Rule 615 order.</u>

On September 22, 2004, Officers Nelson and Miller had dinner together. (R. at 6.) During their meal, the conversation ranged over topics of common interest. Officer Nelson had testified in the Irving trial that day. (R. at 7.) He related to his dinner companion his recollection of his testimony, including his testimony of having seen Irving hand the drug-filled envelope to Roberts. Officer Nelson's description prompted Officer Miller to recall that he had seen the transfer as well. (R. at 7.)

This dinner conversation between the officers did not violate the Rule 615 order. The trial court's order made reference only to whether and when witnesses could be in the courtroom, exactly as the plain language of Rule 615 provides. At no time during the trial did the court instruct witnesses not to speak to each other. This was no mere inadvertent omission by the court. As demonstrated by the court's denial of Defendant's Motion to Exclude, the trial court did not *intend* that its order should apply to communication outside the courtroom.

Nor does this case fall within the narrow *Miller* exception. In *Miller*, the reading of daily transcripts was held to violate Rule 615. 650 F.2d at 1374. The court concluded that reading transcripts eliminated the need to rely on memory and was thus more dangerous than actual witness presence in the courtroom. *Id.* Here, however, Officer Nelson had to rely on his recollection of his testimony. Then, Officer Miller had to rely on *his* recollection of what Officer Nelson had recalled. These key differences render the officers' conversation far less problematic than either physical presence in the courtroom or the reading of trial transcripts.

In fact, this double reliance on memory is even less problematic than the situation the Eighth Circuit permitted in *Smith*, where an officer in the courtroom was taking notes and relaying information to prospective witnesses. 578 F.2d at 1227. Here, no one was planted in the courtroom taking notes. There was no plot to circumvent the prohibition on access to actual testimony. Two co-workers simply had dinner together and spoke of their day's events, as friends and co-workers often do.

Additionally, prohibiting these officers from speaking to each other likely would have made no difference here. Officers Nelson and Miller had worked together on this case for months. Together, they had arrested the Defendant and worked with the prosecutor to prepare the case for trial. During that process, they would have seen each other daily. Undoubtedly, they had discussed the case on countless occasions. They may well have discussed the case immediately before trial began. Whether or not the officers communicated on September 22, no doubt the prosecutor would have carefully prepared Officer Miller for his testimony the next day. The prosecutor would have highlighted the factual question of the drug transfer and would have told Officer Miller about the status of the testimony on that point. Officer Miller's recollection would have been just as refreshed by that description as it was by the description of his co-worker the night before. In such a circumstance, there is little point in prohibiting a discussion on September 22 that normally could have happened both on September 21 and on September 23.

Further, whether the conversation occurred before or after trial began, the Defendant would have been able to confront Officer Miller with his prior statements and question him about conversations with others—just as the Defendant did. Thus, in either case, the jury would have been fully informed of the circumstances surrounding Officer Miller's testimony. In neither case would there be reason to second-guess the jury's ability to gauge the officer's credibility and the accuracy of his recollection.

Finally, reading Rule 615 beyond its express terms is not necessary to preserve the availability of broad sequestration in appropriate cases. As part of its inherent authority, the court below had the power to impose, *sua sponte*, extra-courtroom restrictions on witnesses. The court did not find those restrictions necessary here. If the Defendant disagreed, the Defendant had the opportunity to request those restrictions, but the Defendant did not make the request. Had counsel sought such an order, and had the trial court issued it, Officers Nelson and Miller certainly would have complied. The Defendant did not seek the order, however, and cannot now bootstrap a routine Rule 615 order into the order Defendant wishes he had sought.

CONCLUSION

Both the plain language of Rule 615 and all available indicators of the drafters' intent show that the Rule governs only physical presence in the courtroom and not conversations such as that between Officers Nelson and Miller. Further, application of Rule 615 according to its express terms preserves the Rule's carefully crafted balance of the rights of parties and the efficient administration of trials. Therefore, the Government respectfully requests this Court to affirm the trial court's denial of the Defendant's Motion to Exclude Testimony.

Respectfully submitted

DATED: ____________________ ____________________

Counsel for the United States

CERTIFICATE OF SERVICE

I, ____________________, do hereby certify that I have this date served a true and correct copy of the Appellants' Brief upon the Appellee's counsel by placing a true copy of the Appellants' Brief in the United States mail, with sufficient postage affixed, and addressed as follows:

DATED: ____________________ ____________________

Counsel for the United States

CERTIFICATE OF COMPLIANCE

This document complies with the typeface requirements of Fed. R. App. P. 32(a)(5) and the type-style requirements of Fed. R. App. P. 32(a)(6).

DATED: ____________________ ____________________

Counsel for the United States

Sample Informal Advice Letter

[date]

Mr. Joseph S. Crimshaw
Crimshaw Plumbing Supply
1245 Glenwood Dr.
Gooding, New State 55832

RE: Crimshaw Plumbing Supply; personnel matter

Dear Joe:

Last week, I said that I would research the question of whether you can require an existing sales employee to sign a covenant-not-to-compete to retain his employment. My research indicates that you can require the employee to sign a non-competition covenant as long as the employee is an "at will" employee and as long as the terms of the covenant are reasonable. I will explain that conclusion more fully below, but first let me summarize my understanding of the facts that have raised this question for you.

Facts: I understand that about a year ago, you hired Steven Lewis to call on potential customers and take orders for plumbing supply products. Lewis told you that he had been selling plumbing supply products for ten years for another company but was recently laid off when that company reduced its work force. He told you orally that he wished to go to work for another established company and stay there until he retires in ten years. I understand that you did not offer him any particular term of employment and that he did not make any promises to you about how long he would stay or whether he would leave and compete against Crimshaw Plumbing Supply. You have now heard a rumor indicating that Lewis is planning to open his own plumbing supply business in about a year and that he will be directly competing against Crimshaw Plumbing. You would like to require Lewis to sign a covenant-not-to-compete with Crimshaw for three years after he leaves Crimshaw's employment.

Issues: These facts raise two issues: (1) whether a current employee can be required to sign a covenant-not-to-compete; and (2) what covenant terms are enforceable.

Research and Legal Conclusions: On the first issue, no statute or reported case in our state has addressed the question of whether continuation of employment can be conditioned on the signing of a covenant-not-to-compete. However, all employment contracts are treated as "at will" employment unless the contract specifies otherwise. Assuming that you did not offer Lewis employment for any particular period of time, he is an "at will" employee. You can terminate an "at will" employee at any time as long as the termination is not for a particular prohibited reason, such as the employee's race, religion, or sex.

While no reported cases in our jurisdiction have dealt with requiring an employee to sign a non-competition covenant, several cases did deal with requiring a current "at will" employee to abide by other kinds of newly instituted rules of employment such as new attendance or dress requirements or new rules requiring particular training or certifications. These cases have uniformly upheld an employer's right to institute new employment rules or requirements and to condition continued employment on compliance with those rules.

Further, I was able to find several cases in other jurisdictions that dealt specifically with requiring a current employee to sign a covenant-not-to-compete, and those cases all permitted the requirement. In those cases, the courts stated that there was no significant difference between requiring the signing of a non-competition covenant and requiring the employee to abide by other newly instituted rules. Although a court in our state would not be required to follow the ruling of a case from another state, these cases do provide additional support for our position.

On the second issue, the cases in our state uniformly hold that a signed covenant-not-to-compete is enforceable if its terms are reasonable. Customary terms set out the geographic area of the restriction, the duration of the restriction, and a description of the restricted activities. The opinions all recite that the restrictions should not be broader than necessary to protect the employer's business. Commonly, durational terms do not exceed one year, and geographic restrictions do not exceed the area of the employer's primary market. The restricted activities are limited to the activities the employee performed for the former employer plus any additional activities for which the employee could profitably use confidential information obtained from the former employer (such as a customer list). Consequently, if you are going to require Lewis to sign a covenant, we should carefully discuss its terms, and I would recommend that you allow our firm to draft the agreement for you so we can help you create terms a court would enforce.

Advice: First, if competition from former sales employees is a concern, as I suspect it is, I suggest that you ask all new sales employees to sign a non-competition agreement with carefully drafted terms. This will prevent future occasions in which the current delicate situation arises.

Second, it appears that legally you can condition Lewis's continued employment on the signing of a covenant-not-to-compete. However, you may want to think carefully about whether to bring the issue to a head in this way. If Lewis has not yet decided whether to start his own business, presenting him with a covenant at this point may push him to decide to leave and begin to compete immediately. Further, presenting him with a legal document and requiring him to either sign it or be fired may cause him to react emotionally. He might feel both strong-armed and suspected of wrong-doing, in which case he might react by doing exactly what you are trying to prevent. Therefore, you will need to assess carefully the risks of acting as compared to the risks of waiting.

If you decide to ask for the non-competition agreement, I suggest that you consider two possible strategies. If Lewis is a valuable employee you would like to keep, consider whether you can devise a promotion or some other increase in status or benefits and present the covenant as part of that new position. If a promotion or increase in benefits is not feasible, you might present the covenant as a new policy applying to a whole category of employees so Lewis does not feel singled out and personally offended.

I hope this information is helpful. I would be happy to discuss this matter with you further. Let me know if you would like us to assist in any other way.

Very truly yours,

Keith Salter
Attorney at Law

APPENDIX F

Cases

LUCY V. ZEHMER

196 Va. 493, 84 S.E.2d 516 (1954)

Supreme Court of Appeals of Virginia

BUCHANAN, Justice.

This suit was instituted by W.O. Lucy and J.C. Lucy, complainants, against A.H. Zehmer and Ida S. Zehmer, his wife, defendants, to have specific performance of a contract by which it was alleged the Zehmers had sold to W.O. Lucy a tract of land owned by A.H. Zehmer in Dinwiddie county containing 471.6 acres, more or less, known as the Ferguson farm, for $50,000. J.C. Lucy, the other complainant, is a brother of W.O. Lucy, to whom W.O. Lucy transferred a half interest in his alleged purchase.

The instrument sought to be enforced was written by A.H. Zehmer on [Saturday,] December 20, 1952, in these words: "We hereby agree to sell to W.O. Lucy the Ferguson Farm complete for $50,000.00, title satisfactory to buyer," and signed by the defendants, A.H. Zehmer and Ida S. Zehmer.

The answer of A.H. Zehmer admitted that at the time mentioned W.O. Lucy offered him $50,000 cash for the farm, but that he, Zehmer, considered that the offer was made in jest; that so thinking, and both he and Lucy having had several drinks, he wrote out "the memorandum" quoted above and induced his wife to sign it; that he did not deliver the memorandum to Lucy, but that Lucy picked it up, read it, put it in his pocket, attempted to offer Zehmer $5 to bind the bargain, which Zehmer refused to accept, and realizing for the first time that Lucy was serious, Zehmer assured him that he had no intention of selling the farm and that the whole matter was a joke. Lucy left the premises insisting that he had purchased the farm.

Depositions were taken and the decree appealed from was entered holding that the complainants had failed to establish their right to specific performance, and dismissing their bill. The assignment of error is to this action of the court. . . .

The defendants insist that the evidence was ample to support their contention that the writing sought to be enforced was prepared as a bluff or dare to force Lucy to admit that he did not have $50,000; that the whole matter was a joke; that the writing was not delivered to Lucy and no binding contract was ever made between the parties.

It is an unusual, if not bizarre, defense. When made to the writing admittedly prepared by one of the defendants and signed by both, clear evidence is required to sustain it.

In his testimony Zehmer claimed that he "was high as a Georgia pine," and that the transaction "was just a bunch of two doggoned drunks bluffing to see who could talk the biggest and say the most." That claim is inconsistent with his attempt to testify in great detail as to what was said and what was done. It is contradicted by other evidence as to the condition of both parties, and rendered of no weight by the testimony of his wife that when Lucy left the restaurant she suggested that Zehmer drive him home. The record is convincing that Zehmer was not intoxicated to the extent of being unable to comprehend the nature and consequences of the instrument he executed, and hence that instrument is not to be invalidated on that ground. It was in fact conceded by defendants' counsel in oral argument that under the evidence Zehmer was not too drunk to make a valid contract.

The evidence is convincing also that Zehmer wrote two agreements, the first one beginning "I hereby agree to sell." Zehmer first said he could not remember about that, then that "I don't think I wrote but one out." Mrs. Zehmer said that what he wrote was "I hereby agree," but that "I" was changed to "We" after that night. The agreement that was written and signed is in the record and indicates no such change. Neither are the mistakes in spelling that Zehmer sought to point out readily apparent.

The appearance of the contract, the fact that it was under discussion for forty minutes or more before it was signed; Lucy's objection to the first draft because it was written in the singular, and he wanted Mrs. Zehmer to sign it also; the rewriting to meet that objection and the signing by Mrs. Zehmer; the discussion of what was to be included in the sale, the provision for the examination of the title, the completeness of the instrument that was executed, the taking possession of it by Lucy with no request or suggestion by either of the defendants that he give it back, are facts which furnish persuasive evidence that the execution of the contract was a serious business transaction rather than a casual, jesting matter as defendants now contend. . . .

If it be assumed, contrary to what we think the evidence shows, that Zehmer was jesting about selling his farm to Lucy and that the transaction was intended by him to be a joke, nevertheless the evidence shows that Lucy did not so understand it but considered it to be a serious business transaction and the contract to be binding on the Zehmers as well as on himself. The very next day he arranged with his brother to put up half the money and take a half interest in the land. The day after that he employed an attorney to examine the title. The next night, Tuesday, he was back at Zehmer's place and there Zehmer told him for the first time, Lucy said, that he wasn't going to sell and he told Zehmer, "You know you sold that place fair and square." After receiving the report from his attorney that the title was good he wrote to Zehmer that he was ready to close the deal.

Not only did Lucy actually believe, but the evidence shows he was warranted in believing that the contract represented a serious business transaction and a good faith sale and purchase of the farm.

In the field of contracts, as generally elsewhere, "We must look to the outward expression of a person as manifesting his intention rather than to his secret and unexpressed intention. 'The law imputes to a person an intention corresponding to the reasonable meaning of his words and acts.' "

At no time prior to the execution of the contract had Zehmer indicated to Lucy by word or act that he was not in earnest about selling the farm. They had argued about it and discussed its terms, as Zehmer admitted, for a long time. Lucy testified that if there was any jesting it was about paying $50,000 that night. The contract and the evidence show that he was not expected to pay the money that night. Zehmer said that after the writing was signed he laid it down on the counter in front of Lucy. Lucy said Zehmer handed it to him. In any event there had been what appeared to be a good faith offer and a good faith acceptance, followed by the execution and apparent delivery of a written contract. Both said that Lucy put the writing in his pocket and then offered Zehmer $5 to seal the bargain. Not until then, even under the defendants' evidence, was anything said or done to indicate that the matter was a joke. Both of the Zehmers testified that when Zehmer asked his wife to sign he whispered that it was a joke so Lucy wouldn't hear and that it was not intended that he should hear.

The mental assent of the parties is not requisite for the formation of a contract. If the words or other acts of one of the parties have but one reasonable meaning, his undisclosed intention is immaterial except when an unreasonable meaning which he attaches to his manifestations is known to the other party. " . . . The law, therefore, judges of an agreement between two persons exclusively from those expressions of their intentions which are communicated between them. . . ."

An agreement or mutual assent is of course essential to a valid contract, but the law imputes to a person an intention corresponding to the reasonable meaning of his words and acts. If his words and acts, judged by a reasonable standard, manifest an intention to agree, it is immaterial what may be the real but unexpressed state of his mind.

So a person cannot set up that he was merely jesting when his conduct and words would warrant a reasonable person in believing that he intended a real agreement.

Whether the writing signed by the defendants and now sought to be enforced by the complainants was the result of a serious offer by Lucy and a serious acceptance by the defendants, or was a serious offer by Lucy and an acceptance in secret jest by the defendants, in either event it constituted a binding contract of sale between the parties. . . .

The complainants are entitled to have specific performance of the contract sued on. The decree appealed from is therefore reversed and the cause is remanded for the entry of a proper decree requiring the defendants to perform the contract in accordance with the prayer of the bill.

Reversed and remanded.

Goldman v. Kane

3 Mass. App. Ct. 336, 329 N.E.2d 770 (1975)

Massachusetts Appeals Court

Hale, Chief Justice.

[Barry Kane represented Lawrence Hill, a law school graduate but not a lawyer. Kane had represented Hill for several years on various matters. In April 1971, Hill signed an agreement to purchase a boat for $31,500 and paid a deposit of $3,150. Hill agreed to pay the balance on May 17. Kane advised Hill about miscellaneous legal matters pertaining to the purchase and registration of the boat. Hill also asked Kane to arrange for the financing of the balance of the purchase price. When Kane could not arrange a loan through a bank, Hill told Kane to sell a piece of real property Hill owned. Kane put the property on the market, but the property did not sell. With one day to go before losing the deposit, Hill told Kane that he was in dire need of the money to complete the sale. Kane told Hill that the timing and Hill's financial circumstances made it "virtually impossible" to get a loan. After several telephone conversations, Kane offered to arrange for Kane's corporation to lend Hill $30,000. However, Hill would have to transfer to Kane's corporation absolute title to the unsold real property, to all of the personal property located on the real property, and to a smaller boat Hill owned. In addition, Hill would have to secure the loan with a mortgage on the new boat. Kane urged Hill not to accept these terms, but Hill insisted. In July 1971, Kane's corporation sold the real property and the personal property located on it for $86,000. Subsequently, Hill defaulted on the loan. Kane seized the boat and sold it. Hill's estate thereafter sued Kane and his corporation, alleging that Kane had breached his fiduciary duty as Hill's attorney. Judgment for the plaintiff; defendants appealed.]

The defendants argue that even if an attorney-client relationship existed the record does not support the conclusion that there was a breach of that relationship. We disagree. The relationship of attorney and client is highly fiduciary in nature. "Unflinching fidelity to their genuine interests is the duty of every attorney to his clients. Public policy hardly can touch matters of more general concern than the maintenance of an untarnished standard of conduct by the attorney at law toward his client."

The law looks with great disfavor upon an attorney who has business dealings with his client which result in gains to the attorney at the expense of the client. "The attorney is not permitted by the law to take any advantage of his client. The principles holding the attorney to a conspicuous degree of faithfulness and forbidding him to take personal advantage of his client are thoroughly established." When an attorney bargains with his client in a business transaction in a manner which is advantageous to himself, and if that transaction is later called into question, the court will subject it to close scrutiny. In such a case, the attorney has the burden of showing that the transaction "was in all respects fairly and equitably conducted; that he fully and faithfully discharged all his duties to his client, not only by refraining from any misrepresentation or concealment of any material fact, but by active diligence to see that his client was fully informed of the nature and effect of the transaction proposed and of his own rights and interests in the subject matter involved, and by seeing to it that his client either has independent advice in the matter or else receives from the attorney such advice as the latter would have been expected to give had the transaction been one between his client and a stranger."

Applying these principles to the case at bar, it is clear that the judge was correct in concluding that Kane, by entering into the transaction, breached his fiduciary duty to Hill. While the defendants contend that Kane's conduct did not constitute a breach of his fiduciary duty because Hill fully understood the nature and effect of the transaction and because Kane advised Hill against it, in the circumstances of this case, Kane's full disclosure and his advice were not sufficient to immunize him from liability. The fundamental unfairness of the transaction and the egregious overreaching by Kane in his dealings with Hill are self-evident. In light of the nature of the transaction, Kane, at a bare minimum, was under a duty not to proceed with the loan until he was satisfied that Hill had obtained independent advice on the matter. The purpose of such requirement is to be certain that in a situation where an attorney deals with a client in a business relationship to the attorney's advantage, the "presumed influence resulting from the relationship has been neutralized." . . .

Judgment affirmed.

Jacobson v. Kamerinsky[1]

Karen Jacobson had gallbladder surgery on June 30, 1984. Her doctor negligently left a surgical sponge in the surgery site when he closed the incision. The sponge caused Jacobson considerable physical difficulty and subsequently resulted in a second surgery to remove it. After the second surgery Jacobson decided to seek legal representation for a medical malpractice claim against her first surgeon. She saw Kamerinsky's office sign, sought his advice, and agreed to retain him to bring her claim. Kamerinsky had been admitted to practice law only ten weeks when he accepted Jacobson's case.

Kamerinsky correctly realized that the surgeon was clearly liable for Jacobson's damages. He tried to negotiate a settlement of the claim with the surgeon and the surgeon's insurance carrier so that litigation would not be necessary. As the weeks and months went by, Jacobson contacted Kamerinsky periodically to learn whether there was any progress on her claim. He would tell her that negotiations were proceeding well and that he should have a settlement for her soon. Several times he told her that he had obtained an expert opinion that leaving a surgical sponge inside the body was clearly medical malpractice. He explained that he had not yet filed suit because, since liability was so clear, he hoped to negotiate a settlement without the necessity of filing suit.

Shortly before the statute of limitations expired, when negotiations had not been successful, Kamerinsky filed suit in the appropriate state trial court. However, he had failed to research the requirements for bringing a medical malpractice action. State law requires that prior to filing suit a medical malpractice plaintiff must first file a charge before the medical Malpractice Screening Panel, complete the Panel's discovery and hearing process, and

1. This is a hypothetical case based on several real cases.

obtain a decision from the Panel. [citation omitted] Failure to go through these steps results in the dismissal of the plaintiff's court action. [citation omitted] The lawyer for the doctor successfully moved for the dismissal of the plaintiff's claim, and the plaintiff was precluded from completing the Screening Panel process and refiling the suit because by then the statute of limitations had expired and the medical malpractice claim was barred.

Ms. Jacobson brought this legal malpractice claim against Kamerinsky, arguing that Kamerinsky's failure to file a charge before the Screening Panel constituted legal malpractice and resulted in $500,000 damage to Jacobson. A jury found in favor of Jacobson and awarded her $425,000 in damages. Kamerinsky appeals, arguing that his error did not constitute malpractice.

A lawyer is held to a standard of competency that meets or exceeds the professional skill and diligence commonly exercised by reasonable and prudent lawyers in this state [citation to state's highest court]. Lawyers are not guarantors of a successful result; nor are they required to surpass human limitations. Lawyers are often called upon to exercise professional judgment in representing and advising clients. A good faith error in judgment is not legal malpractice as long as the lawyer's judgment was reasonable under the circumstances.

Kamerinsky's failure was more than an error in judgment, however. The failure to comply with the filing requirements was readily preventable by proper legal research. The Medical Malpractice Act creates the Screening Panel and the requirement of completing the Panel's hearing process before suit is filed. The debate and ultimate passage of the Act had been covered by the press extensively, the Screening Panel requirement being the most controversial provision of the Act. Even if Kamerinsky was not aware of the Act from the public press coverage, he certainly should have been aware of the Act and its requirements as a result of the prominent coverage of the new requirements by the State Bar Journal and the several Continuing Legal Education programs that explained the Act's provisions.

However, no lawyer should rely on press or state bar journalists to keep apace with statutory changes. Kamerinsky had a duty to conduct thorough legal research concerning statutory requirements for filing a lawsuit. Filing lawsuits is something general practitioners are familiar with doing, and it is well within the area of competence required of all lawyers.

Kamerinsky argues that medical malpractice litigation is a complex and difficult area of the law and that he, as a novice lawyer, should not be held to the standard of an experienced litigator. As we established above, researching and complying with statutory requirements for filing a lawsuit are tasks well within the standard of practice expected of all lawyers. However, even if they were not, Kamerinsky cannot undertake representation on a case without being held to the standard expected of all lawyers practicing in this state. A lawyer must either decline the representation or meet the appropriate standard of competence required for the representation. If bringing a medical malpractice claim requires knowledge or experience that Kamerinsky did not already have or could not obtain, he had no business accepting the case. All clients are entitled to at least the minimum standard of knowledge, skill, and diligence. Further, allowing lawyers to meet a lower standard if they can demonstrate a lower level of skill or knowledge would not encourage lawyers to develop their levels of skill, knowledge, and experience.

Judgment affirmed.

Index